A LEVEL

General Studies

GARETH DAVIES
EDWARD LITTLE

Edinburgh Gate
Harlow, Essex

Pearson Education
Edinburgh Gate
Harlow
Essex

ISBN 0582 44761 5

Designed, edited and produced by Gecko Ltd, Cambridge
Illustrations by Helen Humphreys, Dave Mostyn and John Plumb
Printed in Great Britain by Scotprint, Haddington

Contents

Introduction

What is General Studies?

General Studies has been available as an A level for many years but, like all A levels, the specification has recently been revised. The A level system has often been criticised for being too narrow and specialised and, although the introduction of the new AS qualification allows students to study a wider range of subjects at Advanced level, there is no compulsion to choose A level courses from across the subject spectrum, as there is in some continental countries.

General Studies is an alternative method to achieve breadth and balance. It recognises traditional specialisation but, at the same time, requires a more broadly based approach. The nature of the subject requires knowledge and understanding of three broad subject areas – Culture, Science and Society – and the ability to make connections between them.

General Studies has three main purposes:

- It should encourage you to examine issues and make judgements from a broad base of contrasting disciplines.
- It should allow you to encounter areas of knowledge and interest that might otherwise remain outside your experience.
- It should develop Thinking and Analytical Skills and Key Skills, which can also be of benefit in your other studies.

General Studies should, therefore, reinforce other studies and encourage you to draw on knowledge and understanding gained from your main subjects in order to develop an interdisciplinary approach.

The subject content is arranged in three broad overlapping areas:

- Culture (Unit 1 in the book),
- Science (Unit 2),
- Society (Unit 3).

All courses also have a Synoptic element (Unit 4, the Contemporary World) counting for at least 20 per cent of the final Advanced level mark. For this unit, you must draw together knowledge, understanding and skills developed in other parts of the course, showing how they relate to each other and contribute to a fuller understanding of issues.

Thinking and Analytical Skills

Thinking and Analytical Skills are central to the new specifications and provide coherence to what otherwise might be a disparate and unrelated series of studies.

As you will have discovered, there is often overlap between subjects and disciplines. For example, historical knowledge and skills may be used in English (to appreciate literature and understand the influences on an author), in art (to provide a context and background for artists and their work), in sociology (to provide evidence on which to base theories) and in science (to trace the development of discoveries and knowledge and to set scientific work in context) as well as in the study of history itself. Subject-based knowledge is called 'first order' knowledge.

To be able to critically analyse any piece of writing, you must be able to identify different types of subject knowledge and different types of knowledge about knowledge itself. This is called 'second order' knowledge. You should be able to discuss not only what we know but also why we know and how we know that we know, and to understand the relationships that exist between different types of knowledge. You will learn how to demonstrate awareness of the origin and nature of different types of knowledge, and appreciate differences between knowledge, belief and opinion. You will also learn about different types of argument and how to analyse and evaluate arguments to identify whether they are flawed or justified.

Key Skills

Key Skills help you concentrate on how you learn in order to raise achievement. Employers and university tutors have identified them as an essential tool in developing a flexible approach to work. Key Skills are not unique to any one subject, but should be transferable.

All six Key Skills are assessed at four different levels. If you are working at Advanced level standard, you should be able to reach Level 3. Key Skills are assessed through a portfolio of work demonstrating evidence of achievement. Students must also pass external tests to achieve unit accreditation in Communication, Application of Number and Information Technology. Successfully undergoing assessment in these will result in the achievement of a Key Skills qualification.

Opportunities to practise Key Skills are listed under the title of each section and are included at the end in the Activities box. Further examples of how class work can contribute to the development of Key Skills are given on pages 226–234.

No Key Skills activities are listed in Unit 4, although some of the discussion points can be adapted to generate evidence if required. The suggestions made only relate to Level 3 in the four Key Skills of Number, Communication, IT and Working with Others. This doesn't mean that the two remaining Key Skills are less significant – they ought to be integral and easily identifiable in all parts of a General Studies programme. The activities can be modified to meet the demands of other Key Skills levels.

The General Studies examination

Different types of examination questions

There are several different types of examination question:

- multiple-choice,
- short-answer questions, which may be free-standing or may be related to source material. Short-answer questions require you to write concisely, avoiding the temptation to waste time by producing lengthy answers for a relatively small number of marks,
- structured questions, which may be used either in essay sections or as short-answer questions. Their value is that they give some guidance as to the type of answer required,
- essays and extended writing.

Edexcel, in common with other examination boards, uses source material. It may be used:

- for comprehension and evaluation,
- as stimulus for short or extended writing,
- as data for interpretation,
- for testing thinking and analytical skills.

What are examiners looking for?

The number of marks allocated to a question gives you a broad indication of the length of the required response or at least the amount of time that should be spent answering a question.

Examination questions usually contain key words to direct you to the type of answer required. Familiarity with the different key words can be very useful:

- Words like 'what', 'name', 'describe', 'list' and 'give' are usually asking for simple facts.
- Requests for a straightforward explanation are usually made by using longer phrases like 'Give reasons for', 'explain what is meant by' or simply 'why', 'outline' or 'how'.
- Essay-type questions usually require a level of assessment and evaluation. Key words or expressions may include 'assess', 'evaluate', 'analyse', 'discuss', 'critically examine', 'consider arguments (for and against)', 'explain' and 'do you agree'. These expressions require you to examine alternative views on an issue and reach a justified conclusion. Other key words demanding a conclusion include 'to what extent', 'how far' and 'do you think'.
- Certain types of data response questions may use key words like 'calculate', 'estimate' or 'interpret'.

What are the characteristics of a good essay?

The essay is a principal method of assessment. In most subjects essays are related to a specific area of knowledge. General Studies essays are likely to be less concerned with detailed knowledge and more with how you use what you know to examine a given issue.

Issues chosen for General Studies essays usually involve different points of view and, possibly, areas of conflict. Consequently, you should make sure that answers are not narrow factual narratives, but balanced reviews of all sides of an argument, supported by relevant knowledge and understanding from different disciplines.

The body of the essay should consist of an argument which recognises that the issue involves a conflict of views. Alternative arguments should be presented clearly, fairly and coherently. It is important to attempt a balanced presentation. Your argument should consist of comment supported by relevant evidence, drawn from course content. Your argument should be organised so as to lead logically to a justified conclusion.

You should write for the general reader, who should not be assumed to possess any prior knowledge or understanding of the topic.

Coursework in General Studies

Edexcel allows you to replace at least one specified unit with a piece of coursework. Submitted coursework must meet the same Assessment Objectives as the assessment unit it is to replace.

To be effective, your coursework should meet a number of requirements:

- The chosen title should give a clear direction, purpose and challenge.
- The aims and terminology used should be clearly explained.
- Texts should be clearly cross-referenced and properly sourced, and you should include a full bibliography.
- Work should be carefully planned and appropriately monitored.
- The work should follow a clearly defined structure.
- The issue defined in the title should be discussed and evaluated rather than simply described.
- The work should reach and establish a clear, supported conclusion.
- It should demonstrate your ability to use and apply skills and knowledge from different disciplines.
- It should be appropriate to your interests and ability and not deal with issues that are either too trivial or too demanding for the assessment target level.

Although the content of this book does not specifically address coursework, many of the activities, issues for discussion and suggested resources could provide suitable starting points.

The General Studies Specification

This book is designed for students following the Edexcel Specification. The grids on pages x–xiii show how each double-page spread addresses the requirements of the Specification.

The Edexcel Specification, based on new national Subject Criteria, came into force in September 2000. These criteria ensure that all General Studies programmes share the same basic aims, address the same areas of knowledge and are examined according to the same Assessment Objectives. Thinking and Analytical Skills, central to all Specifications, ensure a sufficient level of academic rigour.

The common aims of General Studies were developed by QCA after consultation with the awarding bodies and teachers and indicate why it is beneficial for students to follow a General Studies programme. They encourage students to:

- develop a greater awareness of human knowledge, understanding and behaviour,
- integrate knowledge from a range of disciplines in order to develop a synoptic view of how the various disciplines relate to one another and how each may contribute to the understanding of the issues being studied,
- appreciate that there are various ways of interpreting different types of information,
- assess the relative merits of evidence in order to understand concepts like objectivity, neutrality and bias,
- think critically, logically and constructively about significant problems, acquire an appreciation of the strengths and limitations of different approaches and demonstrate an ability to justify their own argument,
- develop a critical awareness and understanding of perennial and contemporary issues as well as a greater awareness of historical and contemporary contexts in order to enhance their own skills of evaluation,
- communicate with coherence and clarity in an appropriate format.

The four Assessment Objectives are the same at both AS and A level.

AO1: demonstrate relevant knowledge and understanding applied to a range of issues, using skills from different disciplines.

AO2: communicate clearly and accurately in a concise, logical and relevant way.

AO3: marshal evidence and draw conclusions; select, interpret, evaluate and integrate information, data, concepts and opinions.

AO4: demonstrate understanding of different types of knowledge and of the relationship between them, appreciating their limitations.

The Synoptic Assessment

The Edexcel Synoptic Unit requires candidates to write two essays from a choice of four. They are reminded to draw on knowledge and skills developed in the other five modules. Each essay is marked according to the four Assessment Objectives in the order AO3, AO1, AO4 and AO2.

Assessment of AO3 and AO4

Assessment of Thinking and Analytical Skills is done through AO3 and AO4. Recognising the demands of Thinking and Analytical Skills, Edexcel has put greater weighting of marks for these objectives into A2 rather than AS.

Edexcel has a uniform approach in Units 1 to 5. All contain stimulus material in Section B, to give students the opportunity to demonstrate the ability to analyse and evaluate previously unseen written material. Candidates must show the ability to identify stages in an argument, and different types of knowledge and argument, and to assess whether the conclusion is logically justified. Section B only assesses AO4 and AO2.

Through a piece of extended writing, Section C requires you to develop and present your own argument in order to reach a justified conclusion in response to an essay question. This section only assesses AO3 and AO2.

There is a different approach to the Synoptic Unit (Unit 6). The requirement to write two essay answers means that each Assessment Objective is assessed twice. Answers are marked initially on your ability to marshal evidence to construct a reasoned argument (AO3). After this, the answer is assessed against AO1 and AO4.

How is General Studies assessed?

Like most A level courses, General Studies is a modular examination and consists of six modular assessment papers. Three of these, corresponding to the three broad areas of study, constitute the AS assessment. Most candidates are expected to complete AS during their Lower Sixth year.

Students seeking to convert AS into an Advanced Level qualification must take another three papers (A2). These may be taken either as three separate modules at different times in the course or they may all be taken at the same time as end-of-course examinations.

Edexcel offers a coursework option at AS as an alternative to the Society paper specifying broad areas from which titles may be selected. It allows the use of appropriate work prepared for other courses.

How to use this book

There are four main units in this book:

- Culture,
- Science,
- Society,
- The Contemporary World – this unit asks you to use your awareness of the three other units to discuss more general issues.

There is also a section covering Thinking and Analytical Skills and an appendix which suggests some Key Skills activities.

The grids at the beginning of the book indicate the relevance of each spread to each of the different examination board specifications.

Every unit is subdivided into double-page sections, each dealing with a specific topic. Links to other relevant sections and Key Skills activities are given under the main heading of each section.

Each spread includes:

- background information about the topic,
- source material in the form of written material, tables, graphs, illustrations and photographs,
- a glossary for technical vocabulary,
- issues to be discussed – these provide a starting point for group discussion or individual research, and could be used as a basis for coursework,
- activities – structured and essay questions similar to those on real examination papers,
- Thinking and Analytical Skills activities,
- Where now? – books, articles and websites for further research.

The source material contains information, comments and opinions on the issues. Many of these are deliberately provocative and are designed to stimulate discussion!

The activities can be used either for follow-up work for personal study or to generate coursework. Many are designed to provide you with practice in Key Skills – in particular Use and Application of Number.

Where now? provides no more than a starting point for further work. The books can be found in most public libraries and contain additional material on the topics. Again, web addresses are intended to provide a starting point. (As with any Internet provision they need to be used with care.)

You should supplement the material in this book with your own reading and research. You should aim to read broadsheet newspapers (like *The Guardian, The Times, The Observer* and *The Independent*) and relevant magazines and periodicals (like *New Scientist, The Sunday Times* 'Culture' section and *New Statesman*). Documentaries and discussion programmes (like *Panorama, Tomorrow's World* and *Horizon*) on television are another valuable resource.

Unit 1 Contents and specification coverage

Unit	Section	Culture, morality, arts and humanities Topic title	Edexcel AS	Edexcel A2
1.1		**Understanding and appreciation of the nature and importance of culture**		
	i	What is culture?	•	
	ii	What is high culture and how is it different from folk culture?	•	
	iii	Are popular and mass culture inferior to high culture?	•	
	iv	Will Britain have a multicultural or a monocultural society?		•
	v	Why should the arts be subsidised?		•
	vi	Is high culture preferable to popular culture?		•
1.2		**Beliefs, values and moral reasoning**		
	i	What is the need for moral reasoning?	•	
	ii	What do utilitarians say makes 'right actions' right?	•	
	iii	Should moral conduct result from duty or social contract?	•	
	iv	Is genetic modification morally wrong?		•
	v	Should artists have total freedom of self expression?		•
	vi	Can families be morally justified in the modern world?		•
1.3		**Religious beliefs and experiences**		
	i	Why do some people need religion?	•	
	ii	Are different religions really very different?		•
	iii	Is there any point to religious symbols?	•	
	iv	Do all religions share the same symbols?		•
	v	Can scientific knowledge and religious belief be reconciled?	•	
	vi	Can you be religious and live the life you want to?		•
1.4		**Creativity and innovation**		
	i	Was Michelangelo the greatest artist who ever lived?	•	•
	ii	What made Baroque music different?	•	•
	iii	Why did classical architecture make a comeback?	•	•
	iv	Was Romantic 'sentiment' really self-indulgent?	•	•
	v	Was Monet a genuine innovator or simply a rebel?	•	•
	vi	Why were the 'angry young men' angry?	•	•
1.5		**Aesthetic evaluation**		
	i	What is art?		•
	ii	When is a masterpiece not a masterpiece?		•
	iii	What are the main characteristics of Baroque art?		•
	iv	Is there such a thing as classical style?		•
	v	How romantic was Romanticism?		•
	vi	What impression did the Impressionists create?		•
1.6		**Media and communication**		
	i	Does the UK suffer from media saturation?		•
	ii	Who owns the media?	•	
	iii	Who controls the media?		•
	iv	Does the media encourage violent behaviour?	•	
	v	Does advertising show that people are influenced by the media?		•

Unit 2 Contents and specification coverage

Unit	Section	Scientific horizons Topic title	Edexcel AS	Edexcel A2
2.1		**Characteristics of the sciences**		
	i	Where did the universe come from and where might it be going to?	•	•
	ii	Is our climate changing? What can we do about it?	•	
	iii	Do we need genetic modification?	•	•
2.2		**Nature of scientific objectivity**		
	i	How far can we explain human behaviour with biological theories?	•	•
	ii	Faster than the speed of light?	•	
	iii	How difficult is it for new scientific ideas to be accepted?	•	•
2.3		**Understanding of scientific methods**		
	i	How are scientific theories produced?	•	•
	ii	Radioactivity and the modern atom	•	
	iii	What do we mean by scientific proof and solving problems?	•	•
2.4		**Moral responsibility**		
	i	How can we justify the Human Genome Project and its consequences?	•	•
	ii	Where is medical science taking us?	•	•
	iii	How can scientists influence the outcomes of their work?	•	•
2.5		**Mathematical reasoning and its application**		
	i	Testing hypotheses: what use are statistics?	•	
	ii	Presenting data	•	
	iii	Practical activities	•	
2.6		**The relationship between technology, science, culture and ideology**		
	i	Science, technology and civilised living	•	•
	ii	Is scientific and technological progress always for the best?	•	•
	iii	How do the media deal with scientific and technological change?	•	

The grids indicate where sections will meet the requirements of the Edexcel Specification. Some material will be useful even if it is not indicated in the grids.

Unit 3 Contents and specification coverage

Unit	Section	Society, politics and the economy Topic title	Edexcel AS	A2
3.1		**The nature of ideologies and values**		
	i	What are 'social values'?	•	
	ii	How and why do 'social values' change?		•
	iii	Is old age a problem?	•	
	iv	Can we afford old age?	•	
	v	Is disability a social or personal issue?		•
	vi	Are men still more equal than women?		•
	vii	Is Britain a multicultural or monocultural society?		•
3.2		**Political processes and goals**		
	i	What is the difference between the major UK political parties?	•	
	ii	Can we have both low taxes and high government spending?	•	
	iii	Do we need regional government?		•
	iv	How important are pressure groups in the political process?	•	
	v	Should the voting system be reformed and, if so, how?		•
	vi	What is the European Union and how does it work?	•	
	vii	What has Europe done for Britain?		•
3.3		**Explanation and evaluation of human behaviour**		
	i	What do social scientists do?		•
	ii	How scientific are the social sciences?	•	
	iii	What's the point of work?		•
	iv	How much unemployment do we need?	•	
	v	Who pays the price of unemployment?	•	
	vi	What should the government do about unemployment?		•
	vii	How and why has the use of leisure time changed?	•	
	viii	Should government provide leisure facilities?		•
3.4		**The relationship between law, culture and ethics**		
	i	Why do we need law?	•	
	ii	Does the law make things right?	•	
	iii	What is the point of punishment?	•	
	iv	Should capital punishment be restored?		•
	v	Can we afford legal aid?		•
	vi	Does society benefit from deviant behaviour?		•
	vii	Does Britain need a Declaration of Human Rights?	•	
3.5		**Social and economic trends and constraints**		
	i	What are families and why do we need them?	•	
	ii	How many types of family does society need?	•	
	iii	Have attitudes to marriage changed?		•
	iv	Are single-parent families a social problem?		•
	v	How have demographic changes affected family life?		•
	vi	Is society too youth centred?	•	

Unit 4 Contents and specification coverage

Unit	Section	The contemporary world Topic title	Edexcel AS	 A2
4				
	1	Should ethnic minorities be fully integrated into society?		•
	2	Can a modern society afford not to have an integrated transport policy?		•
	3	How real are soap operas?		•
	4	Is the abuse of drugs killing sport?		•
	5	Should adoption be made easier in this country?		•
	6	Should one person ever be allowed to help another to 'die with dignity'?		•
	7	Will human beings soon be able to live for ever?		•
	8	Should organ donation be made compulsory?		•
	9	Should embryos with inherited diseases be aborted?		•
	10	Do animals have rights?		•
	11	Does the pursuit of science lessen the need for religion?		•
	12	Does society still need religion?		•
	13	Is there anyone out there?		•
	14	Are art and science totally different activities?		•
	15	Why should society fund scientific research?		•
	16	Does more technology lead to happier working lives?		•
	17	Are large multinational companies bad for us all?		•
	18	Should Sunday be a special day?		•

What is an argument?

Links: TA 2; 3; 4; 5

Introduction

Most people use 'argument' to describe a quarrel or disagreement. However, it can also mean the process of giving reasoned support for or against an idea or claim.

An argumentative person need not be aggressive and not only makes simple assertions, but uses evidence to support and justify ideas.

Background

Logical arguments contain several separate but linked statements, consisting of **proposition**, conclusion and argument. The proposition, which may be either explicit or implicit, outlines an issue for consideration. The conclusion, or main claim, is what is being argued for. The conclusion may be at the beginning or end of a passage and should be clearly linked to the proposition. The argument proper consists of statements advanced to support or justify the conclusion, in response to the proposition. Its purpose is to show how a conclusion has been reached. Reasons, based on evidence, advance the argument. Balanced arguments consider all aspects of the subject. Arguments may be objective or subjective. If in favour of the proposition, they are not accepted uncritically, nor are they dismissed out of hand if they are against the proposition.

Arguments aim to establish the reliability or truth of a proposition using reason. Effective arguments are well informed, knowledgeable and thoughtful. Ineffective arguments often rely on unsupported prejudice, **rhetoric** or emotion. The structure and supporting evidence of an argument can, on the basis of reason, be analysed to determine its soundness, validity and justification. An argument may support (positive) or oppose (negative) a proposition. There are several different types of argument:

- **Deductive** or 'sound' arguments present a number of assertions which lead to an inevitable conclusion (provided the assertions are true). Often they are presented as syllogisms. A simple example might be: 'Rain is water. Water is wet. Therefore rain is wet.' Since the conclusion can be deduced from the early statements, the argument is sound. Such arguments move from a general to a specific point.
- **Inductive** reasoning uses observation of specifics to develop a generalisation. A conclusion's accuracy may increase as the available evidence increases. Provided the **premises** are true, the conclusion is more likely to be true than false, although it is possible for premises to be true and the conclusion false. An inductive argument is strong if the truth of its premises makes the truth of its conclusion very likely. Inductive reasoning is less straightforward than deductive reasoning. It is easy to make mistakes in observation and available evidence may be incomplete.
- **Analogy** is often used in arguments about morality and law. (An analogy is a comparison or similarity drawn between two things or ideas.) This requires clear thought about the principles applicable to particular situations. In effect, analogy uses old ideas to develop new knowledge, by explicitly identifying similarities. A simple analogy is a comparison between an electric pump and the human heart. Argument by analogy establishes general principles by comparison and seeks to apply them to specific cases.
- Arguments based on an authority rely on an individual's alleged expertise on a particular subject. Often the claim is made that something must be correct because 'X', who is an expert, says it is. An expert in one field is not necessarily an expert in others and is no more entitled to claim authority than any other person. This type of argument only holds water if valid supporting evidence is presented. Assertions made by individuals, however well qualified, do not alone justify a claim. Evidence consists of facts, not simply opinions.
- Emotional arguments based on feelings, whether the author's or audience's, may be the result of beliefs or experience, rather than objective fact. Although opinions can be accepted or rejected, they cannot, by their nature, be proved true or false simply on the basis of belief. Consequently feelings are not a sound basis for an argument, unless supported by clear evidence.
- Ontological arguments seek to establish the truth on the basis of definition and reason. They do not require detailed knowledge of the world or physical evidence but depend on reason alone, arguing that anything that can be defined and understood must necessarily exist.

Glossary

proposition: a statement or assertion; a problem

rhetoric: the art of persuasive or impressive speaking; language designed to persuade or impress

deductive: reasoning by deduction; inference from the general to the particular

inductive: reasoning based on induction; inferring general laws from particular instances

premises: a previous statement from which another is inferred

analogy: process of reasoning from parallel cases

What do you think?

Read the passage below and identify the conclusion and different types of argument used.

It could be the ultimate test of female friendship. The time-honoured tradition of ladies leaving the room in pairs to powder their noses has been taken one step further with the introduction of the two-person toilet cubicle.

The 'twobicles' have been undergoing trials in nightclubs in Manchester, Glasgow and Kingston upon Thames and may be extended nationwide, allowing women to continue their conversations uninterrupted by the call of nature.

Club bosses believe that the lager-loving 'laddettes' of today have shed their inhibitions to such an extent that using a toilet in front of a friend will no longer raise even the faintest of blushes. The twin toilets are in full view of each other without any separating screens to protect the user's modesty.

'It may come as a surprise to the older generation, but it is a fact that young women like to go to the toilet together,' said the manager of a 1,600-capacity nightclub in Manchester, which unveiled a double cubicle last week. 'Now they won't have to squeeze into one cubicle.'

Previous attempts to give the female lavatory the communal atmosphere of the gents have met with little success. The Lady P, a female urinal was unveiled in March last year to much fanfare but has yet to catch on. However, early reports suggest the twobicle is proving more popular, attracting queues last week while single stalls stood empty. 'It's a brilliant idea which makes it much easier to talk to each other,' said Mandy Fox, 22. 'Men line up at urinals together – this is the same sort of idea. Spending a penny is the most natural thing in the world so I don't see any reason to be prudish about it.'

Jenny Brannigan, 18, queued to sample the novelty with her best friend Serena Carrington, 21, ignoring the empty single cubicles. 'It makes it easier to talk without being overheard,' she said.

First Leisure which owns a chain of 44 nightclubs, is expected to expand the scheme nationwide. However, other companies are more circumspect, believing that the twobicle would stretch even the closest of friendships.

Camilla Chiphowe, 18, who declined to try the twobicle last week, said: 'I wouldn't share a toilet even with my best friend. The girls who use them must have no shame. I'm broadminded, but synchronised peeing is taking things too far.'

There are also concerns that the twobicle will give its users carte blanche to get carried away with their conversation and become distracted from the matter in hand.

'If you allow two women into the same cubicle they'll talk for ever,' said Gill Nightingale from a Liverpool nightclub, which has rejected the idea. 'Queues in the ladies are long enough. The last thing we'd want to do is make them worse.'

Adapted from *The Sunday Times*, 3 September 2000

Issues to be discussed

- In a group, write examples of each type of argument described opposite. Clearly identify **a** the proposition, **b** the conclusion, **c** different reasons given to justify the conclusion, and **d** evidence cited to support the reasons.
- Examine a newspaper or magazine article to identify **a** the proposition and conclusion, **b** the stages of the argument, **c** the types of argument used, and **d** to what extent the conclusion is justified by the reasons and evidence contained in the argument.
- Discuss which type of argument is the most effective. Give reasons to justify your conclusion.

Activities

1. Identify the different stages in the argument in the passage.
2. To what extent are the arguments used supported by evidence?
3. How reliable is the evidence presented?
4. Find two examples of argument based on authority. In what ways might the claim to be an 'authority' be **a** justified, and **b** unjustified. Give reasons for your answer.
5. Find examples of deductive and inductive reasoning in the passage.
6. Find two examples of argument from analogy. How valid are the comparisons made?
7. To what extent is the conclusion of the passage implicit rather than explicit? How far is it justified?

Where now?

Popkin and Stroll, *Philosophy*, Heinemann, 1993

W. C. Salmon, *Logic*, Prentice Hall, 1984

www.dartmouth.edu

www.sussex.ac.uk

plato.stanford.edu

How do we know that we know?

Links: TA 1; 3; 4; 5

Introduction

The words 'know' and 'knowledge' are often used in ordinary speech and have a variety of meanings which most people would claim to understand. 'Knowing something' usually implies that it is believed to be true. In this context, 'knowing' has the sense of personal conviction. It may be used as an alternative to 'believe', 'think', 'acquainted with', or 'familiar with'. It may imply a hunch, a hope or an **opinion**.

Background

Epistemology (theories of knowledge) deals with questions about how knowledge is acquired, its nature and extent, and how claims to reliability can be tested. The issue of certainty is critical. Some theories claim to establish absolute certainty, while others recognise that truth is relative.

Before the eighteenth century, **reason** was regarded as the only way to establish true knowledge. Plato and Socrates taught that things learnt through the senses were unreliable. They claimed knowledge was innate and simply needed to be unlocked. This was done by rejecting sense-based evidence and relying entirely on reason. Such knowledge, when discovered, was certain. It is called '*a priori*' or 'before the event' knowledge, since it is known to be true without reference to experience.

Descartes (1596–1650) established modern rationalism. Starting as a radical doubter, he discovered he could accept certain propositions as true, provided a rational case for them could be established. The principle of his philosophy was based on his discovery 'I think, therefore I am.'

Empiricism developed as an alternative to pure reason. Scientists and philosophers, like Locke, claimed knowledge could be acquired only through the senses, based on experience. Modern scientific research, through which hypotheses are developed and tested by experiment and enquiry, developed from this theoretical position. As information increases, the hypothesis is refined and knowledge becomes more certain. Inductive methods recognise that absolute knowledge may never be acquired, but that enquiry can strengthen probability and certainty.

Knowledge can be divided into 'objective' and 'subjective'. Objective knowledge consists of facts which are generally accepted to be true. It is not influenced by personal feelings. However, subjective knowledge is based on personal feelings and opinions. It may not always be accepted as true by everyone.

An ideal approach is one that combines reason and investigation. This is called '**a posteriori**' or 'what comes after' because truth can only be established empirically.

Beliefs, often equated with knowledge, are generally personal, involving trust or confidence. Beliefs may not lend themselves to empirical investigation. An individual may be convinced of the truth of a proposition, but others may feel there is insufficient evidence or knowledge to guarantee certainty. Belief may come from revelation, experience or reason. Statements of belief, though expressed as knowledge, may in reality be little more than expressions of **surmise**, suspicion, opinion, **intuition** or faith and conviction.

Beliefs only become knowledge when the truth of a proposition can be established to the satisfaction of believers and others. To believe in someone or something (like God or a religious teaching) means to trust. To believe the truth of a proposition requires conviction based on sufficient reliable evidence. Throughout history people have firmly believed in propositions which have been subsequently disproved.

Moral values are closely linked to belief. For those who believe in absolute standards and truths, it is logical to claim to know what is right or wrong. The truth of such claims may be **verified** or challenged on the grounds of reason. At one extreme this knowledge is comparable to opinion, while at the other it comes closer to true knowledge (for example, where a moral judgement – 'it is wrong to kill' – is generally accepted). In this sense, people may claim to know the correct conduct towards others and would call this innate knowledge.

Truth and falsity are essential features of knowledge. Rationalism is aimed at establishing absolute truth, so that knowledge is certain and beyond challenge. Empiricists recognise that because knowledge is incomplete, 'truth' is only provisional. A proposition is accepted as true on the basis of available evidence. Truth, therefore, is what corresponds to available facts and falsity is what does not. It is impossible to know or believe anything that is demonstrably untrue.

Glossary

opinion: judgement or belief based on grounds that may be short of proof

reason: the intellectual faculty of humans whereby conclusions are drawn from premises

surmise: make a guess

intuition: immediate mental conclusion not based on reasoning

verified: examine in order to establish truth

What do you think?

Do you agree that reason rather then experiment is the only way to develop true knowledge?

Only about half the hydrogen gas in the early universe ended up in galaxies like our own – the rest went missing. Now astronomers claim they've found it. 'A substantial amount of it appears to be in superhot clouds hiding in intergalactic space,' says Todd Tripp of Princeton University.

Astronomers suspected that a huge amount of hydrogen had gone missing because deuterium – heavy hydrogen – was once abundant in interstellar space. The deuterium is thought to have been forged in the first few minutes after the Big Bang, but it is easily converted into helium if there is a lot of hydrogen about. 'The scarcity of deuterium [today] tells us that when it was born there was about twice as much hydrogen around as we see today tied up in galaxies and galaxy clusters,' says Tripp.

One explanation for the disappearance of the hydrogen was that it became so hot its atoms lost their electrons. Since atoms can't emit or absorb light without electrons, the hydrogen effectively became invisible. According to theorists, this could have happened if some hydrogen was 'shock-heated' to over 100 000 °C as clouds of the gas collided at incredible speeds. 'The stuff that remained cool congealed into galaxies,' says Tripp. 'The stuff that was hot was simply too hot to be held together by gravity and got left out.'

Tripp and his colleagues have now found evidence of the 'left-out stuff' by pointing the Hubble Space Telescope at a distant quasar. They found slices had been taken out of the quasar's spectrum by highly ionised oxygen in gas clouds between the quasar and earth. The oxygen atoms had lost five electrons, which could be because they were being remorselessly bombarded by a huge number of superhot particles. Tripp's team has extrapolated these results to the whole universe. 'Our calculations show there's easily enough [hydrogen] nuclei to substantially alleviate the missing hydrogen problem,' Tripp says.

'Finding evidence for an amount of hydrogen gas equivalent to that in all the stars and galaxies is clearly a major achievement,' says David Hough of Trinity University, Texas. But he adds that all the ordinary matter in the universe accounts for only a few per cent of all the matter there is.

There is ten times as much 'dark matter' as ordinary matter and its identity remains elusive. What's more, it has recently been discovered that empty space contains twice as much 'dark energy' as ordinary and dark matter combined. 'Astronomers have got a long way to go,' Hough says.

Confirmation that the universe contains a prodigious amount of dark energy has just been found by a team led by David Wittman of Bell Labs in New Jersey. They conclude from the way the matter of the universe bends light from distant objects – a phenomenon called gravitational lensing – that there is not enough matter, including dark matter, to make space 'flat'. But recent measurements of the 'afterglow' of the Big Bang confirm that the universe is indeed flat – so vast amounts of dark energy must make up the deficit.

Adapted from *New Scientist*, 13 May 2000

Issues to be discussed

- Should 'belief' be described as 'knowledge'? Justify your answer.
- If there is such a thing as innate knowledge, where does it come from and how can it be recognised?
- What is intuition and how does it contribute to knowledge?
- Some people claim that they know things intuitively. To what extent can such knowledge be counted as knowledge?
- Write your own examples to show the difference between objective and subjective knowledge.

Activities

1 From the passage identify:

a examples of belief for which the author does not provide valid justification,

b belief that is justified,

c opinions which are presented as though they were knowledge,

d opinions which are clearly opinions,

e rational or empirical knowledge.

2 Identify the stages of the argument.

3 How effectively does the evidence presented justify the conclusion reached?

Where now?

Popkin and Stroll, *Philosophy*, Heinemann, 1993
www.britannica.com
plato.stanford.edu

W. C. Salmon, *Logic*, Prentice Hall, 1984
www.infidels.org
www.unco.edu/philosophy

What are fallacies?

Links: TA 1; 2; 4; 5

Introduction

In order to reach and justify conclusions, arguments provide reasons to support propositions. The quality of an argument depends on accurate reasoning, not factually correct supporting evidence. Sound arguments can be built on faulty evidence and **erroneous** ones on faulty logic. Arguments in which reasons do not support the conclusion are **fallacious**. When analysing an argument, different types of fallacy must be recognised.

Background

Accent is a type of fallacy more easily recognised in speech than in the written word. It occurs when the meaning of a phrase is changed, simply by altering the way it is emphasised. In written form it can be quite difficult to spot. An example, taken from an old song, is 'What is this thing called love?'. Stressing different words can change the meaning. So it might become: 'What! Is this thing called love?' or 'What is this thing called, love?' or as the songwriter perhaps intended, 'What is this thing called love?'.

Citing an authority, whether an individual or a written work, can be a **valid** form of argument. However, just because people are expert in one field, doesn't make them expert in all things. This type of argument may only be reliable if the person quoted is an established authority in the area under discussion, but an equally **eminent** authority might take a different, conflicting view. This type of fallacy can occur when appeal is made to an unnamed authority, whose views cannot therefore be evaluated.

Anecdotal evidence is a simple but very common form of fallacy. It is acceptable to use personal experience to illustrate a point being made. However, this does not in itself provide proof of an argument. Anecdotal evidence can seem very persuasive to those wishing to be persuaded, but lacks conviction for others who have not shared the experience. To be acceptable as evidence, rather than simply as illustration, anecdotes must be independently verifiable.

Beliefs are often used as evidence, but can be fallacious. Just because one, or many people, believe a thing is true, does not make it true. Belief may determine what is understood to be 'acceptable' or 'unacceptable' behaviour or it may reflect common practice (such as 'it is wrong to drive a car without insurance'). However, when used as evidence in an argument, belief must be verifiable. A similar type of fallacy is the appeal to 'common practice'. Just because 'everybody' does something, does not necessarily make it right.

Using threats or force to 'persuade' acceptance of a proposition may succeed in its aim, but is still a fallacy. This type of fallacy is often used by politicians and others in powerful positions. Threats may be direct or indirect, but are not valid arguments.

Arguments against the individual are common, but are fallacies. Personal abuse or criticism directed at an individual rather than his views are examples. The truth of an assertion does not depend on the personal qualities of the person making it. Another form is derogatory reference to an individual's personal circumstance. For example, the credibility of the deputy prime minister, John Prescott, speaking on the value of public transport, was undermined by references to his 'two Jags'. Circumstances may affect credibility, but should not undermine the soundness of an argument.

Arguments from ignorance, which claim that something must be true because it has not been proved false, are fallacies. Lack of evidence may lead to inference, but does not provide proof.

Arguments that are based on the belief that frequent repetition (or 'ad nauseam') makes something true are fallacies. They may encourage acceptance that what is said is true, but they do not produce a sound argument.

Circular argument (or 'begging the question') is fallacious because it works by accepting as true and presenting as a premise, the conclusion that is to be established. This type of argument is very common. After reaching and establishing a conclusion, it is easy later to repeat it as an assertion, but this is not evidence of truth. An example of this type of reasoning is: 'If this action were not wrong, it would not be illegal.'

Causal arguments are often fallacies. Simply because two events occur at the same time does not mean that they are causally related. In particular, if one event occurred before another, it cannot be assumed that the first event was the cause of the second. The argument is a fallacy if other causal factors are ignored.

Glossary

erroneous: wrong, incorrect; false judgement

fallacious: a failure in reasoning which renders an argument invalid

valid: actually supporting an intended point or claim

eminent: respected, distinguished, notable, outstanding

What do you think?

Examples of common fallacies:

a

A: 'God must exist.'

B: 'How do you know?'

A: 'Because the Bible says so.'

B: 'Why should I believe the Bible?'

A: 'Because the Bible was written by God.'

b

A: 'I believe that fox hunting is morally wrong.'

B: 'You would say that, you don't live in the country.'

A: 'What about all those arguments I gave you to show it was wrong?'

B: 'Those don't count. You're jealous because you're too poor to hunt and so you want to spoil my pleasure. Anyway you only repeated what you read in the paper. You can't think things out for yourself.'

c

'I think that hairstyle suits you perfectly.'

d

'The prime minister is a clever and important person. If he says that Italy is the best place to go on holiday, it must be right because he ought to know what he's talking about. I'd prefer to listen to him than to you.'

e

'Yesterday John gave his girlfriend £20. It was stolen from her. It was John's fault that she was robbed, because it wouldn't have happened if he hadn't given it her.'

f

'Belief in God is universal. Everyone believes in God.'

g

'You don't have to go to church to be religious. Most people say they believe in God but don't attend church. They can't all be wrong, can they?'

h

'It is wrong to smoke. Everyone knows that smoking causes lung cancer. If you smoke you will get lung cancer. You deserve what you are going to get.'

i

'People don't read much now since the introduction of television and computers. Obviously watching TV and playing computer games stops them reading.'

j

'Life can't exist in other galaxies. Scientists have been looking for evidence for the last hundred years and haven't found any. If life did exist we would know about it by now.'

k

'Last week I read in *The Sunday Times* that more people wanted William Hague than Tony Blair to be prime minister. *The Sunday Times* is a quality newspaper. If they say it, it must be true.'

l

'Young people today are more caring than their parents. Last week I fell over in the street. A young boy came over to see if I was all right. His mother told him to leave me alone. She said I was probably drunk.'

Other common fallacies

Use www.infidels.org or www.us.nizkor.org to research the meaning of these fallacies:

amphiboly	appeal to novelty
appeal to common practice	appeal to popularity
appeal to pity	appeal to ridicule
appeal to emotion	appeal to tradition
appealing to the gallery	biased sample
appeal to flattery	burden of proof
appeal to nature	non sequitur
analogy	red herring
slippery slope	straw man

Activities

1 Identify each of the fallacies given above.

2 Construct your own examples of the different types of fallacy described on the previous page.

3 Write out, with examples, definitions of the fallacies listed above or other common fallacies.

4 Examine a newspaper report and find examples of different types of fallacies that have been used.

5 Why can a form of argument sometimes be valid and at other times contain fallacy?

Where now?

Popkin and Stroll, *Philosophy*, Heinemann, 1993

www.intrepidsoftware.com

www.unco.edu/philosophy

www.dartmouth.edu

W. C. Salmon, *Logic*, Prentice Hall, 1984

www.infidels.org

www.sussex.ac.uk

Why are arguments sound?

Links: TA 1; 2; 3; 5

Introduction

The reliability of an argument can be assessed in two ways. It can be assessed on factual accuracy or it can be evaluated on grounds of logic. Critical analysis is about examining the quality of the reasoning used and the logical relationship between premises and conclusion. It is not concerned with the accuracy of factual evidence.

Background

Factual accuracy is an important measure of the acceptability of a conclusion, but it must be kept completely separate from logical evaluation. It is perfectly possible for an argument to be sound, even if its supporting evidence is **flawed**, provided that the premises are sufficient to support and justify the conclusion on grounds of reason. Evidence can be factually accurate and yet fail to support a conclusion, in which case the argument will be unsound.

In successful arguments, all the premises are true (though not necessarily factually accurate) and provide sufficient evidence to support the conclusion. An argument is not successful if there are true statements that could be made and which would change the nature of the argument. If changes expand the argument so that the original premises could no longer support it, it would be unsound and therefore unsuccessful.

Deductive arguments can be sound or unsound, but are never 'good'. An argument may only be described as 'sound' if all its premises are true and its conclusion is valid. Conversely, if the premises cannot guarantee the conclusion, either because there is no logical relationship or because a different conclusion could just as easily be drawn from them, the argument is unsound. Sound arguments can be based on false premises, even if they are untrue, provided they support the conclusion logically. Similarly, where the premises are true, but do not logically support the conclusion, the argument must be unsound. Arguments containing fallacies are unsound, even when most of their premises are true. A sound argument cannot have a false conclusion.

Valid arguments are those that have premises which guarantee the conclusion because no other conclusion could be drawn from them. The conclusion is **entailed** by the premises and must follow. A valid argument can only have a false conclusion if at least one of its premises is false. However, the conclusion of a valid argument cannot be false if all of its premises are true.

A good argument is either a sound deductive argument or a strong inductive argument, based on true premises. An inductive argument is described as strong, or **cogent**, if the truth of the premises makes the truth of the conclusion highly likely. A weak inductive argument is one in which, even if the premises are true, the conclusion is no more likely to be true than false. Valid arguments and strong inductive arguments may be 'good' even if their premises are false, provided **inferences** drawn from the premises cannot be faulted logically. That is, the reasoning is good, even though it is based on false premises.

A rationally compelling argument is a 'good' argument when the premises are all known to be true and no equally good argument can lead to a different conclusion. Rationally compelling arguments may be described as 'proof', although those disciplines that talk of proof usually establish their own particular rules of proof.

Rhetorically effective arguments generally succeed by persuading hearers of the truth of their claims by non-rational means. A rhetorically effective argument can be logically weak. Similarly a sound argument can be rhetorically ineffective. Logical criticism should be concerned with the quality of reason rather than rhetoric. Often rhetoric, in logical terms, can be a fallacy.

Additional terms:

- Contraries: it is not possible for both of two statements to be true, although both can be false.
- Contradictories: it is not possible for both statements to be either true or false. That is, one must be true and the other false.
- Logically consistent: it is possible for all statements in a set to be true or for a single statement to be true.
- Logically inconsistent: it is not possible for all statements in a set to be true or for a single statement to be true if it is self-contradictory.
- Necessarily true: a statement cannot be false.
- Contingent statement: a single statement is neither a contradiction nor a necessary truth.
- Logically equivalent: it is not possible for one statement to be true when another is false. That is, both statements must be true or both must be false.

Glossary

flawed: blemished, imperfect or fundamentally weak

entailed: involved as an inevitable part or consequence

cogent: clear, logical and convincing

inference: a conclusion reached on the basis of evidence and reasoning; the process of reaching such a conclusion

What do you think?

Critically examine the arguments presented in the passage below and write a reasoned response to its conclusion.

The credibility of America's presidency has been undermined by recent events in Florida. The destiny of a great nation should not be determined by the vagaries of a single, relatively unimportant, state. Something needs to be done, and done fast, to ensure this farce is never repeated.

Florida is called the Costa Geriatrica because of its large number of retired men and women. Many people in their late sixties and beyond lose both their physical and mental faculties and are no longer able to make sound judgements. We wouldn't let senior citizens take part in the Olympics, because they aren't up to it physically. So why should they be allowed to vote, when they aren't up to it mentally? Look at the number of elderly voters in Florida! Now look at the number of electors who claimed they voted for the wrong man because the ballot 'confused' them! Now ask yourself, do you want them to choose the next president?

We all know old people can't cope with technology. But modern voting needs efficient, up-to-date electronic voting systems. People who can't handle the vote shouldn't be allowed to use it. Voting should be left to those who know what they're doing. It's obvious! Old people can't vote properly.

Old people live in the past and don't understand the modern world. They're too set in their ways and won't change. Most of them probably voted for Bush because they thought he was his father, not because they agreed with his policies – if they ever knew what they were. Their prejudices have robbed us of the liberal president we need.

All they want is to cut taxes so they can keep most of their income. They don't want to give welfare to the poor in deprived areas. They reckon they're entitled to an easy life. High taxes mean less income for them to spend on their 'little luxuries'. You can't expect them to think of other people rather than themselves. So, if they're that selfish, why should they be allowed to vote?

They claim we only have free elections now because they risked their lives in the last world war. What's that got to do with it? They allowed the last war to happen – and the one before that! So they needn't feel good about fighting in it. It doesn't give them the right to tell us what to do.

Anyway, why should the whole country have to wait for Florida to make its mind up? If they can't complete the count like other states they shouldn't be counted at all.

Therefore we've got to ask whether all citizens should continue to have the vote as of right. All young people are denied the vote because of their presumed immaturity, even though many of them can make better informed judgements than their parents. The same blanket exclusion should apply to all over the age of, say, 68. Fifty years is long enough for anyone to have a 'democratic right'. They should give up and retire gracefully.

It's obvious really. Old people have had their chance. We should take the vote away from them and let the people who know what they're doing make the decisions.

Source: Gareth Davies

Issues to be discussed

- Is the argument presented above a good argument? Justify your opinion.
- Do you agree that it doesn't matter if evidence is inaccurate, provided it logically supports a conclusion?
- Would you describe the argument above as either rationally compelling or rhetorically effective? Give reasons to justify your answer.
- In the passage above identify the conclusion and the main stages in the argument.
- Is the author successful in justifying the conclusion?
- How effective are 'persuader' words in an argument?

Activities

1 Identify a small argument inside the main argument.
   a What type of argument is it?
   b Identify the types of knowledge it uses.
   c Does the author justify his conclusion?

2 Compare articles on a current political issue taken from two opposing newspapers. What devices are used by each of the writers to 'prove' their argument?

3 In the passage above, identify at least one example of each of the following fallacies:
   a appeal to authority,
   b appeal to anecdote,
   c appeal to belief,
   d arguments against the individual,
   e causal arguments.

Where now?

B. Skyrm, *Choice and Chance*, Dickenson, 1975
www.infidels.org
www.sussex.ac.uk
www.criticalthinking.org/university
W. C. Salmon, *Logic*, Prentice Hall, 1984
plato.stanford.edu
www.unco.edu/philosophy

How can you tell if a conclusion is justified?

Links: TA 1; 2; 3; 4

Introduction

Arguments are about defending and justifying your opinions by presenting a reasoned case in support of a conclusion. It is very easy to be taken in by persuasive language and **spurious** reasoning. The art of critical thinking is to analyse the logic of an argument in order to establish whether a conclusion is supported – it is not about distinguishing fact from opinion, but rather distinguishing acceptable from questionable claims.

Background

Evaluating an argument involves several stages. The premises and conclusion must be identified. There is no mechanical way to do this, other than by thoughtful and careful reading of the text. Looking for terms like 'since', 'for', 'because' and 'however', which often introduce premises, can help. Hidden or unstated assumptions, taken for granted by the author, are essential steps in the logical development of an argument. It is therefore important to identify and analyse unstated premises. Some statements are not premises, have no relevance to the argument and should be disregarded.

Conclusions may be introduced by 'therefore', 'consequently', 'hence' or 'it follows that'. These words all imply 'this [conclusion] follows from those [premises]'. Ask: 'What is the author trying to show or convince readers about?' or 'What position is being defended?' Answers help to identify the conclusion.

Identify those features of argument that everyone must, reasonably, accept. If the truth of the premises:

- guarantees the truth of the conclusion, it is valid,
- makes the conclusion more likely to be true than false, the argument is strong,
- does nothing to make the conclusion more likely to be true than false, it is ineffective.

If premises are true:

- and valid (logically, not factually), the argument is sound and the conclusion cannot be false,
- but inductive, the conclusion is more or less likely to be true; to assess this, identify other arguments for and against the conclusion to reach a judgement,
- but a weak argument is offered, the conclusion is likely to be false. If it seems attractive, better supporting arguments must be found. However, a questionable or false conclusion means at least one of the premises is false. The argument must be rejected and an alternative conclusion that fits the premises must be developed.

If a false conclusion is based on:

- an inductive argument, additional premises must be found,
- a weak argument, both should be rejected.

Useful guidelines:

- A reader's willingness to bet on the outcome of an inductive argument is a good test of its success.
- How good an argument is depends on the quality of the reasons given for asserting the conclusion is true.
- Are statements simply assertions or is a conclusion being argued for? If yes, what is being argued for?
- Examples are not logical arguments. They may illustrate meaning, but they cannot demonstrate truth.
- If a claim is being argued for, supporting reasons must be given. Causal explanations or personal belief are insufficient to support a claim of truth.
- Logically weak fallacies result in unsound conclusions.
- Argument statements should be arranged in a logical order to avoid **ambiguities** and other defects.
- Qualifying terms like 'may', 'might', 'perhaps' or 'could' often show a **fudged** conclusion.
- Emotive language can obscure the message and hide inadequate factual support or illogical arguments.
- Without supporting evidence there can be no argument, merely unsupported assertion.
- Logical correctness depends on the relationship between premise and conclusion, not on factual truth.

Justification of a conclusion depends on argument and evidence. There are two issues to consider. First, are the premises factually true? Second, is the argument logically correct? These issues should be dealt with independently. Justification can fail on either or both counts. If the premises are false, the justification is inadequate. If the argument is logically incorrect, it is unsatisfactory. However, neither of these proves a conclusion is false.

Glossary

spurious: false or fake; reasoning which appears to be valid, but is not

ambiguities: having more than one meaning; unclear because it doesn't distinguish between alternatives

fudged: presented in a vague or inadequate way to mislead; adjustment of facts so as to present a desired picture

What do you think?

Write a reasoned response to the argument in the passage below. Justify your conclusions.

What happens when you create a society in which marriage is not encouraged, let alone rewarded? And when the tax and benefits system means unmarried mothers are often better off financially without a man around the house? The answer is that you foster places where lone-parent families are the norm and fathers helping to bring up their children are a rarity. For most of the women involved this is a matter of deliberate choice. Men are needed to get them pregnant in the first place and for financial support for the child, usually informal, afterwards. Beyond that they are largely irrelevant.

Trends are clear. In the past quarter of a century, the proportion of children being brought up in lone-parent households has more than tripled, rising from 8 per cent to 25 per cent. Two-fifths of children are born out of wedlock. Britain, of course, has the highest rate of teenage pregnancy in western Europe. Evidence shows decisively that children who perform best at school and succeed in later life are from stable two-parent families. No other arrangements come close.

Without the responsibility of fatherhood, men often become feckless, drift between jobs and descend into crime. Why behave maturely when there is no family pressure to do so? The blight on British society, and the damage done to the country's image abroad, is not solely due to 17-year-old yobs high on alcohol or drugs – every country has those. It is more the tattooed thirty-something marauding male who in the past would have been subject to the civilising influence of marriage and an active role as a father.

It would be easy to dismiss such trends as the natural consequences of modern society, where individual freedoms are greater, long-term commitment is no longer so greatly valued and marriage has ceased to be the norm. But it would be a mistake. Recent American experience, beginning with the pioneering 'tough love' strategy of Wisconsin, which required all welfare claimants, including single mothers, to make themselves available for work, shows that something can be done. In New Jersey, existing single mothers on benefit who have further children will receive no extra welfare.

Britain, however, is stuck at first base. The New Deal for single parents is an expensive failure that puts little pressure on lone parents to take up work if they have no desire to do so. 'Family-friendly' measures, such as the working families tax credit and the children's credit, deliberately do not discriminate between traditional families and lone-parent households. In this government's politically correct world, children will receive little help from the state if they are being brought up in a nuclear family whose head happens to be a higher rate taxpayer. But they will get plenty if their mother is a lone-parent by choice. The married couple's allowance, meanwhile, was a casualty of the chancellor's reforming zeal.

It doesn't have to be like this. The decline of family was not inevitable and is not irreversible. But the government has to recognise the problem and then show the leadership and resolve to act on it. Sadly, neither looks likely.

Adapted from *The Sunday Times*, 3 September 2000

Issues to be discussed

- What proposition is being considered?
- Where is the conclusion? Is it stated or implied?
- What is the point of the argument?
- What reasons are offered to convince the reader of the truth of the conclusion?
- Are there any hidden assumptions?
- Is the reasoning complete?
- Is the argument based on assertion or reliable evidence?
- Is the evidence offered valid, relevant and accurate?
- Are claims complete or are relevant arguments omitted?
- Does the argument deal with opposing viewpoints?

Activities

1 From a quality newspaper or magazine, choose an article containing an argument.
a What are its proposition and conclusion?
b Identify the stages of the argument.
c What different types of knowledge are used?
d What types of argument are used?
e Is the argument strong or weak?
f Is the evidence used:
i factually accurate **ii** logically reliable?
g Is the conclusion justified?

Where now?

Popkin and Stroll, *Philosophy*, Heinemann, 1993
webpages.shepherd.edu
www.us.nizkor.org
W. C. Salmon, *Logic*, Prentice Hall, 1984
plato.stanford.edu
www.sussex.ac.uk

(i) What is culture?

Links: 1.1 (ii); 1.1 (iv) **Key skills:** WO1; WO3.2; WO3.3; C3.1b; C3.1a; N3.1; N3.2; N3.3

Introduction

The term 'culture' is used by a variety of disciplines to mean quite different things. Its meaning is determined by the particular needs and perspectives of those using the term. It originates from a Latin word meaning 'cultivation' or 'tending' and at first related mainly to farming.

Background

The original idea of culture came from farming, where the process of growing, developing and improving crops is termed 'cultivation'. To scientists, culture means the artificial development and growth of bacteria or other organisms in the laboratory. Social scientists use the term to describe the values, norms and material goods characteristic of a specific social group. They recognise many different cultures and often use 'culture' as an alternative to 'society'. In its broadest sense this definition encompasses all socially transmitted behaviour patterns. It is regarded as unique to humanity.

E. B. Tyler, in *Primitive Culture* (1881), described culture as 'that complex whole which includes knowledge, belief, art, morals, law, custom and any other capabilities and habits acquired by man as a member of society'. Aimee Cesair told the World Congress of Black Writers and Artists, 'Culture is everything. Culture is the way we dress, the way we carry our heads, the way we walk, the way we tie our ties – it is not only the fact of writing books or building houses.'

Other writers have focused on a narrower view of culture. The poet and critic Matthew Arnold wrote that culture is 'to know the best that has been said and thought in the world' (1873) and 'it is properly described as the love of perfection; it is a study of perfection' (1869).

J. S. Mill said 'a cultivated mind is one to which the fountains of knowledge have been opened, and which has been taught to exercise its **faculties**' (1863).

In this sense culture must be taught and learned, it cannot be transmitted biologically or genetically. As a result, some individuals may be described as 'cultured' while others are dismissed as 'uncultured'. A cultured person has been educated to understand and appreciate the finer things of life, in contrast to the majority who cannot, for whatever reason, do so.

Culture is often categorised by those human activities collectively described as 'the arts', including painting, sculpture, dance, music, literature and architecture. There is some debate as to whether more recent developments such as film, television, video and other electronic forms of communication should be counted as culture.

Is culture **elitist**? For some, every aspect of all art forms should be included in the definition of culture. Others claim that it should be restricted to include only the finest examples, identified according to specific **criteria**. For many, culture includes the old and excludes anything modern. This has led some to identify different types of culture. 'High' culture, presented as the culture of the discerning few, is distinguished from 'popular', 'folk' or 'mass' culture, which carry overtones of criticism and even rejection.

Glossary

faculties: aptitude for any special kind of action; a mental power, like reason

elitist: belief that the best and most talented members of society should control culture

criteria: the standards by which anything is to be judged

unkindled: literally not set on fire, unlit, hence culturally unawakened and unaware

uncouth: uncultured, uncivilised, literally not known

Issues to be discussed

- Should the term culture be restricted to the arts or should it have a broader meaning?
- How justifiable is it to distinguish between 'high culture' and 'mass' or 'popular' culture?
- What criteria should be used to determine whether a work of art or literature is counted as culture?
- Why should film, TV and video not be counted as cultural?
- How and why is culture often regarded as elitist?

Where now?

J. Storey (ed.), *Cultural Theory and Popular Culture, a Reader*, Harvester Wheatsheaf, 1994

Giddens et al, *Polity Reader in Cultural Theory*, Polity Press, 1994

www.wsu.edu:8001 www.britannica.com

What do you think?

Do you have to be cultivated to appreciate culture or should it be accessible to everyone? Explain and justify your view.

Culture is a pursuit of our total perfection by means of getting to know the best which has been thought and said in the world.

Culture has one great passion, the passion for sweetness and light. It is not satisfied until we all come to a perfect man; it knows that the sweetness and light of the few must be imperfect until the raw and **unkindled** masses of humanity are touched with sweetness and light. We must have a broad basis, must have sweetness and light, for as many as possible. Those are the flowering times for literature and art and all the creative power of genius, when the whole of society is in the fullest measure permeated by thought, sensible to beauty, intelligent and alive. Only it must be real thought and real beauty; real sweetness and real light.

Plenty of people will try to give the masses an intellectual food, prepared and adapted in the way they think proper for the masses. The ordinary popular literature is an example of this way of working on the masses.

But culture works differently. It does not try to win them with ready made judgements and watchwords. It seeks to make the best that has been thought and known in the world current everywhere; to make all men live in an atmosphere of sweetness and light, where they may use ideas, as it uses them itself.

Great men of culture, the true apostles of equality, are those who have had a passion for carrying from one end of society to the other, the best knowledge, the best ideas of their time; who have laboured to divest knowledge of all that was harsh, **uncouth**, difficult, abstract, professional, exclusive; to humanise it, to make it efficient outside the clique of the cultivated and learned, yet still remaining the best knowledge and thought of the time, and a true source, therefore, of sweetness and light.

From M. Arnold, *Culture and Anarchy*, Cambridge University Press, 1932 quoted in J. Storey (ed.), *Cultural Theory and Popular Culture, a Reader*, Harvester Wheatsheaf, 1994

Audience at a Proms concert.

Activities

1 Using the entertainments page of a local or national newspaper, identify the different cultural activities available.
a In a group, define the characteristics of 'high', 'popular', 'mass', 'minority' and 'folk' cultures.
b List the activities advertised in the paper, under the appropriate heading. Comment on any trends or pattern you can identify.

2 Debate the view that 'Culture is what your butcher would have if he were a surgeon' (M. P. Poole, 1938).

3 You have been given the task of arranging a cultural event (art, music or literary) to appeal to a large and varied audience.
a Outline the programme you would propose.
b Write a brief justification for your choice of programme.
c Design advertising material to encourage support for your programme.
d Produce a costing for your programme, including permissions, room hire and performance fees.

Thinking and analytical skills

1 Outline the stages in Arnold's argument.
2 Identify different types of knowledge and argument used in the passage.
3 To what extent and in what ways might Arnold's conclusion be found unsatisfactory?

(ii) What is high culture and how is it different from folk culture?

Links: 1.1 (i); 1.1 (iii); 1.1 (vi) **Key skills:** WO3.1; WO3.3; N3.2; N3.3; IT3.1; IT3.2; C3.1b

Introduction

It is claimed that only people of discernment and educated tastes can appreciate high culture. Forms of artistic expression not conforming to high culture are often dismissed as inferior. It is also claimed that each society develops its own cultural forms to meet its own needs.

Background

High culture is the cultural form traditionally favoured by wealthy upper-class people. It embraces activities valued by **dominant groups** in society who often see it as the only true cultural form. High culture reflects the standards and values of the ruling class who believe that only the **elite**, and not the uncultured masses, can unlock its mysteries. They have the power and influence to define what high culture is.

This exclusivity is enhanced by high prices that place this form of culture beyond the financial reach of ordinary people. The use of specialist **jargon** increases cultural inaccessibility. Lip service may be paid to increasing access to the masses, but little practical is done to achieve this. In the UK, London tends to be the centre of high culture. Other parts of the country are dismissed as '**provincial**'.

Folk culture was the cultural and artistic form of ordinary people in earlier times. In recent years it has been absorbed by other cultural forms, thanks to the expansion of the mass media. This is the culture of the people, rather than culture produced for the people, and consists of dance, music, sculpture and carvings, literature and painting. Surviving examples, often corrupted by commercialisation, include Morris dancing, folk songs and perhaps poetry (such as the work of John Clare).

True folk culture was generated spontaneously in local communities. Though broadly similar, significant variations existed between villages within relatively small areas. Acknowledged masters trained practitioners to develop the necessary performance skills.

Today, folk culture has lost its unique characteristics. It used to be unique to particular localities or social sub-groups, but today has been generalised so that it belongs to the whole society. Much modern folk culture has been 'rediscovered' and is now often mass produced for commercial purposes. Modern folk artists often lack the cultural roots of their predecessors. Folk culture used to be separated from high culture by class divisions, but today is the preserve of middle-class enthusiasts, following hobbies.

Western culture resulted from the merger of western European and latterly American national cultures. The internationalism of eighteenth-century aristocrats, whose Grand Tour provided them with an introduction to all that was 'best' in culture, was an important influence.

Nineteenth-century imperial expansion exported Western cultural forms throughout the world. Native culture was usually regarded as inferior. In the twentieth century, the mass media has encouraged cultural **globalisation** and cultural imperialism. Western culture has become dominant. The rich variety of indigenous cultures is often dismissed, downgraded or merged with Western culture.

Glossary

dominant group: the group in society that has cultural, economic and political supremacy; ruling class

elite: literally the best or most talented members of society; hence those with the power to define values

jargon: language full of unintelligible terms to the ordinary person; language used in a specialist way

provincial: manners, speech, narrow views associated with the countryside rather than the cultural capital

globalisation: the development and diffusion of worldwide social and economic ties

Issues to be discussed

- Why is high culture regarded as belonging to the upper and middle classes?
- In what ways is it necessary to be educated to appreciate high culture?
- Can cultural imperialism be justified? If so, how?
- How effectively has folk culture been rediscovered?
- Is there such a thing as true folk culture? What are the criteria by which its worth should be judged?

Where now?

J. Storey (ed.), *Cultural Theory and Popular Culture, a Reader*, Harvester Wheatsheaf, 1994

I. Davies, *Cultural Studies and Beyond*, Routledge, 1995

www.sosig.ac.uk www.wsu.edu:8001

What do you think?

To what extent do you think it is valid to claim that the only true culture is high culture? Explain your answer.

Working classes prefer arts to 'snobby' football

A higher proportion of adults in lower-income groups participate in the arts than play sport – while their upper- and middle-class counterparts are turning from opera to football.

These are the surprising results of research commissioned by the Arts Council. Its chairman says the cash is needed to serve the entire community. 'The arts can no longer be categorised as an upper- or middle-class pursuit. Even in lower-income groups, half the adults participate in the arts.' Football has become a middle-class obsession.

A poll conducted by MORI has shown that more than 60 per cent of people from all social classes think their life is enriched by the arts, while almost 75 per cent agree there should be public funding of arts projects. Nearly 95 per cent of skilled manual and unskilled workers feel that all schoolchildren should learn a musical instrument, read poetry or take part in other arts activities.

The Arts Council attributes much of this increased interest to the over £1 billion in Lottery money spent on the arts around the country in the past five years, much of it on smaller projects such as new theatres, bands, choirs and community arts projects.

Roger Lewis, managing director of Classic FM and the son of a steelworker from Wales, says 34 per cent of listeners are from lower social groups. 'Snobbery has no place in classical music in this day and age.'

From *The Sunday Times*, 25 June 2000

How effectively does this cartoon support or challenge Roger Lewis's opinion that 'Snobbery has no place in classical music in this day and age'?

Activities

1 In a group, identify different types of high and folk culture shown on television. Examine the output of terrestrial channels and calculate the amount of time (including repeats) devoted to each cultural form on each channel for seven days.
a Show your figures in appropriate graphic or tabular form, to compare the five channels.
b Write a brief commentary to explain your graphs.
c Compare your results with viewing figures for the week. What are your conclusions?

2 Investigate the claim that lower social groups are more interested in the arts than they are in football. Using OHTs, tables and graphs, present a verbal report of your findings and conclusions.

3 Collect evidence (pamphlets, leaflets and posters) of folk culture available in your area. Examine the evidence and identify reasons for the apparent popularity of folk culture.

Thinking and analytical skills

1 Identify and outline the stages of the argument in the passage.
2 To what extent is the author able to justify his argument?
3 What additional types of knowledge or argument could you use to support its conclusion?

(iii) Are popular and mass culture inferior to high culture?

Links: 1.1 (vi); 1.1 (iii) **Key skills:** WO3.1; WO3.2; C3.1a; C3.3; N3.2

Introduction

It is often suggested that, while high culture is aimed primarily at the upper classes, popular culture exists for ordinary people. Advocates of the view that popular culture is a contradiction in terms, claim that no art form can simultaneously appeal to the majority and possess true cultural value. Since limited appeal (as in opera and ballet) is often taken as proof of cultural value, they claim that it follows that popular culture must be inferior.

Background

Popular culture often has a negative ring. It literally means 'of or carried on by the people', with 'people' referring to the majority or to lower social classes and income groups.

Television illustrates this distinction. At first only one broadcasting channel existed. Then commercial television – intended to have more popular appeal – was introduced. Viewing habits and a preferred channel seemed to reflect a social and cultural status.

The implication is that popular art forms appeal deliberately to a majority audience because qualities that make them inaccessible have been removed. Popular culture seems to make few demands on **discernment** or taste.

A simple definition of popular culture is 'well liked by many people'. This includes many television programmes (like soaps and game shows), popular music and cinema. It is also possible for high culture to be popular, through the work of performers like Pavarotti or Lesley Garrett. Similarly, the adaptation of Jane Austen's books for cinema and TV has attracted millions. Popular culture can become high culture, as happened with the works of Shakespeare.

Popular culture has been defined as 'the **authentic** voice of the people', originating spontaneously rather than being imposed by a dominant group. However, it is often suggested that it fails to meet required cultural standards. Many critics of popular culture define the criteria for judging high culture. Some claim the ruling classes use popular culture to control other social and economic groups.

Mass culture is often used as a synonym for popular culture. The masses comprise large **disparate** groups, have little in common and lack shared values. Mass culture, it is claimed, is produced for commercial rather than artistic reasons. Its development and spread, in contrast to folk culture's appeal to distinctive groups, is largely thanks to the mass media.

Manufacturers determine what is popular, as with any commercial product, by responding to market forces. Customers play no part in the creative process. Audiences are neither homogenous nor discriminating,but customers retain some powers of **discrimination** and control.

Significant questions about popular culture include:

- Who precisely are 'the people'?
- Who determines how popular culture will develop?
- How and when does popular become high culture?
- Does popular automatically mean inferior?
- How does the media promote popular culture?
- How important is education in selecting, promoting and transmitting ideas about what is good?
- Whose values are reflected in culture?

Glossary

discernment: appreciation of qualities, insight, mental sharpness

authentic: genuine, of undisputed origin, trustworthy

disparate: essentially different, diverse in type

discrimination: the ability to recognise differences, to make a distinction between

Issues to be discussed

- Is there any real difference between mass culture and popular culture?
- To what extent is it true to say that the appeal of popular culture is artificial, owing more to advertising than taste?
- If a high cultural art form becomes popular, does it lose the qualities that made it great?
- What criteria should be used to judge whether a work of art belongs to popular or high culture?
- Can *Coronation Street* and *EastEnders* be described as cultural?

Where now?

J. Storey (ed.), *Cultural Theory and Popular Culture, a Reader*, Harvester Wheatsheaf, 1994

I. Davies, *Cultural Studies and Beyond*, Routledge, 1995

www.sosig.ac.uk www.wsu.edu:8001

What do you think?

'It doesn't matter whether popular culture is produced by the people or for the people, since its main purpose is to keep them in their place.' Examine the arguments for and against this view.

For about a century, Western culture has really been two cultures; the traditional kind – let us call it 'high culture' – that is chronicled in the textbooks and a 'mass culture' manufactured wholesale for the market. In the old art forms, the artisans of mass culture have long been at work; in music from Offenbach to Tin Pan Alley; in architecture, from Victorian Gothic to suburban Tudor. It has also developed new media of its own, into which the serious artists rarely venture: radio, the movies, comic books, detective stories, science fiction, television.

It is sometimes called 'popular culture', but I think 'mass culture' a more accurate term, since its distinctive mark is that it is solely and directly an article for mass consumption, like chewing gum.

The historical reasons for the growth of mass culture since the early 1800s are well known. Political democracy and popular education broke down the old upper-class monopoly of culture. Business enterprise found a profitable market in the cultural demands of the newly awakened masses and the advance of technology made possible the cheap production of books, periodicals, pictures, music, and furniture in sufficient quantities to satisfy this market. Modern technology also created new media, which are especially well adapted to mass manufacture and distribution. The phenomenon is thus peculiar to modern times and differs radically from what was hitherto known as art or culture.

It is true that mass culture began as a parasitic growth on high culture. It is also true that mass culture is to some extent a continuation of the old folk art – the culture of the common people. But folk art grew from below. It was a spontaneous expression of the people, shaped by themselves. Mass culture is imposed from above, fabricated by technicians hired by businessmen; its audiences are passive consumers, their participation limited to the choice between buying and not buying.

From D. Macdonald, 'A Theory of Mass Culture' quoted in J. Storey (ed.), *Cultural Theory and Popular Culture, a Reader*, Harvester Wheatsheaf, 1994

Great classics of literature, like Jane Austen's *Emma*, have been made accessible to the masses through film and television.

Activities

1. In a group, examine the different types of popular high and folk culture. Draw up a questionnaire designed to discover attitudes to different cultural forms. Administer the questionnaire to a wide sample. Analyse your results and present your findings in a report.
2. Discuss ways in which the distinction between high and popular culture is maintained. Write a brief report to explain how high culture could be made more appealing to the masses.
3. What criteria should be used to judge culture?
4. Make a list of the different forms of modern media that have developed in the last 50 years.
   a Discuss the truth of the statement: 'Serious artists rarely venture into these media.'
   b List reasons that might justify your conclusion.
5. Is it true to describe the participants in mass culture as passive?

Thinking and analytical skills

1. Identify the different stages in the argument presented in the passage.
2. What different types of knowledge are used in the passage?
3. Is the author's conclusion justified **a** in the passage, and **b** by the photograph? Explain your answer.

(iv) Should Britain have a multicultural or monocultural society?

Links: 1.1 (i); 1.1 (vi); 4.1 **Key skills:** IT3.2; N3.1; N3.2; N3.3; C3.1a; C3.3; C3.1b

Introduction

It is easy to understand culture in terms of our own, shared British cultural heritage. This understanding may include common western European traditions or be extended to recognise American influences. Lip service is often paid to Britain being a multicultural society, recognising that many UK citizens have vastly different cultural backgrounds. However, the meaning and importance of multicultural are often unclear.

Background

Britain's cultural heritage has been created by waves of invasion, conquest and migration, and by import through commercial and **imperial** links. The UK population is an **amalgam** of ethnic groups, each contributing their own traditions to a common culture. Peoples of the Celtic fringe, while subscribing to the common culture, have retained aspects of their own culture. Welsh, Irish and Scottish languages survive. National identity is preserved through distinctive music, literature, dance and sport.

Migration since the 1950s has led to significant numbers of Asian, African and Caribbean people coming to Britain. Each group has brought with them its own cultural traditions, which owe little to European influence.

Minority groups often form close-knit communities in urban areas. People of Asian background generally retain traditional culture, particularly in film, music, religion, food, dance and literature. This has helped maintain an independent cultural identity. African and Caribbean people have also retained many of their cultural traditions.

Culture helps to create and maintain a sense of identity and of community, but it can lead to division. Cultural differences can result in tension and sometimes conflict, resulting from a combination of ignorance, suspicion and, at times, fear. Tension often exists between generations, with older people trying to preserve their heritage while younger people seek to combine it with, or replace it by, the dominant culture.

The Commonwealth Immigrants Act (1962) virtually ended inward migration. By 1999, 42 per cent (c. 375,000) of the black population and 64 per cent (1.2 million) of Asians were under the age of 35. Most were born in the UK and have therefore grown up as part of the dominant culture.

Politicians often refer to multicultural Britain, implying that all cultures have equal status. In reality, this is not accurate. Almost 95 per cent of the population share a common cultural background; the remainder have different cultural origins, even though almost half were born in Britain.

Possible future developments are:

- Minority and majority cultures become integrated, with disparate traditions merging to produce a new, richer culture. This has happened in the past, but it requires time, tolerance and respect for the various traditions. If successfully achieved, the outcome would be a truly **monocultural** society.
- Aspects of minority culture may be absorbed by the dominant culture. This is already happening, as can be seen by the popularity of Asian food and Caribbean music.
- Different cultures may develop independently, either in isolation or with some level of harmony and tolerance.

If one of the latter two options is successful, Britain will become a genuinely multicultural society. The alternative is the possible **perpetuation** of conflict.

Glossary

imperial: pertaining to an empire, with reference to when Britain controlled much of the world

amalgam: a mixture of substances

monocultural: a country in which there is a single culture rather than several

perpetuation: to make permanent; to ensure continuity

Issues to be discussed

- Should Britain be described as a multicultural society?
- Why has it been more difficult to absorb the culture of Asian than of European and Caribbean groups?
- What steps should the government take to establish greater cultural tolerance?
- Is culture a useful measure of the strength of society?
- What are the potential advantages and disadvantages of each of the three possible future developments outlined above?

Where now?

R. Hoggart, *The Way We Live Now*, Chatto and Windus, 1995

www.scre.ac.uk www.icpa.arc.co.uk www.sosig.esrc.bris.ac.uk

What do you think?

'As culture defines national identity, it is vital that the entire population shares a common culture.' Examine arguments for and against this statement.

The term cultural racism is being used with increasing frequency to draw attention to a shift in the focal point of much racism from physical features to cultural characteristics. It involves prejudice against individuals because of their culture. The culture of minority groups is seen as flawed and standing in the way of their progress. It does not involve belief in the existence of any biological incapacity to change. On the contrary, change is exactly what is sought. Minorities are encouraged to turn their back on their own culture and to become absorbed by the majority culture. Insofar as they refuse to do so, this is thought to justify inferior treatment and discrimination. Cultural racism usually involves stereotyping.

It demands cultural conformity where it is neither necessary nor perhaps even desirable and penalises people unjustly for failure to conform. It may be seen as an attempt to legitimise existing power differences. Opposition to cultural racism does not require the belief that there is no need for any shared values in society. Nor does it involve the belief that different cultures are all equally good or that one should never criticise other cultures. What it does involve is the claim that to insist on cultural conformity, where such an insistence is not justified, is a form of domination and oppression.

In 1986 Seidel claimed that for the New Right 'the problem of race lies in the fact of cultural differences'. The presence of different cultures in a single country, in their view, is likely to cause unacceptable social divisions. They argue that this problem can only be overcome by the assimilation of minority groups, but if they resist assimilation, the only 'radical policy that would stand a chance of success is repatriation'.

From M. Halstead, *Education, Justice and Cultural Diversity*, Falmer Press, 1988 quoted in M. O'Donnell, *A New Introductory Reader in Sociology*, Nelson, 1993

Percentage of people born in the UK by ethnic group and age, 1997–98

	Under16	16 – 24	25 – 34	35+	All
White	98	96	95	95	96
Black Caribbean	94	87	86	17	56
Black African	61	36	27	6	33
Other Black groups	97	94	88	57	87
Indian	96	81	37	1	44
Pakistani	93	65	35	5	54
Bangladeshi	84	40	–	–	47
Chinese	77	41	–	–	26
None of the above[1]	87	61	3	16	56
All ethnic groups[2]	97	93	91	92	93

[1] Includes those of mixed origin [2] Includes those who did not state their ethnic group

Source: *Social Trends 29*, The Office for National Statistics, 1999; www.statistics.gov.uk

Activities

1 Use www.statistics.gov.uk to research the actual number of people represented as percentages in each of the categories shown in the table.
a Construct a table to show these figures.
b Choose any two ethnic groups from the table and construct graphs to show the number in each age group who were born in the UK.
c Calculate the total proportion of each ethnic group not born in the UK.

2 Discuss the possible consequences of a government introducing a policy of racial repatriation. List arguments for and against such a proposal.

3 What activities exist in your area for people with minority culture interests? Use listings or reports in the library or in a local paper to help you gather information. Other sources of information are questionnaires and interviews with members of ethnic minorities. Present your findings in a report.

Thinking and analytical skills

1 Outline the stages of Halstead's argument about 'cultural integration'.
2 To what extent do the types of knowledge and argument used by Halstead support his conclusions?
3 In what ways and to what extent does the table support or weaken Halstead's assertion?

(v) Why should the arts be subsidised?

Links: 1.1 (i); 1.1 (ii); 4.15 **Key skills:** N3.2; N3.3; C3.3; C3.1a; C3.3

Introduction

Reasons for subsidising the arts include **altruism**, the quest for personal pleasure or prestige, political influence, tax relief on expenditure and commercial advantage.

Sources of patronage are individuals, commercial organisations and state-appointed public bodies. Debate exists about the best level of state funding and subsidy.

Background

State funding of the arts has fluctuated in Britain. Comparisons are often made with the relatively high arts funding in Germany and France. From 1950 the level of state funding gradually increased, reaching a peak in the mid-1960s under Jenny Lee, Labour's first Minister for the Arts. In the 1980s, Thatcher's government significantly reduced funding in the belief that activities should be commercially viable or privately sponsored. In the 1990s, state funding began to increase again.

Criticism is levelled at the distribution of funds because of the belief that money is wasted on elitist culture and could better support more popular art forms. The Arts Council says it aims to 'give the maximum benefit to the public by supporting arts projects that make a significant and lasting difference to the quality of life'.

State funding comes from four sources:

- Occasional direct government grants to particular causes. This has declined recently.
- Local Authorities can raise revenue to fund cultural activities, but few spend their full **entitlement**.
- Official bodies, like Arts Councils, receive annual grants for distribution.
- The National Lottery distributes income to worthy causes in the arts, through the Arts Council.

Why subsidise the arts? Because it:

- demonstrates the nation's cultural health,
- maintains **parity** with European practice,
- enables certain threatened art forms to survive,
- makes the arts more widely available,
- keeps costs and prices at a lower level,
- protects and preserves our heritage,
- encourages tourism, generating government **revenue**,
- encourages experiment, talent and new art forms,
- maintains breadth and opportunity of experience,
- encourages expensive stars to perform in the UK,
- allows activities that might otherwise be too costly,
- reduces dependency on commercial values,
- increases accessibility to the arts throughout the UK,
- complements commercial sponsorship.

Why not subsidise the arts? Because:

- it is elitist, subsidising minority-interest art forms,
- money could be better spent on more deserving causes,
- people should pay for what they want,
- the criteria for allocating funds are unclear,
- it encourages inefficiency, waste and poor experiments,
- too much subsidy goes to prestige projects in London,
- costs and stars' fees are inflated,
- subsidies discourage private sponsorship,
- it reduces direct **accountability**,
- it creates and preserves artificial divides between subsidised high art and unsubsidised popular art,
- Lottery subscribers who don't favour the arts don't get value for money.

Glossary

altruism: behaviour based on regard for others rather than regard for self

entitlement: something a person can claim the right to

parity: equality or equivalence

revenue: the state's annual income from which public expenses are met

accountability: taking responsibility for things done

Issues to be discussed

- Do subsidies to the arts protect values or just self-interest?
- Are prestige projects like the Royal Opera House justified?
- What cultural activities deserve to be subsidised? Justify your conclusions.
- Do you agree that art forms which are not financially self-supporting do not deserve to survive?
- Does it matter if UK subsidies are less than European ones?

Where now?

R. Hoggart, *The Way We Live Now*, Chatto and Windus, 1995

J. Storey (ed.), *Cultural Theory and Popular Culture, a Reader*, Harvester Wheatsheaf, 1994

www.artscouncil.org.uk www.culture.gov.uk www. nlcb.org.uk

What do you think?

'Good art doesn't need subsidy because audiences will pay for it.' Critically examine this statement.

I am an unrepentant, unreconstructed anti-Domer. At least £800 million, much of it Lottery money, has been earmarked to pay for a temporary construction plonked down miles from anywhere on a poisoned promontory on the Thames estuary. Meanwhile our capital city will be unable to boast of a single grand public building erected in honour of the millennium. Where will be the equivalent of the 1951 Royal Festival Hall? History will surely conclude that the Millennium Commission has let us down.

These reflections are prompted by a modest but inspiring success story I came across this summer in mid-Wales. Ten years ago a young man named Andrew Lambert used a £10,000 legacy to buy the freehold of a disused chapel in his home-town of Machynlleth. With the help of his music-loving parents and of a sympathetic trust fund, Andrew turned the Tabernacle into a 400-seat concert hall, which is now home to an annual week-long chamber music festival.

For its tenth anniversary season this vigorous organisation was granted Welsh Arts Council lottery money (£60,000) topped up by grants from the Tourist Board and local councils to build a handsome new entrance to the Tabernacle, just right for a multipurpose meeting place.

For the price of Greenwich Dome you could create literally hundreds of such local art centres, and establish an endowment fund to help keep them running, and still have enough to pay for a new cultural complex in our capital. Here endeth the lesson.

From an article by H. Burton, *CLASSIC fM* magazine, November 1997

Government spending on the arts

	1992–93 outturn	1993–94 outturn	1994–95 outturn	1995–96 outturn	1996–97 estimated outturn	1997–98 estimated outturn	1998–99 plans
Culture, media and sport							
Museums and galleries	259	262	270	268	264	264	253
Other arts and heritage	490	484	494	516	508	510	472
Libraries	172	159	186	216	151	141	127
Films	22	24	26	26	24	23	23
Tourism	60	59	62	62	64	64	64
Sport and recreational	50	54	53	54	52	50	49
Broadcasting	57	61	67	71	74	19	76
Administration	16	23	22	21	22	24	23
Total arts spending	**1,127**	**1,127**	**1,180**	**1,235**	**1,159**	**1,096**	**1,088**
Total central government expenditure	191,591	208,707	215,007	229,147	232,947	240,200	252,200

Source: Government Public Expenditure Statistical Analysis for 1998–99; www.statistics.gov.uk

Activities

1 Using the figures in the table, construct graphs to show government spending on the arts. Comment on any trends your graphs show.

2 Calculate the percentage change in government spending on the arts as a proportion of total government spending between 1992 and 1999. Explain briefly:
a Which area of the arts experienced greatest growth?
b Which area of the arts experienced least growth?

3 Write a reasoned reply to Burton's article, from the point of view of the Arts Council.

4 In a group, discuss what permanent memorial to the millennium you would like erected in your locality. Make an illustrated presentation outlining your proposal and including your justification for seeking Arts Council funding. How else might you raise necessary funds?

Thinking and analytical skills

1 Outline the stages in the argument in the passage.
2 List the different types of knowledge and argument used to support the conclusion.
3 Identify any particular strengths and weaknesses in the argument.

(vi) Is high culture preferable to popular culture?

Links: 1.1 (ii); 1.1 (iii); 1.5 (ii); 4.3 **Key skills:** WO3.1; WO3.2; C3.1a; C3.3

Introduction

Culture consists of socially transmitted and learned patterns of behaviour. It is therefore a reflection of society itself. At the same time, culture – in its selected and defined form – helps to shape society. Since no cultural forms are totally static, society's perception of culture changes continually.

Background

Aldous Huxley wrote, 'Culture is like the sum of special knowledge that accumulates in any large united family and is the common property of all its members.' Culture is a means of communication within and between generations, and between societies separated by time or space. Effective communication requires shared language, experience and understanding. Cultural confusion comes when language conveys different meanings to different people.

Each generation views its own culture as definitive and fears declining standards and values in the future. Some feel other cultures are inferior because they are different. Each generation has its own definition of true culture. However, true culture is continually evolving.

The real debate ought not to be about qualities. If culture really is 'the best that has been said and thought' (Arnold), we should recognise good and bad in every art form, through the generations. The important issue is how cultural forms are evaluated and categorised, to distinguish the worthwhile from the **shoddy**. Emphasis is too often placed on the 'dumbing down' effect of mass cultural forms. Insufficient stress is given to modern cultural creativity and innovation. High culture is not all good. Art that is highly valued today is a fraction of original output. High art survives through a process of selection and sifting. Only the best will survive. Future generations will reject some of today's highly regarded works, while regarding as high culture modern works that we perhaps dismiss as insubstantial and **transitory**.

Taste is personal. Some presume to define 'good' and 'bad' art, basing evaluations on clear criteria or personal feelings. Too often judgements are based on snobbery and prejudice rather than genuine appreciation. Responses do not, of themselves, make art better or worse. The opinions of others should not be blindly accepted.

Aspects of culture must be judged in their own right. People should judge art on their own terms and not according to the values of others. Art, of whatever age, that has something to say to its audience is different from work produced primarily for sale. Training of one's critical faculties can create in any person, of any social background, the ability to question and judge critically, not accepting anything simply on face value or according to received wisdom. Art of quality, of whatever **genre** and age, should create feelings of satisfaction in the individual. Art which is mass produced and where the response is predetermined may be pleasing, but may not be great art.

Glossary

shoddy: anything of worse quality than it claims to be; counterfeit, pretentious, trashy

transitory: not permanent; lasting for a short time

genre: kind of style

Issues to be discussed

- Are there universal standards by which to judge good, bad and great works of art? If so, can people be educated or trained to use them?
- Does familiarity make a work of art more acceptable?
- Does society shape culture or culture shape society?
- Can people enjoy high and popular culture at the same time and in the same way?
- Must good art have something to say?

Where now?

R. Hoggart, *The Way We Live Now*, Chatto and Windus, 1995

J. Storey (ed.), *Cultural Theory and Popular Culture, a Reader*, Harvester Wheatsheaf, 1994

www.artscouncil.org.uk www.culture.gov.uk www.natlotcomm.gov.uk

What do you think?

'Culture is simply a matter of personal taste. The good is what we like and the bad is what we don't like. There is no more to be said.' Assess and evaluate arguments for and against this opinion.

We need to distinguish three levels of culture, even in its most general definition. There is the lived culture of a particular time and place, only fully accessible to those living in that time and space. There is the recorded culture, the culture of a period. There is also, as the factor connecting lived culture and period cultures, the culture of the selective tradition.

When it is no longer being lived, but survives in its records, the culture of a period can be very carefully studied. Yet the survival is governed, not by the period itself, but by new periods, which gradually compose a tradition. A selective process is evident in every field of activity. Theoretically a period is recorded; in practice, it is absorbed into a selective tradition. Both are different from the culture as lived.

As well as reducing the number of works, this new process will also alter expressed valuations. When 50 years have passed, reasonably permanent values will have been arrived at. The selective tradition thus creates, at one level, a general culture; at another, the historical record of a particular society; at a third, most difficult to accept and assess, a rejection of considerable areas of what was once a living culture.

Within a given society, selection will be governed by many kinds of special interests, including class interests. The traditional culture of a society will always tend to correspond to its contemporary system of interests and values, for it is not an absolute body of work but a continual selection and interpretation. It is natural and inevitable that the selective tradition should follow the lines of growth of a society, but because such growth is complex and continuous, the relevance of past work in any future situation is unforeseeable.

From R. Williams, *The Long Revolution*, Chatto and Windus, 1961 quoted in J. Storey (ed.), *Cultural Theory and Popular Culture, a Reader*, Harvester Wheatsheaf, 1994

A modern version of Shakespeare's *Macbeth*.

Activities

1 As a group, list and discuss five examples of one of the following which you think deserve to survive into the next century as good examples of modern culture. Explain and justify your choice:
a television programmes,
b popular music,
c dance forms,
d novels or magazines.

2 Conduct a survey of people representing different age groups, asking them what they consider to be the qualities that will enable a work of art to be described as 'good art'. Analyse these responses and present your findings in a brief written report.

3 What is the justification for producing a modern version of a classical artwork?

Thinking and analytical skills

1 Summarise the main points of Williams' argument, identifying the strengths and weaknesses of his conclusion.

2 What types of knowledge and argument are used in the passage?

3 What evidence might you use to **a** support, and **b** challenge Williams' conclusion?

(i) What is the need for moral reasoning?

Links: 1.2 (ii); 1.3 (i); 3.4 (ii); 4.6 **Key skills:** C3.3; C3.1a; N3.1; N3.2; N3.3

Introduction

Every society has standards which are used to control behaviour. These are either embodied in rules or laws or, more frequently, consist of customs that dictate a moral outlook and lifestyle. Such norms are transmitted by families, education, and religious institutions and are upheld by sanctions.

Background

Ethics is the philosophical enquiry into moral values. It investigates how individuals and groups should behave. First, what goals should individuals have to experience a good life? Second, how should individuals in a 'good society' deal with one another? Ethical enquiry tests the **rational** basis of moral judgements. Moral values are examined on the grounds of rational justification.

There are many ethical questions concerning our behaviour. Although some routine, relatively trivial, day-to-day issues do not require much thought, issues that are more challenging require greater thought using accepted principles. Ethics, dealing with such issues, involves reasoning *about* basic and general principles, and *from* them identifying appropriate individual or group behaviour for particular circumstances. Applied ethics focuses on specific issues such as abortion, euthanasia or pollution.

Even though society's norms govern how people live, questions do arise about the kind of behaviour that is best:

- Individuals may oppose societal values and customs because these limit personal freedom of action. They may question whether one belief system is superior to another and which, for them, is better.
- Everyone has different social roles that can lead to internal conflict. In seeking to reconcile such conflict, individuals must prioritise their needs and wants.
- People choose occupations and lifestyles. Changing circumstances may dictate revising these choices. This requires that they analyse their options to decide what is best for them.
- Societies develop and change over time, making some practices and standards seem less appropriate. Individuals must choose whether it is best to live as before or to change to meet new conditions.
- Complex modern societies have pluralistic standards. Individuals must choose which are best for them and how best to relate to people who make different choices.
- Some people do not passively accept being told how to behave. They prefer to think about transmitted standards, developing their own **rationale** for adopting or rejecting them.
- Some believe certain 'absolute' standards should apply to all societies and circumstances. They may try to identify these in order to modify and improve their own behaviour. To do this, it is necessary to analyse what is good and true.
- Strong personal views do not make opinions right. 'Good', 'right', 'best' and 'true' are subjective judgements. Moral judgements require a level of **objectivity** in which personal feelings are less important than rational evaluation.

Glossary

rational: endowed with reason; sane, sensible, moderate; of or based on reasoning, rejecting what is unreasonable

rationale: a reasoned exposition; statement of reasons; the logical basis of an argument

objectivity: dealing with outward things and not with feelings, thoughts or emotions

dogmatism: inflexible teaching as though beyond challenge; authoritative

scepticism: doubting the truth of a received teaching

Issues to be discussed

- What does the term 'a good life' mean for **a** an individual, **b** a group, and **c** society as a whole?
- Is society weakened or strengthened if people challenge received values and standards of behaviour?
- Do you agree that routine, relatively trivial, day-to-day issues do not require great thought?
- What are the arguments for and against individuals constructing their behaviour to meet their own desires rather than the needs of society as a whole?
- Can a society with pluralistic values survive?

Where now?

P. Taylor, *Principles of Ethics, an Introduction*, Dickenson, 1975
McInerney and Rainbolt, *Ethics*, HarperCollins, 1994
R. Billington, *Living Philosophy*, Routledge and Kegan, 1993
www.ets.vidaho.edu/center_for_ethics
www.ethics.acusd.edu
www.ethics.ubc.ca/resources

What do you think?

'Really moral people don't have to think about what to do, they know what is right automatically.' Evaluate the arguments for and against this opinion.

We can think of the process of moral growth as moving away from both complete **dogmatism** and complete **scepticism.** Neither of these conditions can provide reasons for or against moral beliefs. Moral maturity occurs when an individual has the capacity to be open minded about his moral beliefs, defending them by reasoned argument when they are challenged and giving them up when they are shown to be false or unjustified, always holding them tentatively, always willing to listen seriously to arguments on the other side.

Moral growth occurs as an individual develops the capacity to reason about his moral beliefs. He is able to think clearly, calmly and coherently about any set of moral norms. He learns how to give good reasons for accepting and rejecting such norms or else he learns the limits of moral reasoning. But his conclusions are arrived at on the basis of his own reflection.

Even if he ends up with moral norms that happen to be in general agreement with those of his own society, they are of his own choosing, so long as he can show why he thinks they are the norms he ought to follow. The process of critical reflection, however, will often lead a person to disagree with his society.

How can this shift be accomplished? The answer lies in ethics, the philosophical study of morality. For ethics is nothing but the most systematic and thorough endeavour to understand moral concepts and to justify moral norms. We are striving to be clear and rational in our thinking to arrive at the principles of a universally valid moral system. Ethics deals with the most vital issues we shall ever confront in practical life and it alone can provide an adequate foundation for moral growth.

From P. Taylor, *Principles of Ethics, an Introduction*, Dickenson, 1975

'So I find this law at work: when I want to do good, evil is right there with me' (Romans 7v21, New International Version).

Activities

1 Choose an area of social conflict – like a dispute over a hedge or right of way – recently reported in your local press. Collect evidence of how this is reported in the media.

a List arguments for and against the particular issue.
b From the press reports identify examples of **i** objective reporting, and **ii** subjective reporting.
c On the basis of your study, write a brief, reasoned report outlining what you consider to be the best solution for the community.

2 Construct a questionnaire to investigate opinions on whether young people are entitled to develop their own moral views or whether they should accept their parents' views without question. Your sample should include people from a variety of ages and, if possible, ethnic groups.
a Analyse your responses and present your findings in appropriate graphic or tabular form with a written commentary.
b Make a presentation about your findings.

Thinking and analytical skills

1 Identify the different stages in the argument outlined by Taylor.
2 What different types of argument are used in the passage?
3 To what extent is the conclusion justified by the arguments and evidence presented in the passage?

(ii) What do utilitarians say makes 'right actions' right?

Links: 1.2 (i); 2.4 (i); 4.1 Key skills: C3.1a; C3.3

Introduction

Determining whether actions are right or wrong, good or bad, involves moral reasoning. **Normative** reasoning is based on the concept of ordered moral standards and rules of conduct or norms. By referring to these standards (linked to factual knowledge about circumstances) an individual can determine what is right in any situation.

Background

Normative ethical systems can be divided into teleological and deontological reasoning. Teleological systems claim an action is morally right if it brings about good consequences. Good or bad consequences make an action right or wrong. According to deontological systems, an action is right if it accords with moral principles, based on the ultimate principle of duty to society; it is wrong if it does not.

Utilitarianism, though recently criticised, has dominated **consequentialist theory** since the early nineteenth century. Its leading **exponents**, Jeremy Bentham and J. S. Mill, claimed that all actions have identifiable, measurable consequences. The theory is that, since no action is good or bad in itself, these qualities come from whether the action brings about a desirable end. Bentham described **utility** as pleasure, Mill used happiness, while Moore, a later utilitarian, used **intrinsic** good. Effectively these terms are interchangeable. Each agreed that actions that bring about an overall increase of happiness or reduction of unhappiness are good and those that increase pain or decrease pleasure are wrong or evil.

The critical question is: whose happiness? Utilitarian theories are universal as they state that the happiness or unhappiness of all individuals is of equal worth. It is not sufficient to count one's own or family's or friends' happiness, we must take into account the total happiness created by our actions for all people.

Utilitarian decision making follows this pattern:

- Identify alternative courses of action.
- Calculate and quantify the probable total amount of pleasure and pain the consequences of each action will produce.
- Choose the action that is most likely to maximise pleasure and minimise pain, in global terms.

Morally, a person must act to achieve maximum happiness. It is morally wrong to act in any other way. Where two courses of action potentially have the same happiness outcome, choice of action is **indifferent**, even if the results of one action seem fairer than the other.

Practically, this is not possible in everyday life. Delay caused by calculation may increase rather than diminish happiness. Decisions are usually reached by a common-sense view based on past experience. In a new situation, utilitarians seek to analyse possible consequences in order to apply existing principles to new conditions, since the theory teaches that it is the consequences, and not the acts themselves, which are morally wrong.

Critics claim the theory ignores the fundamental moral concept of justice. Justice and utility may be incompatible, since justice, in effect, teaches that it is always morally right to increase one person's happiness at the expense of another.

Glossary

normative: relating to or based on norms

consequentialist theory: the doctrine that an action is right or wrong depending on whether its consequences are right or wrong

exponent: a person setting out a view or a teaching

utility: usefulness, profitability

intrinsic: belonging naturally to something, inherent, essential

indifferent: neutral, having no inclination for or against something; neither good nor bad

Issues to be discussed

- Do you agree that the happiness of every person is of equal worth? Consider examples from your experience, which **a** support this view, and **b** challenge it.
- Are all consequences morally important?
- Should the happiness of animals be taken into account when making moral judgements?
- Is murder always wrong if **a** the death of a person reduces unhappiness for the majority, and **b** if there are no obvious consequences for others?

Where now?

P. Taylor, *Principles of Ethics, an Introduction*, Dickenson, 1975
McInerney and Rainbolt, *Ethics*, HarperCollins, 1994
R. Billington, *Living Philosophy*, Routledge and Kegan, 1993

www.frank.mtsu.edu
www.ethics.acusd.edu
www.ethics.ubc.ca/resources

What do you think?

'"The greatest happiness of the greatest number" is a sound basis for making moral decisions.' Explain and evaluate this view, critically examining arguments for and against it.

We can readily understand why many people have found utilitarianism both obvious and attractive, and why it has been and still is extremely influential. It seems uncontroversial that morality should have a lot to do with people's happiness. Furthermore, happiness isn't meaningless; we're not totally puzzled by what someone means when they say they're happy and we do know what courses of action are likely to make us or other people happy and act on this basis.

In addition, the utilitarian view of the guidelines by which happiness may most confidently be assured seems entirely praiseworthy. The stress laid on impartiality, unselfishness, altruism seems to transcend self-interest and take into account the interests of all concerned. It is not too difficult to give such guidelines our backing. The basic criterion by which we test everything we do – 'the greatest happiness of the greatest number' – seems, for once, clear and rational, and having the virtue of simplicity.

Utilitarianism also seems to be flexible; no law or principle or institution is sacrosanct or unchallengeable. We can't defend things or ideas merely on the basis of authority or tradition: we have to justify them on the 'principle of utility'. So, if you criticise utilitarianism, you don't have to do so on the basis that happiness and morality have nothing to do with each other. The question is not whether happiness ever is or should be a factor in this process, but whether it is the only thing we should ever take into account.

From R. Billington, *Living Philosophy*, Routledge and Kegan, 1993, p.139

The scene after a pop concert. Is this outcome justified if there are more happy concert goers than miserable residents?

Activities

1 Consider and comment on each of these actions from a utilitarian point of view:
a Income tax is raised by 2p in the pound in order to give pensioners a minimum income of £90 per week.
b Examiners raise the minimum mark required to gain a grade E in General Studies to reduce the number of students passing.
c All students staying at school or college until age 18 are paid a weekly grant of £50.
d Married but not single women are paid £1,000 for the birth of a first child and £750 for every other child.
e Retirement age is raised to 70 from 2008.

2 Discuss and produce a definition of happiness.

3 Debate the view: 'My happiness is more important than anyone else's.'

4 Conduct a survey to investigate what people would be prepared to forego in order to increase the happiness of people suffering in Africa or India or Liverpool.
a Create a table to show your findings.
b Write a brief report outlining your conclusions.

Thinking and analytical skills

1 Identify the different stages in the argument developed by Billington in the extract.
2 What types of knowledge and argument does he use?
3 To what extent does Billington justify his conclusion?

(iii) Should moral conduct result from duty or social contract?

Links: 1.2 (i); 1.2 (ii); 2.2 (i) **Key skills:** C3.3; C3.1a; C3.2; C3.1b

Introduction

Moral reasoning is concerned with motives for behaviour and consequences. It is often claimed that human nature is the same in all societies. There are two opposing views of human nature. One claims we are essentially altruistic, while the other insists our conduct is motivated by self-interest.

Background

Altruism is concern for the well-being of others, even if this leads to personal inconvenience, loss or suffering, irrespective of possible reward. Christians believe the death of Jesus perfectly illustrates altruism. Most moral codes include the principle 'love your neighbour as yourself'. For altruists, a good life is one spent helping others.

The behaviour of the self-interested is motivated by their desire to satisfy personal wants. They often fear that others will seek to take advantage of them. For them, a good life means fulfilling their own desires. Selfishness, its most extreme form, excludes the needs of others.

Absolute standards should apply at all times, to all people, in all circumstances. These values must be **objective** and universal and not alter according to changing circumstances, beliefs, emotions or customs. (For example, slavery, if morally wrong today, must have been morally wrong in 2000 BC.) The aim of moral reasoning is to identify moral absolutes and apply them in society. The real issues, if they exist, are who defines them, where do they come from and what happens when two moral absolutes conflict.

Relativism emphasises variety and differences between cultures, where moral values are relative to a specific society, time and circumstances. Values shared by two or more societies are not absolute – moral standards alter through changed circumstances, needs, beliefs and knowledge. Moral relatives and moral absolutes are mutually exclusive.

Hobbes, in the seventeenth century, developed the 'Social Contract' theory. He argued that in their search for satisfaction, people are motivated by self-interest. In a 'state of nature' lacking legal and political systems, each individual can do as they choose. In organised societies mutual obligations exist and are based on self-interest rather than altruism. Individuals agree to obey society's rules in return for its protection. If either party to the contract breaks the agreement, both are automatically released from any further obligation to the other. Moral obedience rests on fear of sanctions, not duty to others. Moral choice is **subjective** and relative.

In the eighteenth century, Kant argued that reason defines moral requirements that are familiar to all. We know we should undertake certain moral actions, even without personal benefit, and should not commit immoral acts, even if we could escape discovery. Each individual's duty is to promote the well-being of others. These values, based on a '**categorical imperative**', are universal, objective and absolute. The categorical imperative is derived from human reason and not an external supernatural source. Reason determines whether actions are moral or immoral. The criteria for judging actions is, 'What would happen if everybody else did that?' This theory demands that society treats each individual as a rational being able to behave in a rational way. As such, each individual is intrinsically valuable.

Glossary

absolute: complete, perfect; not relative or comparative; unqualified, unconditional; without relation to other things

objective: dealing with outward things and not with thoughts or feelings; facts uncoloured by emotions

relativism: comparative in relation to something else; emphasises the variety and difference of cultures

subjective: belonging to the consciousness or thinking as opposed to the real or external

categorical imperative: something that must be done, irrespective of consequence; actions should be guided by 'think what would happen if everybody did this'

Issues to be discussed

- Identify five moral values that might be considered moral absolutes. Give reasons to justify your choice.
- What arguments are there **a** in favour of, and **b** against the idea that there are moral absolutes?
- Identify five relative moral values. How might circumstances cause them to change from moral imperatives to moral choices?
- In what ways can reason teach us that certain types of behaviour are either moral or immoral?
- How might **a** Hobbes, and **b** Kant test the morality of an action?

Where now?

P. Taylor, *Principles of Ethics, an Introduction*, Dickenson, 1975
McInerney and Rainbolt, *Ethics*, HarperCollins, 1994
R. Billington, *Living Philosophy*, Routledge and Kegan, 1993

www.depaul.edu/
www.funrsc.fairfield.edu
www.ethics.ubc.ca/resources

What do you think?

'You ought to be moral, even if it makes you unhappy or imposes severe burdens on you.' Critically examine arguments for and against this view.

Many philosophers have claimed that the best way to live is to treat other people and oneself according to morality. We all have some understanding of what it is to live a moral life. Some actions are easily identified as moral actions and other actions are clearly immoral. Some think that moral standards are relative to cultures and historical periods. However, most defenders of the view that the moral life is the best life think that there are objectively true moral standards. Different moral theories attempt to state exactly what it is to be moral. All theories of morality share some basic features. Morality always includes requirements about how people are to be treated by others. It always imposes some restrictions on acting from selfish interests. For example, morality prohibits harming other people just because you enjoy doing so.

Morality sets some goals for what you should and should not do with your life. Wasting abilities or resources that could contribute to the welfare of others is generally forbidden by morality. You are supposed to disapprove of immoral actions, to encourage other people to act morally and to support those who are the victims of seriously immoral treatment.

Why is living morally the best way to live? Some philosophers claim that it is in a person's self-interest. Living morally brings most satisfaction of informed wants and provides for the proper treatment of other people. It is the intrinsically right or good way to live, whether or not it allows you to satisfy your wants. Being moral is always more important than selfish interests or concern for anything else, such as art, science or environment. Being moral always has priority over any other interest whenever the two conflict. Morality commands without conditions. You should do your moral duty.

From McInerney and Rainbolt, *Ethics*, HarperCollins, 1994, pp. 20–21

Many people find it easier to pretend that social problems do not exist, rather than try to do something about them.

Activities

1 Collect and examine examples of advertisements from the press concerning **i** charitable appeals for an international disaster, and **ii** luxury goods.
a Compare the use of language to appeal to altruism and self-interest.
b How do the visual images used make moral demands?

2 Make a list of 'ought' and 'should' statements from a newspaper. Divide them into **a** moral imperatives and **b** moral choices. What conclusions can you draw from your lists?

3 Debate the opinion that 'you don't have to be moral to be good'.

4 It is often claimed that the Ten Commandments are no longer relevant to modern society. Either **a** produce an alternative list for the twenty-first century, or **b** justify the retention of the original list.

Thinking and analytical skills

1 Identify the different stages of the argument in the passage.

2 What different types of knowledge are used in the passage to support the argument?

3 How effectively is the conclusion of the passage justified by **a** the argument, **b** the evidence presented, and **c** evidence like that in the photograph?

(iv) Is genetic modification morally wrong?

Links: 1.2 (i); 1.2 (ii); 2.1 (iii); 2.4 (i); 4.9 **Key skills:** IT3.1; IT3.2; IT3.3; C3.3; C3.1a; C3.2

Introduction

Genetic modification is an inescapable fact of modern life. Some see it as evidence of the inevitable march of scientific progress, while others consider it to be the most serious social and **ecological** threat facing humanity. As the speed and range of developments increase, scientists and society at large are being faced with many significant ethical as well as practical issues.

Background

Genetic modification has developed because of scientific discoveries about DNA and the genetic code. Farmers and scientists have always used **selective breeding** to improve animals and plants. Recent discoveries have made it possible to transfer genetic material from one species to another, creating **transgenic organisms**. Scientists aim to develop desirable and eliminate undesirable characteristics.

The application of these techniques to farming, medical research and eliminating disease is expanding rapidly. It is now possible to genetically modify plant and animal life in ways not possible in traditional selective breeding. Concern about its possible medium- and long-term effects is growing.

Should scientists be responsible for deciding on the proper application of their discoveries? Should society control scientific research? Politicians, the media and pressure groups as well as society as a whole all claim a decision-making role. Decisions can be made on economic, practical or ethical grounds. Moral reasoning is concerned about the moral right and wrong of genetic modification.

Utilitarians are concerned with consequences and the increase of human happiness, rather than actions. Before reaching a conclusion, they must identify and quantify all potential positive and negative consequences. However, while it is easy to identify some positive benefits to society from genetic modification, there is considerable doubt about its possible harmful effects. A utilitarian must therefore estimate likely consequences in order to determine whether the sum total of human happiness will be increased or decreased.

Absolutists, often influenced by religious beliefs, feel that moral right and wrong are defined in natural universal law by an external force and that absolute moral laws are unchallengeable and binding on everybody. These laws must be examined to see whether genetic modification breaches them. However, it is also necessary to determine whether circumstances allow natural laws to be set aside. Otherwise, however great the potential benefits for humanity, genetic modification is wrong and must be opposed on moral grounds.

Motivists believe that morality is determined by underlying motives. Actions generated by good intentions, designed to benefit humanity rather than the individual, are morally good. Scientists who develop techniques because their duty is to serve humanity act morally. However, if they, or others, use their discoveries for selfish ends, it is morally wrong. Adverse effects, resulting from well-intentioned actions, are not morally wrong.

Genetic modification presents many scientists with a moral conflict. On the one hand, they have a duty to use their research for the good of human society. On the other, their vocation is to expand the sum total of human knowledge. Some would claim it is their duty to make discoveries and the responsibility of others to make moral decisions about the application of their knowledge.

Glossary

ecological: biological area dealing with living organisms, habits, modes of life and relations to surroundings

selective breeding: scientific breeding, using animals or plants with preferred characteristics, to improve the breed

transgenic organisms: where genetic material from one species has been artificially transferred to another

organisms: individual animal or plant, having connected or interdependent parts

Issues to be discussed

- Should ethical controls be placed on genetic modification?
- Should non-genetically modified organisms be available for people who are morally opposed to genetic modification?
- Are the present needs of society as a whole more important than the fears of possible future consequences?
- Should the producers of GM foods be concerned with moral issues rather than profit?
- Does genetic modification challenge any natural laws?

Where now?

Wellcome Trust Lab Notes 1, 2000; www.wellcome.ac.uk
www.genwire.com
www.environment.detr.gov.uk
www.greenpeace.org
www.biotech.or.th/
www.genewatch.org
www.hedweb.com/
www.newsbank.com

What do you think?

Examine arguments for and against the view that the beneficial consequences of genetic modification are morally more important than any possible negative effects.

Professor Watson insists that playing around with plant DNA to make them resistant to insects is justified. 'Seeds,' he says, 'have always been bred to be bug-resistant – by natural selection, plants that didn't have these compounds died out. You have to be able to judge the danger before you introduce bans. You can't just say "this is going to cause harm to the environment" when you don't know if that is true.'

This principle is, he believes, 'antithetical to the liberty which has allowed civilisation to flourish to prevent scientists from doing something good, because you say there is some unknown thing that might go wrong. Change has always been resisted.' As a scientist, Watson believes we can improve society but that people like Greenpeace or Prince Charles won't let us.

Watson's determination to beat nature is most evident in his work on the human genome. His only ethical fear is that it won't be used. It is disuse rather than misuse of genetics which is the real danger. By this he means that people's fear of the unknown and of playing God with their own and their unborn children's lives will limit the genome's capacity for good.

'We balk at genetics because of its association with Hitler and eugenics. But that is in the past. Now the state has the capacity to make genetics available to everyone and I believe all breakthroughs should be licensed so they are widely available. But because of fears about initial hostile public opinion, governments aren't allowing people access to genetic tests. The danger is that the pro-life lobby and the fearful ones will stop us using the technology to improve our lives. It's all very well believing in the survival of the fittest – but it's not much fun if you happen to be the weakest.'

From *The Sunday Times*, 26 March 2000

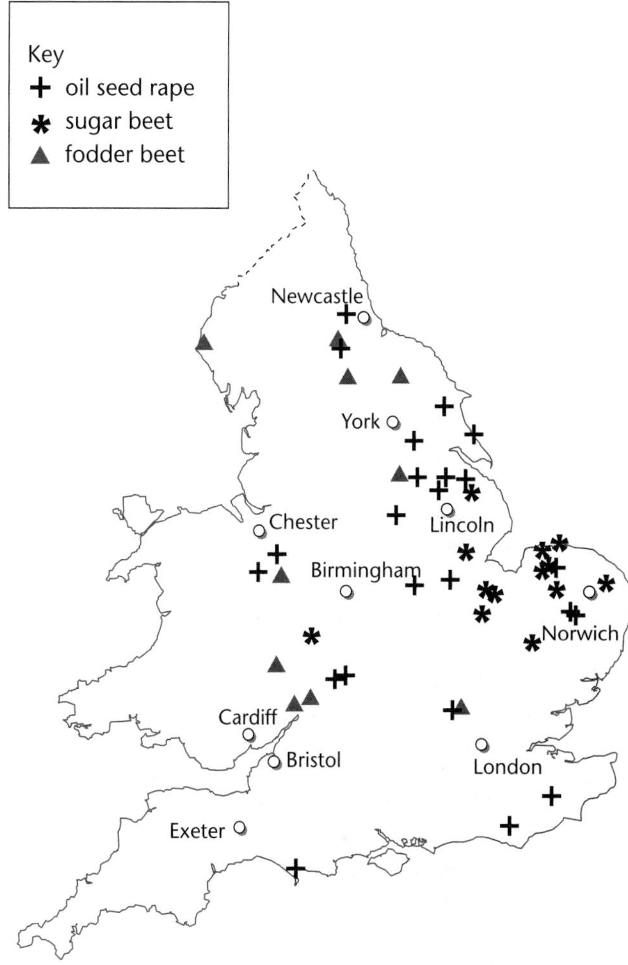

The location of sites approved by government in 2001 for genetic farming experiments in England and Wales.

Activities

1 Choose an issue relating to genetic modification that is in the news at present. Using the websites listed and other sources, investigate the way in which the press reports the issue. Write a report on your findings, including references to:
a the amount of space given to pro and anti arguments on the topic,
b the type of language used to support pro and anti comments,
c the images used to support the arguments,
d the use of any statistical evidence presented.

2 Debate the view that science exists to discover ways of improving society and that it is not the job of science to make moral judgements.

3 Choose one area of genetic modification that interests you and research it, using the Internet. Make a list of moral issues that are raised.
a Put them in order of importance to you.
b Identify who should be taking the necessary moral decisions.
c What knowledge is required to make these decisions?

Thinking and analytical skills

1 Identify the stages in the argument presented by Professor Watson in his interview.
2 What different types of knowledge and argument are used in the passage?
3 To what extent does Watson fail to justify his conclusion?

(v) Should artists have total freedom of self-expression?

Links: 1.2 (i); 1.2 (iv); 1.2 (vi); 1.4 (i); 1.5 (i); 1.5 (ii); 3.4 (vii) **Key skills:** IT3.1; IT3.2; IT3.3; WO3.1; WO3.2; C3.3; C3.1a; C3.1b

Introduction

Freedom of expression encompasses morality, law and the rights of artist and audience. The audience includes those directly addressed as well as those who engage indirectly with the work in question. Should artists have total freedom to do and say as they wish or ought they to be restricted by the feelings, concerns and reactions of others?

Background

Laws about **obscenity, libel, slander** and official secrets restrict freedom of expression, yet society's understanding of what is offensive often needs to be clarified by the courts. Personal freedom, limited by law, requires the exercise of judgement.

Article 10 of the European Convention on Human Rights states, 'Everyone has the right to freedom of expression. This right shall include freedom to hold opinions and to receive and impart information and ideas without interference by public authority and regardless of frontiers' and 'The exercise of these freedoms may be subject to such … restrictions or penalties as are prescribed by law … for the protection of the health or morals … or reputation or rights of others …'.

Morally this issue raises several questions:

- Ought artists to have total freedom of expression?
- If they should, ought they to use it?
- What, if any, self-imposed restrictions should there be?
- Who should decide restrictions on artistic freedom?
- What sanctions should be imposed if moral codes limiting artistic freedom are broken?
- Should the same moral limits apply to all art forms or should restrictions for some (television or literature) differ from others (visual arts or music)?
- Should great artists and works of art face the same restrictions that apply to lesser ones?

Conflict inevitably exists between what the creative artist needs to say and what an audience wishes to hear. Artistically and culturally, many people are conservative and easily offended by what is different or new. Moral judgements may simply disguise lack of artistic taste and poor judgement. Artists, by definition creative, look for new things to say and new ways in which to say them. However, not all **innovations** are great art or improve society. Do demands for artistic freedom simply seek to justify inferior work and disguise lack of talent?

Those making ethical rather than cultural judgements about artistic freedom should consider:

- Consequences for society: how will society benefit?
- Will the sum total of human happiness be increased?
- What are the artist's underlying motives? Does he seek to challenge, offend or explore?
- What are the motives of the audience? Does it seek to appreciate, judge or find fault?
- Is the artist fulfilling a duty to humanity?
- Does the action offend **natural law**?
- Does tolerance result from indifference, judgement or a broad-minded approach to art and freedom?
- Would restrictions remove an artist's right to choose?
- Is the judgement 'it is morally wrong' a disguised version of the expression 'I don't like it'?

Glossary

obscenity: something repulsive, filthy, loathsome, indecent

libel: a written statement that is damaging to a person's reputation; false and defamatory statement

slander: a false report, spoken maliciously to damage a person's reputation

innovation: a novelty, something new or different

natural law: absolute law, established by an external authority, which is, or should be, binding on all people at all times and under all circumstances

Issues to be discussed

- What is meant by 'freedom of artistic expression'?
- How might freedom of expression **a** harm, and **b** benefit society?
- How might **a** a utilitarian, and **b** a follower of Kant view the question of freedom of artistic expression?
- Do you agree that art should be about communication and not about pleasing an audience?
- Should artists practise the teaching of 'to thine own self be true' irrespective of the consequences?

Where now?

McInerney and Rainbolt, *Ethics*, HarperCollins, 1994

R. Hoggart, *The Way We Live Now*, Chatto & Windus, 1995

www.ncfe.net www.artscouncil.org.uk

What do you think?

Artists should be free to do what they want, when they want and how they want. Critically examine this view, justifying your response.

'Either kill me or take me as I am,' said the Marquis de Sade, 'because I'll be damned if I shall ever change.' His catalogues of sexual variation, mixed with anti-authoritarian rantings are a deliberate and maniacally focused expression of the vision of natural man as a monster. All of us know there are crimes we could commit, even want to commit, but for some reason, don't. The Marquis imagined a world in which all restraint was gone and all crimes committed.

Now his memory is to be revived: de Sade, the godfather of the contemporary impulse to let it all hang out, however weird and vile 'it' may be, is back. But why is he once again fashionable?

The last time de Sade was revived, in the Sixties and Seventies, was predictable. His books were widely published for the first time and he became an aspect of the age's libertarian aspirations. 'If it feels good, do it,' we said.

When in the Seventies, de Sade's novel *Juliette* was to be republished, fierce campaigns were launched against it and *The Times* argued that it should be suppressed under the Obscene Publications Act. In the event it wasn't banned, and his three main works are widely available.

Of course, even if we had banned it, we could still buy it from amazon.com. Like so much else in the globalised, wired world, it's there if you want it. Sex is being consumerised like everything else and the ideology of consumerism requires the maximum elaboration of choice.

From an article by B. Appleyard in *The Sunday Times*, 16 April 2000

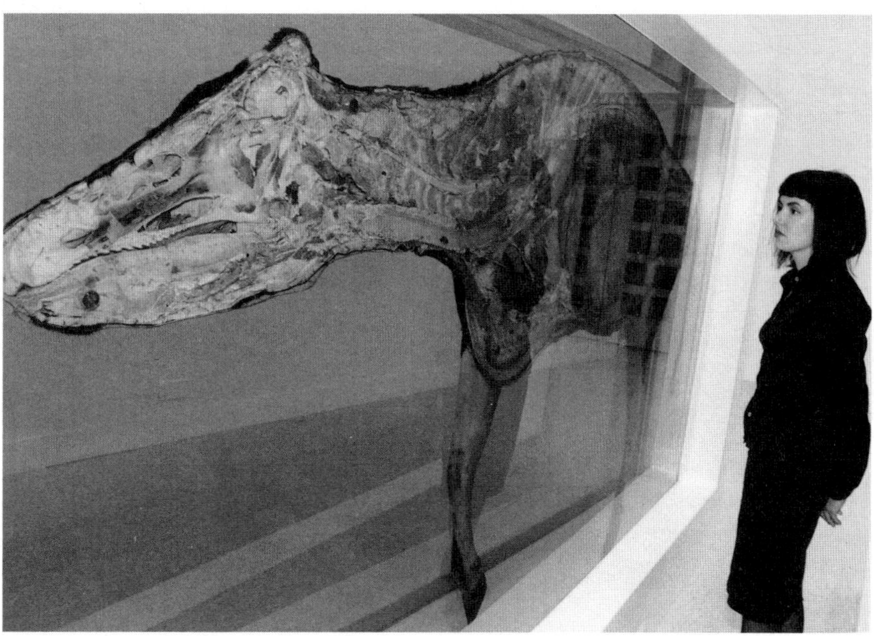

***Mother and Child Divided* by Damien Hirst, 1995. Is this real art or is it taking advantage of freedom of expression?**

Activities

1 Use the Internet to research the way in which the government of the former USSR forced the composer Shostakovitch to modify his style to fit in with the ideology of the state.

2 Make a list of arguments for and against artists having total freedom of expression.

3 Should public money be used to support artists who are prepared to offend rather than to please their audience?

4 Censorship is often justified because it protects society against work that is offensive, obscene, pornographic or just bad. Working in a group, write clear definitions of each of these words to make the differences between them apparent and enable a person using them to distinguish different qualities.
a Which, if any, of the terms you have defined would justify banning a work of art?
b Explain your findings in a presentation.

Thinking and analytical skills

1 Identify the stages in the argument in the extract from *The Sunday Times*.

2 What different types of knowledge and argument does the author use to support his conclusion?

3 How valid is the author's conclusion?

(vi) Can families be morally justified in the modern world?

Links: 1.2 (i); 1.2 (iv); 1.2 (v); 3.5 (i); 4.5; 4.9 **Key skills:** N3.1; N3.2; N3.3; IT3.1; IT3.2; C3.1a

Introduction

The nature of family has been the subject of considerable debate in recent years. As a result of social and economic changes, the traditional structure of the family has been challenged and its purpose has been questioned. Some, particularly those with a feminist perspective, claim that the family is **immoral** as well as a form of **oppression**.

Background

Family, which is involved in most aspects of society, raises many moral issues. Traditionally most people accepted and, to some degree, conformed to what society dictated 'ought to be'. As social beliefs changed, the benefit to society of conformity has been questioned. This issue can be examined from different moral perspectives.

Natural law views argue that the traditional family pattern and associated values are right and that other structures are **flawed** as they fail to meet absolute standards. The New Right may support this moral view.

Existentialism emphasises the importance of individual freedom of choice. It argues that there is no single correct pattern and that individuals must choose for themselves what is best for them in terms of family organisation and structure.

Utilitarians, concerned with consequences rather than actions, believe that any structure that increases total human happiness and reduces pain, is good. They may support family diversity and social perspectives that regard traditional family structures as exploitative and oppressive.

Kant's view is that people have a duty to society. Reason should dictate that an individual's conduct must be in the best interests of society, even if it does not please the individual. However, objective reason can justify a variety of family structures. Rationally, family ought not to simply serve the emotional needs of individuals.

Some issues involved:

- Is the traditional two-**heterosexual**-parent family the only right one or are others as valid?
- Can surrogacy be morally justified?
- What moral rights and responsibilities should **surrogate** parents and children have towards each other?
- Are single-sex parents and families acceptable?
- Should divorce laws be more restrictive?
- Should marriages be preserved at all costs?
- Do reconstituted families harm or benefit society?
- Should the state provide in the same way for both alternative families and traditional families?
- What mutual commitments and responsibilities should participants in broken families have and for how long?
- If family is important, should adoption be made easier?
- Do 'family values' exist? If so, should the state, society, and families support and encourage them?
- Should children have any moral responsibility or commitment to the care and support of aged and infirm parents?
- What 'rights' ought children to have and how should they be protected and enforced?
- What rights and responsibilities should parents have towards their children?

Glossary

immoral: opposed to morality; morally evil, vicious, dissolute

oppression: overwhelming with superior weight, numbers or superior power; to lie heavily on or weigh down

flawed: imperfect, blemished

heterosexual: a person who is attracted to members of the opposite sex

surrogate: deputy, substitute for; hence a mother bearing a child on behalf of another

Issues to be discussed

- To what extent should the nature and organisation of families be guided by moral laws rather than by personal choice?
- How do believers in natural law reconcile possible conflict between followers of different religions in terms of their views about the 'right' family structure?
- How might supporters of each of the moral perspectives described above regard the issue of abortion?
- Can the nature of family be considered rationally and objectively?

Where now?

McInerney and Rainbolt, *Ethics*, HarperCollins, 1994

N. Jorgenson, *Investigating Families and Households*, Collins Educational, 1995

www.sosig.esrc.bris.ac.uk

What do you think?

'There is no moral justification for continued reliance on the traditional form of family.' Analyse and evaluate this statement, giving reasons for your conclusions.

In some Western societies the belief that the family is oppressive has led to vigorous advocacy of alternative lifestyles. This issue brings us back to the problem of defining the family, for if variations in arrangements we think of as families make it difficult to delimit the family, then it is difficult to say what constitutes an alternative to the family. For example, is a communal endeavour in which several nuclear families share accommodation and pool resources to be seen as an alternative to the family or as a group of families? Moreover, the definitional problem does not end when we draw a boundary round the family, for there is the further problem of drawing boundaries round the family alternatives.

However, advocates of alternative lifestyles, like most conventional people, appear to identify the family with a nuclear family unit based on legal marriage and biological parenting. They then identify as alternatives, sexual and parental relationships which break with legal marriage and/or biological parenting. Further, advocates of alternative lifestyles appear to be thinking of a specific nuclear family form, namely a unit which is independent of kin and privatised (that is, the conjugal family). The search for a non-privatised arrangement may therefore be part of the alternative lifestyle endeavour. In addition, the nuclear family may be identified with the sexual division of labour and gender inequality, and some alternative lifestyle endeavours involve attempts to restructure sexual and parental relationships in ways that will restructure the sexual division of labour and bring women equality with men.

From F. R. Elliot, *The Family: Change or Continuity?* Macmillan, 1986, quoted in M. O'Donnell, *New Introductory Reader in Sociology*, Nelson, 1993, pp. 190–91

A traditionally structured extended family.

Activities

1 Conduct a survey of approximately 50 people to identify **a** the family type they belong to, and **b** what family means to them.
  i Analyse your results.
  ii Show your findings in appropriate graphs.
  iii Comment on your findings.

2 Discuss and list arguments for and against the traditional nuclear family compared to possible alternatives.

3 Working in a group, compile a glossary of terms (with meanings) used for different family types. Using the Internet (www.statistics.gov.uk and www.europa.index), investigate the proportion of the population in the UK who fall into each category of family. Compare your figures with those for other European countries. Show your findings in appropriate graphs or tables and comment on them.

Thinking and analytical skills

1 What are the stages in the development of the argument in the passage?
2 Identify different types of knowledge used by the author to support his argument.
3 What are the strengths and weaknesses of the author's conclusion?

(i) Why do some people need religion?

Links: 1.2 (iii); 1.3 (ii); 1.3 (v); 1.3 (vi); 4.11; 4.12 **Key skills:** Wo3.1; WO3.2; N3.1; N3.2, C3.1a; C3.1b

Introduction

Religion has been important in establishing different cultures. Each society develops its own religion. Different religions, despite persecution, suppression or challenge by social, economic and scientific developments, are remarkably resilient, largely because of their followers' commitment and belief.

Background

Few definitions of religion gain general acceptance. One extreme says it is belief in the **supernatural** while the other claims it is any belief system. Although communism, humanism and even football have been described as religions, most religious organisations usually fall into the first category.

Characteristics of religion usually include:

- belief in gods or other supernatural beings,
- distinguishing between **'sacred'** and **'profane'**,
- agreed ritual centred around sacred objects,
- a supernaturally defined and sanctioned moral code,
- religious feelings (awe, wonder, guilt) aroused in the presence of sacred objects and during acts of worship,
- a world view that provides an explanation of the individual and his place in the universe in terms of religious teachings,
- a social organisation bound together and given purpose by religious belief,
- an individual's life based on this world view,
- answers to life-questions.

Belief is central to religion, influencing personal behaviour. It is more than simply knowledge. Belief implies acceptance of things known to be true and rejection of the untrue. It depends on faith in a superior power, which may see man and god intimately involved with or totally separated from one another.

Believers justify religious faith because:

- Consolation comes from the idea of an almighty being, aware of and concerned with his creatures.
- Comfort is found in believing their god is preparing a glorious future for them in an afterlife.
- The fear of inevitable death creates a desire for continued existence in some future form.
- They hope that suffering now will lead to glorious future reward, while the wicked will suffer punishment.
- Belief gives a sense of direction and purpose based on obedience to clear guiding precepts.
- Religion justifies a moral god-given code, which is binding on all people at all times. It creates a sense of continuity, consistency and certainty in life.
- It provides answers to searching life-questions like 'Why am I here?', 'Does life have purpose?' and 'After death, what?'
- It gives a sense of community and belonging.
- It encourages individuals to perform acts of self-sacrifice.
- It provides the certainty of an unchanging 'right' and 'wrong' not fixed or changed by mankind.

Other justifications for religion include:

- strengthening society,
- answering 'unanswerable' questions,
- imposing social control,
- **validating** moral and social control.

Glossary

supernatural: possessing qualities greater than nature; out of the ordinary

sacred: consecrated or held dear to a deity; made holy by religious association

profane: not belonging to what is sacred or biblical

validate: make valid, ratify, confirm

Issues to be discussed

- Is it possible to develop a generally acceptable definition of religion? If so, what is it? If not, why not?
- In what ways can religious belief be described as a method of social control?
- Is it possible to be religious without believing in a supernatural power?
- Many physicists find it easier than biologists to believe in a supernatural power. Why is this?
- Is it possible to experience religious feelings without being committed to any particular religious belief?

Where now?

J. Bird, *Investigating Religion*, Collins, 1999

R. Billington, *Living Philosophy*, Routledge and Kegan, 1993

plato.stanford.edu www.britannica.com

What do you think?

Critically examine arguments for and against the view that religion is simply 'morality touched with emotion'.

A precise definition of religion is probably impossible. Matthew Arnold defined it as morality touched with emotion.

The more deeply we probe into early religion, the more clearly we perceive how little it has to do with morality, however strongly it might be touched with emotion. A second element was an infantile, but nonetheless genuine, physical science. Surrounded with unknown influences, tormented with terrors of spirits of all kinds, men searched timidly into the causes of these plagues, and leapt eagerly at the first possibilities that presented themselves for avoiding or mitigating them. Any man who professed to know was a man of 'science'. The science might be mistaken, but it was nonetheless dominating. Antagonism between physics and religion did not exist in early times. On the contrary, religion was the natural development of physics and without physics could scarcely have arisen. The priest was the professor and the minister was the medicine-man. People went to them for explanations of natural phenomena and for relief from the fears those phenomena aroused.

Thus, while not every philosophy is a religion, every religion is a philosophy. Religion, to be worth anything, must cast out fears, allay bewilderment, solve perplexities: and this cannot be done without the formation of theories. No-one can conceive an object of worship unless he has first reflected on the 'causes of things'. It needs philosophy to conceive of 'powers' and to believe they can be conciliated.

Such belief cannot arise unless the believer has first thought about the universe. That he first wondered about it is, of course, true; wonder is the necessary preliminary to examination.

From E. E. Kellett, *A Short History of Religions*, Gollancz, 1957, pp. 9–13

Charismatic worship: religious experience or emotional release?

Activities

1 In a group, devise a questionnaire and conduct a survey to investigate the nature of people's religious beliefs. Your investigation should cover what people believe and the reasons they give for holding their beliefs. Your survey should include people of different ages and, if possible, different ethnic origins. Analyse your findings and present a report using numerical, graphic and written forms.

2 Debate the view: 'Religious belief gives the elderly comfort and hope but has little relevance for the young.'

3 Imagine you were developing a new religion for the twenty-first century. Make a list of the five most important beliefs that you would include. Give reasons to justify your choice.

4 In a group, discuss and develop a full definition of what you understand by 'religion' and 'belief'.

Thinking and analytical skills

1 What conclusion does Kellett reach? Identify the stages by which he arrives at his conclusion.

2 Give examples of different types of knowledge used in the passage to develop the argument.

3 How effectively does Kellett support and justify his conclusion?

(ii) Are different religions really very different?

Links: 1.3 (i); 1.3 (iv); 4.12 **Key skills:** IT3.1; IT3.2; N3.1; N3.3; C3.3; C3.1a; WO3.1; WO3.2

Introduction

Belief systems consist of ideas held to be true by groups or individuals and provide explanations of events, answers to the meaning of life and guides for conduct and behaviour. Individuals may develop their own life philosophy or, more frequently, may inherit their belief system from previous generations.

Background

Belief systems that are based on the concept of a divine force are religious; those that are centred on this world and emphasise a human, not divine, agency are **secular**. There is overlap, but each system has distinctive ideas of 'right' and 'true'. Most belief systems offer answers about the universe and the nature and purpose of life. Some claim monopoly of truth, while others are more tolerant of conflicting ideas.

The major religions originated in different parts of Asia. The Middle East produced the **monotheistic** faiths: Judaism, Christianity and Islam. They have similar Holy Books, morality, ethics and **doctrine**. From India came **polytheistic** religions, like Hinduism, described as an 'evolving religious tradition rather than a single separate religion' and Sikhism. They emphasise lifestyle more than theology. Eastern Asia contributed Taoism, Shintoism and Confucianism. Buddhism, originating in India, rapidly spread eastwards. Some claim these are philosophical approaches to life in the present world, not true religions, since they require no belief in an omnipotent deity.

Animism, developed in primitive societies, is the belief that impersonal supernatural forces, demons or spirits are present throughout the universe and exist in all aspects of life. These are not gods to be worshipped. Rather, they are powers for good or evil in a person's life, which must be coped with.

Pantheism teaches that divinity is present in all life (animals, insects and plants). Since every action is performed by beings containing divinity there is neither absolute good nor evil. Every action performed is an expression of divine nature. Right and wrong are relative and not absolute terms.One person's right is often another's wrong.

Theism is belief in an almighty creator overseeing human affairs who reveals himself to humanity in various ways, explaining the universe and providing salvation. It is divided into monotheism and polytheism. It is sometimes claimed that the Hindu religion (which appears to have many gods) is, in reality, monotheistic. The different gods are manifestations of the single god Brahma. Polytheistic religions may have one supreme god, superior to all others.

Deism teaches that a supreme being created a perfect universe; he does not intrude in moral decisions or impose demands on humanity. This view developed in the eighteenth century to combine traditional religion with new science.

Panentheism (literally 'all in god') claims that divinity, the underlying essence of all life, has no boundaries to existence or power.

Atheists positively reject belief in any supernatural power, but agnostics feel that inconclusive evidence makes either belief or unbelief equally unjustifiable.

Glossary

secular: concerned with worldly affairs; not sacred

monotheistic: belief that there is only one god

doctrine: that which is taught; a body of religious beliefs

polytheistic: belief in many gods

theism: belief in the existence of a god, supernaturally revealed to man and sustaining a personal relationship with his creatures

Issues to be discussed

- Why is it that all the world's great religions originated in Asia?
- Should Buddhism and similar belief systems be thought of as philosophies rather than as religions?
- What grounds are there for the belief that all gods are simply different aspects of the same supreme being?
- Does religion simply provide an excuse to avoid personal responsibility for actions?

Where now?

J. Bird, *Investigating Religion*, Collins, 1999

N. Smart, *The Religious Experience of Mankind*, Collins, 1984

www.kcmetro.ccmo.us www.britannica.com

What do you think?

To what extent are pop stars and sports idols modern gods in a new religion for the twenty-first century?

Religion is a six-dimensional organism containing doctrines, myths, ethical teachings, rituals, social institutions, animated by religious experiences. To understand key ideas of religion, such as God and nirvana, one has to understand the pattern of religious life directed toward these goals.

God is the focus of worship and praise and is to be defined in relation to worship. God and gods are essentially the foci of men's worship and ritual activities. To say that there is a God is therefore different from saying there is a Creator. God may be creator: but primarily he is the object of worship.

When comparing religions, we are not confronted by some monolithic object, namely religion. We are confronted by religions. Each religion has its own style, its own inner dynamic, its own special meaning and its uniqueness. Each religion is an organism and has to be understood in terms of the interrelation of its different parts. Though there are resemblances between religions, these must not be seen too crudely.

It is correct to say that some religions are monotheistic, worshipping a single God. But the conception of God can vary subtly. It is like a picture. A particular element, such as a patch of yellow, may occur in two different pictures. One can point to the resemblance. Yet the meaning of one patch of yellow can still be very different from the meaning of the other.

So although we are inevitably drawn to compare religions in order to make sense of the patterns of religious experience, we have to recognise that each religion must be seen essentially in its own terms. We have to have a sense of the multiplicity of man's religious life. We are not only concerned with religion; we are concerned also with religions.

From N. Smart, *The Religious Experience of Mankind*, Collins, 1984, pp. 31–32

A Christian interpretation of Ancient Greek gods feasting on Mount Olympus: *The Banquet of the Gods*, a ceiling painting by Raphael (1483–1520).

Activities

1 Research the number of people in 1950 and today who **i** regularly attended places of religious worship, **ii** claimed membership of a religious group or organisation, and **iii** claimed belief in God or a supernatural power.
a Show your findings in appropriate graphs.
b Compare your figures with attendances at football matches (or other sporting events) or pop concerts in the same two periods.
c Write a brief report, commenting on your findings.

2 Devise a questionnaire to investigate why religion seems to be more attractive to older than to younger people and to women rather than men. Administer your questionnaire to a range of people of different ages and ethnic backgrounds. Analyse and comment on your findings.

3 In groups, discuss and make a presentation on why religion appears to be declining in the West but is developing rapidly in parts of Africa and eastern Europe.

Thinking and analytical skills

1 What are the main stages in Smart's argument?
2 Identify, with examples, the different types of knowledge and argument he uses.
3 What is Smart's conclusion? To what extent does he successfully justify it?

(iii) Is there any point to religious symbols?

Links: 1.3 (i); 1.3 (iv) **Key skills:** WO3.1; WO3.2; C3.1a; IT3.1a; It3.2; IT3.3; C3; N3.3

Introduction

Symbols used in everyday life can usually be easily interpreted, provided their underlying reason is understood. They are used as a type of shorthand to convey simple messages. More complex symbols require explanation. In the same way, symbols have played an important part in many different religions.

Background

Symbols are used in all religions, whether primitive or modern, to convey religious 'facts' and communicate religious experiences. They exist to convey meaning to believers and to strengthen their awareness of the **holy**. In many religions the use of symbology is increasing after a period when its popularity declined. Religious symbols are often stylised and standardised in form. Outsiders may easily understand some symbols, but others require detailed knowledge of the beliefs and practices of a religion before they can be fully comprehended.

'Symbol' is derived from ancient Greek, *symbolon*, and means a token. A symbol represented a greater whole and guaranteed its existence and truth. In ancient times, when a business agreement was made, an object was broken in half. One part was given to each of the participants as a symbol or token of their agreement. The fact that both parts could be fitted back together showed that the agreement could not be broken. This idea was adopted to represent the relationship said to exist between a worshipper and his god. A religious symbol represented one half of a binding agreement. Symbols were developed to be concise, to indicate a larger context and deeper meaning. To be effective, a symbol must be understood and accepted by a group who agree on its meaning.

Religious symbols convey the relationship between man and the sacred world, but can also deal with relationships in the social and **material** worlds. At the same time, as 'pictures of meaning', they can reveal generally accepted truths, while concealing mysteries from the **uninitiated**.

In religion, the key to understanding a symbol is the truth or reality it reveals. Revelation may be immediate or may be gained slowly as an understanding of religious truths develops. A single symbol may be given a variety of meanings by different groups, as has happened in the Christian religion with the **Eucharist**.

The formation of symbols can usually be traced back to particular religious experiences. Every encounter with a symbol is intended to renew the memory of a religious experience. They are intended to be a concentration of collective experiences rather than the subjective construct of an individual's creative process. Symbols may be abstract expressions, stylised representations or naturalistic figures. They are often associated with the early origins of a religious movement and, as such, have strong spiritual and emotional associations for believers. Over time, the meanings given to symbols can change or be perverted. The form of a symbol may be transformed or exaggerated as additional meanings are built on the original concept. It is possible for a single symbol to have a number of different meanings. For example, the wheel or circle can represent the universe, the sun, the underworld or even the eternal continuity of life. As a result, interpreting symbols can become the subject of **theological** dispute and even **schism**.

Glossary

holy: consecrated, spiritually perfect, belonging to God

material: unspiritual; concerned with bodily things

uninitiated: not admitted to a group's rites or beliefs

Eucharist: the Lord's Supper; the consecrated elements of bread and wine

theological: dealing with the knowledge of God

schism: the division of a group into opposing factions

Issues to be discussed

- Are religious symbols more appropriate to non-literate societies than highly educated ones?
- Do symbols lose their value if their meaning is hidden from ordinary people?
- Has interest in religious symbols revived?
- How do symbols convey the relationship between mankind and the spiritual world?

Where now?

N. Smart, *The Religious Experience of Mankind*, Collins, 1984

J. R. Hinnells (ed.), *A Handbook of Living Religions*, Penguin, 1991

www.britannica.com www.amazingmysteries.com

What do you think?

'Religious symbols are only of value to believers who have been granted the secret knowledge needed to interpret them.' To what extent can this opinion be challenged or supported?

In every phase of history, Christians have solemnly taken bread and wine, read the words of Jesus at the Last Supper, offered prayer and eaten and drunk. Few Christian communities do not follow this custom, though a few have substituted articles of local fare for bread and wine.

There are immense differences in the external actions of the various Christian communities. Some have sumptuous language, dress and music meant to indicate the very presence of the King of Heaven and ritual to mark his appearance among men. Others recall the domestic simplicity of the original meal which the rite repeats. There are communities where people stand as though in the heavenly courts with the risen Jesus among them. In some they receive the consecrated bread and wine kneeling, as in solemn adoration of the Lord present at the feast; and others where they sit, as though his guests.

These things underline its importance for Christians. But the significance attributed is as varied as its forms. Some use the language and ideas of expiatory sacrifice to take away sin. Some associate it with a special and particular presence of Christ. Others stress the nature of broken bread and poured-out wine. Others eschew any suggestion that the rite has effect in and of itself or requires the presence of a consecrated priest, insisting that it is a solemn commemoration of his self-offering.

The names given reflect these differing ideas: Mass, Eucharist, Lord's Supper, Communion. The idea of communion underlies them all. Its original significance as a shared meal has never quite been lost. The ultimate discipline has always been exclusion from the table, but welcome to the table is the ultimate sign of acceptance.

From J. R. Hinnells (ed.), *A Handbook of Living Religions*, Penguin, 1991, pp. 89–90

Rushton Triangular Lodge, built in the sixteenth century, to represent in symbolic form the mystery of the Holy Trinity.

Activities

1 In a group, identify other commonly used Christian symbols. Research their origin and meaning. Present your findings in a table. Use these categories:
a Biblical origin,
b church tradition,
c shared with other religions,
d origin and/or meaning uncertain.

2 Debate the view that the use of symbols creates an oversimplified view of religious beliefs.

3 Use a computer to design a sheet showing 10 different Christian symbols. Do not name them.
a Using this as a prompt, investigate how familiar people are with the meanings of these symbols.
b Write a brief report on your findings and the conclusions you draw from them.
c Present your findings in at least two different, appropriate tables or graphs.
d Write a brief commentary explaining which graph or table most clearly explains your findings.

Thinking and analytical skills

1 Outline the main conclusion of the passage and the stages of the argument presented.
2 Identify, with examples, different types of knowledge used in the passage.
3 To what extent is the author able to justify his conclusions?

(iv) Do all religions share the same symbols?

Links: 1.3 (i); 1.3 (ii); 1.3 (iii) **Key skills:** C3.3; C3.1b; C3.1a; WO3.1;WO3.2

Introduction

The many different religious symbols can be put into three categories. Most symbols are visual. Others are symbolic actions or gestures, especially in worship. The third group is linguistic, including different types of sound. Some symbols, though not holy, are signs leading to 'the holy' and guaranteeing its efficacy.

Background

Spaces and buildings are often powerful symbols of the sacred. Holy places, designated as areas of worship, may be symbolically set apart by trees, sacred stones or other signs. In many religions worshippers entering sacred places remove their shoes and wash their hands and feet so as not to **defile** the sanctuary. Ground plans, ornamentation and sacred architecture often have spiritual significance. **Orientation** of churches, mosques and temples points worshippers to sacred locations. Domes can represent the vault of heaven and the empty Holy of Holies in Jewish or Shinto buildings, and prayer niches in mosques represent the presence of the Deity. Cross-shaped churches reflect the crucifixion of Christ. The location of doorways, sacred pathways and the position of furniture often have great spiritual significance. Bell towers, **minarets** and steeples are a reminder of the finger of God.

Colours can have special significance and one colour can have a different meaning in different religions. White may represent purity, joy or festivity, but can also show sadness and death. Each period of the Christian year is associated with a different colour. In the Maya religion, colours represent different directions (red symbolises east; white, north; black, west and yellow, south). Buddhist priests wear saffron robes and their **mandala** consists of different coloured sands: white represents purity, blue the vastness and truth of doctrine, and red, warmth and compassion. Precious stones and metals often have religious significance related to their colour.

Time and the sacred calendar have symbolic meanings. For Buddhists, the wheel shows continuity and the passage of time. In Ancient Greek religion, time was represented by a winged, lion-headed figure standing on a globe encircled by a snake. Fixed points in the religious year, such as Christmas or Easter for Christians and Divali for Hindus, have a symbolic meaning associated with belief, religious experience and worship. Many religions set aside certain days in the week, month or year, while others have specially designated years.

Animals and plants can have real symbolic value. Some gods possess animals' attributes. In many polytheistic religions deities are often represented as animal or part-animal/part-human. Christianity uses the lamb and the fish as symbols. Plants too can have a symbolic role. A god may appear as a plant or, like Demeter or Ceres, be regarded as the creator of plants and represented as an ear of corn. Trees (like the tree of knowledge, the tree of life, the fig tree and the grapevine) are important in both Jewish and Christian symbolism. Religions like Islam and Judaism forbid the representation of the human or divine form.

Liturgical symbols are important in most religions and may include vestments, sacred objects, holy books, music and ritual.

Glossary

defile: make dirty, pollute, corrupt

orientation: place buildings so as to face east; place or position exactly with regard to compass directions

minarets: slender turret linked to a mosque: used to call the faithful to prayer

mandala: geometrical design used as an aid to worship

liturgical: set of formularies for public worship

iconoclasm: attacks on cherished beliefs or institutions; the destruction of images used in religious worship

Issues to be discussed

- Why do different religions use similar symbols to convey different meanings?
- Do secular symbols (like football colours, team pictures or team chants) have religious qualities?
- Why does the family (mother, father and children) have symbolic significance in many religions?
- **Iconoclasm** often occurs during religious reformation. What are the reasons for and consequences of this?

Where now?

N. Smart, *The Religious Experience of Mankind*, Collins, 1984

J. Ferguson, *Religions of the World*, Lutterworth, 1979

www.kcmetro.cc.mo.us/ www.fastlae.net

What do you think?

Critically examine the origin and meaning to believers of one symbol used in a religion of your choice.

Mandala

Seven-branch candlestick.

Shiva.

Celtic knot.

Yin-yang.

Wheel (Hindu Sun god).

Tasbih (Islamic prayer beads).

Kara.

Wheel and throne (Buddhism).

Celtic cross.

Buddhist footprint.

Star of David.

Crescent.

Activities

1 Gestures and hand movements can have symbolic meaning in some religions. Investigate the meaning of such gestures in one religion and present your findings in the form of an annotated poster.

2 Identify the religions to which each of the symbols depicted above belong. Choose any three of these symbols and explain what meaning they have for a believer.

3 Choose any religious symbol not represented above and make a brief presentation, explaining its origin and the part it plays in the life and work of a believer.

4 Arrange to meet and interview a local religious leader. Investigate the nature and importance of the different symbols used in his or her religion and place of worship.

5 Make a plan of a place of worship, marking on it any symbolic features or objects. Explain their significance.

Further research

1 Investigate the symbolic use of numbers and/or alphabetic letters in any one religion. Outline the part they play in the lives and worship of believers.

2 Investigate the symbolic role of silence and 'emptiness' (such as an empty throne or the missing Buddha) in religious worship.

(v) Can scientific knowledge and religious belief be reconciled?

Links: 1.3 (i); 1.3 (ii); 2.1 (i); 2.2 (iii); 4.11; 4.12; 4.13 **Key skills:** N3.1; N3.2; N3.3; C3.1a; C3.3

Introduction

Religion and science deal with overlapping areas of human experience. Science looks for answers to significant life questions which are usually the concern of religion, such as how the universe and life originated, the purpose of life and the nature of death. Scientific discoveries raise moral issues that challenge the principles of religious faiths.

Background

Traditionally, religion and science were intertwined. Religious leaders, often the 'scientists' of their day, claimed a **monopoly** on true knowledge. In western Europe, the Christian church controlled the activities of scientists, forbidding investigations that might conflict with church **dogma**, banning false teaching and threatening punishment for those involved.

Empirical methods developed by scientists after about 1650 began to challenge the church's authority. In the eighteenth century, philosophers argued that the two disciplines should be kept apart. Darwin's theory of evolution (1859) posed a threat to the authority of religion. Many of the faithful were unable to reconcile the conflicting theories of 'special creation' and 'accidental development' and their faith was undermined. Some scientists claimed religion threatened their research.

Scientific ideas about the origins of the universe and of mankind are now based on evolution, although some scientists accept there must have been an original creative act. There are two main scientific theories. The more traditional view was that the universe had existed in a 'steady state'. More recently, many scientists have accepted the 'Big Bang' theory which teaches that the universe came into existence as the result of a sudden convulsive event.

Most religions state that the universe and the animal kingdom resulted from special acts of creation. These claims are recorded in sacred books and generally demand belief in the existence and intervention of a supreme being.

The Genesis story of creation, taught by Judaism, Islam and Christianity, claims God created the universe, earth and mankind, in six days. His creative acts follow a logically structured pattern. However, the Bible claims to be God's revelation of Himself to humanity and not a scientific textbook.

Buddhism teaches that the earth and all life, both good and bad, were created from nothing by an ever-existing spiritual force. Eventually the material world will be destroyed and emptiness restored.

Chinese mythology claims the first life was born inside a great **cosmic** egg which, after separating, formed the opposites of the universe (yin and yang). The two halves of the egg became heaven and earth. The death of Pan-gu (the original being) produced the sun and moon (his eyes), rivers (his blood), thunder (his voice) and mountains (his body). Indian creation myths teach that in the beginning, water and fire combined to produce a golden egg from which came Brahma. The splitting of the egg created heaven and earth.

Freeman Dyson, a physicist, wrote 'Science and religion are two windows that people look through, trying to understand the big universe outside and why we are here. The two windows give different views, but both look out at the same universe. Both views are one-sided. Neither is complete. Both leave out essential features of the real world. And both are worthy of respect.'

Glossary

monopoly: exclusive possession of the trade in a commodity or thing

dogma: principle or teaching as laid down by a religious organisation; arrogant declaration of opinion

empirical: based or acting on observation and experiment, not on theory

cosmic: of the universe or cosmos, as opposed to the earth

Issues to be discussed

- Why did churches limit freedom of scientific thought and discovery in the Middle Ages?
- Does it matter if science and religion develop different answers to the same questions? Consider this in relation to **a** the origin of the universe, **b** the origin of life, and **c** the causes of human behaviour.
- Why do people talk about the 'theory of evolution' but 'creation stories' (or 'myths'). Does this terminology influence understanding and acceptance of the ideas put forward by science and religion?

Where now?

N. Smart, *The Religious Experience of Mankind*, Collins 1984
J. Ferguson, *Religions of the World*, Lutterworth, 1979

www.britannica.com
www.fastlae.net

What do you think?

'Science and religion deal with different aspects of knowledge and should not trespass on each other's territory.' Critically examine arguments for and against this view.

It does not seem reasonable to believe that all the heavenly bodies following their respective orbits to perfection could have developed from an accidental beginning. The evidence that the universe was designed by a Supreme Being far outweighs any possibilities that it all just happened by chance. Let me present a few ideas to support this view:

- Our earth is just the right distance from the sun so that we get exactly the right amount of heat to sustain life. Mercury and Venus would be far too hot and the planets from Mars out would be too cold to support life, as we know it. So far, scientists have not found evidence of any life on other planets, except for the possibilities of some very primitive plant life on Mars.
- If the rotation of the earth had been one-tenth its present rate, the length of our days and nights would have increased by ten times. This would cause our vegetation to burn up during the long day, while at night any plant life would be sure to freeze.
- The composition of the atmosphere is about 78 parts nitrogen and 21 parts oxygen. It has been demonstrated that too much nitrogen would slow down the body so that death would finally result. Too much oxygen would also be harmful. It doesn't seem likely that this ratio could have developed by accident, since many accidents in chemistry result in explosions – especially since nitrogen is the basic ingredient of most explosives.

There seems to be no possibility that a universe of such perfection could have developed entirely by chance.

From D. Riegle, *Creation or Evolution?*, Zondervan, 1971, pp. 18–21

Is this how humankind developed or were we specially made?

Activities

1 What other 'scientific' evidence might Riegle have produced to support his claim that the universe is the result of design rather than accident?

2 Imagine you were in a debate opposing Riegle's views. What scientific arguments could you use to challenge the points he makes? What other evidence might be presented to show that the universe is the result of accident rather than design?

3 Do the following research:
a Find out the diameters of the sun and the planets in the solar system.
b What is the distance of each of the planets from the sun?
c Calculate the scale that you would need to use to show the exact size and position of each of the planets in relation to the sun if you drew the sun 2.5 cms in diameter.

Thinking and analytical skills

1 What are the stages in the argument presented by Riegle?

2 Identify, with examples, the different types of argument and knowledge used in the passage.

3 To what extent does Riegle's evidence justify his argument?

(vi) Can you be religious and live the life you want to?

Links: 1.3 (i); 1.3 (ii); 1.3 (v); 3.1 (i) **Key skills:** N3.1; N3.2; N3.3; C3.1a; C3.2; C3.3

Introduction

Most religions offer their followers the prospect of a better future life, either through **reincarnation** or by attaining a state of blessedness, variously described as nirvana, the Isles of the Blest, heaven, paradise or God's kingdom. Whatever is offered, believers are given a sense of purpose and incentive to follow their chosen religion.

Background

Lifestyle can play a significant part in religious life. In some religions leading a good life is a way to achieve promised reward, but in others, like Judaism and Christianity, following a moral code is a response to what God has already done for you. Most religions offer ethical codes, either directly revealed by divinity or indirectly through prophets, teachers or leaders. Such codes, contained in sacred writings, may need interpreting before they can be applied.

Hindu ethics teach that the consequences of a person's actions will return in a future **incarnation**. This is not reward and punishment, but is inescapable consequence. Motivation is essentially self-centred rather than 'other centred'. Hindus believe a state of bliss can be achieved by following one of four different paths:

- sensual pleasure (*karma*),
- practical usefulness and economic prosperity (*artha*),
- righteous behaviour and ritual purity (*dharma*),
- abandoning all wordly ties (*moksha*).

Buddhists aim to achieve nirvana by focusing on the eight-fold path. 'Right action', the fourth of these, specifies five ethical **precepts**. Buddhists should not:

- kill, but show love that does no harm,
- take what is not given, but practise charitable giving,
- misbehave sexually, but be pure and self-controlled,
- speak falsehood, but be sincere and honest,
- take drugs or intoxicants, but recognise the need for self-discipline.

Believers suffer the consequences of their actions. Good actions will lead to a more favourable next life, but evil will lead to a lower order. Buddists should follow their own duty, not seek to meet other's needs.

Judaism's ethical teaching is based on the Ten Commandments and a **covenant** with God. Man's duty is to respond to God's love by loving fellow men through a practical lifestyle. Two basic principles of behaviour are respect for individuals and for all creation. Man has a moral debt to God, requiring repayment. Christian ethics grew from Judaism. Although based on the Ten Commandments, the key to Christian living is love for God and for fellow men. Christianity stresses the importance of lifestyle.

Islamic life, based on the five Pillars of Wisdom, includes a requirement to give **alms**. Possessions are not simply for personal enjoyment but should be used responsibly to benefit others. The Koran prohibits gambling, alcohol and eating pork. Believers are instructed to live in truth, honour, justice and trustworthiness.

Glossary

reincarnation: the entrance of the soul, after death into another human or an animal body

incarnation: embodied in human flesh, hence referring to the state of reincarnation when it has occurred

precepts: divine command, moral instruction

covenant: bargain, contract, agreement in which both parties are committed to specified actions

alms: donation, charitable relief of the poor

Issues to be discussed

- Are the ethical demands of religion intended to be a form of social control rather than a means to build individuals up in their faith?
- Many religions have similar ethical codes. Does this similarity mean that the different religions have a common origin, have copied from each other or base their ideas on universal absolutes?
- Choose any three ethical principles mentioned above. How might they be justified to a modern audience on **a** religious, and **b** secular grounds.
- Are ethical codes binding if they are not based on supernatural authority?

Where now?

N. Smart, *The Religious Experience of Mankind*, Collins, 1984

J. Ferguson, *Religions of the World*, Lutterworth, 1979

www.britannica.com

www.fastlae.net

What do you think?

To what extent do you agree that organised religion is more about giving a sense of purpose to life than about laying down systems of conduct that must be observed?

Throughout history we find that religion usually incorporated a code of ethics. To some extent, the code of ethics of the dominant religion controls the community. Quite obviously, men do not always live up to the standards they profess.

Even so, there is no doubt that religions have been influential in moulding the ethical attitudes of society. It is important, however, to distinguish between moral teaching incorporated in doctrines and social facts concerning those who adhere to the faith in question. For instance, Christianity teaches 'Love thy neighbour as thyself'. As a matter of sociological fact, a lot of people in 'Christian' countries fail to come anywhere near this ideal. The man who goes to church is not necessarily loving nor is the man who goes to a Buddhist temple necessarily compassionate. Consequently, we must distinguish between the ethical teachings of a faith and the actual sociological effects and circumstances of a religion.

In technologically primitive societies, where the priest, soothsayer or magician is closely integrated into the social structure, religion is not just a personal matter: it is part of the life of the community. But even in sophisticated communities, churches exist as institutions to be reckoned with. They are part of the 'establishment'.

This social shape of religion is, of course, to some extent determined by religious and ethical ideals and practices. Conversely it often happens that religious and ethical ideals are adapted to existing social conditions and attitudes. It is important to distinguish between the ethical and social dimension of religion. Doctrinal, mythological and ethical dimensions express a religion's claims about the invisible world and how men's lives ought to be shaped: the social dimension indicates how men's lives are in fact shaped by these claims and the way religious institutions operate.

From N. Smart, *The Religious Experience of Mankind*, Collins, 1984, pp. 19–21

Church membership in the United Kingdom

Thousands

	1970	1980	1990	1995
Christian Church membership				
Trinitarian churches	8,122	7,554	6,693	6,361
Non-Trinitarian churches	285	353	359	522
All Christian church members	9,407	7,907	7,152	6,883
Other religions				
Muslim	130	306	495	580
Sikh	100	150	250	350
Hindu	80	120	140	155
Jewish	120	111	101	94
Others	21	53	87	116
All other religions	451	740	1,073	1,295
All religious groups	9,858	8,647	8,225	8,178
Total UK population (approx.)	55,928	56,352	57,808	59,000

Source: *Social Trends 29*, The Office for National Statistics, 1999; www.statistics.gov.uk

Activities

1 **a** Construct appropriate graphs or charts to show the distribution of membership of religious groups in the UK in **i** 1970, **ii** 1980, and **iii** 1990.
b Comment on any trends you can identify.

2 Construct a line graph to show the changes in religious membership of each religious group between 1970 and 1995. Explain, with suggested reasons, any trends you can identify.

3 Discuss the view that Britain is just as religious as ever and that the only difference is that people worship with different religious groups.

4 Make a table to show the similarities and differences between the ethical teachings of the major world religions.

5 Research the teachings of three major religions on birth control, euthanasia and animal research.

Thinking and analytical skills

1 Identify Smart's conclusion and the stages of the argument he develops in order to reach it.

2 What flaws might a critic of Smart find in his argument?

3 Give examples of different types of knowledge used in the passage.

(i) Was Michelangelo the greatest artist who ever lived?

Links: 1.5 (v); 1.5 (vi); 4.14 **Key skills:** C3.1b; C3.2; C3.3; C3.1a; IT3.1; IT3.2

Introduction

A period of cultural revival is known as a renaissance or rebirth. Originally the Renaissance referred to the period of European history from the fourteenth to the sixteenth centuries when there was a revival in the values and artistic styles of the ancient world. It marked the end of the **Middle Ages**.

Background

Italian painters and poets in the sixteenth century who modelled their styles on ancient Rome described their efforts as a 'rebirth'. In the eighteenth century the term rebirth was broadened to include other developments which took place in the period c.1450–1600, including the rise of individualism, scientific inquiry, geographical exploration and the growth of secular values.

Humanism inspired the spirit of Renaissance. It:

- focused on human achievements,
- stressed compatibility between philosophical truths,
- emphasised man's dignity.

Humanism stressed creativity and self-control, helped to develop new knowledge, encouraged freethinking and promoted enquiry and investigation.

Art benefited most from this new approach, with the development of the new methods of painting and sculpture founded on observation of the visible world, firm mathematical principles and scientific inquiry. The Renaissance, which began in Italy, rapidly spread to other parts of Europe.

Alberti (1404–72) described Renaissance man as 'a man who can do all things if he will'. He believed that man's capacity for development was unlimited. Gifted Renaissance figures developed skills in areas of knowledge, physical development, social accomplishment and the arts. The ideal man was an accomplished poet, architect, painter, sculptor, classicist, mathematician, scientist and musician. Alberti, Leonardo da Vinci, and Michelangelo **exemplified** these qualities.

Michelangelo Buonarrotti (1475–1564) trained as an artist and spent most of his life in Rome and Florence. Judged the greatest living artist of his time, he was accomplished in many different fields, but regarded himself primarily as a sculptor. As well as being one of the most powerful and influential Renaissance artists and sculptors, he was also a noted poet and architect.

His preferred material was white marble. His early work showed great technical ability and was classically influenced. Based on careful anatomical studies, his sculptures have religious and mythical themes and are often **allegorical**. Famous works include various Pietas and David. Much of his later work was left unfinished.

His painting produced his best-known works, including the ceiling of the Sistine Chapel and the Last Judgement. He only left one easel painting, the remainder of his work being **frescoes**. He preferred to work alone. His frequent use of nudes upset later generations. His architecture, an occasional activity, produced several masterpieces, like St Peter's Dome and Rome's Capitol.

His style, massive and monumental, was influenced by classical principles. He tried to create a general impression rather than simply represent the real textures of cloth and flesh. Much of his work shows movement, but his human forms are often idealised.

Glossary

Middle Ages: the time between the classical world and the Renaissance

humanism: a rationalistic outlook attaching prime importance to human interests; a movement away from medieval scholarship towards classical thought

exemplified: a typical example of something; illustrated

allegorical: constituting an allegory that is a story or picture that can be interpreted to reveal a hidden meaning

frescoes: a type of watercolour painting done on wet plaster on a wall or ceiling, in which the colour is absorbed and fixed in the plaster as it dries

Issues to be discussed

- To what extent do you agree with Alberti that 'a man can do all things if he will'?
- Why did the Renaissance start in Italy and what enabled it to spread and influence the rest of Europe?
- How and why did Michelangelo exemplify the qualities of Renaissance man?
- Examine why the church and merchants were among the most important patrons of artists during the Renaissance.

Where now?

Wolf and Millen, *Renaissance and Mannerist Art*, Abrams, 1968

B. Whelpton, *Art Appreciation Made Simple*, W. H. Allen, 1970

www.artchive.com www.sunsite.dk www.michelangelo.com

What do you think?

Choose a single Renaissance work of art. Critically examine claims that it is a masterpiece.

Just how did Filippo 'Pippo' Brunelleschi, early fifteenth-century Florentine goldsmith, clockmaker, sculptor and inventor, work out how to build the largest masonry dome in the world – the one surmounting Florence cathedral? For a long time, nobody quite understood how he had done it. He died in 1466, shortly before his masterly lantern on top was completed. By then he was so famous that his every movement was public. Pippo was arguably the first personality architect, the first to be recognised as a designer of genius in his own time.

Brunelleschi is one of those Renaissance men much admired by modern architects, particularly those of the high-tech school. Pippo found technological solutions for aesthetic problems. Shortly before he took on the dome, for instance, he invented (or perhaps rediscovered) the laws of perspective in painting, thus changing the whole course of Renaissance art and architecture.

A design (in the form of a model) for the dome had existed for fifty years. Florence's ministry of public works finally held a competition to find out how to do it, which Pippo won. Pippo struggled for three decades as he got his dome built by unconventional means – because it was too big to use any known techniques. He had to invent everything to make this possible – including the world's first counterweighted tower crane. Pippo needed no props or scaffolding. He invented safety harnesses: only one mason fell to his death as the dome was built, a miraculous safety record for the time.

Filippo Brunelleschi's extraordinary achievement is that, in the end, there is the dome of Santa Maria del Fiore. To have your name on that makes you more than a short, ugly master mason with personal problems. It makes you a superman. We know that. And so, most certainly, did Pippo.

From *The Sunday Times*, 9 February 2000

Brunelleschi's dome, Florence cathedral.

Activities

1 Investigate and make a short presentation on the contribution of one of the following to the development and/or spread of Renaissance ideas:
a the development of printing,
b the fall of Constantinople in 1453,
c the development of scientific enquiry.

2 Select two examples of paintings or sculptures by different artists on a religious theme of your choice. Write a report to compare the way each artist has dealt with the subject.

3 Research another period which historians have labelled 'renaissance'. To what extent do you feel the label is either deserved or justified?

4 Compare examples of Renaissance architecture with buildings of Ancient Rome or Greece. In what ways do Renaissance buildings show classical features?

5 Discuss whether there is any justification for talking about a twentieth century renaissance. Give evidence to support your arguments.

Thinking and analytical skills

1 Outline the stages in the argument to show that Brunelleschi was a creative genius.
2 How does the author use different types of knowledge to support his argument?
3 To what extent do you feel that the author's conclusion is justified?

(ii) What made Baroque music different?

Links: 1.5 (ii) Key skills: IT3.1; IT3.2; C3.2; C3.1b; N3.3

Introduction

The early seventeenth century was a major turning point in musical development, although the influences that resulted in Baroque music began earlier. A key feature, was the growth of distinctive musical styles in various European countries. A move away from **polyphony** had begun, as had the advance of true instrumental music. Though religion remained a major influence, new forms of secular music were developing.

Background

The seventeenth century was a time of experiment. New musical forms took shape and became established. This required a new, expanded musical vocabulary, new instruments, new forms and new techniques. Major areas of influence were Catholic Italy and Protestant Germany. By about 1700 the various strands merged to flourish as the 'high Baroque' of Vivaldi, Bach and Handel.

Italy was first to influence change. Polyphonic style or *stile antico* was retained for sacred music, but *stile moderno* was developed for secular use. Music's new vocabulary allowed for a distinction between sacred and secular, and vocal and instrumental. The new, more theatrical style emphasised solo voices and encouraged expressive harmony.

Opera began in Florence in an attempt to rediscover Greek theatre. **Recitative**, use of chorus and soloists, dancing and, a structured overture developed in Rome, but the first public opera house opened in Venice in 1637. In the 1670s, Opera Seria, with classical and mythological themes, evolved in Naples. It introduced improvised, embellished **arias**, sung by soloists. The leading composer was Alessandro Scarlatti. His stylised form dominated operatic music and stifled innovation for a century. Church music was influenced by this desire for drama. The cantata, a new form of vocal work, was used in Italy for secular or sacred texts, but in Germany church cantatas evolved as a recognisably different form. Separate vocal and instrumental sections were balanced with arias and recitatives. J. S. Bach perfected the cantata as a setting for chorus and congregation in the early eighteenth century.

Cantata and opera merged to produce oratorios. These were operas for concert performance. Though lacking a dramatic setting, they retained many dramatic musical features and were popularised in England, thanks to Handel.

Instrumental music originally supported vocal works, but developed a separate identity in the Baroque, including sinfonias, choral preludes, sonatas for different combinations of instruments, *concerto grossi* and overtures. By the 1730s, composers were using each of these forms independent of choral works. Composers were helped by the development of new instruments and combinations of instruments.

The spread of ideas occurred in spite of poor communications because wealthy gentlemen, future patrons of the arts, completed their education with the **Grand Tour**. Travelling Europe, they developed a taste for new cultural forms. As patrons of artists, composers and architects, they often sent their employees to study in Italy, under masters like Corelli, Scarlatti and Vivaldi. Music and other art forms became truly international, developing a genuinely common language, vocabulary and style.

Glossary

polyphony: having many (equal) sounds or voices; music in two or more parts, each having its own separate melody

recitative: narrative or dialogue sections of opera where words are declaimed rather than sung

arias: a long, accompanied song for solo voice

Grand Tour: a cultural tour of Europe conventionally undertaken by young men of the upper class in the eighteenth century

Issues to be discussed

- Why has religion been such a significant influence in the development and performance of music?
- To what extent was the development of different musical traditions in Italy and Germany simply a result of religious differences?
- In recent years Baroque music has increased in popularity. What are its attractions to modern audiences?
- Do you agree that since Baroque music is artificial, enjoying it today must be an acquired taste?

Where now?

G. Hindley, *Larousse Encyclopedia of Music*, Reed International, 1971
J. R. Martin, *Baroque*, Allen Lane, 1977
www.islandnet.com www.britannica.com

What do you think?

Choose a work of art produced in the Baroque period. Critically examine whether it justifies the title 'Baroque'.

To define 'Baroque style' is impossible. The very diversity of styles is one of its distinguishing features. The sober realism of the Dutch school bears no resemblance to the high-flown imagery of the Roman Baroque, and neither shows any affinity to the noble classicism of the age of Louis XIV.

Attempts have been made to define a coherent stylistic vocabulary for the Baroque period. To look at the Baroque as a succession of phases in an international development, is especially useful in dealing with the representational arts.

The first or 'Early Baroque' phase, essentially a naturalistic one, originated in Italy, and its pioneering figure was beyond doubt Caravaggio.

The second generation, or 'High Baroque', found its fullest realisation in the sensuousness and colourism of Rubens. To this phase also belong the great achievements of Italian masters like Bernini, in the fields of painting, sculpture and architecture. Luxuriousness and sensuality are equally conspicuous in the decorative arts. Such works, regarded because of their exuberance and voluptuousness as typical of the Baroque period as a whole, should be viewed as products of the sensualistic stage.

The third, or classicistic, phase in which the opulent and emotional qualities of 'High Baroque' were supplanted by a more rigorous order, clarity and composure, began in Rome in the early 1630s. The growing strength of the classicists challenged the more flamboyant Roman artists. Poussin – the most rational and disciplined seventeenth century master – became the chief representative of this phase. It won its greatest victories in French art and architecture.

If a fourth 'Late Baroque' stage can be distinguished, it is that of the later Louis XIV style, with its decorative reworking of the classic vocabulary. The great Baroque masters had all lived out their lives: the earliest Rococo artists had not yet come upon the scene.

From J. R. Martin, *Baroque*, Allen Lane, 1977, pp. 26–29

The Calling of St Matthew **was commissioned in 1597 as one of three large paintings for a church in Rome. Caravaggio created public astonishment by replacing a traditional subject with dramatic contemporary realism.**

Activities

1 Research the contribution of one of the great figures in Baroque art or sculpture. Make a presentation, using illustrations, to explain the importance of their contribution to the development of the Baroque style, paying particular attention to one work.

2 Use the Internet to compare Bernini's design for the main front at St Peter's in Rome with either the Palace of Versailles or one of the great houses designed by Vanbrugh. Make a list of similarities and differences between the two designs. Is there sufficient similarity for both to be described as Baroque?

3 Conduct a survey to establish modern attitudes to one particular piece of Baroque music. Present your findings in written and tabular form.

Thinking and analytical skills

1 Summarise the argument presented by Martin on the subject of Baroque style.

2 What different types of knowledge does he use to support his conclusion?

3 To what extent is his conclusion supported by evidence from the picture or from Baroque music?

(iii) Why did classical architecture make a comeback?

Links: 1.5 (ii); 1.5 (iv) **Key skills:** C3.3, C3.1b; IT3.1; IT3.2

Introduction

The eighteenth century was a period of prosperity and stability in Britain. It was also a period of great building. After about 1720, wealthy gentlemen returning from the Grand Tour began to modernise old buildings in new styles. They were influenced by great Italian masters like Palladio and Alberti, and by the ancient classical buildings.

Background

Alberti, in the sixteenth century, equated classicism with beauty, defining it architecturally as 'the harmony and **concord** of all the parts achieved by following well-founded rules based on the study of ancient works and resulting in a unity such that nothing could be added or taken away or altered except for the worse'.

Colen Campbell revived interest in classical style after 1715. After studying in Rome, he publicised designs by Inigo Jones, Vetruvius and Palladio. Although not a trained architect, he was commissioned to build houses in the new Italianate style. His ideas rapidly became popular and other architects copied them.

Palladian architecture, named after Palladio, had several fundamental principles. Symmetry and a perfectly regular plan were key features. A huge **portico**, consisting of a massive **pediment** over supporting columns, with open stairs leading to the 'piano nobile' dominated the entrance front. The remainder of the exterior was plain. Equal numbers of windows or bays balanced either side of the entrance. Internal decoration was considerably more ornate and flamboyant.

Lord Burlington, the second leading Palladian, visited Italy twice to study Palladio's work. As an amateur, he designed Chiswick House in Palladian style. He was the chief theorist of the movement, working closely with William Kent, the interior decorator.

Later developments saw less originality and more rigid stylisation through the imposition of strict rules of proportion. Country house design was standardised as a large rectangular central block, flanked by pavilions, often containing servants' quarters and service areas. The ground floor was heavily **rusticated**, while upper floors were plain **ashlar** finish, resulting in a stark, severe, often uninteresting appearance. Little attention was given to comfort and convenience, since integrity of design was considered more important. In the 1750s the **Gothic** style, influenced by Strawberry Hill, developed in reaction to Palladian orthodoxy.

Robert Adam (1728–92), who studied in Italy, revived classicism in the 1760s. He built few large houses, but often completed the designs of others, blending his own style effectively with more traditional ones. His main claim to fame rests on internal design and decoration. He believed in total design for rooms, including size, shape, wall ceiling and floor decorations, furniture and furnishings.

Adam accepted basic Palladian principles but developed greater theatricality. Believing that a building's appearance should create a sense of movement, he incorporated flowing curves in place of rigidity of design. Originally influenced by Roman styles, after 1762 he used Greek and Etruscan features in his interiors. These, lighter in style than the Palladian's, used fantastic decorative carving and long flowing lines. The key to his style was delicacy, gaiety, grace and beauty. He said decoration was about feelings, not rigid rules.

Glossary

concord: agreement or harmony between things

portico: a structure consisting of a roof supported by columns; usually attached as a porch to a building

pediment: triangular upper part of the front of a classical building, typically surmounting a portico or windows

rusticated: masonry with deeply sunken joints and roughened surfaces

ashlar: masonry made of large square-cut stones, often used as facing material

Gothic: the style of architecture common in western Europe from the twelfth to sixteenth centuries

Issues to be discussed

- Discuss the claim that much of the attraction of the new architecture was a reaction against Baroque extravagance.
- Why should building activity be encouraged by a 'period of prosperity and stability'?
- Why does an artistic movement lose originality when it becomes fashionable?
- Do you agree with Adam's view that decoration should be about feeling rather than rigid rules?
- To what extent do you agree with Alberti's view?

Where now?

M. Wilson, *The English Country House and its Furnishings*, Batsford, 1977

M. Girouard, *Life in the English Country House*, Yale, 1978

www.encarta.msn.com www.britainexpress.com/history

What do you think?

Critically examine the view that 'You can learn a lot about social attitudes from a study of architectural design.'

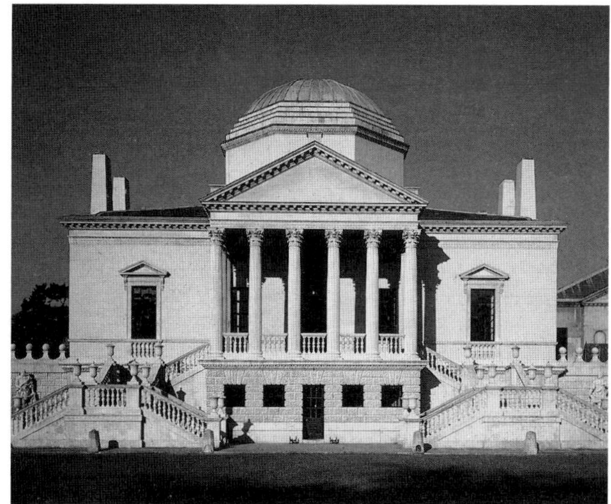

Chiswick House, 1725, Lord Burlington.

Lamport Hall, 1635 and 1732–41, John Webb/ Smiths of Warwick.

Strawberry Hill, 1748–70, Walpole/Robinson.

Kedleston Hall, 1760s, Adam.

Activities

1 Compare the photos. List **a** similarities, and **b** differences between them

2 Using all of the photos:
a Construct a table of different architectural features used in each building.
b Using the evidence of your table and the photos, write a brief illustrated guide to classical architecture.

3 Investigate each of the architectural details you have identified. Using appropriate images, create a poster to illustrate the principal features of classical architecture.

4 Conduct a survey in your town or locality to identify any buildings that have classical features. Investigate the origins of these buildings and use them to illustrate a short presentation on classical style.

Further research

1 Investigate further the contribution to the development of classical style of any one of the contemporaries and successors of either Lord Burlington or Robert Adam.

2 Research the development of Gothic style between the time of Walpole and about 1820.

(iv) Was Romantic 'sentiment' really self-indulgence?

Links: 1.2 (v); 1.5 (v) **Key skills:** IT3.1; IT3.2; IT3.3; C3.2; C3,3; C3.1a

Introduction

The great Romantic authors were primarily poets; to a lesser extent they were writers of prose and letters but there were few dramatists of note. Romantic writing can be found after 1770, but notable developments occurred around 1790. Strong links existed between Romantic literature and the growing European awareness of democracy.

Background

Romanticism was a reaction against the elegant formality and artificiality of the classical style. It encouraged relatively unsophisticated and openly emotional forms of expression. A significant theme was the essential nobility of ordinary people. Writers believed their responsibility was to reflect this and celebrate the prospect of a better life in a better world. Poets like Wordsworth gave a newly discovered and glorious significance to nature.

Blake, Coleridge and Wordsworth were three prominent early Romantic poets. In the preface to *Lyrical Ballads*, Wordsworth wrote 'poetry is a spontaneous outflow of powerful feelings'. This 'manifesto of the Romantics', implied that writers should follow their own interests and feelings and not be limited by established form. It encouraged new perspectives, themes and modes of expression.

After 1805, an increasing awareness of cultural nationalism (as opposed to universal brotherhood) led to renewed interest in collecting and imitating folk culture. Scott's historical novels focused on the (imagined) glories of the **medieval** past. Byron, Keats and Shelley dominated poetry.

Women writers began to emerge, largely due to the new emotionalism and increased middle-class literacy. Mrs Radcliffe's Gothic novels reflected interest in the past while Jane Austen and Mrs Edgeworth wrote about ordinary life. Mary Shelley's *Frankenstein* reflected the prevalent fascination with horror.

Born in the Lake District, William Wordsworth (1770–1850) was influenced by nature, saying that he 'grew up fostered alike by beauty and by fear'. Influenced by the French Revolution, he developed a passionate enthusiasm for **republicanism** and democracy. Later, through relative poverty and depression, he gained sympathy and understanding for the poor. His poetic style developed in response to both these influences and his friendship with Coleridge. In 1798 the two friends published *Lyrical Ballads*, which opened with Coleridge's 'Rime of the Ancient Mariner' and closed with Wordsworth's 'Tintern Abbey'. Though severely criticised by contemporaries, this book heralds the start of **lyrical** English Romantic poetry.

Wordsworth consciously rejected fashionable classicism, favouring short, lyric dramatic verse, dealing with tributes to nature or pictures of simple folk. He aimed to illustrate simple human truths and man's relationship with nature. He believed the real source of poetic truth was direct, **sensuous** experience. His writing was driven by strong emotions, not strict rules of form. In 1800, he wrote of his desire 'to choose incidents and situations from common life and to describe them in language really used by men, tracing in them the primary laws of our nature'. He helped to establish a new poetic style, language and vocabulary.

From 1799, while living in the Lake District, he formed a group called the 'Lake Poets'. Most of his greatest work was completed before 1808. His later poems have been criticised – Byron and Shelley dismissed him as 'dull'. In 1843 he was appointed Poet Laureate.

Glossary

medieval: relating to the Middle Ages (about 1100–1500)

republicanism: belief in government where the people and their elected representatives hold supreme authority

lyrical: expressing the writer's emotions in an imaginative and beautiful way

sensuous: relating to or affecting the senses rather than the intellect

Issues to be discussed

- Is it possible to express emotion and follow rigid rules?
- Why was poetry a more important form than drama in the Romantic period?
- What would you regard as Wordsworth's key contribution to the development of English lyric poetry?
- Why do you think Wordsworth's poetic skills and popularity declined after about 1805?

Where now?

B. Ford (ed.), *The Romantic Age in Britain*, Cambridge University Press, 1989

R. Cronin (ed.), *1798: The Year of the Lyrical Ballads*, Macmillan, 1998

www.kirjasto.sci.fi/wordswo.htm www.britannica.com

What do you think?

To what extent is it true to say that the Romantic movement simply offered an opportunity for second-rate writers to say what they wanted without the disadvantage of rules, structure or even good taste?

While there were many British writers after 1785 whose work would now be referred to as 'Romantic' there was no Romantic movement, as such. If there was one particular writer to whom most others related, it was Coleridge; but he was not a leader with a formulated message or programme, rather a man of unusual gifts and intelligence who had a decisive influence on a number of young writers during their formative period.

What we see when we look at the period as a whole is rather an extraordinary flowering and richness of creativity, involving individual writers who were drawn to think and write in new ways. It is only in retrospect that each can be seen to be pressing to an extreme some element in what would eventually be seen as 'Romantic' thinking and writing.

For young poets such as Wordsworth and Coleridge 'genius' and 'sensibility' were words of power. Genius, although usually intended to convey, specifically, either responsiveness to the spirit of a place or an invocation of one's inward powers, could easily suggest that one thought one's own powers to be unique.

Sensibility was less controversial. Many contemporary poems written for drawing-room readers directed their emotions to small birds and animals or to beggars and outcasts. The inducing of human sympathy was believed to have become more necessary in an age which cried up the virtues of freestanding independence.

Genius and sensibility were vulnerable ideals, however. The appeal to fear and pity on which both were partly based were giving rise to a proliferating fashion for the 'Gothic' – a mode which encouraged writers to play upon such emotions in their readers with little seriousness of purpose.

From J. Beer, 'Literature' in B. Ford (ed.), *The Romantic Age in Britain*, Cambridge University Press, 1989, pp. 57–60

Tintern Abbey.

Lines composed a few miles above Tintern Abbey

These beauteous forms,
Through a long absence, have not been to me
As is the landscape to a blind man's eye:
But oft, in lonely rooms, and 'mid the din
Of towns and cities, I have owed to them
In hours of weariness, sensations sweet . . .
For I have learned
To look on nature, not as in the hour
Of thoughtless youth; but hearing oftentimes
The still, sad music of humanity,
Nor harsh nor grating, though of ample power
To chasten and subdue. And I have felt
A presence that disturbs me with the joy
Of elevated thoughts; a sense sublime . . .
. . .Therefore am I still
A lover of the meadows and the woods
And mountains . . .

William Wordsworth

Lines 23–28, 90–95 and 104–06
Source: From Samuel Taylor Coleridge and William Wordsworth, *Lyrical Ballads*, 1798

Activities

1 Using www.britannica.com, obtain a complete copy of 'Tintern Abbey'. In a group, discuss:
a Does the extract reflect the content of the remainder of the poem?
b What different types of knowledge does Wordsworth use or ask his readers to use?
c How effective is Wordsworth's imagery?

2 Research the life and work of one other Romantic poet. Write a brief report either:
a comparing the poet of your choice with Wordsworth, or
b outlining the contribution your chosen poet made to the development of Romantic poetry.

3 Read Chapter 10 of *Sense and Sensibility*. How does Jane Austen reflect the sentiments of Romanticism?

Thinking and analytical skills

1 What conclusion is Beer attempting to support?
2 Identify, with examples, different types of knowledge or argument used in the passage.
3 To what extent does Beer succeed in justifying his conclusion?
4 How and in what ways does the extract from 'Tintern Abbey' help or harm Beer's argument?

(v) Was Monet a genuine innovator or simply a rebel?

Links: 1.5 (i); 1.5 (vi) **Key skills:** C3.1b; C3.2; C3.3; IT3.1; IT3.2; IT3.3

Introduction

Although Impressionism had a very short life, it led to the development of various new experimental styles. By about 1900 Impressionist ideas even began to influence music. France was the main centre of creativity in both art and music, led by Monet and Debussy respectively.

Background

Claude Monet (1840–1926), generally regarded as the founder of Impressionism, grew up in Paris and then moved to Le Havre. His only interest was painting. He was already receiving commissions at the age of 15.

Eugene Boudin introduced him, in 1856, to the 'new' idea of painting outdoors, rather than in a studio. At first Monet resisted this technique, but eventually adopted and refined it, painting in bright colours to catch the character of light. He said, 'My eyes were finally opened and I understood nature; I learned at the same time to love it.'

In 1859 he moved to Paris, the European centre of art. He became disillusioned with traditional techniques and principles, and refused formal training. He joined the studio of Gleyre, where he met Renoir and Sisley. These three, with very different backgrounds, were all committed to finding new approaches to art. This led to the development of Impressionism. They visited the forests of Fontainbleau to paint, but unlike their contemporaries, who used subdued colours and dark shadows, they filled their paintings with open spaces and sunlight.

Seeking to make his name (and gain Establishment recognition) Monet painted several traditional pictures for exhibition. Though well received, his larger work was severely criticised for being 'broadly handled with a loaded brush, giving a rough surface texture, clearly visible brushstrokes, and sacrificing detail to overall effect'. Further efforts to gain recognition failed, despite careful attention to detail.

Financial insecurity drove Monet to London, where he studied Constable and Turner. Returning to Le Havre he painted 'Impressions: Sunrise' which gave the name 'Impressionism' to the new movement. Critics said his paintings were 'sketchy and unfinished – just like first impressions'. The 1870s were the **pinnacle** of Impressionism. Many of Monet's student friends visited him at Le Havre to benefit from the clarity of light which they contrasted with the murky conditions of Paris. It was during this period that many of the important features of Impressionism developed.

At that time the French artistic establishment attempted to control artistic standards and techniques through an annual exhibition. Most of the Impressionists were barred from this exhibition as they were regarded as being too experimental. As a challenge to the establishment, the group (including Renoir, Manet, Degas, Cezanne and Sisley) staged the first of several unofficial exhibitions in 1874. It was a disaster, as were efforts to raise money by selling paintings. These setbacks did not affect the quality of Monet's paintings, which never became gloomy or **sombre**. Undeterred, he continued to perfect his style.

After 1883, following his wife's death, he settled in Giverny. The Impressionist group disintegrated as the members started to develop individual styles. In 1892, while painting a series of pictures of Rouen Cathedral, Monet discovered that all aspects of a scene changed as light altered. He became obsessed by the effect of changing light and devoted the remainder of his life to its study. Despite failing sight he continued to paint until his death, concentrating on a series of studies based on his lily pond.

Glossary

pinnacle: high pointed piece of rock, or architecture, hence the most successful point

sombre: dark or dull; oppressively solemn or sober

Issues to be discussed

- Why did Impressionism have such a 'short life'?
- What do you think the advantages and disadvantages might be of painting outdoors?
- What are the lasting effects of Impressionism?
- Why has Impressionism affected art and music but not literature and architecture?
- How true is it to claim that all new ideas will meet opposition from traditionalists? Justify your opinion.

Where now?

B. Whelpton, *Art Appreciation Made Simple*, W. H. Allen, 1970

www.geocities.com/Paris/Gallery

www.columba.edu/ www.ndirect.co.uk

What do you think?

Critically assess the importance of the role of any one artist in establishing and developing Impressionism.

Straightforward, naturalistic landscape painting continued as the popular style in France for almost a hundred years, but at a critical moment its place was taken by photography. The three great lovers of nature in the late nineteenth century, Monet, Cezanne and Van Gogh, had to make a more radical transformation.

Curiously, it came from looking at ripples – the sun sparkling on water and the quavering reflection of masts. Monet and Renoir both followed the ordinary naturalist style. But when, in 1869, they came to those ripples and reflections, patient naturalism was defeated.

All one could do was to give an impression – an impression of what? Of light, because that is all that we see. Monet's words – 'light is the principal person in the picture' – gave a kind of philosophical unity to their work. Our awareness of light has become part of that general awareness, that heightening of sensibility, which seemed almost to give us new senses. When one thinks how many beautiful Impressionist pictures there are in the world, and of what a difference they have made to our seeing, it is surprising how short a time the movement lasted. The periods in which men can work together happily inspired by a single aim last only a short time. After twenty years the Impressionist movement had split up. One party thought that light should be rendered scientifically, in touches of primary colour, as if it had passed through a spectrum. This theory was too remote from the first spontaneous delight in nature.

On the other hand, Monet, the original unswerving Impressionist, attempted a kind of colour symbolism to express the changing effects of light. He turned to the water lily garden and the enraptured contemplation of the clouds reflected on its surface was the subject of his last great masterpieces.

From K. Clarke, *Civilization*, John Murray, 1969, pp. 288–90

La La at the Cirque Fernando **illustrates Degas' ability to show suspended movement. Proportion creates a sense of size, by contrasting the tiny figure with the massive room. A sense of excitement and tension is created by the composition of the figure, especially her crossed ankles and outspread arms. However, Degas also shows that La La is fully in control. Light and colour are used to increase impact.**

Activities

1 Make a presentation arguing for or against the view that 'painting not photography is the best way to show nature'.

2 Some critics claim that Degas was an Impressionist, but others say he was not. Research his career and work, then write a short report giving your own view.

3 Make a list of any of Degas' paintings that you think justify the title 'Impressionist'. Give reasons to support your choice.

4 Compare either one of Monet's paintings of water lilies or the work of another Impressionists painter with *Snow storm* or *Waves Breaking on a Lee Shore* by the English artist, Turner. Make a list of similarities and differences between them. (Use the Internet to find copies of these paintings, unless you are able to view real works in an art gallery.)

Thinking and analytical skills

1 Identify Clarke's conclusion and the different stages of his argument.

2 What different types of knowledge and argument are used in the passage about Impressionism?

3 How successfully does Clarke justify his conclusion?

(vi) Why were 'the angry young men' angry?

Links: 1.1 (iii); 1.5 (i); 1.5 (ii) **Key skills:**N3.1; N3.2; N3.3; C3.2; C3.3

Introduction

The Second World War was a significant turning point for each of the literary genres. Social and cultural attitudes were changing rapidly and mass education was creating a new reading public. The vast literary output was influenced by different experimental ideas. This led some critics to claim that there were no longer any great literary figures.

Background

The fear of social, economic and cultural disintegration was a threat to stability in the post-war years. Traditional literary forms seemed inappropriate in the face of the ever-present threat of renewed chaos and a pessimistic view of humanity's future. Left-wing idealists were disillusioned and many writers became increasingly sceptical and **cynical**. In the 1960s society rejected traditional moral values, embraced the new permissiveness and accepted inter-generational conflict.

Drama reflected these new attitudes most clearly. Initially established authors continued using pre-war style. In 1955 Samuel Beckett's *Waiting for Godot* created considerable shock, introducing continental 'non-realist'-style theatre and dramatising a sense of **futility** and isolation.

The movement known as the 'Angry Young Men' emerged the following year. These young authors, who had not been active in the war, demonstrated their scorn and disaffection for the establishment. The label came from criticism of a John Osborne play. Mostly working class and educated at **red-bricks**, they were contemptuous of the Oxbridge elite. Their plays reflected raw anger and frustration with the drab post-war world. Heroes were usually rootless, working-class male rebels who viewed society with disdain, rejected authority, yet sought upward mobility. Writers included Osborne, Pinter, Wain, Amis, Braine, Sillitoe Kops, Delaney and Wesker. They succeeded by verbalising contemporary frustrations.

John Osborne (1929–94) despised the mediocrity of his lower middle-class background. After several unsuccessful jobs he was attracted to theatrical work. His first successful play, *Look Back in Anger* (1956), is regarded as a representative work of the movement. The play, in fairly traditional form, used unusual and unexpected content. The hero, Jimmy Porter, rebels against traditional lower-middle-class **mores**. On the edge of middle-class respectability, he feels marginalised and resentful, frustrated by barriers to his progress imposed by privileged people, who monopolise better jobs. He vents his frustration on his middle-class wife and her friends. The play sharply expressed a resentful generation's anger and frustration, but offered no solution.

The Entertainer (1957) used a metaphor of the declining music hall to condemn Britain's imperial collapse. *Luther* (1961) portrays the historical figure as a rebellious hero. Osborne continued writing about decline, frustration and anger, and attacked contemporary values in his later plays. His style created actable roles, restored the art of the **tirade** and used passionate, scathing speeches for dramatic effect. His main contribution was to change the direction of British theatre. Earlier authors presented well-drawn pictures of upper- or middle-class life. Osborne created vigorous, realistic examinations of contemporary working-class issues.

Glossary

cynical: believing that people are motivated purely by self-interest or are concerned only with their own interests and disregard accepted standards to achieve them

futility: a pointless state, producing no useful result

red-brick: universities founded in the late nineteenth and early twentieth centuries; not having the status of Oxbridge

mores: the customs and conventions of a community

tirade: a long speech of angry criticism or accusation

Issues to be discussed

- Why was there disillusion and frustration after the end of the Second World War?
- Does literature reflect or create popular feelings?
- What evidence is there of disillusion and frustration in other art forms at this time?
- How has the role of traditional art forms been affected by the development of new, more popular forms (like television, film, video and recordings)?
- Does the rise of popular culture mark the end of high culture?

Where now?

D. Daiches, *A Critical History of English Literature*, Secker and Warburg, 1969

B. Ford (ed.), *The Cambridge Cultural History – Modern Britain*, Cambridge University Press, 1992

www.encarta.msn.com www.britannica.com

What do you think?

'In the last 50 years British culture has entered a new Dark Ages from which it may not emerge.' Critically examine this view with reference to any one art form or the creative work of one individual.

London has been going through the annual collapse of values known as London Fashion Week. All over town, people with huge budgets and tiny brains have been primping and posing. And as usual I have had to read paragraphs of gibberish claiming that art and fashion are growing closer together. Someone writes it every year.

Fashion, the cuckoo of popular culture, has been using an assortment of modern galleries and London museums as venues for the drunken wastage of resources that are known as fashion launches. A few artists have gone to some of these parties. But art and fashion are not growing closer together. How can they? They are the opposite of each other. Art is driven by an appetite for truth; fashion is driven by an appetite for concealment. One has given us Rembrandt. The other has come up with shoulder pads.

A couple of exhibitions have opened in London that make the difference between art and fashion easier to distinguish in detail. One mimics the moods and attitudes of fashion culture in order to show it up for the ugly, deceitful, vapid, superficial and misogynistic culture it is. And the other is a well-meaning photography exhibition called Imperfect Beauty, which sets out to tackle fashion's ruthless pursuit of untruths. But does it badly. I wish I could recommend it to you as an aesthetic experience in its own right. But it is a mess.

The point is to show what kind of work goes into the creation of a typical fashion image. This ought to have been a valuable exercise. But it manages to be more confusing than revealing. All that emerged clearly for me was the ego of the stylist. There is an essential silliness to fashion folk that no amount of timid exhibition-making can disguise.

From an article by W. Januszczak, *The Sunday Times*, 1 October 2000

Has the angst of popular culture in the 1950s been replaced by sickly sweet images in the 1990s?

Activities

1 Investigate the plays performed at a local professional theatre during the space of twelve months.
a Make a table to show when they were written.
b Obtain the theatre attendance figures and calculate which plays were **i** most popular, and **ii** least popular. Show your findings in an appropriate graph.

2 Collect reviews of pop and classical concerts.
a Make a list of features that are regarded as desirable in each type of concert, according to the critics.
b Identify similarities and differences between them.
c Compile a questionnaire to investigate the qualities that people look for in a concert.
d Write a brief report to outline your findings.

Thinking and analytical skills

1 Identify the stages in the argument that 'fashion is not art' in the extract.
2 Identify and illustrate different types of argument or knowledge used by the author.
3 Does the quality and style of argument used by the author undermine the validity of his conclusion?

(i) What is art?

Links: 1.5 (ii); 4.14 **Key skills:** IT3.1; IT3.2; IT3.3; C3.3; C3.1a

Introduction

Aesthetics is the philosophical study of beauty and taste. Most people know what they like, but have difficulty explaining why. Similarly, people can say whether a thing is beautiful, but cannot define criteria to assess the nature of beauty. Aesthetics helps clarify issues concerning the world of experience called 'art'.

Background

Most art critics agree the term 'art' should only apply to man-made objects. No natural object, however beautiful or aesthetically pleasing, is a work of art because it is not humanly produced, although an artist working on natural objects, like rock or wood, can turn them into works of art. Painting, music, poetry, buildings, cars or cities may be included in this definition. Whatever man does to an object is art. Aesthetics judges whether it is good or bad, beautiful or ugly, helpful or harmful.

The way critics use the term 'art' is often narrow in meaning and may be applied to objects that individuals respond to 'aesthetically'. Art can be subdivided into 'fine' and 'useful' art. Fine art consists of objects created to generate aesthetic responses (like sculpture, music, poetry and paintings). These, designed to be enjoyed for their own sake, may not possess utility. Useful art exists to serve practical purposes, but may possess aesthetic qualities which are of secondary importance. Useful art can include cars, dishes, furniture and lights.

Architecture is a problem, since buildings are intended to be useful, even if they are designed to be attractive. However, while most buildings are designed to be aesthetically pleasing, some become accepted as works of art.

The term 'art' may be restricted to the visual arts, effectively excluding music, drama, dance and poetry. Sometimes it is used to distinguish good art from products not considered worthy of the title 'art'. A third, related meaning can apply to the artist's skill or the process of producing art.

Interpretation of art involves several critical areas:

- Art is produced in a context that includes the social and economic circumstances of the time and of the artist. The artist's attitude and intention, the work's relationship to the artist's other work and to other artists and the role and requirements of customer or **patron** are significant. All factors, known or unknown, that helped to shape a work in an artist's mind are important.
- The work of art itself, the outcome of the artist's thought, intentions and creativity, influences how it is interpreted. Artefacts are physical evidence of communication between artist and audience, but the audience may not interpret a work as the artist intended.
- Audiences seeing, reading or listening to art will be influenced by the work. This influence owes as much to the **perception** of the audience as to the artist's intentions. Reactions may be both aesthetic and non-aesthetic, and responses are shaped by the culture and circumstances of the audience.

An observer's involvement with a work 'for its own sake' is aesthetic. Aesthetic experience belongs to the consumer, whereas artistic experience belongs entirely to the creator.

Glossary

patron: a person who gives financial or other support to a person, organisation or cause

perception: the ability to see, hear or become aware of something through the senses; a way of regarding, understanding or interpreting something – hence intuitive understanding and insight

Issues to be discussed

- To what extent is it fair to say that natural objects are not works of art? Give reasons to justify your answer.
- Is it reasonable to make a distinction between fine art and useful art, since both are the result of creativity?
- Why, with the passage of time, can useful art suddenly become fine art?
- Does an observer need to know anything about an artist's background or stylistic rules in order to appreciate a work of art?
- What makes a work of art valuable?

Where now?

N. Cook, *Music, Imagination and Culture*, Clarendon Press, 1990

J. Armstrong, *Looking at Pictures: an Introduction to the Appreciation of Art*, Duckworth, 1996

www.britannica.com www.thispoetry.com www.educacao.pro

What do you think?

'Everything man-made is a work of art. It is only necessary to understand it, to appreciate it.' Assess arguments for and against this view.

The work of art is not a slice of life. No school of realism produces replicas of some visible part of reality and says, 'This is what reality looks like.' No portrait painter who has anything important to say, says only that. The self-portraits of Rembrandt and Van Gogh say more about the sitter and the painter, than merely, 'This is what he looks like.' Similarly no novel, no poem is simply a slice of life. The school of French novelists (of whom Zola was perhaps the most important) really believed they were presenting a slice of life. But Zola's account of the life of his old friend Cezanne was highly sectarian, not regarded as realistic by Cezanne and Monet, and led to a breach between the painters and the writer.

No work of art is simply a presentation of reality, nor is it simply an abstract pattern, either of paint, music or words. Every so often people say, 'The best work of art is simply realistic'; and others reply, 'The best work of art is simply abstract.' But in fact the great works of art have been produced when neither of these extremes has been held. A work of art is in some sense an experiment in living shared with the artist.

A work does not exist on the canvas, in the book, until you breathe life into it! The artist creates the work, but the spectator recreates it. Every time you look more closely at the work it suddenly comes to life with greater depth. A more informed 'reading', not only tells you more about the work, but actually makes it live in a deeper way. That is part of the act of recreation – simply getting more out of what the poem or the portrait says by knowing more about it.

From J. Bronowski, *The Visionary Eye*, MIT Press, 1978

***Self-portrait*, *1661–62* by Rembrandt.**

***Self-portrait*, *1887* by Van Gogh.**

Activities

1 Study the two self-portraits.
 a Using only the paintings as evidence, make a list of all the things you can learn, understand or deduce about each of the artists shown.
 b Using the Internet, research one of the two artists to check the accuracy of your list.
 c Repeat your list, dividing it into three sections headed 'Supported', 'Contradicted' and 'Not proven'.
 d Using the 'Contradicted' list, write brief comments to explain why your original judgement was inaccurate.

2 Discuss the differences between a portrait painted by an artist and a police photo-fit picture.
 a What similarities and differences exist between the two pictures?
 b What differences exist between the purposes of the artists?
 c What are you able to learn about the people shown in the portrait and the photo-fit?
 d Why is one considered art and the other not?

Thinking and analytical skills

1 Identify the conclusion and the stages in the argument presented by Bronowski.
2 What are the strengths and weaknesses of the different types of knowledge and argument used by Bronowski?
3 How effectively does Bronowski justify his conclusion with the evidence he presents?

(ii) When is a masterpiece not a masterpiece?

Links: 1.5 (i); 1.5 (v) **Key skills:** C3.1a; C3.1b; C3,3; IT3.1; IT3.2; IT3.3

Introduction

Art criticism is a way of judging the value and aesthetic qualities of art objects. Critics usually make judgements based on predetermined criteria, which can apply equally to all works of art in a particular genre or medium that interests them. Art criticism is therefore the practical application of aesthetic theory.

Background

Aesthetic theory developed in the eighteenth century. Before then art criticism consisted of broad, vague generalisations about the moral purpose and higher ideals of truth and beauty. Little detailed scrutiny was given to individual works. In 1757 Edmund Burke distinguished between the **sublime** and the beautiful in art. His views were influential, challenging earlier principles of criticism. He argued for the need to analyse and understand human attitudes to these qualities.

The term 'aesthetics' was developed in the 1730s to express the idea that 'sensuous perception must be **emancipated** from traditional limitations'. It was claimed that 'perception' was not a **transitional** stage in the acquisition of knowledge about art, but was itself a type of knowledge to be discovered and understood. From this developed the idea that art's significance lies in what we perceive (when listening, viewing or reading) rather than in what we see.

In 1988 Barrett, an art critic, argued that aesthetics deals with three distinct 'meanings'. Aesthetics concerns sensual perception (or pleasure), beauty (or value) and superior taste. The first two may remain constant through time, but the third is vulnerable to historical circumstances and changing fashion and taste. In the past, fashion changed slowly. Today, media and commercial pressures cause rapid change. This raises the issue of whether aesthetic judgements deal with absolute or transitory values.

Various criteria exist for aesthetic judgements:

- Can anyone make aesthetic judgements or is certain knowledge and understanding required?
- Are the arts elitist or popular?
- Do judgements made in one historical, geographical or social context apply in all others?
- Do absolute rules exist for making judgements?

Aesthetic questions:

- How is **avant-garde** art legitimised?
- Is the value of art measured in terms of intrinsic qualities or commercial worth?
- Should art be valued for its own sake as a beautiful object or in relation to other works?
- Is an artefact 'art' if it is deliberately designed to generate a particular response?
- Does it matter if the viewer's interpretation differs from the creative artist's?
- Is aesthetics about emotional experience or technique?
- Is there any place for politics in the production of art?
- Why does some art survive and some disappear?
- Is there a difference between art and entertainment?

Glossary

sublime: of such excellence, grandeur or beauty as to inspire great admiration or awe

emancipate: to set free, especially from legal, social or political restrictions

transitional: the process of changing from one state to another or a period of such change

avant-garde: new and unusual or experimental

Issues to be discussed

- Discuss whether, in an age of film, true art has lost its ability to shock.
- Is it more important to ask 'how we should approach a work of art' or 'why should we engage with it at all'?
- Is aesthetic criticism how the establishment seeks to retain a monopoly of appreciation of the arts?
- What happens to great art when it is commercialised? Can it remain great art?
- What criteria should be used to judge the quality of a piece of art?

Where now?

I. Davies, *Cultural Studies and Beyond*, Routledge, 1995
N. Cook, *Music, Imagination and Culture*, Clarendon Press, 1990
J. Armstrong, *Looking at Pictures: an Introduction to the Appreciation of Art*, Duckworth, 1996
www.educacao.pro.br www.britannica.com

What do you think?

Choose any work of art that you have studied and which you believe to be a masterpiece. Explain your reasons.

Although we may disagree about a theory, the impact of a masterpiece is something about which there is astonishing unanimity. Changes of taste may keep the amateur amused but we can agree that masterpieces exist, and are the work of great artists in moments of particular enlightenment. The artist will, I suppose, be moved by the subject.

Two characteristics of a masterpiece are: a confluence of memories and emotions forming a single idea, and the power of recreating traditional forms to become expressive of the artist's own. This instinctive feeling of tradition is not the result of conservatism.

The human element is essential to a masterpiece. The artist must be deeply involved in the understanding of his fellow men. Certain portraits are masterpieces because in them a human being is recreated.

But can mere imitation be the basis of masterpiece? If form predominates there is a loss of vitality and humanity. If subject predominates, the mind releases its hold. In both cases the chance of a masterpiece is diminished.

Many think those large elaborate works in which a painter has put in everything he knows to show his complete supremacy in his art are masterpieces. Masterpieces are not painted by 'professionals'. Artists must use the language of the day, however degraded, even if it is incomprehensible to the majority.

A masterpiece is above all the work of an artist of genius, absorbed by the spirit of his time in a way that makes his individual experience universal. If he lives in a time when many moving pictorial ideas are current, his chances of creating a masterpiece are increased. If the acceptable subjects of painting are serious themes, touching us at many levels, he is well on his way. But in the end a masterpiece is the creation of genius.

From K. Clarke, *What is a Masterpiece?*, Thames and Hudson, 1979

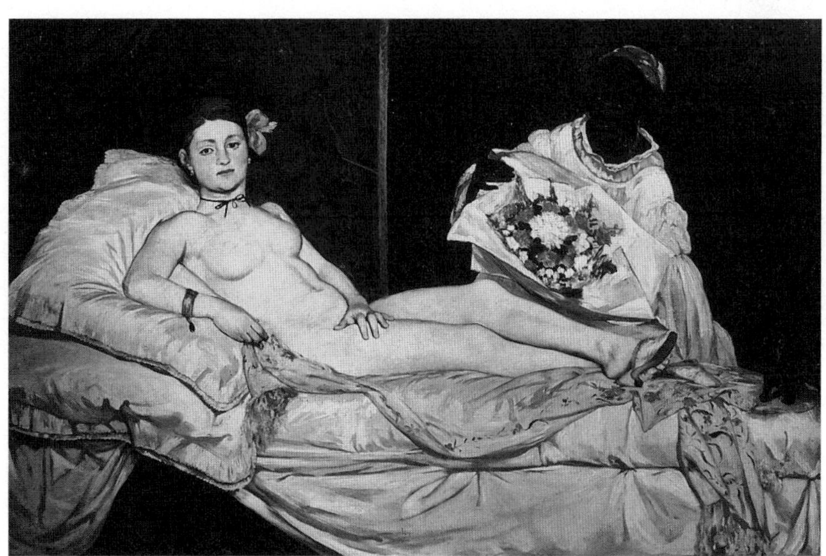

'Manet's *Olympia*' wrote Kenneth Clarke, 'is a masterpiece all right.'

Activities

1 In a group, discuss what you understand by the term 'masterpiece'.
  a Write a short but complete definition of your understanding of the term.
  b Make a list of the qualities that you would expect to find in a masterpiece.
  c Compile a list of masterpieces in each of the arts and, where appropriate, collect illustrations of them.

2 Select a work of art and write a brief description of its qualities.

3 Research the work of a contemporary artist or group of musicians. Make a presentation to explain why you feel that their work will survive into future generations.

4 Create a timeline from about 1400 to the present day and mark on it examples of great artists and writers.

Thinking and analytical skills

1 Identify the stages in the argument presented by Kenneth Clarke.
2 Illustrate, with examples, different types of knowledge used by Clarke.
3 How successful is Clarke in justifying his conclusion? Identify the strengths and weaknesses of his argument.

(iii) What are the main characteristics of Baroque art?

Links: 1.4 (i); 1.4 (iii); 1.5 (i) Key skills: C3.3; IT3.2; IT3.3; C3.2

Introduction

Today Baroque describes various seventeenth and early eighteenth century art forms. Originally applied to music, it now includes painting, sculpture and architecture. In 1888 a German art critic first used the term as a stylistic designation and tried to set down a systematic formulation of its chief characteristics.

Background

The origin of the term 'Baroque' is uncertain. Some trace it to an Italian word 'barocco' meaning any contorted idea. An alternative derivation is from Spanish 'barueco' meaning an irregularly shaped or imperfect pearl. Eighteenth-century art critics used it to show contempt for recent art forms, which they believed had declined from the **classical** standards of the **Renaissance**.

'Baroque' did not define any stylistic features, but rather showed disapproval. It was applied to anything bizarre, exuberant, irregular or that departed from established stylistic rules. Later it was extended to include anything regarded as odd, grotesque, exaggerated or over-decorated. Not until the early twentieth century did critics adopt the term generally to describe a distinctive artistic style.

The style was a response to three broad social and cultural tendencies, which traditional art forms could not satisfy:

- After the **Counter-Reformation**, the Catholic church looked for an artistic form to express religious thought and stimulate faith, and found it in a new style of painting.
- Absolute monarchs consolidated their position and a new prosperous and powerful middle class emerged. Both desired art that would show their wealth and power.
- A new interest in nature and realism developed.

The **patronage** of powerful men encouraged the exploration of new forms of artistic expression. Baroque influence spread through most European countries and many colonies. Developments occurred at different times in different countries and in different art forms. First seen in Italy in painting and sculpture around 1600, it did not really reach northern Europe until the century's end. Baroque music and architecture developed more slowly, continuing to influence style in the early eighteenth century. Throughout this period Classical ideals and influence continued to have some impact.

Principal features of the Baroque style include:

- vast scale, implying infinite space and power,
- a greater sense of perspective, realism and dramatic effect,
- the rise of pure landscape painting,
- a sense of the complexity of the natural world,
- a sense of movement, energy and tension,
- strong contrasts of light and shade,
- undulating lines conveying a sense of motion,
- human figures shown as individuals not generalisations,
- intense spirituality, linked to man's relative insignificance,
- concern with the inner workings of the mind,
- vivid colours, luxury and contrasting textures,
- an emphasis on sensual not intellectual responses,
- new forms, languages and vocabulary,
- a desire to emphasise a sense of physical immediacy.

Glossary

classical: ideas and principles based on Ancient Greek and Roman style; hence a form of art representing an exemplary standard within a traditional, long-standing style

Renaissance: the revival of interest in art and literature under the influence of Classical forms (c. 1400–1600)

Counter-Reformation: a movement for reform in the Roman Catholic church in reaction to Protestantism

patronage: support (usually financial) given by a patron

Issues to be discussed

- What problems might be encountered in trying to define the various art forms of over a century ago under the single heading of Baroque?
- Why is the term Baroque not used to describe literature?
- To what extent does the building shown opposite illustrate the characteristic features of the Baroque?
- Why did religion play an important part in the development of Baroque art and music?

Where now?

J. R. Martin, *Baroque*, Allen Lane, 1977
B. Whelpton, *Art Appreciation Made Simple*, W. H. Allen, 1970
www.britannica.com www.encarta.msn.com www.islandnet.com

What do you think?

With reference to one specific art form (art, music, architecture) assess the view that Baroque style is without merit.

The art we call Baroque was a popular art. The art of the Renaissance had appealed through intellectual means – geometry, perspective and knowledge of antiquity – to a small group of humanists. The Baroque appealed through the emotions to the widest possible audience. The subjects were often obscure, but the means of communication were popular. Caravaggio, the earliest and, on the whole, the greatest Italian painter of the period, experimented with lighting, and gained thereby a new dramatic impact. Later Baroque artists delighted in emotive close-ups with open lips and glistening tears. The huge scale, the restless movement, the shifting lights and dissolves – all these devices were to be rediscovered in the movies. The extraordinary thing is that the Baroque artists did it in bronze and marble, not on celluloid. In a way, it is a frivolous comparison because films are often vulgar and ephemeral, whereas the work of Bernini is ideal and eternal. He was a very great artist. He not only gave Baroque Rome its character, but was the chief source of an international style that spread all over Europe, as Gothic had done and as the Renaissance style never did.

All art is to some extent an illusion. It transforms experience in order to satisfy some need of the imagination. One can't help feeling that affluent Baroque, in its escape from the severities of the earlier forms ended by escaping from reality into a world of illusion. Art creates its own momentum and there was nothing it could do except become more and more sensational. The sense of grandeur is no doubt human instinct, but carried too far it becomes inhuman.

From K. Clarke, *Civilization*, Murray, 1969, pp. 186–92

The main entrance to Blenheim Palace, a Baroque palace designed for the Duke of Marlborough, 1705–32.

Activities

1 Examine the picture of Blenheim Palace (constructed in the early eighteenth century by Vanbrugh).
a List any features that support the passage.
b List any features you can identify which do not support the passage.
c Write a brief report on the subject of whether Blenheim Palace is built in the Baroque style.
d Conduct further research to find evidence to support or challenge your conclusion (start with www.encarta.msn.com or www.britannica.com)

2 Make a chart showing the different characteristics of Baroque painting, art, music and architecture. Using this evidence, write a short passage responding to the view that there was no distinctive Baroque style.

3 Investigate the availability in your locality of Baroque works of art. Show their location on an annotated map.

4 Compile a list of performances of Baroque music advertised in the local or national press during a single month. Construct a table to show this information organised by **a** composer, and **b** type of composition.

Thinking and analytical skills

1 What are the stages in the argument presented by Kenneth Clarke?
2 Identify, with examples, different types of knowledge and argument used in the passage.
3 How far is Clarke able to justify his conclusion in this passage?

(iv) Is there such a thing as classical style?

Links: 1.4 (ii); 1.4 (iv); 1.5 (ii) **Key skills:** C3.1b; C3.2; C3.3; IT3.1; IT3.2

Introduction

When applied to the arts, classical has three different but related meanings. It describes work produced by, or based on, Ancient Greco-Roman artistic style and can therefore mean 'the best of its type'. By extension, it applies to the stage in the cyclical development of art when a style is at its fullest and most **harmonious**.

Background

The eighteenth century is often referred to as 'the Classical Age', although other periods were influenced by classical ideals. In the arts an aesthetic attitude and the use of rules and forms replicating 'the noble simplicity and calm grandeur' of Greco-Roman art developed. Archaeological excavations at Pompeii revived interest in classical ideals like **harmony**, clarity, restraint, universality and idealism. Many artists favoured styles that were logical, moralising, solemn and with fixed ideals.

Classicism was a reaction against the exaggerated sensuousness and triviality of the Baroque period. Its **impetus** increased after the leaders of the French and American Revolutions encouraged the formation of links with the ancient democracies.

Visual artists favoured classical aesthetic qualities of harmony, proportion, balance and simplicity. They aimed to show beauty in traditional terms. Rules were designed to ensure excellence of execution, stressed line not colour, firm lines not curves, closed compositions not limitless spaces, and the general not the particular. Sculptors used white not coloured marble and calm stillness not dramatic twisting poses.

Portraiture was preferred to landscape, which simply formed an often idealised background. Poses were carefully composed to imitate ancient statues. Contours were firm and lighting harsh.

Composers began to react against Baroque style after 1720. They wanted a less formal but more elegant style, one that was delicate, **frivolous**, entertaining and immediately appealing. The result, called Rococo, was often artificial and sentimental. Audience response and enjoyment were increasingly important.

Rococo music was transformed and refined into classical style by Haydn, Mozart and Beethoven. Instrumental music was more important than vocal and the shape of orchestras and chamber groups was standardised. Rules of composition were established, with correctness becoming more important than emotion; these rules often replaced inspiration. Formal structure demanded simplicity. Musical phrases were shorter, better balanced and regular. Volume was used to create dramatic climaxes. Different musical forms were standardised.

Poetry was increasingly dominated by strict rules based on Greek and Roman authors. Writing developed an elegant formalism, often at the expense of deep feeling. Favoured qualities included order, symmetry, decorum and clarity. Emotion and enthusiasm were repressed.

Prose,which lent itself more effectively to the new social and economic circumstances, was the principal literary form. Apart from Pope, who polished poetic couplets to perfection, the greatest authors wrote prose. Fielding and Richardson established the novel as a major new art form. Pamphlets, magazines and newspapers flourished.

Glossary

harmonious: tuneful, not discordant; free from conflict

harmony: the combination of simultaneously sounded musical notes to produce chords, having a pleasing effect; agreement or concord

impetus: a driving force; the force or energy with which a body moves

frivolous: not having any serious purpose or value; carefree and superficial

Issues to be discussed

- Identify similarities and differences between the classical styles found in painting, sculpture, music and literature.
- Can you have strict stylistic rules and inspiration?
- Compare poetry written by Pope and Cibber. In what ways do they differ?
- Is Rococo style (in painting or music) more correctly part of the Baroque than of the classical period?
- What do you understand by the phrase 'audience response and enjoyment was increasingly important'?

Where now?

B. Ford (ed.), *Cambridge Cultural History, Volume 5*, Cambridge University Press, 1992

www.britishliterature.com www.encarta.msn.com

What do you think?

Alexander Pope wrote 'what oft was thought, but ne'er so well expressed'. Examine the arguments for and against this view as a judgement on any single art form in eighteenth-century classical style.

If one word provides a keynote for the many and varied responses to art during the first half of the eighteenth century, it is 'taste'. Essays were written on taste; newspapers argued about taste; and everybody strove to exhibit good taste. A writer in 1756 complained, 'In this superabundance of taste few can say what it really is, or what the word signifies.'

While philosophers struggled to define exactly what taste was, many commentators were more than happy to point out examples of good and bad taste. The Baroque, for example, was very definitely bad taste. Pride, opulence and display for its own sake were roundly condemned.

The ability to display informed value-judgements about art was a social indicator. If you really wanted to insult a man, you criticised his taste. A proper appreciation of the beautiful was, in one sense, a moral act.

Many early Georgians believed that appreciation of art was a matter of coming up with the right judgements. What was – and what was not – beautiful was seen as the reasoned application of unchanging aesthetic criteria. Indeed, the idea of individual taste was virtually a contradiction in terms, since taste involved the cool, rational understanding of how particular works of art displayed or adhered to rules. Joyous Romantic stirrings of the soul were dangerously subjective emotional responses at odds with Neoclassical principles of clarity, order, and harmonisation of parts within the whole.

It follows that appreciation of art becomes a matter of understanding, a straightforward intellectual process. Knowledge of the rules of taste is applied to the experience of an aesthetic object and a value-judgement formed. There is, in theory, no room for a difference of opinion, as long as there is a consensus on the rules to be applied.

From A. Tinniswood, *A History of Country House Visiting*, Blackwell, 1989, pp. 80–85

Apollo and Daphne **by Matthias Rauchmiller (1645–86).**

Venus **by Antonio Canova (1757–1822).**

Activities

1 Research the life and contribution of an English eighteenth-century artist, composer or writer. Make a presentation, using images, to explain his or her contribution to the classical revival.

2 In literature, the early eighteenth century was sometimes called the Augustan Age. Investigate the reason for this and explain its relevance to classical style.

3 Using appropriate tables, show **a** points of similarity in classical styles in art, literature and music, and **b** points of difference in classical styles in art, literature and music.

4 Investigate the availability of classical works of art in either a local art gallery or country house. Make a list of the artists represented. Find at least three other examples of their work.

Thinking and analytical skills

1 What conclusion does Tinniswood reach about the nature of good taste in the eighteenth century?

2 How effectively does he justify his conclusion?

3 Indicate, with examples. the different types of knowledge he uses.

(v) How romantic was Romanticism?

Links: 1.4 (iii); 1.4 (v); 1.5 (iii) **Key skills:** C3.2; C3.3; C3.1a; IT3.1; IT3.2; IT3.3

Introduction

Romanticism in art, architecture and literature is often associated with the period 1780 to 1850, but in music it is dated between the later years of Beethoven (1820) and the death of Mahler (1911). Each of these art forms is closely interrelated. Two important influences were the growing socioeconomic pressures of industrialisation and an awakening political awareness associated with the American and French Revolutions.

Background

Romanticism was both an artistic style and an **aesthetic** attitude. It developed as a conscious rejection of classical principles and practices, emerging first in Germany and Britain. Its influence rapidly spread to most European countries, developing a distinctive but universal style. Later, individual national characteristics emerged. Classical ideals continued to overlap with and influence Romanticism, especially in architecture and among the more conservative painters, musicians and writers.

New characteristics and attitudes included:

- a deeper appreciation of the beauties of nature,
- emotions were more highly valued than reason,
- sensory experiences and feelings were preferred,
- introspection was encouraged,
- a belief that the artist was a creator not a copier,
- imagination was seen as a route to deeper understanding and knowledge of truth,
- a desire to return to the traditions of the past,
- a willingness to explore new and strange ideas.

A key idea for most Romantics was '**sentiment**'. This resulted in open displays of emotionalism and a sense of national identity. These feelings influenced the artist's choice of subject matter.

Architecture reflected Romantic ideals by actively rejecting classical simplicity, **symmetry** and formality. In Britain the new Medieval and Tudor revivals imitating older traditional forms were very influential, but became increasingly strange and **exotic**. The most outlandish example was George IV's Royal Pavilion, built in a dramatic oriental style. Romantic architecture, with its irregular lines and elaborate decoration, was light-hearted and fanciful.

Music emphasised originality and individuality. Early Romantic composers like Beethoven and Schubert retained classical form, but allowed passions and emotions free reign. Later composers experimented with form, developing new types of composition, like tone poems. Rhythm and tonal colour were major expressive agents. Composers could display emotions more readily as the quality of instruments and the size and proficiency of orchestras increased. Some, like Dvorak, Greig and Tchaikovsky, reacting against German domination, developed clearly nationalistic styles, often based on traditional folk melodies.

From about 1770 a number of artists challenged traditional topics and styles. They experimented with new themes, contrasted light and shade, often developing unique visionary images. They showed a new awareness of nature. Landscape painting, led by Turner and Constable, stressed colour, atmosphere and dramatic light effects, aiming for a sense of awe and grandeur.

Glossary

aesthetic: concerned with beauty or its appreciation

sentiment: exaggerated and self-indulgent feelings of tenderness, sadness or nostalgia

symmetry: the quality of being made up of exactly similar parts facing each other, or around an axis

exotic: strikingly colourful or unusual; originating in a distant country

Issues to be discussed

- Why and how did the socioeconomic effects of the Industrial Revolution influence the style of artists in the Romantic period?
- How might the characteristics listed above influence the work of artists, architects or musicians?
- What is the difference between sentiment and sentimentality?
- Why were the Romantics so interested in portraying nature in their work?
- Show how Classical ideals continued to affect art.

Where now?

B. Ford (ed.), *The Romantic Age in Britain*, Cambridge University Press, 1989

R. Hughes, *Nothing if not Critical*, Collins, 1990

www.tam.itesm.mx www.britannica.com

What do you think?

'Romantic artists were more concerned to evoke emotion and feeling than to show life as it really was.' Critically examine this view, with particular reference to at least one artist of the Romantic period.

The period 1785–1851 was one of intense activity in the arts. We think of great names and great movements, but what lay behind this flowering of activity? It was a time of profound change in the way people lived.

Much Romantic art stood in opposition to classicism, which revered tradition and took formal order as an assumption of the arts.

Romanticism extolled the virtues of innovation; explored realms of chaos in human experience; gave emphasis to the artist's overriding responsibility to maintain integrity; looked forward, while seeing quite different versions of the past in which Shakespeare and Milton are at least as important as the Greeks and Romans.

The Romantic artist saw himself as providing a better model for the health and intelligence of the individual by helping to ensure that the whole soul of man, rather than the merely rational faculties, is engaged.

The process of social change reminded the Romantics of the limitless potential of the human mind. These great poetic and painterly landscapes, with flashing waterfalls and sudden avalanches of words, sound, colour are reminders of the constant possibility of change. They therefore remind us of the impermanence of human life.

The Romantics were trying to describe the indescribable. The wonder of it is that, given the internal strain of their programme, they proved able to supply us, across the European spectrum, in literature, painting and music with some of the most brilliant, memorable and glowing images that the arts have produced.

From B. Ford (ed.), *The Romantic Age in Britain*, Cambridge University Press, 1989, pp. 18–21

'The Honeymoon' by T. Rowlandson, from The *English Dance of Death*, 1815. The 'gaffer' shares a glass with 'death' while his young wife flirts with her lover through the open window.

Activities

1. Research the contribution of Turner or Constable to English art in the Romantic period. Present your findings in a short report using appropriate images.
2. Visit an art gallery and consider paintings and sculptures from the Romantic period. List the different artists. Construct a table of features **a** common to all examples, **b** shared by most examples, and **c** unique to few examples.
3. What are the distinctive features of buildings created in the Gothic Revival style? What distinguishes them from genuine Gothic buildings?
4. Listen to a recording of the slow movement of one of Beethoven's early symphonies and one written by Tchaikovsky or Mahler. In a group, discuss any variations in the sound achieved by the two composers. How does the quality of sound create a feeling of emotion?

Thinking and analytical skills

1. Identify the stages in the argument presented by Ford.
2. What types of knowledge does he use to support his views?
3. What is his conclusion? To what extent do you think he is successful in justifying his conclusion?

(vi) What impression did the Impressionists create?

Links: 1.5 (iv) **Key skills:** C3.1a; C3.2; C3.3

Introduction

The Impressionist movement started in France around 1865 and lasted for about 20 years. It was a reaction against the stranglehold of France's artistic establishment. It began in the last years of the **decadent** Third Empire and flourished in the period of social, economic and political uncertainty following France's defeat in the Franco-Prussian War.

Background

Paris was Europe's artistic centre during Napoleon III's reign. Artists, keen to learn, experiment and become established, gravitated to Paris and the Salon, the headquarters of French art. The Salon upheld traditional approaches, regulated standards and limited innovation.

The Academie Suisse provided a cheap **venue** for young painters to meet, develop new techniques and exchange ideas. It attracted many dissatisfied artists whose work the Salon had rejected. They included Monet, Renoir, Pissarro and Sisley. Working together, they influenced each other's development. Others, who later adopted their style, included Degas, Cezanne and Manet.

Light was the key to Impressionists who were concerned to accurately depict the reality of what they saw. Their interests were nature, landscape and sunlight. Significant stylistic features included use of colour and the depiction of changing effects of light on natural objects, like ripples on water. Traditionalists, who preferred imaginative or idealised paintings to reality, opposed them. Impressionism was criticised as sketchy and unfinished.

Monet's style influenced the others. In the 1860s his emphasis changed and he began to manipulate colour, tone and **texture**. The group painted outdoors instead of in studios.

Traditional landscape colours of muted greens, grey and browns were replaced with brighter, sunnier tones. Objects were built up from separate spots of pure colour. Figures were hazy and indistinct to convey outdoor reality. They preferred informal groupings to traditional formal compositions and were fascinated by different light qualities at different times of day.

They held seven exhibitions between 1874 and 1886 independently of the Salon. In 1874 they were mockingly labelled 'Impressionists', after a painting by Monet. They felt this truly described their aim of conveying 'visual impressions'. After 1886 the group broke up, as members followed individual stylistic interests. Some, especially post-Impressionists like Cezanne, wanted a more substantial, **coherent** and permanent style. The movement was, however, revolutionary and freed Western art from traditional techniques and subject matter.

Musical Impressionism is mainly associated with Debussy. The Impressionists' approach to beauty influenced him, but he did not develop techniques simply to mirror art. Other Impressionist composers included Ravel, Delius, Respighi and Szymanowski. Their style is often dismissed as subtle, but fragile – 'vague mood music'. Key characteristics are restraint, understatement, a static mood and challenging colourful effects. They were fascinated with the beauty of pure sound as an end in itself. Impressionism reacted against Romantic excess.

Glossary

decadent: luxurious self-indulgence; the process, period or manifestation of moral or cultural decline

venue: a place where something, especially a sporting or cultural event, happens

texture: the feel, appearance or consistency of a surface or substance; hence in art the representation of the tactile quality of a surface: hence in music or literature the quality created by the combination of elements in a work

coherent: something logical and consistent, able to hold together

Issues to be discussed

- Why do many developments in the arts occur at times when there is social, political or economic upheaval?
- What are the advantages and disadvantages of artists painting landscapes outside rather than in studios?
- Do establishment groups, like the Salon, inevitably oppose the work of innovators? Does it matter?
- Is realism more important in art than imagination and idealism?
- Do painters who leave viewer's eyes 'to merge raw colours' fail to fulfil their responsibilities as artists?

Where now?

B. Whelpton, *Art Appreciation Made Simple*, W. M. Allen, 1970
G. Hindley, *Larousse Encyclopedia of Music*, Reed International, 1971
www.columbia.edu/jns16/monet-_html/impressionism.html
www.ibiblio.org/wm/paint
www.geocities.com/Paris

What do you think?

Critically examine the unique contribution of any single Impressionist artist or composer, or a single work of art, to the development of Impressionism.

Claude Debussy (1862–1918) was the founder and most important representative of the Impressionist movement in music. His composing style inspired many later composers and its influence survives to this day. The most important characteristic of Debussy's music is its visual power – images and scenes hidden within the music, never conveyed directly, but always coloured by the artist's imagination. The composer's impressions of reality sound magical and mysterious, as if they were trying to offer an insight into some great, unnamed mystery surrounding us.

Although he associated little with musicians, he enjoyed the company of the leading Impressionist poets and painters. Their influence is felt in his first important orchestral work, 'L'aprѐs-midi d'un faune'. This work established the style of Impressionist music and initiated Debussy's most productive period. In about 1910 he developed cancer, which sapped his strength during his last years. Debussy's style was one of the most important influences on twentieth century music. He refused to submit to the rules of traditional musical theory, stating, 'There is no theory. You have only to listen. Pleasure is the law.' He rejected the overblown forms and the harmonic style of the post-Wagnerians such as Mahler and Strauss. He preferred understated effects similar to those achieved by the French Impressionist painters and poets. 'Pelleas et Melisande', the most significant Impressionist opera, has been called a masterpiece of understatement. He wanted his music to sound improvisatory, as though it had not been written down. Many of his compositions are miniatures, which often have fanciful titles such as 'What the West Wind Saw' and 'Deaf Leaves'. He created a subtle pianistic style that made new demands on performing technique and blurred sonorities were achieved by a new use of the damper pedal. His best-known composition is probably 'Clair de Lune'.

From jagor.srce.hr/~fsupek/debussy.html.

***Landscape with Viaduct: Montagne Sainte Victoire* by Paul Cezanne (1839–1906).**

Activities

1 Compare a recording of an Impressionist piece of music (like Debussy's 'La Mer') with an Impressionist painting on a similar theme.
  a Which do you think is the more successful in evoking atmosphere?
  b Give reasons to explain and justify your views.
  c Make a list of similarities and differences in the effects achieved by each work of art.

2 Investigate and write a brief report about the contribution made by any one composer, besides Debussy, to the development of Impressionism in music. You should, where possible, illustrate your report with appropriate sound images.

3 Debate the view that Impressionism is more about revolt against established practices than about the creation of a new vocabulary and style of artistic expression.

Thinking and analytical skills

1 Identify the conclusion and different stages of argument in the passage about Debussy.
2 What different types of knowledge and argument are used in the passage?
3 How effectively does the author of the passage justify his conclusion?

(i) Does the UK suffer from media saturation?

Links: 1.6 (ii); 1.6 (iii); 1.6 (vi); 2.6 (iii); 4.3 **Key skills:** N3.2; N3.3; C3.3; N3.1; C3.1b

Introduction

A medium is any form of communication involving the spoken or written word, sound or visual images. Until recently communication was usually a two-way process. In the last century new forms of mass communication developed as a result of technological advances. The printing press, developed in the fifteenth century, is often claimed to be the first instrument of mass communication.

Background

The mass media have become an integral part of everyday life for the majority of the population. The media act variously to provide information, entertainment, ideas and opinions. For most people, their knowledge of the world and the meaning they give to events is shaped for them and delivered to them in a readily digestible form through the mass media. Media consumption is essentially passive, involving reading, watching or listening. At one level, the influence of the media can be measured in the average amount of time spent reading, listening or watching and, at another level, by the part they play in shaping attitudes, values and behaviour. It has been suggested that the mass media bind individuals into society as a whole and without the media a modern lifestyle would not be possible.

Time devoted to the media varies between individuals and may be affected by social class, gender, age and **affluence**. For many people the most time-consuming medium is television, occupying on average the equivalent of one day a week in viewing time. Since the mid-1980s cinema attendance has increased considerably and just over half the population regularly buys a national daily newspaper. Video games have an increasing hold on young people, especially boys in their early teens, and absorb the time of many young adults.

Owners of the mass media are motivated by profit, which depends on market share. Consequently output is geared to particular sections of the market. Many critics fear that the search for a mass market inevitably means that quality of output will be sacrificed in order to attract a larger audience. This has been described as '**dumbing down**'.

Advertising is important in financing the mass media. Advertisers who seek access to the largest possible group of **consumers** invest in those parts of the media able to deliver an audience. Consequently, producers, seeking maximum income, gear their output to attract large audiences, so attracting advertising revenue. This encourages production geared to specific markets. About 25 per cent of advertising expenditure is invested in television, 50 per cent in newspapers and magazines, 10 per cent into **direct mailing,** 3 per cent into commercial radio and 1 per cent into cinemas.

New technologies not only affect developments in the mass media but also potential audiences. Almost all homes have televisions, radios and videos, but newer forms of media, like computers and video games, DVD players, the Internet, satellite and digital television can be expensive. This may create a two-culture society, where some cannot share fully in the experience of others.

Glossary

affluence: abundance of riches or wealth

dumbing down: reducing the content of media product to a level of considerable simplicity in order to attract the largest possible audience; hence a lowering of standards

consumer: (in the economic sense) the user as opposed to producer of an article

direct mailing: advertising material sent through the post directly to customers, often at random or using commercially available lists of names and addresses

Issues to be discussed

- Why does the mass media have mass appeal?
- Does it matter if some sections of society do not have full access to all of the mass media?
- From your own experience think of examples of advertising influencing mass media output.
- Would the mass media be more acceptable as a form of communication if it were more interactive?
- What are the implications of describing audiences as 'media consumers'?
- Was the printing press the greatest technical innovation in terms of the development of the mass media?

Where now?

O'Sullivan, Dutton, Rayner, *Studying the Media*, Arnold, 1998

P. Trowler, *Investigating Mass Media*, Collins, 1996

A. Giddens et al, *The Polity Reader in Cultural Theory*, Polity Press, 1994

www.theory.org.uk www.uclan.ac/uk users.aber.ac.uk/dgce/media

What do you think?

Critically examine arguments for and against the view that the mass media are about commerce rather than culture.

The written text is one type of communications medium, whether this takes the form of a newspaper, novel, scientific treatise or political pamphlet. Painting and music, while they might not involve print, clearly also are communicative forms. To these we must add the electronic media of communication which have become so important in our day – radio, television, videos, tapes and computer communication systems.

When printed or electronic media reach very large numbers of people we speak of mass media. A mass is a large aggregate of people distinct from a 'group', 'crowd' or 'public'. A mass is usually very large, numbering up to many millions of people, is widely dispersed and its members have no direct contact with one another. It is without any sense of collective identity.

Characteristic of the mass media is that communication is primarily a one-way process. The consumer plays no direct role in the creation of the cultural product. That product is commercially produced and marketed in much the same way as other types of goods in modern societies. The media form a set of 'open' channels of communication, which can be received by anyone in the society. Since the media can affect public opinion, however, they are normally linked with various forms of state regulation or control.

A good deal of research and thinking centred upon the 'effects' of the mass media upon the audiences exposed to them. The study of media effects has very often been prompted by moral or normative considerations. Thus there has been a continuing concern to discover how far levels of crime, and particularly criminal violence, are affected by media representations. Such research has also been fuelled by more diffuse concerns that the mass media are creating cultural forms that produce a spineless, apathetic citizenry.

From Giddens et al, *The Polity Reader in Cultural Theory*, Polity Press, 1994, pp. 2–5

Types of television programme watched by age (1997)

UK Percentages

	4–15	16–24	25–34	35–44	45–54	55–64	65 and over	All aged 4 and over
Drama	24	29	27	26	26	25	24	25
Light entertainment	17	18	17	16	15	14	15	16
News	9	10	12	14	16	18	19	15
Documentaries and features	10	13	15	15	15	16	14	14
Film	10	14	14	14	14	13	11	13
Sport	6	8	7	8	8	8	10	8
Children's programmes	23	5	6	3	2	2	2	5
Other	2	3	3	3	3	4	5	3
All programmes	**100**	**100**	**100**	**100**	**100**	**100**	**100**	**100**

Each column shows the breakdown of viewing times per age group, e.g. 4–15 year olds spend, on average, 24% of their viewing time watching drama programmes. Data for terrestrial channels only. Source: *Social Trends 29*, The Office for National Statistics, 1999; www.statistics.gov.uk

Activities

1 Using the figures on page 72, construct an appropriate chart to show the distribution of advertising expenditure between the various media forms. Comment on any possible implications of the figures.

2 Using the figures in the table, construct appropriate graphs or charts to show the proportion of different types of programme watched **a** by young people aged 4 to 15, **b** by people aged 35 to 44, **c** by people aged over 65. Comment on the graphs.

3 Conduct a survey of people aged **a** 15–18, **b** 25–30, and **c** 40–45 to discover:
i which different forms of mass media they use,
ii how long they devote weekly to each mass media form,
iii what are the attractions of each of the mass media?
Present your findings in written and graphic form.

4 Keep a diary of your viewing habits during a complete week. Construct a table to show your findings. Comment on these findings.

Thinking and analytical skills

1 Identify the main stages of the argument in the passage, and the point being made by each stage.
2 Identify examples of objective and subjective argument in the passage.
3 To what extent is the conclusion of the passage supported and justified by the argument and evidence?

(ii) Who owns the media?

Links: 1.6 (i); 1.6 (iii) **Key skills:** IT3.2; IT3.3; N3.3; C3.1b; C3.3

Introduction

The twentieth century saw great expansion in the variety and forms of the media as a result of new technologies. These developments have been accompanied by changes in ownership and structure. The process of consolidation of control has been matched by diversification and the development of **cross-media organisations**.

Background

Ownership of UK media divides into two main groups. All media, except broadcasting, are privately owned. At first the state controlled broadcasting exclusively, but a mixed pattern of public and private ownership now exists. State control is exercised in various ways, by:

- general oversight, subtle pressure and suggestion,
- regulations and regulatory bodies like the Independent Broadcasting Authority (IBA),
- people who support government thinking are appointed to influential media committees,
- legislation (like the laws of slander, libel and obscenity),
- the Competition Commission,
- direct and indirect funding.

Private sector ownership falls into two unequal groups. Independents, usually relatively small, are often newly formed companies set up to exploit new niches. Theoretically **autonomous** and free from larger companies' direct control and influence, in practice successful ones may be taken over and absorbed. The complexity of media production and the interrelationship of different aspects mean that few companies are totally independent. The term covers a range of meanings, stretching from media giants to small-scale businesses.

Conglomerates dominate the media. In each of the media, between 4 and 6 companies control approximately 90 per cent of output. Giants in one sector may dominate other sectors, as a result of **mergers** and acquisitions, leading to excessive concentration of control. This:

- removes competition and increases market share,
- acquires newly developed techniques,
- allows diversity to spread economic risks,
- increases profitability,
- integrates **complementary** businesses in production and distributive processes. **Integration** may be horizontal (companies in the same sector) or vertical (companies in different but related sectors).

Media conglomerates can benefit from new developments, especially technological, as they have the financial resources for investment and survival. They are often **trans-** or **multinational** corporations, which can exploit globalisation and the world market. Theoretically, new technology enables competition to develop, but high costs restrict success to the wealthiest.

Multi-marketing is a vital sector of the media. Conglomerate profits, benefiting already from economies of scale, are raised through sales of linked goods. Music soundtracks, spin off books, TV series and licensed merchandising boost film profits and raises public interest. Cross-media ownership promotes products.

Glossary

cross-media organisations: companies that have interests in several different media rather than just one

autonomous: possessing personal freedom, independence of will, able to take independent decisions

mergers: two or more companies joining or uniting

complementary: serving to complete something

integration: combining parts into a whole

transnational: companies operating in several countries

multinational: a company with a home base in one country but operating in several

Issues to be discussed

- What are the arguments for and against public rather than private ownership of the media?
- Should citizens of one country be allowed to own a large part of the media in another?
- Is the consumer better served by a small number of large media companies or a large number of small companies?
- To what extent do multi-marketing and cross-media ownership exploit customers? Does it reduce freedom of choice?

Where now?

O'Sullivan, Dutton, Rayner, *Studying the Media*, Arnold, 1998
P. Trowler, *Investigating Mass Media*, Collins, 1996
www.findarticles.com www.theory.org.uk

What do you think?

How far do you agree that ownership of the media is about profits and power rather than service to customers?

The AOL-Time Warner megamerger is staggering on account of its sheer size – the combined value of the two companies bears comparison with the GNP of several of the United Nations' less affluent members.

It is also surprising because it involves one of those vast US-based media empires, like Disney-ABC, Viacom or News Corps, which make other countries' media enterprises pale into insignificance. Time Warner – itself the product of a merger just a decade ago between two giants of the entertainment business, the magazine publisher Time and films and music conglomerate Warner Bros – looked so huge as to be impregnable to takeover and utterly uninterested in merging with any other.

In the UK, any impact the merger has will be indirect. Online companies and media groups alike may look longingly at what AOL and Time Warner have achieved (and at the potential for cross-media promotion and advertising deals which it represents). But there are few credible candidates in the UK for a similar deal and they are tiddlers in comparison with AOL and Time Warner.

Much more likely in the UK are new combinations of old media. The mooted merger of Carlton and United News and Media is one such, as would be a possible takeover of either company by Granada. Another was last week's takeover of Chris Evans' Ginger Media by Scottish Media Group.

However, Ginger's original takeover of Virgin Radio showed some of the same thinking as AOL's merger with Time Warner, namely a desire to acquire an asset with real value to bolster what was at the time a rather flaky-looking investment in the talents of one man.

From *Marketing Week*, 20 January 2000.

Although mergers can lead to economies of scale, not all benefit individuals.

Activities

1 Using the British Humanities Index or users.aber.ac.uk/dgc/media, research the media holdings and influence of a modern media tycoon. Present your findings in a factfile with a short commentary.

2 Investigate the way Silvio Berlusconi used his position as a media tycoon in Italy to advance his political ambitions. Make a written or oral presentation of your findings. Is what he did an abuse of or an understandable use of his power?

3 Find out the company that provides either television or the local free newspaper in your area. Investigate whether it is part of a conglomerate or an independent and present your findings in an appropriate form.
a If it is a conglomerate, investigate and list the different media and non-media interests it has. How many of these complement its newspaper or TV work?
b If it is independent, investigate and construct a table to show whether it controls or buys in essential services.

Thinking and analytical skills

1 What is the main conclusion of the passage?
2 To what extent does the knowledge used in the passage justify the conclusion?
3 How effectively are the different stages of the argument structured?

(iii) Who controls the media?

Links: 1.6 (i); 1.6 (ii); 1.6 (v) **Key skills:** C3.2; C3.1a; C3.3

Introduction

Investment in the media is potentially very rewarding financially. Control of a television channel was once described as 'a licence to print money'. Other reasons for media ownership include the opportunity to influence public opinion, the chance to promote personal views and the opportunity to play an active part in the political life of the country.

Background

Editorial freedom is a traditional feature of the British media and is particularly important to the press, broadcasters and filmmakers. In theory, owners do not interfere in day-to-day production, formulation of policy or opinion. In practice, owners always have direct or indirect influence – the extent varies according to the owner's personality, relationship with editorial staff and prevailing circumstances.

Indirect influence comes when owners determine the general thrust of opinion. Their power to hire and fire ensures that employees broadly sympathise with their opinions. Staff not meeting these demands may be dismissed. Some owners seek to influence day-to-day production, especially in areas of particular interest to them.

The manipulative model sees media control as the way in which the ruling classes promote class views and interests. They are, it claims, **conservative** or **reactionary** in attitude and are determined to preserve the **status quo**. By controlling the 'means of production of ideas', they are able to **manipulate** content and mould their audiences' thought processes. Small, powerful groups exploit the media in their own interests, not in the public good. The rich and powerful are enabled to increase wealth and power. The variety of media allows different audiences to be targeted appropriately, to maximise owners' influence.

The **hegemonistic** model rejects the manipulative model, arguing that media people, by background and nature, whether owners or producers, promote a single dominant ideology while ignoring others which are equally valid. Media people are recruited from a small, homogeneous social group which shares similar ideas and aspirations. The pursuit of ideology rather than profit is important for them. Media values are regarded as 'the norm' and the media supports the status quo. **Radicals** are rarely given opportunity. This view claims real control lies with professionals who shape content rather than owners who determine general thrust.

The pluralist model argues that different parts of the media cater for different social segments. The media does not operate solely in the interests of powerful social groups. It claims that the media performs a social, not an economic or political function aiming to inform, socialise and entertain through ongoing communication. Content and language are geared to the interests and wants of each audience. Audiences, not owners or journalists, determine bias, since they use their purchasing power to shape the media. Media control is not sinister, but simply responds to audience demand.

Glossary

conservative: inclined to maintain the existing order

reactionary: tending in a reverse or backwards direction, hence opposed to change

status quo: the position as it is, unchanged

manipulate: to manage, or handle with skill, to achieve a desired outcome; to mould or shape

hegemonistic: belonging to the leading or ruling group

radicals: seeking fundamental change rather than minor variation

Issues to be discussed

- Examine each of the models of media ownership. Discuss the arguments for and against each of them?
- Compare the way a news story is presented by different newspapers owned by a single media conglomerate.
  a What similarities and differences are there?
  b How does newspaper presentation differ from television or radio broadcasts on the same topic?
- Are media owners motivated by the public good or by the quest for power and profit?
- Is the power of the audience a myth or reality?

Where now?

O'Sullivan, Dutton, Rayner, *Studying the Media*, Arnold, 1998
P. Trowler, *Investigating Mass Media*, Collins, 1996
www.nene.ac.uk users.aber.ac.uk/dgc

What do you think?

Analyse arguments for and against the view that media owners have too much power and should be controlled.

The contribution which the mass media make to the political climate is determined by the influences which weigh most heavily upon them.

The first and most obvious derives from the ownership and control of the 'means of mental production'. The mass media are overwhelmingly in the private domain.

Rather obviously, those who own and control the capitalist mass media are most likely to be men whose ideological dispositions run from soundly conservative to utterly reactionary; and in many instances, the impact of their views and prejudices is immediate and direct, in the sense that newspaper proprietors have often closely controlled their editorial and political line and turned them, by daily intervention, into vehicles of their own particular views.

Those who own or ultimately control the mass media do not always seek to exercise a direct and immediate influence upon their output. Quite commonly, editors, journalists, producers, managers, etc. are accorded a considerable degree of independence. Even so, ideas do tend to 'seep downwards', and provide an ideological and political framework whose existence cannot be ignored. But it is at least expected that they will spare the conservative susceptibilities of the men whose employees they are, and that they will take a proper attitude to free enterprise and much else besides. The existence of this framework does not require total conformity; general conformity will do. This assured, room will be found for a seasoning, of dissent.

From R. Milibrand, *The State in Capitalist Society*, Weidenfield and Nicholson, 1973, quoted in P. Trowler, *Active Sociology*, Collins, 1987

In November 2000 porn magazine publisher Richard Desmond bought the *Daily Express*. Two months later the editor Rosie Boycott resigned after refusing to carry out the new owner's instructions.

Activities

1 It is claimed that Murdoch changed the style of his newspapers when he bought them. Compare the style and political stance of a recent editorial in either *The Times* or *The Sunday Times* with a comparable copy from 1980 or earlier. (Murdoch took over in 1981.)
a What similarities and differences can you see in style?
b What political similarities and differences can you see?

2 Write a report on your findings, starting 'In my study of *The Times*/*The Sunday Times* editorial, I believe that Rupert Murdoch's purchase has affected the paper as follows …'. Conclude your report with a list of further evidence you would require in order to test the accuracy of your findings.

3 In a group, discuss the passage. What other influences, besides the interference of owners, might the author have had in mind? Explain and justify your conclusions.

4 Debate the view that 'owners are entitled to tell their employees what to write since they pay them'.

Thinking and analytical skills

1 What different types of knowledge might the author use if he wrote today rather than in 1973?

2 To what extent are the views of the author **a** objective, **b** subjective, **c** biased, and **d** fallacious?

3 To what extent, and how effectively, does the evidence used justify the conclusion of the passage?

(iv) Do the media encourage violent behaviour?

Links: 1.6 (i); 1.6 (v); 1.6 (vi); 3.4 (i); 3.4 (vi); 4.3 **Key skills:** N3.1; N3.2; N3.3; C3.1a; C3.3

Introduction

Critics often blame the media for declining social standards, claiming ordinary people are easily influenced. The mass media, especially the visual media of film, television, video games and videos, are held responsible for the recent apparent increase in violence. Controls 'to protect young people' are often demanded.

Background

Visual media in the 1990s, associated as it often is with the portrayal of extreme violence, may simply reflect real life today or it may affect viewers' attitudes. Some claim the media adversely affect standards, but others argue they benefit society. Conclusive proof either way is lacking since feelings cloud judgements.

Although screen violence has declined, the 'moral majority' claim that the media continue to be a negative influence. They draw parallels between media and real-life violence, arguing that constant repetition of a message creates an environment where the unthinkable becomes acceptable. Concerns are increased by the rapid growth of visual media. Videos, by their nature, cater for private repeat viewing and reinforce content-based 'messages'.

News reports create **moral panics** as they draw attention to incidents, raise public expectation and give them disproportionate importance. Recent demands for a **paedophile** register and subsequent public disorder appeared to be media-inspired.

Violence on the screen can lead to copycat behaviour. This was seen in urban riots in the early 1980s, after broadcasts of disturbances in Liverpool. The judge in the Bulger case blamed James Bulger's murder on this phenomenon. Some argue that those inclined towards violence may be encouraged by what they see on screen. **Correlations** exist between increased aggression and high levels of viewing 'video nasties' or playing video games.

Repetition of violence may **desensitise** viewers, removing any sense of disturbance. The previously unacceptable can become 'normal'. Slow motion, replay and freeze frame on videos can heighten effects, requiring increasing levels of violence to achieve similar levels of viewing satisfaction. Consequently, high levels of violent or aggressive behaviour may become accepted as normal in everyday life.

Counter-arguments to these views include:

- Research evidence can be interpreted in various ways.
- Correlations between screen and real violence may be because potentially violent people enjoy such material.
- Violent behaviour can only be understood in context.
- Real violence shown on the news can be more **explicit** and shocking than fictional violence.
- The media can sensitise people to problems of violence, leading them to develop greater awareness.
- The amount of violence is exaggerated.
- Audiences, as individuals, respond individually.
- Viewers are rarely totally passive. They interpret and give meaning to what they see, based on their own values and experience.
- Violent or aggressive behaviour is multi-causal.
- Catharsis, through identification with fictional beings, is a recognised way of releasing violent tendencies.
- Audiences are generally skilled 'readers' of the media and can sensibly judge and respond to what is seen.

Glossary

moral panic: an exaggerated, media inspired response to initially minor socially deviant activities

paedophile: an adult who is sexually attracted to children

correlations: corresponding to each other

desensitise: remove sensitivity of feeling

explicit: stated in detail, leaving nothing implied

Issues to be discussed

- If the media encourage violent behaviour in viewers, why don't all viewers behave violently?
- Do the media create 'moral panics' or simply report events?
- How true is it that viewing is a two-way activity?
- Is the news more likely to encourage violent behaviour than fictional programmes?
- How justified are critics who claim that TV cartoons encourage violent behaviour in children?
- What do you understand by the term 'moral majority'?

Where now?

Bell, Joyce and Rivers, *Advanced Level Media*, Hodder and Stoughton, 1999

P. Trowler, *Investigating Mass Media*, Collins, 1996

sosig.esrc.bris.ac.uk users.aber.ac.uk/dgc

What do you think?

How justified is the claim that the media can only encourage a particular type of behaviour in people who are already inclined in that direction?

In the 1990s a number of violent films such as *Reservoir Dogs, Child Play 3, Pulp Fiction* and *Natural Born Killers*, have become the focus for the one vital question of the media violence debate: does exposure to screen violence have an effect on audiences?

There are those who believe that exposure to screen violence has a negative effect on audiences and can result in:

- individuals imitating violent events on screen,
- audiences becoming desensitised to violence.

There are others who believe that exposure to media violence has a limited effect and that other factors such as social background are more significant.

A large body of American research claims to prove scientifically that the media have an effect on audiences. A number of studies have attempted to find out the long-term effects of exposure to screen violence. One study observed that the best predictor of whether someone will commit a violent crime aged 30 was the amount of television that they watched aged 8.

Belson in 'Television violence and the Adolescent Boy' (1978) attempted to prove that a boy's exposure to violent television led to aggression. Despite his attempts to monitor the integrity of the data, some commentators pointed out some surprising contradictions. Howitt, for example, has pointed out the fact that 'heavy and light viewers of television violence are less aggressive than middle-range viewers'. In other words, if the levels of violent television were increased, violence in society as a whole would decrease. All violence effects studies should be treated with caution as data can often give conflicting results.

From Bell, Joyce and Rivers, *Advanced Level Media*, Hodder and Stoughton, 1999, pp. 23–24

JUDGE RAPS VIDEO NASTIES FOR MURDER OF LITTLE JAMIE

Sentencing eleven-year-old Jon Venables and Robert Thompson for the torture and brutal murder of innocent toddler two-year-old Jamie Bulger, the judge at Preston Crown Court said, 'I suspect the exposure to violent video films may, in part, be an explanation.'

One of the two boys' parents had hired the horror video Child's Play 3 only days before the horrific killing ...

Activities

1 Make a list of, then research, moral panics encouraged by the media. Why do you think these happened?

2 Make a list of ways in which the visual mass media may benefit society rather than harm it.

3 Discuss whether television producers should be restricted in what they show.

4 Make a survey of violence on television. Choose one channel and watch it for the same hour each day for a week (the best time is either 8 pm to 9 pm, or 9 pm to 10 pm)
a Calculate the number of minutes of violence you see each day.
b Make a table with your figures, listing different types of violence.
i Calculate the percentage of viewing time that was devoted to violent behaviour.
ii Calculate the proportion of violent acts where the perpetrator seemed to escape punishment or criticism.
iii Show your figures in appropriate graphic form.
iv Compare your findings with a partner who has studied a different channel.
v Write a brief report commenting on your findings.

Thinking and analytical skills

1 List the main stages in the argument in the passage.

2 Identify examples of subjective and objective knowledge contained in the passage.

3 Does the author fully justify his conclusions?

(v) Does advertising show that people are influenced by the media?

Links: 1.6 (ii); 1.6 (iii); 1.6 (iv) Key skills: N3.3; N3.2; C3.3; C3.2; C3.1a

Introduction

Advertising is vital to the mass media, since it delivers essential revenue, although it directly provides content. The growth and profitability of the advertising industry show that advertisers believe it is worthwhile and generates profit. Continued investment in advertising shows belief that it can influence human behaviour.

Background

Commercial broadcasters and newspapers need advertising revenue to survive. Most **tabloids** rely mainly on income from sales, but **quality newspapers** and glossy magazines depend on advertisers. Free papers use editorial comment to attract audiences for advertisers. Products failing to deliver audience lose revenue and close.

All media use self-advertisement to establish and maintain market interest. Cinema and pop music use videos, 'same-name' branded products and pre-release material to raise their profile and encourage sales. These are almost a separate media form in their own right. The influence of advertising on media content is a major concern. It is less significant in pure entertainment, but may create undesirable bias in information and news media.

Advertisers, like all commercial organisations, must maximise profit. Blanket advertising, often an ineffective use of resources, is used for essential products, like household goods, where size of audience is more important than type. Such goods may be advertised in mass circulation newspapers or **prime time** broadcasting.

Luxury goods are aimed at specific audiences, who often have high levels of disposable income. Advertisers try to target ideal audiences. Key factors include audience size and social profile such as age, gender, social class and disposable income. Such audiences are often found through quality newspapers and glossy magazines. Cinema ideally targets the youth market, audience quality being determined by film type.

Broadcasters aiming to attract and retain large audiences may modify programme making and **scheduling**. Political bias can be influenced by the need for revenue. Preferred target audiences are often conservatively inclined and reluctant to buy left-of-centre products. Editors may slant content to attract such groups, so retaining their appeal to advertisers. Mass circulation tabloids, less dependent on advertising revenue, are theoretically free to adopt a liberal line. But, needing to attract a large audience, they must adopt one popular with their readers.

The influence of adverts on individuals is often disputed. Few statistics are published to show how effective advertising is, but specific campaigns have been shown to affect sales. Advertising seeks to promote attainable desires. In spite of recent improvements, gender and role stereotypes are still continually reinforced.

Adverts seem most effective when associated with memorable catch phrases, tunes or characters. Problems can develop if audiences accept adverts simply as entertainment. Another problem, 'narrow-casting', occurs through focusing excessively on attractive audiences. Larger, less attractive and less profitable ones (elderly, poor and working class) may feel ignored or marginalised.

Glossary

commercial broadcasters: companies existing for profit, not as a government controlled public service

tabloids: newspapers of a certain size and type, e.g. *The Mirror*, *Sun* or *Daily Mail*; named because of their shape

quality newspapers: often called broadsheets because of size and shape, e.g. *The Times* or *The Guardian*

prime time: peak time viewing between 7 pm and 10 pm when largest audiences are attracted and advertising rates are highest

scheduling: the process of deciding when programmes are shown

Issues to be discussed

- Does advertising really influence people's behaviour?
- To what extent are broadcasters influenced in their programming by the need to attract advertising revenue?
- Why do cinema adverts usually target the youth market?
- What controls should exist on advertisers?
- Consider a well-known and popular TV advert. Is there evidence of **a** stereotyping, **b** questionable content, **c** attempts to create unrealistic desires, and **d** targeting particular audience groups?
- Why do tabloids depend less on advertising revenue?

Where now?

O'Sullivan, Dutton, Rayner, *Studying the Media*, Arnold, 1998

P. Trowler, *Investigating Mass Media*, Collins, 1996

www.adasoc.org.uk users.aber.ac.uk/dgc

What do you think?

Does the success of advertising show the influence of the media? Explain and justify your opinion.

Women's magazines have always had two audiences: the women who buy the magazine and the advertisers who place their advertisements in the magazine. Without the latter, most magazines would have to double their cover price. Often, then, a magazine will aim not so much at attracting a particular section of the female population, as at attracting a particular segment of the advertising market. Therefore, although it is true that readers attract advertising, it is also true that particular readers attract particular advertising and therefore advertising revenue. For a magazine to survive it has to ensure a complex combination of the right readership for the right advertising. This can mean identifying first the source of advertising revenue and then shaping the magazine to recruit the right readership for the advertisements. In this way the pressures of the market can determine to a large extent not only the range of magazines available, but also their actual contents. Magazine advertisements, like the magazines themselves, provide a terrain on which to dream, and thus generate a desire for fulfilment (through consumption). Paradoxically, this is deeply pleasurable because it also always acknowledges the existence of the labours of the everyday.

Desire is generated for something more than the everyday, yet it can only be accomplished by what is for most women an everyday activity – shopping. What is ultimately being sold in the fictions of women's magazines is successful and therefore pleasurable femininity. Follow this practical advice or buy this product and be a better lover, a better mother, a better wife, a better woman. The problem with all this from a feminist perspective is that it is always constructed around a mythical individual woman, existing outside, for example, powerful social and cultural structures and constraints.

From J. Storey (ed.), *Cultural Theory and Popular Culture, a Reader*, Harvester Wheatsheaf, 1994, pp. 147–48

Sources of revenue for newspapers in 1986

Percentages

Type of publication	from adverts	from sales
Popular daily	27	73
Popular Sundays	31	69
Quality dailies	58	42
Quality Sundays	66	34
Regional dailies	61	39
Regional weeklies	84	16
Consumer magazines	41.5	58.5

Source: P. Trowler, *Investigating Mass Media*, Collins, 1996, p.146

Distribution of advertising revenue between the media

Percentages

	1938	1948	1954	1965	1975	1985
Type of publication						
National papers	25	14	17	20	17	17
Regional papers	27	31	31	24	29	23
Magazines	15	13	19	11	8	6
Trade journals	12	16	13	9	9	8
Other	2	1	1	1	2	5
Production costs	5	8	6	4	5	6
Total press costs	**86**	**82**	**87**	**70**	**70**	**62**
Television	0	0	0	24	24	31
Poster & transport	8	14	9	4	4	4
Cinema	3	4	3	1	1	1
Radio	3	0	1	1	1	2

Source: P. Trowler, *Investigating Mass Media*, Collins, 1996, p.144

Activities

1 Comment on any trends shown in the tables.

2 Calculate the difference in the total percentage of advertising revenue spent on the press in 1948, 1965 and 1985. Suggest reasons for any differences.

3 Construct appropriate graphs for the figures given in the second table for each type of publication, showing the proportion of total advertising revenue it attracted for each year. Label your graph clearly and comment with suggested explanations on any trends you can identify.

4 Research the type of adverts contained in tabloid and quality national newspapers and a local or regional free newspaper.

5 Examine three types of newspaper. Write a short report on the number of adverts (exclude personal adverts), the proportion of the newspaper they occupy and any similarities or differences between adverts in the different newspapers. Construct a table to show the different goods advertised in each paper.

Thinking and analytical skills

1 Identify the stages in the argument presented by Storey.

2 What different types of knowledge and argument are used in the passage?

3 Does the author successfully justify his conclusion?

(vi) Is there any justification for censorship?

Links: 1.6 (ii); 1.6 (iii); 3.4 (vi) **Key skills:** C3.2; C3.3; IT3.1; IT3.2; C3.1b; C3.1a

Introduction

Censorship involves restricting free expression of ideas or preventing access to information. Official censorship is rare in Britain in peacetime, but informal or unofficial censorship can take place at any time, and affect any media. Some people believe censorship is essential to protect the vulnerable in society, but others claim it infringes civil liberties.

Background

Censorship ranges from deliberately withholding facts to presenting false details. Between these extremes lies biased presentation of ideas to create a desired result. Various groups can impose censorship in different ways. Many countries legally control media output, establishing regulatory bodies to enforce official or unofficial codes of practice. Additionally self-imposed legal and authoritarian controls exist to limit personal freedom.

Totalitarian **regimes** control the media to bolster their power and shape popular opinion. Opponents are denied media access or are presented negatively. Censorship is inappropriate in democracies in which people ought to be fully and accurately informed if the democracy is to be effective. Nevertheless, indirect or direct censorship still exists. The UK media is relatively free of state control but restrictive powers exist, to be used if necessary.

In peacetime the UK press is rarely censored, but it is an important weapon in wartime. News can be withheld or falsified 'in the national interest'. In the 1991 Gulf War, influenced perhaps by the USA, politicians encouraged self-censorship, using government guidelines. The Official Secrets Act limits publication of items 'against public interest' and D notices restrict press use of 'off the record' government-originated information.

Regulatory bodies exist to oversee the media. Although officially independent of the government, some members are often government appointments. Their role is to ensure proper observation of regulations and codes of conduct. Legal action provides more effective censorship. Libel, slander and obscenity laws offer protection by giving individuals **recourse** to law. They encourage self-censorship, since fines and costs imposed by courts can be punitive.

Authoritarian censorship occurs when power is used to enforce personal views. Examples include media barons using press ownership to publicise their own opinions, politicians 'leaking' information to give the news a particular slant or parents restricting their children's reading and viewing opportunities.

Self-censorship is exercised when media people restrict their own freedom because of possible harm to others. Journalists may suppress stories, editors remove offensive material and producers reduce gratuitous sex or violence.

Liberty is a pressure group that exists to promote civil liberties, freedom of information and oppose all forms of censorship. Their opponents, arguing that one person's freedom exercised irresponsibly threatens another's civil rights, favour either full-blown censorship or at least more **rigorous** regulation and control. Mrs Mary Whitehouse established the National Viewers' and Listeners' Association in 1963 to campaign for greater media control, claiming that relaxation of controls had contributed to declining standards. Members of the Association want the government to protect the vulnerable, especially the young, and believe that limiting civil liberties is a price worth paying to protect society.

Glossary

censorship: literally fault-finding; the process of imposing limits on what can be printed or broadcast.

regime: the method of government, prevailing system

recourse: resorting to a possible source of help

authoritarian: favouring obedience to authority rather than individual freedom

rigorous: severe, strict or harsh; strict enforcement of rules

Issues to be discussed

- To what extent is it true that 'limiting civil liberties is a price worth paying to protect society'?
- Is self-regulation an effective form of censorship and control in **a** the advertising industry, and **b** the press?
- Should the freedom of expression of the National Viewers' and Listeners' Association be restricted? If so, how and by whom?
- Can censorship be justified in a democratic society?

Where now?

O'Sullivan, Dutton, Rayner, *Studying the Media*, Arnold, 1998

P. Trowler, *Investigating Mass Media*, Collins, 1996

www.liberty.org.uk users.aber.ac.uk/dgc

What do you think?

If producers won't voluntarily reduce the excessive amount of sex and violence in the media, then the government must introduce rigorous censorship to protect the vulnerable. Do you agree?

'Entertainment TV violence turns viewers off'

Television shows too much graphic violence, despite evidence that viewers do not like it, according to a broadcasting watchdog. The National Viewers' and Listeners' Association report on television violence comes days after a judge said violent films played a part in the brutal killing of a student by two of his friends.

The group says it found 1,200 scenes involving guns and 798 violent assaults in 269 films it picked at random from the post-watershed schedule on terrestrial television. Its survey also found 107 arson or bombing attacks with knives or other weapons and 44 scenes involving illegal drugs.

Director of the Association, John Beyer said broadcasters must take a moral stand to stop screening violent films and halt the increase in violence and anti-social behaviour. Citing the example of a student murder, he said: 'How many more examples do we have to put up with? How many more murders before someone does something about the violence?'

Mr Beyer accused broadcasters of having a ratings-geared agenda out of step with public opinion. He said recent polls had said that as many as 92 per cent of those surveyed thought TV was too violent. 'I think the broadcasting authorities, particularly the BBC, should take a more responsible line,' he said. 'Whether there is a market for this sort of thing is not really the right question. I think the demand is a function of the supply and if we cut the supply there will not be the demand.'

From a BBC news report, BBC online network; news6.thdo.bbc.co.uk, 10 May 1999

THE Sun

FREE MINCE PIE FOR YOU TODAY DETAILS PAGE 15

20p

Friday, November 26, 1993

Brave Roy's cancer is back

For the sake of ALL our kids...

BURN YOUR VIDEO NASTY

FRENCH REVOLUTION

PLAY £26,000 SUN BINGO AND £48,000 NOUGHTS AND CROSSES – PAGE 40

The front page of *The Sun*, 26 November 1993. *The Sun* reflects public belief that the killers of James Bulger were influenced by watching violent videos.

Activities

1 Select a newspaper article about either **a** an international conflict, or **b** a violent incident. Edit the article, as though you are a censor, to remove any material that you think might not be 'in the public interest'. Write a brief report on the decision-making process you used. How is the revised article different to the original?

2 Research the work of either Liberty or the National Viewers' and Listeners' Association. Make a reasoned presentation to explain why people should support or oppose the organisation you have chosen.

3 Discuss whether parental control of their children's viewing is responsible behaviour or authoritarian censorship.

4 Some years ago the works of Enid Blyton were removed from libraries because they were said to be unsuitable for children. To what extent do you think librarians or politicians today would be justified in using their position in this way?

5 Should people in the public eye (like pop stars or politicians) be entitled to privacy in their private lives?

Thinking and analytical skills

1 Identify the stages in the argument presented in the news report.

2 Identify examples of subjective and objective knowledge used in the passage.

3 To what extent are the conclusions in the passage based on opinion or interpretation rather than on objectivity?

(i) Where did the universe come from and where might it be going to? Links: 1.2 (iii); 2.2 (i); 2.3 (iii); 4.11; 4.13 Key skills: C3.1b; IT 3.1

Introduction

Everyone who has ever lived has probably wondered how our world came to be. We cannot help but be conscious of time passing: we see day following night, birth and death, and seasonal change. If days, nights, living things and seasons have beginnings and ends, then it is reasonable to believe that the world itself began at some point and presumably will end at some point.

Background

Religious beliefs

Creation stories are often based on everyday, observable objects, events and living things. The Judaeo-Christian account in Genesis describes a Creator and Supreme Being who made light and darkness, night and day, and everything else. Such accounts were originally intended to be literal and were supposed to be the revelation of a prophet or thinker. Belief in the literal truth of Genesis led many Christians to think that the world was created a few thousand years ago, based on the genealogies described in the early books of the Bible.

Scientific theories

Astronomy is an important science, not least because of its usefulness for navigation and geography. Theories of creation and the structure of the universe, produced by Greek and Roman philosophers, were part of Western academic thought until the sixteenth century. At this time our understanding of the relationship between the earth, sun and heavenly bodies changed radically. It had been believed that the earth was the centre of the universe (geocentricism), but astronomical observations, made more accurately and with better instruments (notably the telescope), threw up many anomalies. These issues were ultimately resolved by the work of Copernicus, Kepler, Galileo and Newton. The regular **elliptical** paths of the planets around the sun were explained simply, using gravitational forces. The motion of the earth and planets around the sun, and the moon around the earth described our system in a way that enabled more accurate predictions, which were subsequently confirmed by observation.

With more and better telescopes and clocks, astronomical measurements were very important for accurate and safe navigation. At the same time, the nature of the universe caused much speculation. More powerful telescopes showed that there were more stars, fainter and further away, everywhere one looked. Did this mean that the universe stretched onwards and outwards for ever? In 1823, Heinrich Olbers identified a paradox: if the universe extended infinitely and contained stars, then everywhere you looked in the sky would at some point end in the surface of a star. In which case, why was the night sky dark? Even though the stars were very far away, light from them would eventually reach us and every part of the night sky would be equally illuminated. This made the idea of an infinite universe seem less likely.

Glossary

astronomy: the study of the universe and the laws covering its behaviour

elliptical: from ellipse, a regular oval shape

cosmology: the branch of astronomy which covers the origin and evolution of the universe

Milky Way: the galaxy which contains our solar system

galaxy: a vast collection of stars

radio astronomy: a branch of astronomy which uses radio waves rather than light to observe the sky

Issues to be discussed

- Is it possible both to hold a religious belief about the origin of the world and to accept the current view on the origin and evolution of the universe?
- If astronomers and cosmologists cannot carry out experiments, how can they test their theories?

Where now?

Stephen Hawking, *A Brief History of Time* (chapters 1–3), Bantam Press, 1988

www.physics.gla.ac.uk/introPhy/Famous/index.html

www.astro.uni-bonn.de/~pbrosche/hist_astr

www.cv.nrao.edu/fits/www/yp_history.html

www.fits.cv.nrao.edu/www/astronomy.html

What do you think?

What is a scientific revolution?

There have been many times in history when established ideas suddenly become impossible to hold and a revolution occurs. Often these are associated with one or two key individuals. In astronomy and physics some of these people are as follows:

- Aristotle and Ptolemy were classical scholars who were mainly responsible for the classical Western view of the universe, in which all heavenly bodies moved around the earth, often in very complex paths.
- Copernicus and Kepler developed the idea that the planets circled the sun in elliptical orbits.
- Galileo showed moons circling Jupiter and, consequently, planets circling the sun (among other things). He was made to recant his view by religious authorities.
- Newton developed the fundamental laws of motion and described the gravitational force that explained how the orbits of the planets were maintained.
- Einstein demonstrated the interchangeability of matter and energy, and showed that time can vary depending on the velocity of the object

In the first half of the twentieth century, the idea of a 'steady-state' universe became popular with **cosmologists**. In view of Einstein's demonstration that matter and energy were interchangeable, it seemed possible that matter might disappear as energy from some parts of the universe and appear in other parts. If the total amounts of energy and matter were constant, then the universe would be steady and stable. The question of a beginning and end was thus side-stepped – it would have neither. In one version of this theory, stars at the edge of the universe disappeared and matter was created in the 'empty' space between the galaxies. This matter gradually collected together to form new stars. If this model was correct, then discussion of what existed 'before' or 'after' the universe came into being was not a scientific problem.

The American astronomer, Edwin Hubble, made landmark discoveries in 1924 when he observed galaxies outside the **Milky Way** (our own **galaxy**) and in 1929 when he found that these galaxies were moving away from us. The furthest galaxies were receding fastest. The universe was expanding, very rapidly so, at the edge. A galaxy at the edge of the universe could be travelling away from us at a speed approaching that of light. This is startling enough, but if we run time backwards, there must have been a time when all the galaxies were very close together and, ultimately, crammed into a single tiny point. This phenomenon (known as a 'singularity') becomes the starting point of our universe; subsequent events became known as the 'Big Bang', since when all matter has been flying away from this point.

The Big Bang has become the best description physicists currently have of the origin of the universe, because it fits observations made by astronomers, **radio astronomers** and particle physicists. Although the idea can be expressed quite simply, the physics of the situation is not easily grasped by the layman. One obvious question is: how did the singularity arise? Another is: what is the ultimate fate of the universe? Two possible answers for the last question are being explored. Some physicists suggest that the expansion will continue indefinitely; others believe that the expansion will slow down, stop and then all matter will be drawn back by gravitational forces to again form a singularity. The latter has the neatness of symmetry, but there is more evidence to support the former proposition.

Activity

In groups, select one of the revolutionaries listed above and prepare a poster or presentation that clearly shows the nature of their discovery or theory and the idea that it replaced.

Thinking and analytical skills

1 What are the key features of a scientific revolution?
2 Why were Copernicus's and Kepler's ideas such a shock to the world?
3 Outline the stages of the argument in favour of the Big Bang theory.

(ii) Is our climate changing? What can we do about it?

Links: 2.3 (iii); 4.2 **Key skills:** C3.1b; IT 3.1

Introduction

It is a human characteristic to want to know why things happen. Science is an elaboration of this need for explanations and to be in control. Scientists, quite rightly, disagree with one another. Many think that scientific disagreement is a fundamental weakness but it is, in fact, a formidable strength. Climate change, in particular, is a topic rife with disagreements.

Background

Good science helps us to:

- ask the right questions,
- constantly question the answers we receive,
- use the answers to plan further action.

Since climate change profoundly affects our future existence, we should try to understand why this subject is so difficult and controversial.

Since the earth was formed, its climate has changed, although conditions in the regions containing living organisms have stayed within a narrow range for billions of years. The chemical composition of the atmosphere, the chemical composition of the oceans and lakes, and the earth's temperature changed significantly when living organisms first appeared. One of the major prehistoric changes, for example, was the conversion of the atmosphere from an **anaerobic** to an **aerobic** state when the highly reactive gas oxygen was released in large quantities. It is believed that this was caused by the development of green, **photosynthetic** plant life.

How good is the evidence for changes in the atmosphere that happened millions of years ago? If we find fossils in ancient rocks that are similar (but not identical) to plants alive today, we reason that their metabolism must have been similar, therefore the atmosphere must have contained carbon dioxide in order for them to photosynthesise. The scientist needs to crosscheck this circularity with other, independent evidence.

In the time life has been on earth, continents have broken up and drifted, and the climate has changed on these continents from tropical to arctic. This has all been deduced by the forms of fossil organisms. There is now evidence of **cataclysmic** events such as the collision of a **meteor** or **comet** with the earth and of times of massive volcanic activity. Such events have profoundly altered atmospheric conditions and the evolution of life on earth – and could do so again.

Scientists have evidence of recent changes in the concentration of carbon dioxide, the depletion of ozone in the high atmosphere of polar regions and drifts in mean monthly temperatures. There is agreement that **global warming** is taking place, but many dispute its extent and significance. The main problem is how to distinguish between random, small, 'natural' fluctuations that may last for days, years, hundreds or thousands of years and underlying long-term changes that will profoundly alter our environment. Climate scientists have to bring together the observations and evidence of prehistoric events with those from the comparatively tiny changes that have taken place in the last few hundred years.

Glossary

anaerobic: no oxygen available

aerobic: with oxygen available

photosynthesis: the use of light energy by green plants to build up organic compounds

cataclysmic: catastrophic

meteor: small fragments of rock circling the sun which occasionally hit the earth

comet: a small body of ice and dust orbiting the sun in a highly elliptical path

global warming: the steady rise in the average temperature of the earth's surface

Issues to be discussed

- Why is climate change such an important issue for economic development, for social development and for scientific development?
- Why bother with changes that are so far back in the past and so far distant into the future?
- Are we likely to be able to control the climate?

Where now?

www.newscientist.com/nsplus/insight/global/faq.html
www.ncdc.noaa.gov/ol/climate/globalwarming.html

What do you think?

Why can't we make reliable forecasts of changes in climate?

The weather is a very frequent climate change. In temperate climates, seasonal changes are produced by the fact that the earth is tilted on its axis and therefore more radiation per unit of surface area arrives in summer compared with winter. Records which have been kept for many years show that, on average, these seasonal changes are quite uniform and steady. In tropical zones, where the sun delivers roughly the same energy throughout the year, there are wet and dry periods that are also, on average, constant. Even though weather forecasting is ridiculed as being unreliable, even perverse, we spend enormous amounts on measuring instruments, satellites, the most powerful computers in the world and the personnel to operate them. The presentation of forecasts has even become part of the entertainment industry. So why don't we do better at forecasting more than a day or two ahead?

Surely the physical laws covering the phenomena of air pressure, airflow, density, solar radiation and the rest are not that complicated? Well, maybe not, but it is obvious that there are many variables and many possible interactions of those variables. We can spot an event – a cold front moving or a Caribbean hurricane – that has a good chance of moving in the same direction for a few hours or days, depending on the surrounding systems. But it is not yet possible to do much more than this. For many years the British Meteorological Office produced long-term forecasts for the next month, but these proved to be as often wrong as they were right and they were abandoned.

Forecasting has had an interesting mathematical spin-off: work on chaotic systems. Chaos theory, which sounds like a contradiction in terms, is now a well-established branch of mathematics. Studies of the regularities in such systems emphasise an important point: the critical importance of the initial conditions. Infinitesimal differences in these can cause wildly different outcomes for any given situation. A classic example is the suggestion that the beating of a butterfly's wings in the Amazon rainforest might cause a hurricane in the North Atlantic.

Weather is a small temporary fluctuation in the climate, although it may not seem like that to the flood or hurricane victim. Since it is impossible to determine the initial conditions adequately, the direction and speed of the part of the atmosphere containing rain clouds or a warmer body of air can only be predicted with a chance of success which becomes smaller the further ahead that we wish to look.

Predicting climate change is weather forecasting on a grand scale. We accept that there is evidence of longer term changes and that we can afford to ignore the small fluctuations that affect whether we have a barbecue next weekend or not. Human activity can undoubtedly change the environment. Burning fossil fuels and clearing forests with fire increases atmospheric carbon dioxide. Since we have evidence of increased mean levels of carbon dioxide in the atmosphere and a corresponding mean temperature rise, we predict that if the carbon dioxide in the air continues to increase in the same way, then the increase in mean temperature could be between 0.5 and 1.7°C within 50 years. The effect of this change is debatable and many other factors – the amount of water vapour in the atmosphere, cloud cover, the amount of ice and snow (which reflect back energy which would be absorbed by darker grass and forests) – come into play.

Dire predictions have been made of the rise in sea levels, shrinking of polar ice caps and the desertification of north Africa and southern Europe. International agreements to reduce the release of carbon dioxide and other 'greenhouse' gases are hotly disputed by governments. Some scientists are concerned that a small change may make it more likely that a drastic change will result (a positive feedback effect) that may then become irreversible. This is where computer models become essential, since the interaction of all the factors requires huge mathematical calculations.

So will global warming, on the scale indicated, have much effect on us? We still don't know. It would seem that the best strategy is to do as little as possible to alter the atmosphere until we understand more.

Activities

1 Find out about the Kyoto agreement. Produce a poster showing the international actions that have taken place as a result.

2 List and present to your group the possible effects of a rise in sea level of say, 10 metres, on your local community.

Thinking and analytical skills

1 What forms of reasoning are used to support the conclusion in the passage?

2 Give examples of the types of knowledge used in the passage.

3 Using the knowledge in this section, construct an argument to support an active policy of controlling carbon dioxide emissions.

(iii) Do we need genetic modification?

Links: 1.2 (iv); 2.4 (i); 2.4 (iii); 4.9 **Key skills:** C3.1a; IT 3.1

Introduction

The discovery of **DNA** and the way in which it behaves as genetic material helps us to explain how living organisms are similar and how they are different. It has provided medicine with tools that have the potential to cure intractable diseases, and agriculture with ways to change the nature of crops more quickly than by selective breeding. But is this all a good thing?

Background

Genetics has made incredible progress in the last 50 years. We now understand that many characteristics are passed from parents to children, that these characteristics are the result of the action of proteins, that proteins are composed of chains of amino acids in a specific order and folded into a specific shape, that the order of the amino acids is determined by a section of a DNA molecule (a gene) which contains a code for this purpose, and that DNA can produce exact copies of itself. Almost every day discoveries are made which are consistent with this understanding.

We know that all the physical characteristics of an organism (and perhaps some behavioural characteristics as well) are affected by genes, although the environment can affect the way in which a gene expresses itself.

Although DNA seems to copy itself exactly most of the time, mistakes can and do occur. There is an efficient DNA repair system, so most mistakes are repaired immediately. In some micro-organisms exposed to high radiation levels, the DNA repair system is very effective. If a mistake persists, even if it is just a change of one amino acid, it can profoundly affect the working of the protein so that it becomes completely ineffective. These changes are gene mutations and are usually damaging, but they may be useful and lead to long-term changes (evolution).

It is possible to transfer genes from one individual to another, producing genetic modification. Genes may, in certain circumstances, be transferred between individuals of different species. There are several ways in which this can be done:

- Hybridisation is a process that occurs in nature; a **hybrid** possesses a mixture of genes from parents of different varieties or species.
- Genes for specific drug resistance can be readily and naturally transferred between different kinds of bacteria. This is a major problem when the gene is in a harmless bacterium and is transferred to a disease-causing bacterium, which may then be resistant to the drug used to treat the disease. For this reason, **antibiotic** drugs should never be used except to treat a bacterially caused disease. The practice of dosing farm animals liberally with antibiotics has been banned.
- Genes can be inserted into cells using a virus as a carrier (vector).
- Genes may also be injected into cells directly, using a '**gene gun**'.

Once in the individual, the gene may have to be 'switched on'. Genes may vary in their activity in cells in different organs.

Glossary

DNA: deoxyribonucleic acid, a long chain molecule in the nucleus of the cell

hybrid: an organism which has parents of different genetic origin, often two different species

antibiotic: a drug which kills or de-activates bacteria

gene gun: a microscopic device for inserting DNA physically into a cell

Issues to be discussed

- Why should we want or need to transfer genes from one organism to another?
- What ethical issues might arise from the transfer of genes between individuals of one species or between individuals of different species?
- How are topics like this reported in the press?

Where now?

www.health.upenn.edu/ihgt/index.html
www.health.upenn.edu/ihgt/info/prospcts.html

What do you think?

What sort of problems occur with gene modification techniques?

One possible use of gene transfer would be to replace a mutant gene (for example that for cystic fibrosis) with a normal gene (gene therapy). There are many problems with this attractive idea. It is not possible, with current techniques, to replace such a gene in all the body cells of a foetus, let alone an adult. There may be ways to achieve this in the future, but not soon and not without some ethical problems – what would happen, for example, if someone wanted an entirely new set of genes?

Gene therapy has been attempted (so far without permanent success) to treat affected organs rather than the whole body, for example, the lungs of cystic fibrosis patients. This would be useful as an alternative to an organ transplant, with its attendant problems of rejection.

In the future, if a defective gene is identified early enough in the fertilised egg or young embryo, it may be possible to insert the gene in all of the small number of cells. This would only be possible if the family history indicated a problem. Why not just prevent the egg from developing?

The ethics of remedying a genetic defect in an affected person is one thing, but genetic modification has much more debatable applications, notably in agriculture:

- Transferring a gene conferring resistance to a herbicide into a crop plant so that weeds growing in the crop can be sprayed with the herbicide, killing them but leaving the crop to prosper.
- Transferring a gene for the production of a natural insecticide into a crop plant in the hope that less or no insecticide will be needed.
- Transferring genes that control or delay the ripening of soft fruit so that less fruit is wasted through over-ripening and subsequent decay.

In these examples, the genes transferred may come from organisms completely different from the host. In addition, the genes may be produced artificially in the future.

The genetic outcomes of these procedures are, in fact, little different from the genetic modifications brought about by plant and animal breeding over thousands of years. Everything you eat has been genetically modified from the wild ancestors of food plants and animals. The differences are that gene transfer is quick and that it can be more controlled and specific.

It is important, however, to discover whether the genes and the proteins they produce are harmful to those who eat the modified crop, and to ensure the genes are not subsequently transferred from the modified organisms to other wild organisms with potentially unknown consequences.

Activities

1 Find out as much as you can about the current state of gene therapy. Are we moving further forward?

2 If genes transferred into a crop plant can move into wild plants, can genes that the plant possesses 'naturally' do the same?

Thinking and analytical skills

1 What experiments do you need to carry out to discover if genes transferred to a crop plant are not harmful to **a** consumers, or **b** local wild organisms?

2 Using the passage above, produce an argument to justify genetic modification of human beings.

(i) How far can we explain human behaviour with biological theories? Links: 2.1 (iii); 2.2 (iii); 2.4 (i); 3.3 (i); 3.3 (ii); 4.9 Key skills: C3.1a; C3.1b; IT 3.1

Introduction

Socio-biology has developed as an attempt to explain human behaviour and social development, using the concepts of genetics and natural selection. It has passionate devotees and critics. Its hypotheses, predictions and conclusions test the objectivity of all scientists.

Background

We have often looked, and are still looking, for simple explanations for human problems and issues. The **spurious** claims of some scientists have caused untold misery to millions of people through the ages. There have been thousands of fantastic fads: phrenology, for example, taught that character and behaviour were determined by the natural irregularities of the skull. In the nineteenth century, Lombroso claimed that potential criminals could be distinguished by certain facial characteristics. More cynical were Hitler's attempts to produce a pure Aryan race through selective human breeding. While none of these abuses is part of socio-biology, the problems and explanations it deals with are of great human interest and raise significant moral and ethical questions. A very big issue is how far social behaviour is genetically determined and how far it is modified by the environment.

Darwin thought that natural selection worked on individual organisms – if an individual was well adapted, it would have more offspring than one less well adapted. In modern genetic terms, it would pass on its genes, some of which contributed to its better adaptation, to its offspring.

Some modern evolutionists, notably Richard Dawkins, regard the gene itself as the subject of natural selection and the organism as a convenient vehicle for carrying genes about and ensuring their survival.

Some biologists believe there are genes to determine aggressive and cautious behaviour. Their reasoning goes like this: if genes are to ensure their own survival, then their aim is to ensure that copies of themselves are replicated in offspring. One way of ensuring this would be to make the organism look after its offspring. Parental care is quite usual in nature, but it clearly requires an expenditure of energy and probably some increase in personal risk. However, the investment of energy and increased risk may be worthwhile if genes are passed on to more offspring. If this is so, there must be genes for **altruistic behaviour**.

Altruistic behaviour is difficult to explain using the traditional view of nature and the struggle for survival in which organisms are involved (which so caught the imagination of the Victorians). An organism that sacrifices itself, or accepts additional risk, would seem to be doomed in the evolutionary race and its characteristics would disappear from the population.

If, however, altruistic behaviour by any organism could be shown to increase the chances of survival of genetically related individuals, then the costs may well be less than the benefits. It would also be neat if we could show that altruism is family-linked and that individuals are more protective of those with whom they have more genes in common than of unrelated members of the population. Experiments in many species have shown this to be so and this might also explain human family groupings and allegiances.

This idea also explains some apparent oddities of the animal world, such as the existence of the social insects (bees, ants, wasps, termites and others) that have castes, each with a defined role, where workers display extreme self-sacrificial behaviour. With bees, the workers are all female and have all their genes in common with their mother, the queen.

These ideas are proving extremely fruitful in explaining the life-histories and behaviour of many animals.

Glossary

socio-biology: a branch of biology which attempts to find explanations for human social behaviour using purely biological and genetic concepts

spurious: not genuine

altruistic behaviour: sacrificing oneself for the benefit of others

Issues to be discussed

- If the HGP (see 2.4 (i)) is successful and genes for specific types of human behaviour can be isolated and transferred, what are the implications for **a** human geneticists, and **b** social institutions?
- Is it possible to show that altruism always contains hidden rewards?

Where now?

S. J. Gould, *The Mismeasure of Man*, Penguin, 1981
Richard Dawkins, *The Blind Watchmaker*, Longman, 1984

What do you think?

Do we need genetics to improve human behaviour?

Biological ideas can become highly controversial when we apply them uncritically to the human species. Many human conditions and behaviours have either organic or genetic origins. Huntington's disease is a well-known example of a genetic disease, which produces changes in behaviour before physical changes occur. The possession of an extra chromosome causes physical differences: Downs' syndrome is an example. People with extra or missing X and Y-chromosomes also possess several unusual features. In the late 1960s and early 1970s, several American investigators reported that the chromosome numbers (karyotype) of prisoners in some American jails were unusual and, in one investigation, an extra chromosome was linked with a distinctive body type – very tall with long limbs. Quite incorrectly, this syndrome was also linked with criminal behaviour. The investigators had not carried out any control surveys and their work was quickly discredited. However, their suggestions were seized upon by those who believed that criminality could be an inborn defect and therefore that all we had to do to clean up society was to identify and round up all such individuals to prevent them from carrying out crimes.

Some socio-biologists believe that genes exist for all aspects of human behaviour, which is an extension of the idea of selectively useful altruism. This leads us to a particularly sterile, and almost certainly incorrect, view that all our behaviour is programmed by our genes. This is known as genetic determinism.

A classic subject for divided scientific opinion is the inheritance of intelligence and the postulated existence of racial differences in intelligence. Here intelligence is interpreted as an aspect of human behaviour. Controversy about the inheritance of intelligence has run hot for the last 100 years, since genetics began as a scientific activity. Mountains of evidence, some genuine, some spurious and some even fraudulent, has accumulated. Some of the controversy originates in the meaning of 'intelligence', but there is a fairly common understanding of the term. We can give unequivocal answers to two questions:

- Is intelligence inherited and therefore influenced by the activities of genes? If it is, it is subject to natural selection and the adaptive advantages of intelligent behaviour should be measurable. There is evidence that intelligence does have a genetic component, so the answer is 'yes'.
- Is intelligence open to environmental modification? This is undoubtedly so – you would not be reading this if that were not the case.

Are there lessons we should learn and strategies for society to adopt as a result of the scientific evidence for the causation of human behaviour? Yes, but we must set about them with caution. Maybe advances in genetics and the information gained from the Human Genome Project will enable us to isolate genes that have a profound influence on specific behavioural traits. Maybe gene therapy will find ways whereby genes could be transferred to embryos or even young children and activated. Maybe we could create ethical reproductive regimes to enhance some human beings.

At this moment, all of this is a long, long way off. But it is worth thinking about the implications of such work and discoveries so that we are prepared for the future. We know now that we can modify behaviour by upbringing and education as well as by medical treatments – that is, by modifying the environment rather than the genes. There is much evidence that small changes, applied early, can have small but highly significant long-term effects. For example, some nursery enhancement programmes for disadvantaged children are known to have had effects lasting into adulthood. Our energy and resources are finite and limited and should be saved for pushing on with the possible.

Activity

Find out about the life and work of one of the following: Cyril Burt, E. O. Wilson, Richard Dawkins, W. Hamilton, or any leading socio-biologist, and present a short talk on their key ideas to the rest of your group.

Thinking and analytical skills

1. What conclusion does the writer reach?
2. Present an argument for a totally environmental explanation of human criminality, justifying any assumptions you make.
3. What forms of knowledge are required in the study of human intelligence and its inheritance? Justify your selection.

(ii) Faster than the speed of light?

Links: 2.1 (i); 2.3 (iii); 4.14 **Key skills:** C3.1b; IT 3.1; IT 3.3; PS 3.1

Introduction

We use the word 'revolution' to mean a turning over of governments, institutions and ideas. Big revolutions in scientific ideas are often associated with one or more scientists whose thinking generated them. Sometimes a key experiment is the catalyst for the change. Galileo's observation on falling bodies is one example; another, closer to our time, is the Michelson–Morley experiment.

Background

Light travels, very fast, in straight lines and can be reflected, refracted and diffracted. Isaac Newton, who spent 40 years studying it, was puzzled by the fact that sometimes light behaved as though it was formed of particles and sometimes of waves. He was in no doubt, however, that light had to travel in 'ether' which filled apparently empty space. This substance was not detectable but the behaviour of light seemed to demand that there was a medium capable of carrying waves through millions of miles without losing the initial energy. The existence of the ether was unquestioned until the late-nineteenth century.

Classical thinkers were convinced that light moved at infinite **speed**, although this was questioned by a few. Disagreement persisted until Galileo's time, although people realised that if the speed was finite, it must be exceedingly fast. In 1676, a Danish astronomer, Roemer, investigated anomalies in the timing of the eclipses of Jupiter's moons, when measured at different times of the year. He suggested that the maximum delay of 1,320 seconds over the expected time was due to the distance the light had to travel across the earth's orbit; in other words, the path the light took was that much longer. The diameter of the earth's orbit was then thought to be 182,000,000 miles and a simple division results in a value of 138,000 miles per second. This was an astonishing result and within one order of magnitude of the best figure we now have – a good result considering the inaccuracies of measuring instruments. Roemer then used this figure to predict anomalies in the timings of other eclipses which were all confirmed.

A challenge to later scientists was to measure the **velocity** of light more accurately – and in a terrestrial setting as the astronomical methods took too long. It was achieved by Fizeau, the French physicist, in 1849 and subsequently by his countryman, Foucault, whose result was 185,000 miles per second. Albert Michelson, an American navy scientist, read Foucault's paper and devoted much of his life to perfecting methods for measuring the speed of light as accurately as possible. He, like most others, accepted the existence of the ether. Once he had built an instrument for measuring the velocity of light, he wanted to investigate the medium in which light travelled. If the ether affected the velocity of light, then if the ether itself was moving, the velocity would depend on the motion of the ether. Earth was travelling through space, which was assumed to be full of stationary ether, so that if you could measure the velocity of light in the direction of the earth's motion and at right angles to it, there ought to be a difference. Michelson made this comparison with great accuracy, but was stunned to find no difference at all in the velocity of light in different directions. In 1882, he wrote 'the hypothesis of a stationary ether is erroneous', a somewhat conservative conclusion. It was still possible that the earth carried a bag of motionless ether with it but, with his colleague, Edward Morley, Michelson was eventually able to show that in a uniform medium, light travels with the same velocity in all directions. This critical measurement established the velocity of light in a vacuum as a universal constant – c – and was an essential part of the development of the theory of **relativity**.

Glossary

speed: rate of movement of an object

velocity: speed of an object in a particular direction

relativity: the two basic ideas of Einstein's special theory of relativity are **a** the laws of nature are always found to be the same in any frame of reference moving with constant velocity, and **b** the velocity of light in a vacuum always has the same value, in all directions and for all observers

Issues to be discussed

- Why did scientists want or need to know the velocity of light?
- How did Fizeau, Foucault and Michelson measure the speed of something going so quickly?
- Why was the notion of the ether so widely accepted for such a long time?

Where now? Stephen Hawking, *A Brief History of Time*, Bantam Press, 1988

What do you think?

What is a scientific theory?

If the observations and results gleaned from many experiments from different laboratories reflecting the efforts, thoughts and techniques of many different scientists are brought together, an interpretation of strength and beauty may result. By such means a scientific theory or concept is formed. Of course, it is obvious that a theory must be consistent with all the experimental data. Using observations and experimental findings as bricks, we build the structure of a scientific theory.

A theory is our best idea as to how a group of separate facts are related to each other. Such concepts do not emerge automatically from observations and experiments, any more than bricks assemble themselves to form a house. Theories, like houses, must be built, and the style of architecture is dependent on the builder and the time and area in which he works. After many experiments have been run on different aspects of a particular subject, the accumulated information will enable one or a few scientists to propose a general theory bringing all of that information into one interpretation. A theory is a concept which unifies an area of scientific interest. It provides a single scheme of interpretation for a whole group of apparently disconnected facts.

Sometimes a new theory is readily accepted by other scientists as soon as it is proposed. But sometimes a new theory is challenged and a vigorous controversy arises. Battles are waged from the speakers' rostrums of scientific societies and from the printed pages of books and scientific journals. When such a controversy breaks out, there is a great scramble to run more experiments, test new ideas and obtain more evidence in support of one side or another. Sometimes the issue is decisively settled. Sometimes the issue is not settled, but must be abandoned, pending the development of new methods and new evidence. The history of science is made quite exciting by the numerous turbulent controversies which have disturbed its serenity. The birth of a new theory is seldom painless, but if our science is to grow and to have meaning, unifying concepts are essential.

In trying to decide what makes one theory acceptable and another unacceptable, a person is forced to make some value judgements. In the first place, it is quite obvious that not all observations are going to be of equal importance to the subject at hand. The scientist is then required to decide which facts are the most pertinent. Such a decision is a value judgement, and is likely to be a personal opinion, unless the matter can be decided experimentally. Being merely human, a scientist is not able to be completely impartial in his interpretations. As an individual and as a member of a community, he will hold certain philosophical, religious and political beliefs. A scientific theory which is felt to be inconsistent with those beliefs, he will oppose. It is very easy for a person to change his ideas on a subject that is not important to him personally. But it is much more difficult when prior commitments of thought, effort and ideology have been made. This sort of difficulty was the cause of some of the opposition to Darwin's theory on evolution. This type of opposition, or even support, has nothing to do with the scientific merits of a theory, but results from the impact of a theory on personal beliefs. Nevertheless, such personal factors play a role in the interpretations we make of any set of observations, however scientific we may try to be.

From Stanley D. Beck, *The Simplicity of Science*, Pelican, 1959, chs. 3 and 4

Activities

1 In groups, choose a well-known scientific theory and apply the tests for a theory given by the author above.

2 Using available resources, find out about one other scientific experiment of great significance which had a null result. (The Michelson–Morley experiment, which had a null result, is one of the most highly significant.)

Thinking and analytical skills

1 How far does the author support his definition of a theory as 'our best idea as to how a group of separate facts are related to each other'?

2 The author is a biologist. Do you think his view of theories is consistent with other types of scientist?

3 Does the author satisfactorily justify the idea that accepting a scientific theory is dependent on a person's beliefs?

(iii) How difficult is it for new scientific ideas to be accepted?

Links: 1.3 (v); 2.3 (ii); 4.7; 4.16 **Key skills:** C3.1b; IT 3.1

Introduction

There are a few scientific theories that have changed everyone's view of the world. There is no better example of this than the theory of evolution put forward by Darwin and Wallace in 1859. It has had a profound effect on non-scientists as well as biologists. While the evidence for evolution is robust and compelling, it is still denied by minority groups and misunderstood by many others.

Background

The health of science can be judged by the power of newer, more insightful explanations. For almost 2,000 years, human understanding was restricted and stultified by classical orthodoxy. Evolution may be considered one of the most significant explanations, since it has made us change our view of ourselves and the complex world in which we live.

The theory of evolution put forward by Darwin was based on years of direct observation and thinking about the diversity of life in several areas of the world. Darwin was greatly influenced by Malthus's 'An Essay on Population' which identified the causes for fluctuations in human populations. This sparked off in Darwin's mind the notion of the 'struggle for existence'. Another scientific naturalist, A. R. Wallace came to the same conclusion as Darwin and their theory was published in a joint paper in 1859. Its key points were:

- All living things produce more offspring than survive to their normal lifespan.
- All living things vary, giving rise to a struggle for existence that becomes dominated by those with more useful variations.
- Offspring that vary in such a way that they are at an advantage are more likely to survive as a result of competition (survival of the fittest).
- Offspring that survive will pass on these variations to their offspring (inheritance of variations).
- In time, groups of offspring will be better adapted to the places in which they live (natural selection).
- If groups move to different environments or if the environment changes, even in the smallest way, then these groups will vary in different ways and, in time, will not resemble their ancestors.
- Thus new species will arise.

Since Darwin's time, advances in different branches of science are consistent with the theory:

- Geology has supplied ample evidence about the timescale for life on earth and the former existence of organisms and groups that became extinct.
- Genetics has explained the inheritance of variations.
- **Biochemistry** has explained the structure of the gene and has established how they work and can change (**mutation**).
- **Ecology** has established the relationships between the environment and living organisms, and the nature of competition.

Evolution is an explanatory theory. As a predictive theory, its power is general in that it shows that changes in living organisms will arise and the likely nature of these, but not what the specific changes will actually be. Its major philosophical message is that apparently purposeful changes in the structure, behaviour and existence of living things can take place through random events. It is not necessary to assume that living things have been designed by someone.

Glossary

biochemistry: the study of the chemical reactions in living things

mutation: a change in a gene or genes. A mutation may be disadvantageous in some circumstances and beneficial in others

ecology: the study of the relationships between organisms and the environment

Issues to be discussed

- What were the actual views of pre-Darwinian scientists about **a** the origin of life, and **b** the origin of different species?
- What was the effect of the theory on Victorian society and its beliefs in religion, science, economics and politics?
- How did the idea of evolution affect the arts?
- In what ways do fossils and extinction support evolution?

Where now? Ernst Mayr, 'Darwin's Influence on Modern Thought', *Scientific American*, July 2000

What do you think?

Is mutation the result of evolution or degeneration?

Evolutionists believe that genetic mutations are an avenue of positive change in living organisms. In *The Blind Watchmaker*, Richard Dawkins seeks to establish a godless cosmos of chance in which the appearance of design in life has occurred by accident. His evidence relating to biochemical genetics, however, consists of theoretical models of little relevance to the real world. So, what do we actually see in the world around us when we use scientific tools of measurement and observation? Do we see this 'blind watchmaker' at work in any real-life examples, or do we see the opposite?

Literally thousands of human diseases associated with genetic mutations have been catalogued in recent years, with more being described continually. A recent reference book of medical genetics listed some 4,500 different genetic diseases. For example, atherosclerosis (hardening of the arteries) is commonly caused by high blood cholesterol levels, which are hereditary in some families. It has been found that many such families have mutational defects of a cell-surface cholesterol receptor protein. Analysis of genes from people of many different affected families has shown hundreds of different mutations affecting this gene. Likewise, genetic study of many different families carrying the cystic fibrosis gene (CFTR gene) have shown nearly a thousand different mutations of this gene. Some are very harmful, some are less harmful, but none are beneficial.

Many more examples can be given of mutational diseases of virtually every organ and tissue of the human body. Are these mutations confined to rare families or individuals? No, they are spread throughout the world population, though some are more common than others in various subpopulations. Overall, it is estimated that each of us carries five to eight mutations capable of causing serious disease, if paired with another defective gene.

What of positive effects? With thousands of examples of harmful mutations readily available, surely it should be possible to describe some positive mutations if macroevolution is true. But, when it comes to identifying positive mutations, scientists are strangely silent.

The mutation responsible for sickle cell anaemia has been put forward as an example of evolution. Sickle cell mutation, like the many other described haemoglobin mutations, clearly impairs the function of the otherwise marvellously well-designed haemoglobin molecule. It can in no way be regarded as an improvement in our species, even though its preservation is enhanced in malaria-endemic parts of central Africa by natural selection.

What conclusions may be drawn from these few examples, and countless others like them? First, that the human mutation problem is bad and getting worse. Second, that it is unbalanced by any detectable positive mutations. Instead of a 'blind watchmaker', mutations behave like a 'blind gunman', a destroyer who shoots the deadly 'bullets' randomly into beautifully designed models of living molecular machinery. Sometimes they miss, sometimes they maim and sometimes they kill. Thus, the 'blind watchmaker' is an illusion. It is an old-fashioned idol – an invention of the imagination, to which superhuman powers are falsely ascribed.

This research affirms the reality of the past Biblical curse of decay and degeneration on the world of nature, as stated in both the Old and New Testaments. It also highlights the future hopelessness of the human race without the saving intervention of God and His Christ. Mutations continue to slowly harm us. Each generation has a slightly more disordered genetic constitution than the preceding one. Gene therapy may mask the effects, but it will not reverse the underlying degenerative process. A slight but definite ongoing mutation rate, accompanied by a zero rate of positive genetic change, will eventually turn the human genetic code to gibberish. The human race is condemned to a degenerative death, not just as individuals, but as a whole.

In conclusion, the Christian hope stands as the only light in the darkness. Only the creative and regenerating work of Christ, as shown in His creation of all things (John 1:3), His miraculous healings, and in His resurrection from the dead, offers humankind true hope for the future.

From Dr. David A. Demick, 'Mutations – Evolution or Degeneration?', Institute of Creation Research www.christiananswers.net

Activity

1 Not all Christians would accept the view of mutation presented by Dr Demick.

a Research the views of other Christians on this topic.

b Research the position on evolution taken by believers in other faiths.

c Present your results to the group.

Thinking and analytical skills

1. Critically evaluate the evidence presented by the author in order for him to reach his conclusion.
2. In his title the author, perhaps unwittingly, presents evolution as the antithesis of degeneration. On the basis of this article, what do you think is his view of evolution?
3. Identify the types of knowledge he brings to bear on the subject of mutation and illustrate these with examples.

(i) How are scientific theories produced?

Links: 2.3 (ii); 2.3 (iii) **Key skills:** C3.1a; IT 3.1; PS 3.1

Introduction

Chemistry became a fully fledged science in the early nineteenth century, when Dalton and others developed the atomic theory. Inductive thinking produced the theory which provided explanations for chemical observations and made predictions that could then be tested. Chemistry's next leap forward was Mendeleyev's Periodic Classification of Elements, which also made startlingly accurate predictions.

Background

Until the nineteenth century, chemistry had been a 'useful art' in which tried-and-tested processes were used to produce, for example, metals from ores. Many people were seduced by the idea of **transmutation** and the '**Philosopher's Stone**', which could change basic, common substances into valuable, rare metals. No-one had formulated a consistent theory of the nature of matter.

Although several chemists contributed to the atomic theory, John Dalton (1766–1844) is credited for setting it out and testing it rigorously.

The main features of the theory are:

- Matter is composed of minute particles (atoms).
- We can separate particles from one another and join them together, but we cannot create or destroy them.
- Each chemical element has a distinct kind of atom, all of which are the same as the others of that element.
- Each chemical compound has its own distinctive 'compound atoms' all of which are identical to the rest.
- Atoms of one element bear a constant weight relationship with atoms of other elements.

Dalton worked out this relationship of weight between atoms – the atomic weight – for as many elements that he could, using hydrogen, the lightest, as the basic unit. His reasoning is interesting because he consciously used the simplest basic assumptions. For example, he knew that water was composed of hydrogen and oxygen, both elements. He was able to show that in water, eight parts by weight of oxygen are combined with one part of hydrogen. Relative to hydrogen, the atomic weight of oxygen was eight. However, this assumption was wrong, because water molecules contain two hydrogen atoms and one oxygen atom and therefore the atomic weight of oxygen is 16. Nevertheless, this does not invalidate his theory. He produced a set of atomic weights which differ from those we use today, but only because the ultimate particles of compounds have different compositions from those assumed by Dalton, and because of the limited accuracy possible with his apparatus.

Dalton's work illustrates graphically many characteristics of scientific method. His theory was not a logical construct – it may just been a hunch based on extensive observation and reading. He had no evidence, based on his own senses, for the existence of atoms, but the assumption that they existed and behaved according to rules, enabled him to make predictions which he could then confirm by careful measurement. The simple laws of chemical combination are logical deductions from the theory, and the fact that they are borne out in practice gives strong evidence to the real existence of atoms.

If the development of the atomic theory is a good illustration of **induction** and experiment, then the classification of elements into a logical system is an illustration of how this can also produce more good predictions. The work of Mendeleyev fifty years after Dalton depended critically on the atomic theory and the more refined work on the atomic weights of elements that immediately followed it.

Glossary

transmutation: changing one element into another

Philosopher's Stone: a mythical stone thought by alchemists to be the source of all life and able to convert base metals into gold

induction: a form of reasoning, common in science, where generalisations are made by classifying and ordering specific observations, to be tested later by experiment

Issues to be discussed

- Why were the scientific ideas of the classical world influential for so long?
- Why are Aristotle and Lucretius regarded as philosophers and Dalton and Mendeleyev as scientists?
- In Scotland, science has long been described as 'natural philosophy'. Can you justify this?
- Why were scientific discoveries in the early and mid-nineteenth century so significant for European societies?

Where now? www.chemsoc.org/viselements/

What do you think?

How useful is the Periodic Table?

This great and comprehensive scheme, said Mendeleyev, was 'the direct outcome of the stock of generalisations of established facts which had accumulated by the end of the decade 1860–70'. It was warmly welcomed – particularly on account of its predictions. In the table, some thirty of the elements known in Mendeleyev's time are arranged according to his system

The success of the system in grouping together elements which are chemically similar will be very obvious, even at a casual glance; but it will be observed that Mendeleyev was obliged to leave three blank spaces, indicated by the letters [X], [Y] and [Z]. Elements which should fill these gaps were at that date unknown, but Mendeleyev foretold their existence, prophesied that they would be discovered if searches were made, and even deduced their chief properties by a consideration of the properties of the neighbouring elements already known. Such sublime audacity before the hidden secrets of Nature evoked unbounded enthusiasm which was redoubled when, a few years later, all three of the missing elements were discovered and were found to possess the identical properties that Mendeleyev had predicted.

To convey some idea of the accuracy of the forecast, we may compare Mendeleyev's deduction of the properties of the hypothetical element Z with those of the actual metal germanium, which was discovered by Winkler in 1887. Z, said Mendeleyev, should have an atomic weight of 72 and its specific gravity should be 5.5. It should form an oxide ZO_2, of specific gravity 4.7 ; a chloride ZCl_4 – which ought to be a liquid boiling slightly below 100°C. and possessing a specific gravity of 1.9; and a derivative $Z(C_2H_5)_4$ which ought to be a liquid boiling at 160°C and possessing a specific gravity of 0.96. These, then, were the predicted properties.

The actually observed properties of germanium proved to be as follows: it had an atomic weight of 72 and its specific gravity was 5.5. It formed an oxide GeO_2, of specific gravity 4.7; a chloride $GeCl_4$, which was a liquid boiling at 86°C. and possessing a specific gravity of 1.9; and a derivative $Ge(C_2H_5)_4$, which boiled at 160°C and had a specific gravity slightly less than that of water!

Mendeleyev may well be excused the feelings of pride and gratification which these discoveries gave him. Speaking to the Chemical Society in 1889, he said: 'When, in 1871, I described to the Russian Chemical Society the properties, clearly defined by the periodic law, which such elements ought to possess, I never hoped that I should live to mention their discovery to the Chemical Society of Great Britain as a confirmation of the exactitude and the generality of the periodic law.'

From E. J. Holmyard, *The Great Chemists*, Methuen, 1929

Mendeleyev's Periodic Table

Group I.	Group II.	Group III.	Group IV.	Group V.	Group VI.	Group VII.	Group VIII.
H 1 Li 7	Be 9	B 11	C 12	N 14	O 16	F 19	
Na 23	Mg 24	Al 27	Si 28	P 31	S 32	Cl 35.5	
K 39	Ca 40	[X]	Ti 48	V 51	Cr 52	Mn 55	Fe 56 Co 59 Ni 58.7
Cu 63.5	Zn 65	[Y]	[Z]	As 75	Se 79	Br 80	

Activities

1 What are the names of elements X and Y in the table above?

2 How many elements were known in 1800, in 1850, in 1900 and today? Are we likely to discover many more?

3 The periodic classification is based on increasing atomic weight and the grouping of elements that have similar chemical and physical properties. The classification depends on properties of atoms that Dalton would have been staggered to know about. Why?

Thinking and analytical skills

1 How does the passage above support the view that Mendeleyev's idea was a 'great and comprehensive scheme'?

2 What forms of knowledge did Mendeleyev and Dalton use?

(ii) Radioactivity and the modern atom

Links: 2.3 (iii) Key skills: C3.1a; IT 3.1

Introduction

At the end of the nineteenth century, understanding of the atom was still theoretical. It took a clutch of discoveries in physics to produce a theory that could explain both the chemical properties of an element and its compounds as well as the fundamental ways in which elements differ.

Background

Dalton and his successors gave chemistry a useful theoretical concept – the atom – which enabled chemists to develop economically important industries. No-one knew what an atom was really like, other than that it was a very small particle indeed. Electrolysis enabled scientists to show that there was a close connection between an electrical charge and the amount of element released from a solution (electrolyte), namely that a fixed amount of charge (a faraday) will release an amount of element proportional to its atomic weight. This meant that electricity itself must involve charged particles, in other words, that it was 'atomistic'. The discovery of the **electron** by J. J. Thomson in 1897 and the measurement of its charge and mass confirmed this. Electricity was shown to be the result of charged particles. Passing electricity through gases creates charged particles and by measuring how these are deflected by magnetic fields, their charge and mass can be determined. It was also found that positive particles were produced, the mass and charge of which were related to the atomic weight of the element forming the gas.

At this point, the emerging picture of the atom was one of a large, positively charged part with much smaller negative particles (electrons) embedded in it, like a plum pudding. At the same time, however, Ernest Rutherford, one of Thomson's students, was investigating the newly discovered radioactive elements. Becquerel (see opposite) discovered the natural radioactivity of uranium salts. Rutherford studied the radioactivity of radium and found that the radiation was complex – some of it could be stopped by air, some could not. Radiation from uranium was much more penetrating and could pass through thin sheets of aluminium. He called the first alpha (α) rays and the latter, beta (β) rays. Subsequently, he was able to show that alpha rays were particles of helium from which electrons had been removed so that they had a positive charge. When they became neutral, they were identical to natural helium.

Ernest Marsden, one of Rutherford's students, discovered that when alpha particles were fired at thin gold foil, some (about 1 in 10,000) bounced back. Rutherford found this astonishing, because these massive particles should have had no difficulty in passing through a diffuse material. In further experiments, Rutherford found that alpha particles could be deflected (scattered) when passing through a very thin film of metal. He realised that this deflection was caused by the positively charged particles coming very close to, or even hitting, other positive particles that were relatively fixed. In 1911, he reasoned that an atom in the film was composed of a very small, positively charged particle (the atomic nucleus). He went on to suggest that the electrons circled these at a relatively great distance, analogous with the planets circling the sun. Thus, most of the atom was empty space. Although this had first been put forward as a suggestion in 1904, Rutherford's theory was supported by solid results.

In 1919, Rutherford achieved what was believed to be impossible. He bombarded nitrogen gas with alpha particles. Some of the particles joined with the nuclei of the nitrogen atoms, emitting a positive charge – a **proton** or hydrogen nucleus. The outcome was atoms of a different element – an **isotope** of oxygen.

Glossary

electron: the first atomic particle to be detected and measured

proton: a particle forming the nucleus of the simplest element, hydrogen

isotope: a form of an element which differs by the number of particles in the nucleus

luminescence (including fluorescence and phosphorescence): the production of light by excitation of a material rather than heat or burning

Issues to be discussed

- How significant was a new model of the atom?
- Does the model hold true today?
- Rutherford worked with a large number of colleagues and students – was this a new development in scientific research?

Where now? www.gsu.edu/~mstjrh/atomictheory.html

What do you think?

Which discoveries led to the new theory of the atom?

In the last decade of the nineteenth century, two major discoveries led to a revolution in physics. If Roentgen had not discovered x-rays in 1895, someone else would surely have done so. And, eventually, another Becquerel would have made the observations of radioactivity that led to the development of nuclear physics. But Roentgen and Becquerel did play leading roles in this revolution and it is interesting to remember how they came to be in positions to do so. In fact, their stories could scarcely be more of a contrast.

Wilhelm Roentgen had a colourful upbringing during which he was expelled from Technical School as 'an insufferable and disturbing student' – although the circumstances are not clear. His father was a cloth merchant and supported him in going on to university. Although he failed the entrance examination, Roentgen was able to attend classes but not to take an examination. He subsequently heard that the Polytechnic in Zurich admitted students without formal qualifications and he was accepted there. Roentgen qualified with excellent marks as a mechanical engineer, but was more interested in scientific research. He gained a doctorate for a study on gases and his teacher, A. Kundt, took him on as assistant when he became professor of physics in Wurzburg, Germany. After several posts in German universities, during which he established a reputation as a skilled experimentalist capable of working with great precision, he became rector of Wurzburg in 1894. He was a devoted teacher and built much of his own demonstration apparatus. In 1895 he was studying the cathode rays produced by applying high voltages to a closed vacuum tube. The tube becomes luminous when charged. In a darkened room, he covered the tube with black paper to make sure that no light escaped. He was just about to start another experiment when he noticed a weak light about a yard away from the tube – a glow on a fluorescent screen that he was to use later. He was surprised because he knew that cathode rays would not pass through more than a few centimetres of air and therefore could not be responsible. He had discovered the vastly more penetrative x-rays, a sensation at the time. X-rays have been a basic tool of medicine ever since.

Henri Becquerel came from a line of chemists and physicists. His education, in Paris, was straightforward and traditional, and he qualified as a engineer in 1877. He taught at the École Polytechnique and was an engineer for the Department of Bridges and Highways. He became professor of physics and chief engineer in those institutions. He gained a doctorate from research in optics and helped his father in a study of phosphorescence. They investigated the properties of uranium compounds and Henri prepared crystals of potassium uranyl sulphate, which glow strongly when exposed to light. Becquerel was shown some x-ray photographs in 1896 and was told that x-rays seemed to be emitted from the glowing spot on the vacuum tube, where the cathode rays hit it. His interest in this new phenomenon led him to look for a link between x-rays and **luminescence**, and he set out to show that x-rays were emitted by potassium uranyl sulphate when exposed to sunlight. His experiment consisted of wrapping a photographic plate with black paper, putting some crystals on the paper and allowing sunlight to fall on the crystals. On that day, however, the 'sun showed itself only intermittently', but he was surprised to find that the plate was exposed. Some form of radiation was being produced which could penetrate the paper and fog the plate. This happened with other compounds of uranium and it had nothing to do with phosphorescence. Furthermore, if the uranium salts were kept in darkness the activity did not diminish.

Roentgen was awarded the first Nobel prize for physics in 1901, but did not do much more work on x-rays. He considered his work on electrodynamics as more significant. Becquerel continued to do research on radiation and shared the 1903 Nobel prize with Pierre and Marie Curie.

From John Harris, 'On the education of revolutionary physicists: W. C. Roentgen and A. H. Becquerel', *School Science Review*, September 1995

Activity

Find out the names of other scientists who contributed to Rutherford's new theory of the atom and the nature of their discoveries.

Thinking and analytical skills

1 Does the writer justify his view that if these discoveries had not been made by Roentgen and Becquerel, others would have done so?

2 What was the 'critical observation and deduction' made by Roentgen?

3 How 'revolutionary' were these discoveries?

(iii) What do we mean by scientific proof and solving problems?

Links: 2.3 (i); 2.3 (ii); 3.3 (ii); 4.15 **Key skills**: C3.1a; C3.1b; N 3.1; PS 3.2

Introduction

Proving something depends on the nature of the activity. Solutions to problems are arrived at differently in mathematics, science and technology. The public expects socially important problems – 'Should I eat beef on the bone?', 'Is it safe for me to use a mobile phone?' – to have definitive answers. It is not always possible to provide such black-and-white answers, not because scientists are incompetent, but because that is the nature of things.

Background

Mathematicians start with 'axioms' (self-evident truths) and by logical steps (deduction) confirm or extend a mathematical **theorem**. A classic example is Pythagoras's theorem on the properties of right-angled triangles. The important thing is that once the logic is stated, and provided the axioms are true, the proof is absolute and there are no exceptions. So all triangles in the universe conform to Pythagoras's theorem.

Scientific proof is altogether more elusive. Current thinking is that a scientific **theory** can never be completely, everlastingly proven. This is because scientific theories are really causal explanations of how the world is. Since the world is apparently complicated, scientists strive to find an explanation that covers as many circumstances as possible, until we come across an observation that is incompatible with the explanation. Explanations are tested as much as possible and if **experiments** do not cast doubt on the theory, we are happy that the explanation is good enough. It follows that crucial scientific experiments are designed to test if an explanation is false, rather than verify the truth. Millions of children have been told in their science lessons to carry out an experiment to 'verify Boyle's Law' or 'prove that light is necessary for photosynthesis'. The hard fact is that a scientific theory can never be proven true, but we can always hope to prove it false.

Scientists are economical when there are several explanations of observed phenomena that fit the facts. If there is no other way of choosing, we select the simplest – the maxim of parsimony. The principle is that of '**Occam's Razor**' and it is justified because it is more likely that simpler explanations are of more general application and likely to be more powerful, until someone comes along with an experiment to show that we are wrong.

Technology is the use of scientific theories and understanding to satisfy human needs and resolve problems. Technologists are even more pragmatic than scientists and may well use phenomena that do not have full scientific explanations, if they appear to work. Classical medical technology depended for hundreds, and possibly thousands, of years on medical treatments using naturally occurring drugs in plants, although almost nothing was known of their actual effect on the body.

Glossary

theorem: a proposition to be proved by logical reasoning

theory: a generalisation that explains observations of the universe, enables predictions to be made and has been tested by experiment

experiment: a procedure for making observations to test theories and hypotheses

Occam's Razor: the principle that 'Entities should not be multiplied unnecessarily.' William of Occam was a medieval logician and philosopher

Issues to be discussed

- Does it matter that scientific theories can never be proved?
- What is the relationship between mathematics and science – is one dependent on the other?
- What encourages scientists to carry on producing more theories?
- Is it possible to have a 'theory of everything'?
- Do other subjects have theories in the same way as science?

Where now? Simon Singh, *Fermat's Last Theorem*, Fourth Estate, 1997

What do you think?

How do mathematicians, scientists and technologists work?

The close analogy between scientific experiment and technological problem-solving can be seen in the two diagrams below.

Mathematical problem solving can be shown more simply:

Axioms ---➤ Logical relationships ---➤ Proof

The axioms may change. For example, Pythagoras's theorem only applies to two-dimensional right-angled triangles, which can only contain one right angle (try to draw one with more!). Try drawing a triangle on a globe and see how many right angles it can contain. Does Pythagoras's theorem apply to it?

While we're on the subject of proving things, one of the landmark mathematical achievements of the twentieth century was the proof that any mathematical system which sets out to be a complete description of mathematical logic will contain true statements that are not verifiable. In other words, all such systems will be incomplete. Kurt Gödel broke this shocking news to mathematics in 1931, after Bertrand Russell and Alfred Whitehead had spent many years producing what they thought was a complete description of mathematics: the *Principia Mathematica* (1910–13).

Testing scientific explanations (theories)

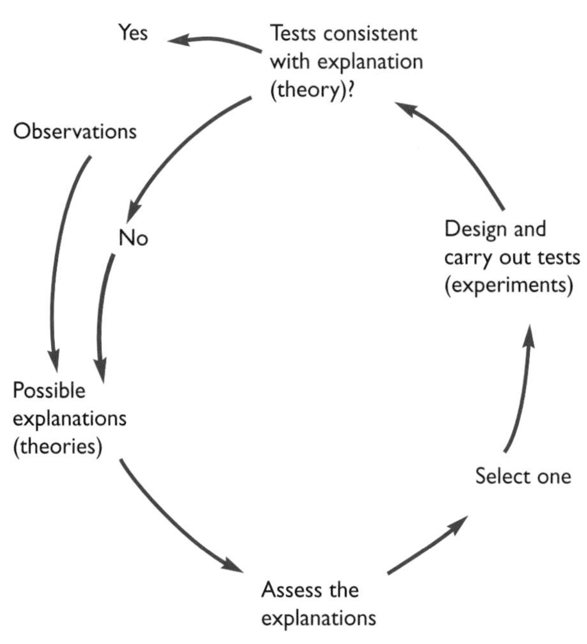

Problem solving in technology

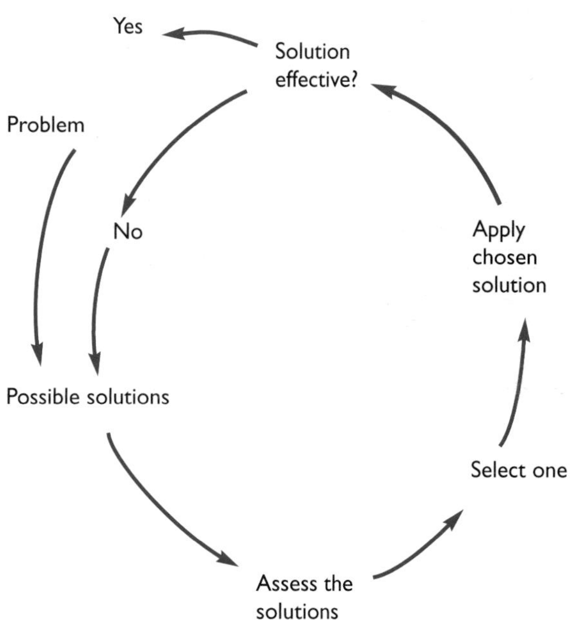

Activity

1 In groups, try to apply the cycles above to the following problems. Before you try, decide whether you are working on a scientific, technological or mathematical problem.

a Fred has impaired hearing. How can we help him hear well?

b Why can Fred only hear sounds of a narrow range of frequencies?

c Prove that the observed speed of sound varies according to the velocity of the observer.

Thinking and analytical skills

1 Is the analogy between testing scientific explanations and solving technological problems more than just an analogy?

2 Is it possible to prove 'beyond reasonable doubt' that a suspect did or did not commit a particular crime?

3 Is social science a science like biology, chemistry or physics?

(i) How can we justify the Human Genome Project and its consequences?

Links: 1.2 (iv); 2.1 (iii); 2.4 (iii); 4.9 **Key skills:** N 3.1; PS 3.2

Introduction

The Human **Genome** Project (HGP) is the culmination of nearly 40 years' work, resulting from the discovery that genes are chemicals the structure of which contain a simple code. It has brought to a head profound issues of morality, ethics, politics and economics.

Background

Genes are parts of **DNA** molecules that produce proteins. Proteins are the stuff of living things – they may be structural (determining the form of the key parts of the cell) or form **enzymes**. Proteins are made up of chains of **amino acids** in very specific sequences. The chains link up so that the protein molecule has a distinct, individual shape. The shape determines how the protein works. The landmark biological discovery of the twentieth century was the unravelling of the DNA code of base pairs that decide how each protein chain is built up from its component amino acids and the way in which the code is copied from generation to generation.

Impact of the Human Genome Project

The atlas of the human genome will revolutionise medical practice and biological research into the twenty-first century and beyond. All human genes will eventually be found and accurate diagnostics will be developed for most inherited diseases. As research progresses, investigators will also uncover the mechanisms for diseases caused by several genes or by a gene interacting with environmental factors. Genetic susceptibilities have been implicated in many major disabling and fatal diseases. Investigators determining the underlying biology of genome organisation and gene regulation will also begin to understand how humans develop from single cells to adults, why this process sometimes goes awry and what changes take place as people age.

While human genome research itself does not pose any new ethical dilemmas, the use of data arising from these studies presents challenges that need to be addressed. To assist in policy development, the ethics component of the Human Genome Project is funding conferences and research projects to consider relevant issues and activities to promote public awareness of these topics.

From *Department of Energy Human Genome 1991–92 Program Report*, June 1992

A private company announced plans this week to sequence the human genome by 2001, four years sooner than the target date set by the publicly funded Human Genome Project. All the data will be made freely available to researchers. 'We decided it would be morally wrong to keep the data secret,' says Craig Venter, founder of The Institute for Genomic Research (TIGR) in Maryland, USA. He estimates that sequencing the genome will cost around $200 million. The new company hopes to make money by identifying single-nucleotide polymorphisms, subtle variations in the same gene that predispose particular individuals to disease and dictate which medicines will work for them. This information, which takes extra effort to tease out, will be sold to pharmaceuticals companies.

From *New Scientist*, 16 May 1998

Glossary

genome: the complete set of genes in one individual

DNA: deoxyribonucleic acid, found in the nuclei of cells and in mitochondria in the cytoplasm

enzyme: a highly specific catalyst composed of protein; enzymes determine whether or not particular reactions take place in living cells

amino acid: a small organic molecule of which 20 are naturally occurring components of proteins

Issues to be discussed

- What are the advantages and disadvantages of knowing the structure of the human genome?
- Who should determine the nature and direction of scientific research – scientists, doctors, governments, business or others?
- Should the human genome be patented?
- Should the person whose DNA has been sequenced have any say in the use of the information gained?

Where now?

'The Business of the Human Genome', *Scientific American*, July 2000

www.ornl.gov/TechResources/Human_Genome/home.html

www.newscientist.com/ns/980523/ngenome.html

www.ncbi.nlm.nih.gov/Genbank/GenbankOverview.html

www.ncbi.nlm.nih.gov/

www.er.doe.gov/production/ober/hug_top.html

www.nhgri.nih.gov/ELSI/

What do you think?

Is the human genome about to revolutionise medicine?

Is the human genome about to revolutionise medicine? A lot of people seem to think so, but a much more cautious view is put forward in a recent issue of the *New England Journal of Medicine* by Dr Neil Holtzman of Johns Hopkins Medical Institutions and Dr Theresa Marteau of Guy's, King's and St Thomas' Medical School in London. 'Although we do not contend that the genetic mantle is as imperceptible as the emperor's new clothes were, it is not made of the silks and ermines that some claim it to be,' they conclude in a metaphoric flourish.

For a start, having a gene that confers a risk of a common disease does not make it certain that you will get that disease. Most such genes are of low 'penetrance', as geneticists say. If they were not, they would have been selected out by evolution because those carrying them would be less likely to have children. Exceptions are diseases that occur only after the reproductive years, such as Alzheimer's. Secondly, even if a gene that confers a high risk of a disease is found, this does not mean that knowing about it makes an effective treatment certain. It is 40 years, the authors remark, since the molecular basis of sickle-cell anaemia was found, but no treatment has yet emerged.

So what about genetic testing, the idea that we can all be warned in advance, through the genes we carry, of the diseases waiting for us in later life? The problem is that the predictive power of the tests is low unless the gene is rare and its effect strong. Such cases are likely to be a small proportion of the total. If two or more genes contribute to an increased risk and must both be present simultaneously, the problem of prediction becomes even harder – and so far there are few treatments that would offer comfort to people found to carry a predisposition to any disease. 'No interventions based on the identification of disease-related genes have yet proved safe and effective,' the authors say.

Possible exceptions are breast or colon cancer, where prophylactic surgery or careful monitoring might prolong life in those who are found to carry unlucky genes. But the extent of improvement is not yet known, nor the effects on quality of life.

Many people, faced with the low predictive value of the tests and the lack of treatments, will simply choose not to be tested at all, say Drs Holtzman and Marteau. The rare cases where testing would help – by showing that an individual was insensitive to a drug, for example – are too uncommon to justify widespread screening. 'Testing in families with a history of the disease would be a more efficient approach but does not a revolution make,' they say. 'In our rush to fit medicine with the genetic mantle, we are losing sight of other possibilities for improving public health,' the authors conclude. 'Differences in social structure, lifestyle and environment account for much larger proportions of disease than genetic differences.'

From *The Times*, 27 July 2000

Activity

Using a simple sampling method, find out what proportion of people of your age would prefer to know whether or not they possessed genes predisposing them to illnesses later in life.

Thinking and analytical skills

1 Critically evaluate the arguments for and against the HGP.

2 What is the answer to the question posed by the writer of the extract in his first sentence? What arguments are used?

3 Is the HGP worthwhile scientifically even if it does not live up to the promises made in 1992?

(ii) Where is medical science taking us?

Links: 2.1 (iii); 2.2 (i); 2.4 (i); 3.1 (iii); 4.7 **Key skills:** C3.1b; N 3.2; IT 3.1; PS 3.4

Introduction

Advances in genetics and in our understanding of the ways in which our bodies work are helping doctors: first, to understand what might be going wrong and, second, to repair or eliminate problems.

Background

The HGP will present us with incredibly detailed data about our genes and the proteins that they produce. Of all our DNA, about 10 per cent forms genes which code for proteins. The rest is unknown and may be 'junk' DNA accumulated through our evolutionary history. On the other hand, it may be important in affecting the functional genes, for example, switching them on and off or moderating their action.

Genomes of organisms that cause diseases will be investigated and enable us to combat their effects. Gene therapy (the manufacture and insertion of genes into living cells) opens up new possibilities for treating inherited diseases and producing genetic modifications quickly.

Advances in human reproductive biology, such as **IVF** and the **cloning** of human embryos, open up other avenues. The objective of these is not, as is commonly supposed, to produce many copies of 'superior' human types nor to enable an individual to attain immortality by producing an identical copy of themselves. Its purpose is to provide supplies of stem cells that are able to grow into different tissues and organs for use in transplant surgery – if the **stem cells** are your own, this removes the problem of foreign tissue rejection.

Nerve cells could treat Parkinson's, Alzheimer's, strokes, spinal cord injuries and multiple sclerosis. Heart muscle cells could treat heart failure or heart attacks; insulin-producing cells, diabetes; and cartilage cells, osteoarthritis. Liver cells would treat cirrhosis or hepatitis; skin cells, burns and wounds; and bone cells, osteoporosis. Retinal cells could treat macular degeneration, which is a common cause of blindness in the elderly, and muscle cells could treat muscular dystrophy.

Advances in our understanding of ageing are allowing individuals to have greatly increased life spans. The average life span of individuals in wealthy developed countries has been rising steadily since 1900. The maximum age to which an individual might aspire has changed less, but recent research shows that this too is slowly rising. More people in these countries live longer, but there is an attendant increase in the diseases of old age (cancer, Alzheimer's, diabetes and stroke) which require medical intervention.

Glossary

IVF: in vitro fertilisation; eggs and sperm are removed from the body, fertilisation is accomplished outside the mother's body, and the developing embryo is implanted in the mother

cloning: the process that produces genetically identical individuals. The offspring of organisms that reproduce asexually are clones (e.g. strawberry runners)

stem cells: unspecialised cells, found in embryos and some parts of the adult, which have the capacity to differentiate into other cells

Issues to be discussed

- Is it possible to justify the cost of the medical procedures outlined above, when the same money spent on providing clean water, improving basic hygiene and making some simple surgical procedures available in poorer countries would alleviate much human suffering?
- What social and moral problems would arise if the average life span of Europeans and North Americans rose to 100 years?
- How can we control or prevent the immoral or unethical uses of medical technology?

Where now?

www.ri.bbsrc.ac.uk/library/research/cloning/cloning.html
www.humancloning.org/seed.htm
www.doh.gov.uk/cloning.htm
www.banneroftruth.co.uk/articles/technological_cannibalism.htm
www.newscientist.com/nsplus/insight/clone/clone.html
www.dspace.dial.pipex.com/srtscot/cloning.shtml
www.geneletter.com/archives/twentyonearguments.html
www.catholicdoctors.org.uk/Submissions/cloning_expert_committee.htm

What do you think?

Should we allow cloning?

A new law explicitly banning the cloning of human beings was promised by the government yesterday in an attempt to draw the sting from opposition to cloning in medical research. The promise was in response to a report by Professor Liam Donaldson, the Chief Medical Officer, which recommends approval for research into therapeutic cloning – a technique with 'enormous potential' for treating a wide range of diseases, from Parkinson's to cancer.

The long-awaited Donaldson Report makes nine recommendations, all of them referring to research rather than treatment. The report's central conclusion is that research into therapeutic cloning – the creation from a patient's cells of an embryo which could be used as a source of material for treatment – should be allowed, but only if there is no other means of achieving the same results.

The same techniques should be permitted for research into diseases caused by faulty DNA in the cytoplasm, the material surrounding the cell nucleus. The diseases are passed on from mother to child, but might be prevented by taking sound cytoplasm from a donor for combining with the mother's own nuclear DNA. The report expressly forbids the creation of hybrids made from human cells and the eggs of other animal species, as well as the use of cloning to produce identical copies of people.

In effect, the report says it is acceptable to clone embryos for research, so long as they are not allowed to live for longer than 14 days. The justification is that stem cells taken from these embryos can form the basis of a new branch of medicine, acting as a source of replacement cells for many tissues in the body. Such cells, Professor Donaldson said, may one day be used to treat a huge range of diseases.

The report was welcomed by patient groups, medical charities and the scientific and medical profession. Both the British Medical Association and the Medical Research Council expressed support. The British Heart Foundation and the Parkinson's Disease Society backed the recommendations. 'Therapeutic cloning offers a tremendous opportunity,' said Professor David Latchman, vice-chairman of the Parkinson's Disease Society's medical advisory panel.

But Cardinal Thomas Winning, chairman of the bioethics committee of the Catholic Bishops of Great Britain and Ireland, said: 'Obtaining stem cells from a human embryo is morally wrong because it involves the destruction of a human life.' Martin Casey of Right to Life said that the recommendations were arrogance and irresponsibility of the worst kind. Therapeutic cloning was being 'offered as a panacea to cure a whole range of serious conditions without any proof that this method is any more likely to produce results than the ethically and morally more responsible route of using adult stem cells'.

The Donaldson recommendations:

- Research permitted using human embryos created by IVF or cloning.
- Licences for such research to be issued by the Human Fertilisation and Embryology Authority, only if there is no other means of doing the research.
- People whose eggs or sperm are used to create the embryos to give specific consent.
- Research which uses nuclear transfer to try to treat mitochondrial disease also to be allowed.
- Research using stem cells from embryos to be monitored to ensure it is achieving benefits.
- No 'hybrids' between human cells and animal eggs.
- Reproductive cloning to remain a criminal offence.
- Legislation to allow the research, if successful, to be turned into treatments to be kept under review.
- Research councils to establish programmes of research into stem cells and consider establishing collections of stem cells for research.

From *The Times*, 17 August 2000

Activities

1 In groups, use the web-based resources to obtain the views of one interest group on the subject of cloning. Present these to the other groups.

2 Construct a 10-point questionnaire to test a younger age group's views on cloning.

Thinking and analytical skills

1 Why do you think the government is to introduce a law banning the cloning of human beings?

2 Describe clearly the differences between reproductive and therapeutic cloning, then evaluate the ethical arguments for and against therapeutic cloning.

3 The Right to Life organisation condemns the Donaldson recommendations. Evaluate the arguments it uses to justify its position.

(iii) How can scientists influence the outcome of their work?

Links: 1.2 (v); 2.4 (i); 2.6 (iii); 4.15 **Key skills:** C3.1a; C3.1b; IT 3.1; PS 3

Introduction

Scientists, since they are ordinary human beings, have views and feelings like everyone else. However, the work that engages them may have an enormous impact on human life and society. Many scientists subscribe to codes of moral and ethical procedures and try to affect the ways in which their innovations are used.

Background

The most famous and enduring code of conduct is that of the medical profession. Known as the Hippocratic oath, it dates from the fourth century BC. It is, however, a strange document and very much part of its time. For example, it requires a doctor to avoid carrying out surgery, as it was then regarded as an activity conducted by lesser mortals. Codes of conduct, some of which are based on the Hippocratic oath, are now established features of most scientific professions.

Many scientists have tried to influence the attitudes of their own nation and others. The ongoing Pugwash Conferences were initiated in 1957 by 22 eminent scientists in response to a manifesto issued by **Bertrand Russell** and Albert Einstein in 1955. Their purpose is to bring together influential scholars and public figures concerned with reducing armed conflict and seeking co-operative solutions for global problems. A basic rule for participation is that individuals always attend in their private capacity and not as representatives of governments or organisations.

It is an unfortunate fact that discoveries cannot be undiscovered. Nuclear weapons have changed the nature of war and politics, although they have only been used twice in anger. Einstein said that if he had known that his work in nuclear physics would lead to the invention of the nuclear bomb, he would never have studied physics. Scientists, as generally moral individuals, would like their work to lead to the greatest good and the least harm. In weapons research, this is a dilemma. How do we regard the rocket research in Nazi Germany that led to a terrifying anti-civilian weapon as well as to the gigantic technological achievement of putting us on the moon? The development of armaments creates a cycle from which it seems impossible to escape – a new weapon is developed, sparking off research in how to defend against it. A successful defence spurs researchers into circumventing it. Ultimately, it is humanity at large, not scientists alone, who must decide what to do about these issues. It is difficult to think of an example of a mad scientist trying to control a country or the world, but there have been plenty of power-hungry rulers and politicians who have directed scientists who either shared their political goals and morality or who were coerced into working for them.

Weapons research is an extreme, but useful, example because it highlights the dilemma. Scientists may well be asked why they participate in research that has unpredictable outcomes, such as the genetic modification of crops, the cloning of humans or the exploitation of non-renewable resources. **Sir Peter Medawar** contrasted two views of scientific activity: messianism, in which scientists strive to make a perfect Utopian world, and meliorism, in which they simply try to make it better.

In tackling the problem of over-population, for example, a scientist might research the best and most innovative methods of birth control. Despite having surmounted formidable physiological problems to create cheap, safe and reliable products, nothing can be resolved unless the politicians and administrators ensure that the population uses them. The idea that scientists and scientific advances alone can make a content and happy world is a delusion.

Glossary

Bertrand Russell: an English mathematician, philosopher and pacifist

Sir Peter Medawar: a distinguished medical researcher and Nobel prize winner

Issues to be discussed

- In what ways does society ensure that scientific research is guided and controlled?
- What is to stop an individual scientist carrying out research that leads to predictable and unwelcome problems?
- Are scientific outcomes always unpredictable?

Where now?

P. B. Medawar, *Advice to a Young Scientist*, Harper Row, 1979

www.brad.ac.uk/acad/sbtwc/other/bw-info.htm

www.euthanasia.com/belgium.html

www.cs.umb.edu/jfklibrary/j072663.htm

www.medword.com/hippocrates.html

www.hol.gr/greece/medicine.htm

www.pugwash.org/index.htm

What do you think?

What factors should be taken into consideration when deciding to support scientific projects?

Until recently, science has responded to human needs haphazardly, by spontaneous growth within a general policy of laissez-faire. Research has followed the inclinations of individuals or has swayed one way or another in response to fashion or to the consensus of the privileged groups who wield scientific authority.

Before embarking on a research programme we tacitly ask questions such as:

- Is the particular topic ripe for exploitation?
- Are there good things to be done in that field?
- Is the subject not too stale and overworked?
- Are good people available to do the research?

These questions are all directed towards the achievement of progress inside that particular branch of science, almost as if for its own sake. The advantage is, of course, that they can often be answered fairly accurately by the scientific experts in that branch. If our aim is simply to 'push back the frontiers of knowledge' by 'pure', 'basic', 'fundamental' research, then they are by no means inappropriate criteria. But the world-wide community of science is too large, and too closely connected with practical affairs, for such a policy to continue. The amount of money available for fundamental research is limited and would be spread too thinly if everybody were to be supported in research of his own choosing. Serious political and economic thought, and the experience of success in military and industrial research, clearly indicates that science should be planned to achieve much more explicit goals outside the scientific community.

In the nature of things, research results cannot be planned in detail. Who can know the outcome of a new experiment? If the result could be predicted, then the experiment would be unnecessary. To draw up a precise programme of investigation is likely to waste effort and can even be self-defeating: the attempt to carry out a preconceived programme merely shackles the imagination in its drive to see things from a new point of view. There is an inner logic of nature that prevents premature success. For example, a determined effort to build a heavier-than-air flying machine would have been fruitless before the invention of the internal combustion engine. And an enlightened project in 1850 to improve the horse as means of transport would surely have failed to invent the automobile!

But the objections to planned research can be overstated. Within normal science, the range of problems worth tackling can be defined and the general prospects of a successful outcome can be assessed. The capacity of the enormous numbers of scientists now at work in the world may well be put to best use in routine tasks within an organised scheme. A method whereby financial support is allocated according to some rough general plan may achieve an overall balance of effort without great constraints on individual scientists.

This is what is now called 'science policy'. The task of the policy makers, whoever they may be, is to observe gaps in the research front or to take account of important social needs such as new sources of energy or the protection of the natural environment and to manoeuvre squads of scientists into the appropriate direction of attack. It is natural then to apply criteria external to science to assess a project:

- Does the research lead to fairly obvious improvements of existing or proposed techniques, i.e. technological merit?
- Does development in the field have important consequences in other fields, i.e. scientific merit?
- Does this research have potential applications of great social value, i.e. social merit?

From John Ziman, *The Force of Knowledge – the Scientific Dimension of Society*, Cambridge University Press, 1976

Activity

Select a major problem in the developing world, such as desertification in Africa, AIDS, catastrophic flooding in Bangladesh, famine.

As a group, develop a science policy to address the problem and assess to what extent science and technology can solve or reduce it.

Thinking and analytical skills

1 Critically examine the arguments for and against Ziman's view that research results cannot be planned in detail.

2 Evaluate possible criteria for judging whether an application has great social value. In modern societies, who should apply these criteria?

3 What is the moral argument in the passage?

(i) Testing hypotheses: what use are statistics?

Links: 2.5 (ii) **Key skills:** C3.1b; C3.2; N 3.3; IT 3.3

Introduction

Statistics is a branch of mathematics and it is used widely in science, particularly in biology, since it enables quantitative analysis of complex problems. Sometimes it is difficult or impossible to find the cause of an observation, but the finding of a **correlation** between observations and measurements helps scientists to see whether further investigation is worthwhile.

Background

There is a widespread belief that 'you can prove anything with statistics'. This is patently untrue because statistics cannot prove anything in a strict mathematical sense. Statistics just tell us how likely or unlikely things are. Scientists commonly set up a **null hypothesis**, make observations to test it and decide how different the results are by statistical methods. For example, it might be suggested that blue-eyed people can see further than those with non-blue eyes. Anecdotal evidence should tell us that this is unlikely to be true. If we wished to investigate this, our null hypothesis would be that there is nothing in it. Therefore, we sample the population (that is find 50 people with blue eyes and 50 with eyes of other colours), apply our vision test on each of the groups and then compare the two. How do we make the comparison?

- Calculate the mean distance seen by the two groups: are they the same, similar or different? How do we decide, if the mean distances are close?
- Count the number of people with better-than-average distance vision in each group. How do we decide whether the distribution curve is different?

In either case, we are not sure whether any difference we find is statistically significant. Is it possible that the results were achieved by chance alone?

This is already a complex problem because we are looking at the distribution of a **variable** (good/poor distance vision) in relation to another (blue/non-blue eyes).

Everyday knowledge tells us that other things – age, gender, illness, among others –might affect our vision. So, if we need to improve our experiment, we could try to take **matched samples**. Even then, there is still a chance that our numbers will not fall out as we predict. We still need to carry out statistical tests to tell us whether our results are achieved by chance.

You will notice that none of this has anything to do with explaining the result. We are only told that two variables are significantly correlated.

How did we come to see the problem? We might just have idly thought 'I wonder if this so?' More likely an observant scientist noticed that blue-eyed people do better in sporting events of a particular kind, or that people with blue eyes seem to wear spectacles less than other people. The scientist would have been using induction and would then have produced the hypothesis on which the experimental measurements are based.

The great experimenter Gregor Mendel carried out thousands of plant breeding experiments, making the breakthrough that showed that inheritance could be explained by particles in the reproductive cells moving into the **gametes** randomly and combining randomly when fertilisation occurs. He had to count seeds or plants with the characteristics he studied to note that they were found in simple ratios, like 1:1, 3:1, 9:3:3:1 in the offspring. Although his ratios were never exact, they were quite close and he used large numbers. Long afterwards, a sceptical statistician pointed out that some of his results were too close to the now-expected results. No-one now really believes that he doctored his figures.

Glossary

correlation: a measure of whether events or variables are associated. Demonstrating correlation does not prove that one event causes another

null hypothesis: the experimenter assumes that the variable will have no effect

variable: a measurable feature in an experiment

matched samples: experimental groups which are as alike as possible

gamete: a sex cell, sperm or egg

Issues to be discussed

- How could results like Mendel's be too good?
- Why can't statistics be used to prove anything?
- How do scientists other than biologists use statistics?
- Why do scientists look for causes?

Where now?

Darrell Huff, *How to Lie with Statistics*, Penguin, 1991
V. Opel, *Mendel*, Oxford University Press, 1984

What do you think?

Why are we so bad at weighing up risks?

It is a strange paradox that in industrialised countries we live longer and healthier lives than ever before, yet we feel less safe. We shudder at the slightest risk to our well-being. Newspapers regularly run scare stories about new technologies or unsafe food, confident that they will whip up public concern. It seems that nothing short of a life completely free of risk will satisfy us. Our attitudes to risk vary widely. We happily continue in activities we know to be risky, such as smoking, driving and sunbathing. At the same time, we worry about others that carry a low health risk, such as taking oral contraceptives.

It is easy to put such reactions down to apathy or a lack of scientific and technical knowledge, fuelled by a media more concerned with their audience share than with a reasoned debate on the protection of public health. Yet public interest in science has never been higher. Far more significant for the public understanding of science is the fact that people tend not to think of risk in purely statistical terms. Surveys show that most people have a good grasp of the relative chance of death they face from various hazards. For example, they know that in any normal year heart disease kills more people than botulism. However, when asked about the overall risks that these hazards pose to their well-being, people's judgements extend far beyond the statistical chances of dying.

We find risks more acceptable if we can choose whether or not to take them, if we can control our level of exposure and if the benefits are clear and immediate. Mobile phones are an obvious example. Despite the sensational media stories, most people have carried on using them. On the other hand, we object to hazards that are imposed on us without our consent, that affect the young or could cause a major catastrophe, or when risks and benefits are inequitably distributed across society.

Often, controversies about risk seem to be more about the politics and ethics than about the science. Thus, scientists and policy makers must go beyond simply 'getting the numbers right' when thinking about risk. The mathematical approach may indeed be counterproductive, particularly with long-term hazards such as radioactive waste disposal, where it is very difficult to predict accurately what the future risks might be.

But the most crucial factor that dictates how people judge risk is trust. Many experts claim that a mistrust of expertise and risk management is now a defining feature of industrialised societies. People have become increasingly distanced from the technologies and organisations that generate the hazards they face. We accept this in some areas: for example, many of us travel by air, though few of us have the technical knowledge to understand how a modern aircraft's electronic systems work, let alone the skill to operate them. We put our faith in a whole host of experts when we fly. Trust becomes particularly significant when things go seriously wrong, as illustrated by the Air France Concorde crash in July 2000.

Food production, for example, has advanced beyond our capacity to understand it. We have to rely on experts. As the BSE crisis unfolded in Britain in the mid-1990s, events contradicted earlier assurances by the government that eating beef was safe. When governments and experts get it wrong, trust disappears. The lesson here is that while trust is hard to gain, it is very easy to lose. The distrust generated by the BSE crisis has spilled over into the public debate about genetically modified organisms. Governments should learn from this.

Lack of trust makes it particularly hard to communicate scientific information. Crucially, if people do not trust the person giving them the message, they will not trust the message itself.

So what is to be done in the face of public scepticism? A first step would be to understand the origins of that scepticism. If the government and scientists want the public to understand scientific issues and to trust them, they must go beyond one-way provision of technical information and engage in a wider dialogue with people. It would be naive to claim that scientists have nothing to learn from society, particularly where long-term uncertainties and ethically charged issues are concerned. Listening, as with anything in life, is risky. But so is not listening.

From *New Scientist*, 12 August 2000

Activities

1 Compare the risks taken in different sports. What are the best ways of calculating risks of injury and death?

2 Analyse the use of statistics in any piece of scientific news publicised within the last month.

Thinking and analytical skills

1 Justify the argument in the passage that people are poor at assessing risks to their health.
2 Give examples of the different types of knowledge referred to in the passage.
3 What conclusions are reached by the writer in relation to the risks in food production?

(ii) Presenting data

Links: 2.5 (i); 2.5 (iii) **Key skills:** IT 3.1; IT 3.2

Introduction

Information and ideas can be presented in pictures or **graphic** displays as well as in written or oral forms. Quantitative measures and complex relationships may sometimes be communicated more effectively in diagrams or charts.

Background

Anyone who produces a diagram or photograph creates an edited view of reality. They have to choose what to show and what to hide. In this way they introduce meaning and interpretation to the diagram and we should always be aware of this. Diagrams are intended to help us understand.

The range of diagrams, graphs and charts used by scientists is very broad, but they fall into three main categories:

- **Data** maps: a good example is the map of central London which showed the cases of cholera in 1854. It was possible to link the cases to a single water pump and to show that the infection was waterborne.
- Time series present data which is sequential. Excellent examples are rainfall and temperature charts.
- Relational graphics: these are the 'straightforward' graphs which show how one or more variables are related to one another. There are numerous forms of these: histograms, bar charts, line graphs, curves of best fit, scatter diagrams, polar graphs, spider diagrams and so on. How each is used is related to the data that the scientist wishes to present.

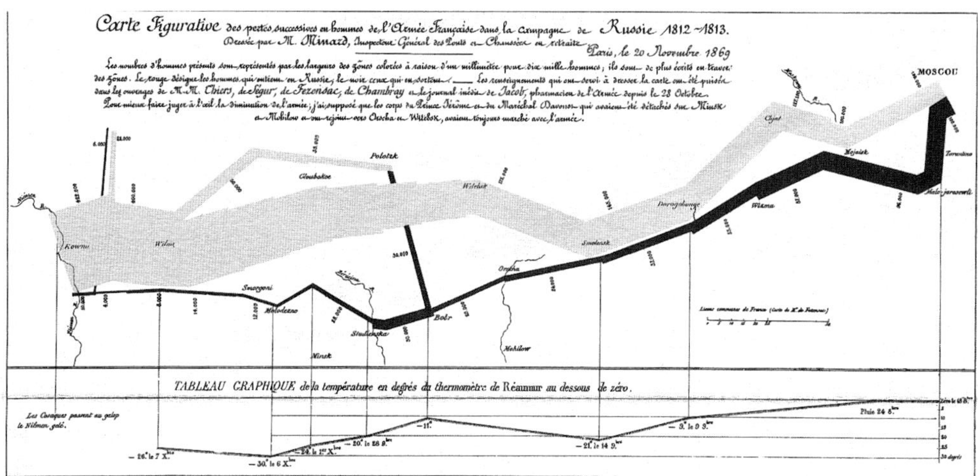

This graphic is a classic, produced by the French engineer C. J. Minard in 1869. It is a combination of data map and time series showing the fate of Napoleon's army during his invasion of Russia in 1812. The width of the grey band represents the size of the army during the march on Moscow and the black band shows his return. The black band is referenced to a temperature graph showing the severe winter conditions. Six variables are represented: size of the army, its location in two dimensions, direction of march, temperature and dates.

Glossary

graphic: any pictorial representation of objects, ideas or data intended to help the viewer understand

data: more than one piece of information (datum: one piece of information)

perinatal: at or around birth

Issues to be discussed

- Do different types of scientists (biologists, chemists, and physicists) use graphics in different ways?
- How does one choose whether to describe data and their relationships or to produce a graphic representation?
- Are pictures always worth a thousand words?

Where now?

E. R. Tufte, *The Visual Display of Quantitative Information*, Graphics Press, 1983

E. R. Tufte, *Envisioning Information*, Graphics Press, 1990

www.official-documents.co.uk/document/doh/tobacco/report.htm

What do you think?

How can complex data on health be presented to the general public?

The lung cancer mortality rate for men fell by an estimated 13.9 per cent over the four years since the start of the Health of the Nation strategy in 1992. Over the same period the mortality rate for women fell by only 2.5 per cent. These data should be interpreted with caution because of the latent period for onset of cancer.

Preliminary figures from the 1996 General Household Survey (GHS) data published in November 1997 show that, for the first time since smoking questions were included in 1972, the prevalence of cigarette smoking has increased for both men and women.

Between 1990 and 1994 the percentage of men smoking cigarettes fell from 31 per cent to 28 per cent and that for women fell from 28 per cent to 26 per cent. In 1996, 29 per cent of men and 28 per cent of women smoked cigarettes, a return to 1992 figures. The increase was only statistically significant for women aged 25–34 (up from 30 per cent in 1994 to 34 per cent in 1996.) In recent years the fall in smoking prevalence among men and women has been levelling out, but it is not known whether the new figures indicate a trend or a short-term fluctuation.

The General Household Survey also demonstrates that smoking prevalence is closely linked with socio-economic status. In the period between 1974 and 1994, smoking prevalence in professional groups fell by a half, but in unskilled manual workers the fall was only a third. This means that, by 1994, unskilled workers were two to three times more likely to smoke than professionals.

Conclusions:

- Smoking is a major cause of illness and death from chronic respiratory diseases, cardiovascular disease, and cancers of the lung and other sites.
- Smoking is the most important cause of premature death in developed countries. It accounts for one-fifth of deaths in the UK (some 120,000 deaths a year).
- The avoidance of smoking would eliminate one-third of the cancer deaths in Britain and one-sixth of the deaths from other causes.
- Smoking prevalence in young people rose between 1988 and 1997 and the downward trend in adult smoking, noted in the UK since 1972, was reversed in 1996.
- A person who smokes regularly more than doubles his or her risk of dying before the age of 65.
- Addiction to nicotine sustains cigarette smoking and is responsible for the remarkable intractability of smoking behaviour.
- Smoking in pregnancy causes adverse outcomes, notably an increased risk of miscarriage, reduced birth weight and **perinatal** death. If parents continue to smoke after pregnancy, there is an increased rate of sudden infant death syndrome.
- Cigarette smoking is an important contributor to health inequalities, being much more common amongst the disadvantaged than the affluent members of society.

Recommendations:

- The enormous damage to health and life arising from smoking should no longer be accepted; the government should take effective action to limit this preventable epidemic.
- The government should require of the tobacco industry:
    - reasonable standards in the assessment of evidence relating to the health effects of the product it sells,
    - acceptance that smoking is a major cause of premature death,
    - normal standards of disclosure of the nature and magnitude of the hazards of smoking to their customers, comparable to that expected from other manufacturers of consumer products.
- Tobacco manufacturers should comply with these requirements independently of specific governmental regulations.
- There is an importance and urgency about the smoking problem that needs to be recognised by both the government and the public.

Source: *Report of the Scientific Committee on Smoking and Health*, The Office for National Statistics, 1998; www.statistics.gov.uk

Activity

Take one conclusion presented above and present it visually in a way that communicates the information in a clear and easily understood way.

Thinking and analytical skills

1 Construct an argument, based on one of the recommendations, which supports the actions suggested to the government.

2 Develop another argument, based on individual responsibility and free-will, which opposes any action by the government on smoking.

(iii) Statistics and their presentation: two practical activities

Links: 2.2 (i); 2.2 (ii) **Key skills:** C3.2; N 3.3; IT 3.3; PS 3.2

Introduction

If you need to be clearer about the uses of statistics, particularly in everyday life, two practical activities might help you. Tackle whichever you wish, in a group, but share your results with others.

Activity 1

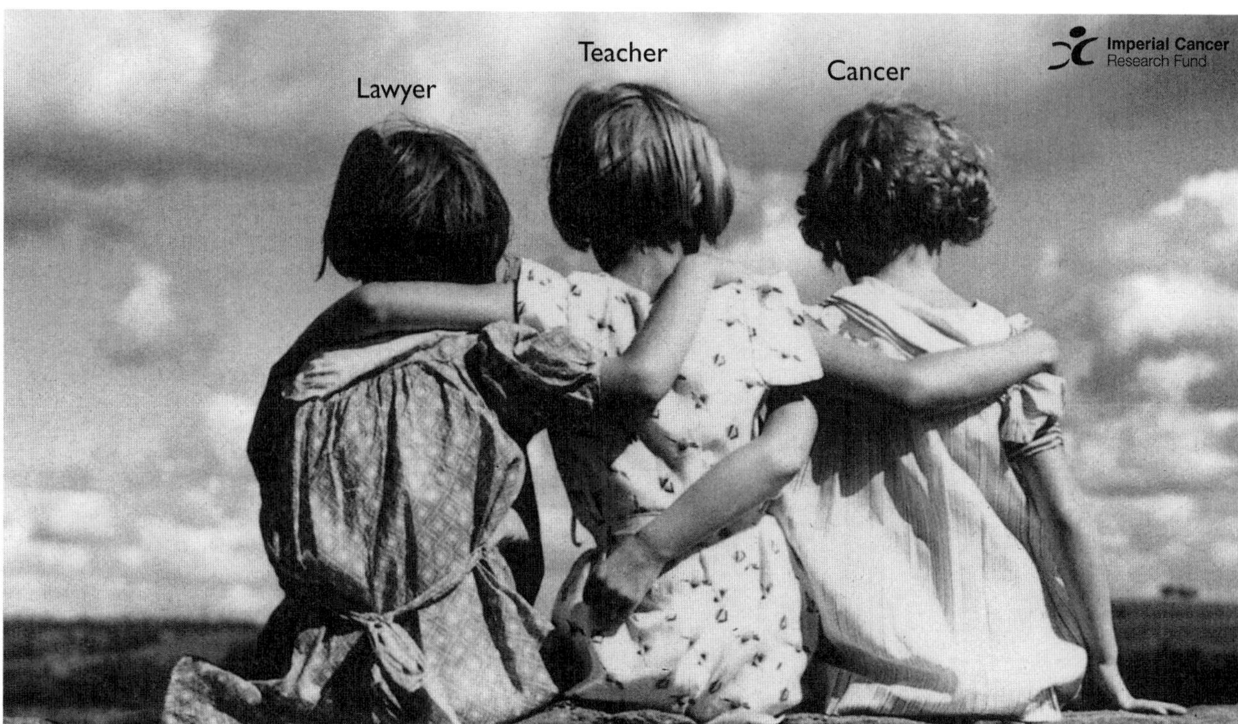

This image is from an advertisement for the Imperial Cancer Research Fund. The text below it reads:
'At least one in every three people will contract cancer. It's a chilling statistic. But at the Imperial Cancer Research Fund, we believe there's good reason to be optimistic about the future. Recovery rates are improving every year, thanks in part to work carried out by our doctors and scientists. Ninety per cent of men with testicular cancer are now treated successfully. Nearly seventy per cent of children survive the most common form of childhood leukaemia. And deaths from cervical cancer have fallen by fifty per cent in the last fifteen years. That's good. But we need to do better. We want to turn one in three to none in three. If you'd like to find out about the work we do, call 0845 601 1891 or visit www.imperialcancer.co.uk. The Imperial Cancer Research Fund. Turning science into hope.'

The advertisement carries messages that are largely statistical.

- Review the piece as objectively as you can. Is there a particular target audience? How are the risks of cancer presented? Are they clear to all readers? Do they reassure or frighten? Is there much science in it?
- Design a new advertisement that presents a similar amount of data on cancer (or any other disease or condition) in a different format or formats. Remember that the intention is to encourage people to donate money and support the ICRF. (Further information and data can be obtained from the sources below.)
- If you have the facilities, demonstrate your work as a web page or as a presentation using a computer.

Where now?

www.aabc.org.uk/facts.htm
www.ash.org.uk/html/about/pubcat.html
www.cancerindex.org/clinks3c.htm
www.hosted.aware.easynet.co.uk/
www.imperialcancer.co.uk

Activity 2

- Survey any conveniently available group of people to find out the sort of risks they might happily accept. For example, would they:
    - Bungee jump?
    - Cycle into a city centre?
    - Travel 1,000 miles nonstop in a plane?
    - Travel 1,000 miles nonstop in a car?
    - Play in a football match?
    - Eat a beefburger?
- You will need to construct your survey very carefully. Be very clear about phrasing the questions you ask and allow people to make graded responses, for example 'Would you bungee jump? – willingly/possibly/no way'.
- You must test your results against the hypothesis that 'People's willingness to undertake an activity is inversely related to the risks of injury in the activity'. In other words, the more risky it is, the fewer people will want to do it (see Unit 2.5 (i)). It would be wise, therefore, to research the risks associated with each different activity before you construct your questionnaire/interview procedure. See the references below, and any others you can find.
- If you have the facilities, present the results as a web page or as a standalone computer presentation.

Where now?

www.driving.co.uk/8london.htm
www.jackellis.co.uk/accident.htm
www.smitha.demon.co.uk/hardwick/hcc/accident.html

Further research

1 For each presentation, assess the validity of the results.
2 When all results are presented, evaluate the arguments for and against the hypothesis.

(i) Science, technology and civilised living

Links: 2.1 (i); 2.3 (iii); 4.2; 4.16 **Key skills:** C3.1a; C3.1b; IT 3.1; PS 3.1

Introduction

Science and technology affect almost every aspect of society. The apparently simple matter of knowing where you are and how to get from place to place is an illustration of a very old, yet still important, technology.

Today new technologies are used to satisfy the energy needs and problems of remote and underdeveloped communities.

Background

Science tries to explain the world as we see it and traces causal links between events. It develops ideas and concepts behind these explanations, it satisfies human intellectual and emotional needs and, not least, it provides the basis of solutions to human problems or the hope that they may be solved in the future. Technology is any response that is intended to satisfy needs or solve problems.

The need to know where you are, the safe boundaries of your activities and how to deal with getting lost is part and parcel of human history. Physical landmarks and a good spatial memory are very useful, and are still employed by some groups today – the Penan forest dwellers of Borneo, for example. Early in the development of civilisation people realised that there were certain landmarks that were stable and predictable and not subject to loss of memory – the sun, moon and stars all move predictably in the sky, in different patterns but without risk of being tampered with.

The apparent motion of the sun enables us to standardise the passage of time and, when you have the concept of a turning, spherical earth and the time of day, it enables you to work out your north-south position.

In order to fix one's position on the earth's surface, two measurements are needed: your north-south position (latitude) and your east-west position (longitude). Latitude is easily determined, provided you can work out when the sun is at its highest point at midday. The length of the shadow cast by a vertical stick and some simple geometry fixes your latitude. The sextant is an instrument that does the same thing by measuring the angle between the horizon and the sun at midday. Finding your east-west position, however, is entirely dependent on having an extremely accurate clock. You have to measure a fixed point in the day – sunrise, for example – in relation to a standard time at an agreed point on the earth. This is the meridian, running through Greenwich. The invention of a sufficiently accurate and robust clock that could be taken around the world occupied much of the life of John Harrison.

Nowadays, a small device, costing relatively little, will read out your latitude and longitude on a screen, to within a few metres. Global positioning (GPS) is dependent on signals broadcast from satellites in geostationary orbits. A network of these surrounds the earth, to the huge benefit of sailors and explorers all over the world. Needless to say, there are military uses for such a system. The device is essentially a computer which receives the signals from several satellites and calculates its position from them. All of this depends on the development of an enormous range of technologies, in turn dependent on the scientific discoveries of several centuries:

- Satellites: Newtonian physics (seventeenth); chemistry of fuels (early nineteenth to mid-twentieth); electronics; computing; metallurgy and materials science.
- Communications: electricity (mid-nineteenth to early twentieth); wireless (early twentieth); computing and digital communications (mid-twentieth).
- Energy: fuels; **photovoltaic cells**; storage batteries.

Glossary

photovoltaic cell: a device that converts light directly into electricity

hydroelectric power: the production of electricity by the use of flowing water to turn a generator

solar power: either the production of electricity through photovoltaic cells or the transfer of thermal energy in sunlight to water

Issues to be discussed

- Why should knowing one's position be important in the development of a community or civilisation?
- What are the advantages to an ordinary citizen of GPS?
- What potential problems are there in becoming dependent on GPS?
- Would we have GPS without the military advantages of such a system?

Where now?

Dava Sobel, *Longitude*, HarperCollins, 1998

www.oneworld.org/ni/issue284/index.html

www.oneworld.org/ni/index4.html

What do you think?

Is small-scale technology better than huge projects?

Different people see the impact of science and technology as good or bad. It really isn't very easy to come to a confident overall judgement, however. For example, why should the Mongolian government (see below) want to ensure that rural families have electricity? The two examples emphasise the benefits to individuals and groups of small-scale, but not necessarily simple, technological projects. Putting the science and technology to one side, who decides and who should decide on the application of technology to satisfy human needs and desires? Certainly not scientists and technologists alone.

The flow of power

A light bulb swings above Juan and José as they do their homework. 'They have a chance of a good education now,' says their grandmother, Maria. 'They have a future.'

For six months of the year the Andean village of Chalán in northern Peru is cut off from the nearest town, Celendín. Candles are expensive so villagers used to go to bed when it got dark. Now all that has changed thanks to the village's new micro-hydro scheme.

Hydroelectric power is a dirty word in more enlightened development circles. But on a small scale, it's quite another matter. Nearly everyone in the village was involved in building their micro-hydro scheme, with help from the UK-based development agency, Intermediate Technology. And the power goes directly to homes, school, workshops, the health clinic, even to the local dentist who says his running costs have dropped by 90 per cent! Anticipating the demand that the Chalán example would generate in the surrounding area, Intermediate Technology has funded a workshop in the town of Cajamarca to make the turbines and equipment necessary for micro-hydro schemes.

Micro-hydro is bringing change to other parts of the world too. In the Himalayas, the Hilly Hydro Project has ingeniously gained World Bank funding. In view of the World Bank's famed preference for mega-schemes, hundreds of separate, environmentally friendly, micro-schemes have been packaged to look like one big project. The micro-hydros will bring power to remote mountain communities and relieve the pressure on firewood in an area which is being rapidly deforested.

Hi-tech nomads

Have *yurt*, yak, **solar** panel, can travel. Mongolian nomads are attaching a new feature to their *yurts* (or tents) these days – photovoltaic cells. Solar technology is actually ideally suited to a nomadic lifestyle. Mongolian nomads, who constitute nearly half the country's population, move their tents about 30 times a year, covering vast distances with their herds of horses, yaks, goats, sheep and camels. Solar panels can be set up and function anywhere, providing there is sun. Not a problem in a land with an average 300 sunny days a year.

When the sun doesn't shine, temperatures can drop as low as minus 30°C. But, as though to compensate for this, photovoltaic cells work even better in extreme cold and the snow reflects additional light.

Traditionally, rural families have depended on wood fuel or animal dung and candles for all their cooking, heating and lighting needs. Now renewable energy is the centrepiece of the Mongolian government's strategy to bring electricity to rural families and so slow down the drift from highlands to cities. A single 40–60-watt solar module can provide a nomadic family with five hours' light, four hours' television and fifteen hours' radio per day. Several hundred photovoltaic systems have now been installed in the country. In the capital Ulan Bator, the Research and Production Corporation for Renewable Energy has been busy assembling and distributing these systems – which come from Europe, the USA and China – and evaluating their performance. The Mongolian Institute of Physics and Technology, meanwhile, is pursuing a photovoltaic research programme of its own.

From *The New Internationalist*, October 1996

Activities

1 Identify the kinds of technology that are applied in one of the scenarios above.

2 Identify the scientific and technological advances that were necessary for these technologies (e.g. electric light – current electricity – materials technology (wires, metallurgy) – generators, etc.).

3 Predict the longer term impact on the communities of the use of the technologies described.

Thinking and analytical skills

'The world's environmental problems are created by major technological projects, such as hydroelectric dams, oil drilling, coal mining and nuclear power generation, and will only be resolved by a return to small-scale community projects.' Critically evaluate the arguments for and against this view, using material from the two extracts above.

(ii) Is scientific and technological progress always for the best?

Links: 2.6 (i); 3.3 (iv); 4.16 **Key skills:** C3.1a

Introduction

The apparently accelerating development of new technologies, the progress of science, and the accessibility and manipulation of inconceivably vast amounts of information are not seen by everybody as a good thing.

Background

There are many examples of the development of new scientific understanding and the development of new technologies that supplant old. For ordinary people, this means that jobs using old technologies may cease to exist and new skills must be learnt.

Just look at how manual labour has changed:

- Manual digging is a simple technology, although the tools that have been invented to support it exploit the basic principles of physics in clever ways. It developed, presumably, when man discovered how to cultivate food that previously had been searched for. The plough, which utilised the muscle power of an animal rather than a human, although physically liberating, required little extra skill. It greatly helped the cultivation of land, however, and the production of food, possibly in amounts which could then be traded.
- Digging the foundations for buildings for ceremonial and religious purposes may have required many workers, but greater numbers could always solve this – more digging just needs more diggers. Digging canals and the foundations for railway lines would, in the end, improve communications and trade.
- The invention of various types of steam engine, at first tied to one place, but eventually mobile, changed this situation completely. Mechanisation meant that more could be accomplished in a shorter time and less labour was needed. The mechanisation of agriculture profoundly affected the distribution of labour and the foundations of English rural life throughout the twentieth century.
- Things have moved on again and now British and European agriculture is undergoing a chemical and genetic revolution that seems to be having as profound an effect as mechanisation once had. The 'chemicalisation' of agriculture is dependent upon but, at the same time, has reinforced a chemical industry which is multinational and which has been criticised for promoting artificial rather than 'natural' ways of improving food production, to the suggested detriment of the health and safety of the population at large.

The majority of people go along with change, perhaps reluctantly, but usually believing that they have little option. There are always others, however, who want to slow down innovation and resist new methods. This will happen for as long as we are capable of thinking up new explanations and new ways of doing things. This tension is not solely the fault of scientists or technologists, who generally are seeking to find ways to do things that will help humankind.

A utilitarian view of science would suggest that it tackles problems that contribute beneficially to society. If so, progress (in the sense of things becoming better) would be guaranteed. Unfortunately, the world, particularly that part occupied by humans, is complicated and very unpredictable. Even things which seem to be good, like spraying tropical areas with **DDT** to kill the mosquitoes that transmit **malaria**, and which show immediate success, turn to ashes when we find that DDT is accumulated in the bodies of all organisms, with various adverse effects.

Glossary

DDT: an insecticide widely used in the mid-twentieth century, but now banned because of its toxic effects

malaria: a very serious disease of warm and tropical regions caused by a blood parasite transferred by mosquitoes

monoculture: farming systems in which a large area is used to grow a single type of crop plant

Issues to be discussed

- How should science and technological activity be controlled?
- A scientific discovery cannot be undiscovered. Is this a justification for slowing or halting scientific progress?

Where now?

James Lovelock, *The Ages of Gaia*, Oxford University Press, 1995

www.ussc.alltheweb.com/go/1/H/news.bbc.co.uk/hi/english/static/events/reith_2000/

www.princeofwales.gov.uk/speeches/speeches_index_5.html

www.sunday-times.co.uk/news/pages/sti/2000/05/21/stinwcopn01002.html

What do you think?

'What chance is there of working with the grain of nature?'

In this technology driven age it is all too easy for us to forget that mankind is a part of nature and not apart from it. And that this is why we should seek to work with the grain of nature in everything we do, for the natural world is, as the economist Herman Daly puts it, 'the envelope that contains, sustains and provisions the economy, not the other way round'. So which argument do you think will win – the living world as one or the world made up of random parts, the product of mere chance, thereby providing the justification for any kind of development? This, to my mind, lies at the heart of what we call sustainable development. We need, therefore, to rediscover a reference for the natural world, irrespective of its usefulness to ourselves – to become more aware in Philip Sherrard's words of 'the relationship of interdependence, interpenetration and reciprocity between God, Man and Creation'.

Above all, we should show greater respect for the genius of nature's designs, rigorously tested and refined over millions of years. This means being careful to use science to understand how nature works, not to change what nature is, as we do when genetic manipulation seeks to transform a process of biological evolution into something altogether different. The idea that the different parts of the natural world are connected through an intricate system of checks and balances which we disturb at our peril is all too easily dismissed as no longer relevant.

So, in an age when we're told that science has all the answers, what chance is there for working with the grain of nature? As an example of working with the grain of nature, I happen to believe that if a fraction of the money currently being invested in developing genetically manipulated crops were applied to understanding and improving traditional systems of agriculture, which have stood the all-important test of time, the results would be remarkable. There is already plenty of evidence of just what can be achieved through applying more knowledge and fewer chemicals to diverse cropping systems. These are genuinely sustainable methods and they are far removed from the approaches based on **monoculture** which lend themselves to large-scale commercial exploitation, and which Vandana Shiva condemned so persuasively and so convincingly in her lecture. Our most eminent scientists accept that there is still a vast amount that we don't know about our world and the life forms that inhabit it. As Sir Martin Rees, the Astronomer Royal, points out, it is complexity that makes things hard to understand, not size. In a comment which only an astronomer could make, he describes a butterfly as a more daunting intellectual challenge than the cosmos!

Others, like Rachel Carson, have eloquently reminded us that we don't know how to make a single blade of grass. And St. Matthew, in his wisdom, emphasised that not even Solomon in all his glory was arrayed as the lilies of the field. Faced with such unknowns it is hard not to feel a sense of humility, wonder and awe about our place in the natural order. And to feel this at all stems from that inner heartfelt reason which, sometimes despite ourselves, is telling us that we are intimately bound up in the mysteries of life and that we don't have all the answers. Perhaps even that we don't have to have all the answers before knowing what we should do in certain circumstances. As Blaise Pascal wrote in the seventeenth century, 'it is the heart that experiences God, not the reason'.

So do you not feel that, buried deep within each and every one of us, there is an instinctive, heartfelt awareness that provides – if we will allow it to – the most reliable guide as to whether or not our actions are really in the long-term interests of our planet and all the life it supports? This awareness, this wisdom of the heart, may be no more than a faint memory of a distant harmony, rustling like a breeze through the leaves, yet sufficient to remind us that the earth is unique and that we have a duty to care for it. Wisdom, empathy and compassion have no place in the empirical world yet traditional wisdom would ask 'without them are we truly human?' And it would be a good question. It was Socrates who, when asked for his definition of wisdom, gave as his conclusion, 'knowing that you don't know'.

From HRH The Prince of Wales BBC Reith Lecture 2000, news.bbc.co.uk/hi/english/static/events/reith_2000//

Activity

The topic of the Reith Lectures 2000 was 'Sustainable development'. Debate the proposition: 'Sustainable development is a contradiction in terms.'

Thinking and analytical skills

1 List the types of knowledge used in the passage and give examples of each.
2 Write in your own words the conclusion reached in the passage.
3 Describe the stages in the argument used to support the conclusion. Is the conclusion valid?

(iii) How do the media deal with scientific and technological change? Links: 2.4 (ii) Key skills: IT 3.1; IT 3.3

Introduction

The public are usually interested in scientific and technological matters, particularly when the topic is medical and perhaps more so when it is bizarre. The media feed this interest, with varying degrees of honesty and integrity. It is instructive to look at the headlines and points seized upon by different sections of the media.

Activity 1

The first successful attempt to clone a mammal – 'Dolly' the sheep – was a media event. The fact that cloning had taken place raised worries and concerns about the possibility of cloning humans. The following are headlines and brief extracts from websites that deal with the topic in different ways.

Government response to the report by the Human Genetics Advisory Commission and the Human Fertilisation and Embryology Authority on Cloning Issues in Reproduction, Science and Medicine

The government's position was made absolutely clear in the response by the minister for public health to a question in parliament on 26 June 1997 when she said, 'We regard the deliberate cloning of human beings as ethically unacceptable. Under United Kingdom law, cloning of individual humans cannot take place whatever the origin of the material and whatever technique is used.' This remains the government's position.

Source: www.doh.gov.uk/cloning.htm

Human cloning: technological cannibalism

We now stand at a crossroads. In 1967, Britain chose abortion and since then 5 million unborn children have died. In 1990, we chose human embryo experimentation and 110 000 tiny lives have been ended deliberately in the pursuit of scientific progress. In 1999, the government must decide whether or not to choose cloning. The temporary 6 months' moratorium that they have placed on cloning is likely only a stay of execution unless we act. It is, therefore, even more urgent that we do so.

Source; www.banneroftruth.co.uk/articles/technological_cannibalism.htm

Cloning Special Report
Everything you always wanted to know ...

Dolly was the first clone of an adult mammal ever born. Ever since Scottish scientists announced her birth, her life was closer to that of a rock superstar than that of a Finn Dorset sheep. Her cast-offs, a sweater knitted from her wool, is a treasured showpiece in a museum. The newspapers fell over themselves to dig out the slightest details of her life: her sexual liaisons made major news ('Dolly's baby's Bonnie – but who is her dad?'). And, to save her nerves, she was shielded from the glaring flashes of the paparazzi.

Now, in the fourth year of Dollymania, it seems a fair time to ask whether she was really worth all that fuss. And the answer, everyone seems to agree, is yes. Initially, the brouhaha was mostly based on shock – no-one really saw cloning adults as anything but an interesting premise for science fiction. Faced with the reality, biologist, doctors, lawyers, ethicists and religious leaders sat down and had a good think about how the world might change.

But as time goes by, the cloning technology that brought Dolly into the world has shown that it isn't a one-hit wonder. Researchers are producing clones from foetal cells with relative ease. Others have shown they can combine cloning and genetic engineering to produce cows and sheep that produce therapeutic proteins. There seems to be no doubt that our future is a future filled with clones.

Source: www.newscientist.com/nsplus/insight/clone/clone.html

Randolfe H. Wicker: world's first pro-cloning activist

Mr. Wicker founded the world's first activist pro-human-cloning group, the Clone Rights United Front (http://www.humancloning.org/users/randy/index.html) on 26 February 1997, immediately after the announcement of Dolly's birth. He organised the first demonstration in support of human cloning on Saturday, 1 March 1997, which was covered live by WABC-AM radio. He spoke out against the National Bioethics Advisory Commission's proposed ban of human cloning on nationally televised newscasts and has been the subject of coverage by the New York Times Sunday Magazine and USA Today. He has appeared on the Leeza Show, the Bey Buchanan Radio Show, the Alan Combs Radio Show and the Curtis Sliwa Radio Show. Mr. Wicker is on the board of directors of the Human Cloning Foundation. As an unpaid volunteer, he handles press inquiries and helps monitor the Human Cloning Foundation's message boards.

Source: www.humancloning.org

Cloning – not so new, after all

I was sitting in the lab busily cloning, the way you do, when the news broke. Someone had cloned a sheep. The wires were soon hot, which happens if you leave the computer too near the lamp, and the whole of human ethics was being thrown into the melting-pot. This, said the media, introduced the new age of molecular genetics and the end of civilisation as we know it.

Source: *Boz* magazine, 47: 14-15, March 1998; www.sciences.demon.co.uk/zclone1.htm

Issues to be discussed:

- What types of knowledge do these different responses draw on?
- What standpoint does each source adopt in relation to cloning?
- Does each source present a valid argument? (You may want to follow the link, if possible, to see more of the original source material.)

Activity 2

- Choose a science news item, which may come from a newspaper, magazine, TV, radio, or online version of any of these.
- Obtain clips, extracts and pictures from as many different sources as you can.
- Analyse each source in terms of:
  - the level and validity of the information it provides,
  - any bias in favour of a political body or any other interest group,
  - the integrity of any arguments it uses,
  - stereotyping of scientists/technologists,
  - appeals to the emotional side of its audience.
- Present your analysis in an informative graphic format.
- Which sources are most reliable and informative?
- What general conclusions about the media and science can you come to as a result of your study?

Where now? P. Trowler, *Investigating Mass Media*, Collins, 1996

Thinking and analytical skills For the activity you have chosen, list and compare the types of knowledge used in each source.

(i) What are 'social values'?

Links: 3.1 (ii); 3.1 (iii) **Key skills:** C3.1b; N3.1; N3.2; C3.3

Introduction

Every human society develops its own distinctive culture. In one sense 'culture' describes 'higher things of the mind' like art, music, or literature. More broadly it defines the total way of life of a society or group, including all aspects of learned, rather than **innate**, behaviour. 'Culture' defines how values, norms and beliefs are expressed.

Background

Values, the abstract ideals that define **fundamental standards**, have considerable impact on the social conduct and behaviour expected of individuals as members of a social group. Such values, formalised as 'norms', are definitive principles or rules governing behaviour. Failure to observe those norms is to reject society's values and may result in **sanctions** to encourage conformity.

Socialisation is how values are transmitted between generations and through which behaviour is modified. Human behaviour is shaped through social experiences.

Primary socialisation is small scale, personal and face-to-face. It is largely the responsibility of family and friends. Primary values like love, sharing and loyalty are learned.

Secondary socialisation is larger scale, involves groups as well as individuals and is less personal and more formally organised. Values learned (like honesty, respect for life and awareness of differences between right and wrong) are of a more general nature and are fitted into a wider context.

It is claimed that, although each culture has its own separately developed value system, there are certain 'universal values' found in some form in most societies. These develop from 'cultural universals'. However, when examined, there can be significant differences in meaning given to these universals.

Individual values exist alongside societal values. Social conflict may occur when differences develop between them. People may accept societal values in theory; yet in practice break them. An individual may accept:

- that drink driving is wrong, but personally may do it,
- that theft is wrong, but take an employer's property,
- equal opportunities but personally be discriminatory.

Values can change over time within a society:

- women were inferior, but today have legal equality,
- old people had high status, but today are marginalised,
- the mentally impaired were believed special, as 'touched by God', but today are understood to suffer physical or psychological disorder,
- marriage was 'for life', but today divorce is socially acceptable and repeat marriage commonplace.

Values may differ between societies. In some:

- female infanticide is acceptable and justified but is illegal and unthinkable in Western society,
- foreigners, as 'barbarians' are excluded from society, but Western society is multiracial and multicultural,
- **polygyny** is practised, but monogamous relations are the Western legal norm,
- kittens, dogs and song-birds are eaten, a practice rejected in Western societies,
- orthodox Jews refuse pork, while pork is acceptable to Hindus who reject beef.

Globalisation and the mass media, has led to greater awareness of differing beliefs, attitudes and behaviour, and has reduced variations.

Glossary

innate: inborn, natural, genetically inherited

fundamental standards: primary or original standards of behaviour from which others are developed

sanctions: any means, whether positive or negative, which enforces a code of values

polygyny: a form of plural marriage where a man has more than one wife

Issues to be discussed

- Does it matter if an individual does not always accept all of society's values?
- Is it better to be 'true to yourself' than to conform to behaviour patterns with which you disagree?
- Are there universal values? If so, what are they and how can they be identified?
- Identify examples of social values that have changed.

Where now?

D. Anderson (ed.), *The Loss of Virtue: Moral Confusion and Social Disorder in Britain and America*, The Social Affairs Unit, 1992

A. Gidden, *Sociology*, Polity Press, 1993

www.un.org/rights50/decla.htm

sosig.ac.uk/

What do you think?

'Social values reflect the opinions of dominant groups rather than the majority.' How far can this view be justified?

A society that is multiracial is likely to enjoy civil peace only if it is not at the same time radically multicultural. By contrast, the multiculturalist demands that minority cultures - however these are defined - be afforded rights and privileges denied the mainstream culture. In effect it delegitimates the very idea of a common culture. It thereby reinforces the radical liberal view that a common allegiance can be sustained by subscription to abstract principles, without the support of a common culture. Indeed, the very idea of a common culture comes to be seen as an emblem of oppression. Accordingly, the large healthy pressures on minority cultures to integrate themselves into the mainstream culture are represented as inevitably the expression of prejudice, racial or otherwise, and so condemnable.

We reach a crux now in the idea and practice of toleration - its bearing on the idea and fact of prejudice. The idea of prejudice is, perhaps, not as simple as it looks. The essence of prejudice as a practice seems to be the discriminatory treatment of people on grounds of their belonging to a group of some sort, where this is not relevant to the matter at issue. Prejudicial law enforcement or prejudicial hiring policies would then be practices in which the treatment of people correlated not with relevant facts about them as individuals, but merely with their belonging to a certain group. Now there can be no doubt that prejudice of this sort can be a great evil against which there can, and ought to be, legal remedies. A consistent rejection of policies based on prejudice would be one that was blind to race, gender and sexual orientation, rather than one that merely reversed earlier or pre-existing prejudicial policies.

From John Gray, 'Toleration and the Currently Offensive Implication of Judgement', quoted in D. Anderson (ed.), *The Loss of Virtue: Moral Confusion and Social Disorder in Britain and America*, The Social Affairs Unit, 1992

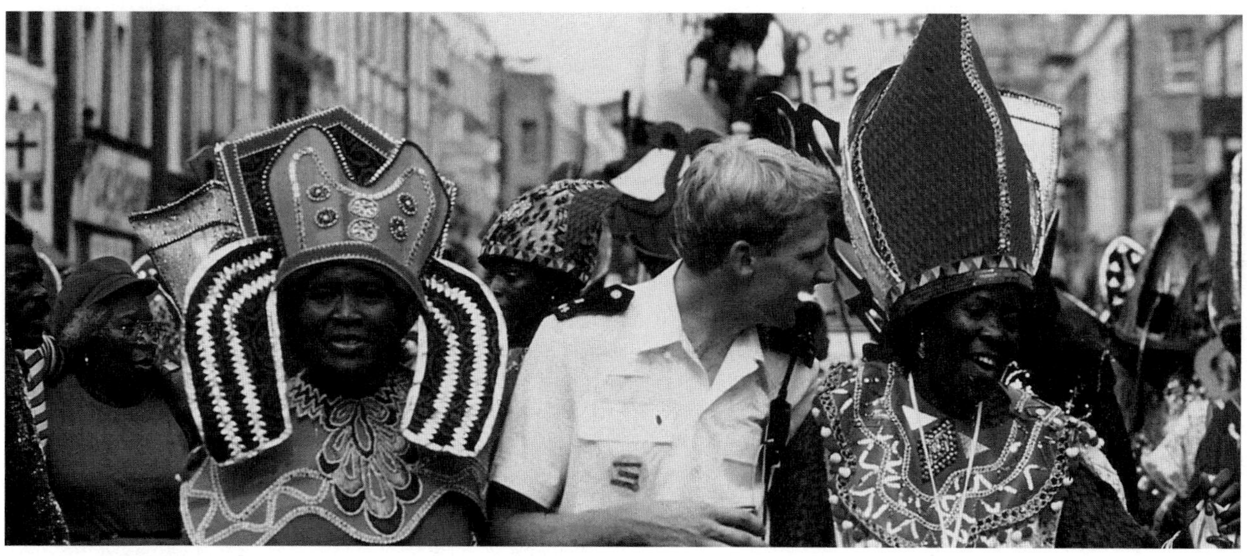

The Notting Hill Carnival: multicultural harmony can exist in Britain.

Activities

1. Choose two examples of what you would regard as 'universal values'. Make a presentation to justify your choice.
2. Conduct a survey of at least 20 different people to identify which present-day values the majority would most like to change. Present your findings in written and graphic or tabular form.
3. Debate the opinion that each person is entitled to develop an individual value system, without reference to the opinions of others.
4. Choose a current issue and examine the way in which it is dealt with by different newspapers and/or television programmes. Describe and explain any differences you have noticed.

Thinking and analytical skills

1. How far, and how effectively, does Gray justify his argument?
2. Do the values shown in the photograph conflict with or confirm the judgements in the passage?
3. How reliable is the photograph as evidence of shared values? Explain your answer.

(ii) How and why do social values change?

Links: 1.1 (iv); 1.3 (v); 3.1 (i); 3.1 (iii); 3.1 (v); 4.12 **Key skills:** N3.1; N3.2; N3.3; WO3.1; WO3.3; WO3.3; C3.2; C3.1a

Introduction

Each culture has its own distinctive values, but few are permanently fixed. Values change in response to pressure or circumstances. Members of small-scale societies, revolving around a common lifestyle, share the same values. In larger, more complex industrial societies, values may vary between groups and sub-cultures, often resulting in value conflict.

Background

Religion has traditionally influenced the development, transmission and defence of values. Religious beliefs have offered answers to '**life-questions**', defined laws, promoted moral teaching, established social structure and imposed sanctions for nonconformity. It provided a link between the supernatural and natural worlds. **Ritual** and ceremony protected society against disaster and loss of supplies.

Religion's role in supporting values has faced challenges from two different directions. The expansion of scientific knowledge has provided 'natural' answers to 'life-questions'. For many, this has reduced the need for supernatural authority. Multicultural and multireligious influences have challenged the unique authority held when there was only a single religion to which most belonged.

Science has, for many people, replaced religion as the supreme authority. By offering explanations of naturally occurring **phenomena**, it has undermined religious authority based on unique access to the supernatural. Humanity has replaced 'god' as the supreme authority for, and source of, values. Religion often was a conservative force, maintaining the continuity of a commonly accepted value system, but humanism and science encouraged social change and adaptation. Consequently different value systems have become increasingly common in society.

Economic circumstances can influence the development of values and value consensus, encouraging change to meet new situations. Simple small-scale societies, which depend on mutual support for survival, will value cooperation and the subordination of individuality. Societies with few material possessions may not place great significance on property ownership. Societies in which wisdom and experience are essential for survival are more likely to respect age than those marked by rapid technological change. Groups facing external threats may value highly military skill and leadership, while complex societies may give prestige to administrators. Some claim that Britain, which placed little value on childhood when infant mortality rates were high, has recently become increasingly child-centred.

Pressure groups and the media can encourage change. They seek to persuade society and government to modify existing values, often by changing the law, in order to gain general acceptance of alternatives. This can be illustrated by the anti-smoking campaign. Smoking is still practised, but most people accept that it is harmful and should not occur in public buildings. Leaders of campaigns for changed values are sometimes called moral crusaders.

Examples of changing values are:

- acceptance of alternatives to marriage,
- attitudes to abortion and divorce,
- employment opportunities for married women,
- care in the community for the elderly and impaired,
- entitlement to the franchise,
- equal opportunities (especially race and gender),
- punishments appropriate for different crimes,
- using medical knowledge to maintain damaged life.

Glossary

life-questions: issues, such as the origin of life, which affect people in all societies

ritual: form of procedure or activity required in a religious or other solemn ceremony

phenomena: something that appears or is perceived but whose cause may be uncertain

norms: a standard pattern or type of behaviour

nebulous: cloudy, hazy, vague or indistinct

Issues to be discussed

- Can society survive without shared common values?
- How has the development of a multicultural society in Britain contributed to changes in society's values?
- Does society need religious belief in order to justify its value system?
- Should one group be able to force its views on society?
- What values are in process of change today? Will it make any real difference to ordinary individuals?

Where now?

Francis Fukuyama, *The Great Disruption: Human Nature and the Reconstitution of Social Order*, Profile Books, 1999

D. Anderson (ed.), *The Loss of Virtue: Moral Confusion and Social Disorder in Britain and America*, The Social Affairs Unit, 1992

sosig.ac.uk/

www.stbrn.ac.uk

What do you think?

Do you agree that value changes are 'stimulated by technological and economic developments'? Justify your answer, referring to at least one change in values occurring in the last 30 years.

Crime and distrust can be linked to changes that have taken place in family structure. That the family has undergone such dramatic change in the past 30 years is obviously related to the two major upheavals of the 1960s and the 1970s: the sexual and feminist revolutions. Many people regard these developments as purely voluntary cultural choices. The Right decries a decline in family values, while the Left sees traditional **norms** as a matter of men who 'just don't get it'. These value changes were stimulated, however, by important technological and economic developments related to the end of the industrial era. It is not that people don't have free will or make moral choices. But moral choices take place within a technological and economic framework that makes certain outcomes more likely in some periods than others.

From Francis Fukuyama, *The Great Disruption: Human Nature and the Reconstitution of Social Order*, Profile Books, 1999, p. 92

Today, there is a babble of confusion on moral issues among the members of the middle-classes, and they can no longer offer the kind of moral leadership they successfully provided in the past. A vociferous middle-class minority has made straightforward and immediate moral issues appear complicated by treating them as social rather than moral questions. Yet, at the same time, the members of this minority have responded with simple-minded moral hysteria to distant and complex problems such as acid rain, the culling of seals, or the owning of tobacco shares by charitable organisations. Where their ancestors saw the just as being those who gave others their due according to their moral deserts and chose civility over brutality, the members of today's middle-class moral minority have instead elevated the **nebulous** concept of social justice.

From D. Anderson (ed.), *The Loss of Virtue, Moral Confusion and Social Disorder in Britain and America*, The Social Affairs Unit, 1992

Have the values of young people changed since the 1950s?

Activities

1 Conduct a survey to identify values that have changed over the last 30 years. Use your results to draw up a questionnaire to be completed by at least 50 people, representing a range of age groups. Present your findings in tabular form.

2 In a group, discuss and identify five present-day values that you would like to change. Design a poster to show the changes you would like to make, and your reasons for doing so.

3 How have ethnic minorities influenced British values?

4 Has the decline in importance of religious belief made any impact on values? Explain and justify your answer.

5 In a group, add to the list of values you think have changed in the UK in the last 30 years. Suggest reasons why these changes have occurred.

Thinking and analytical skills

1 Identify and compare the different types of knowledge and argument used in the two passages.

2 Which of the two conclusions represented in the passages can most easily be justified?

3 To what extent does the photograph support the view that no values are fixed forever?

(iii) Is old age a problem?

Links: 3.1 (ii); 3.1 (iv); 4.6; 4.7 **Key skills:** N3.2; C3.1a; N3.3; C3.3

Introduction

'Old age' is the final stage in an individual's life. The 'fact' of old age is biological since we all age in the natural course of life. However, many of the features of old age are social in origin. The onset of old age, and the development of those characteristics and attitudes associated with it vary through history and between individuals. Most people understand the term old age and can describe qualities associated with it. But not all elderly people seem old.

Background

In traditional societies and in Britain in earlier times, elderly people customarily had considerable social status. Wisdom and experience were respected and people, especially men of great age, were listened to and generally obeyed. They were usually heads of households and owners of whatever property existed. In such societies there was no retirement simply through age. Withdrawal from active economic or social life was most frequently due to mental or physical infirmity. Becoming old was marked by changes in physical abilities and appearance rather than simply chronological age.

In modern Western society the position is usually very different. The elderly are often marginalised, have low social status and frequently have limited resources. Most Western societies have a strongly dominant youth culture, where even the middle-aged are often regarded as having little of worth to contribute to society or the economy. Being old is marked legally by reaching retirement age and has nothing to do with physical or mental ability. In politics and the law, for example, elderly people continue to play an active role long after retirement age.

Historical reasons have contributed significantly to this development. In 1908 the first old–age pension was paid to the elderly poor. It was never intended to provide comfort or **self-sufficiency**. Rather its purpose was to supplement incomes so that families could look after their elderly and infirm members. Since then, Britain has adopted an unwritten and unofficial policy of removing the elderly from paid employment in order to create opportunities for the young. The elderly, having little economic contribution to make, have been treated increasingly as second-class citizens.

Family changes have also contributed to this changed position. In many societies old people were an essential and integral part of the family economy. When too old to work, they often acted as child minders. The decline of extended families and emergence of **nuclear families** has meant that many elderly people have become sidelined and isolated from their children.

Demographic changes have resulted in an increased number of elderly people in the population. As a result many people perceive old age as a problem.

- 1900 **life expectancy** at birth c. 40 years
- 1931 life expectancy at birth 60 years (men 58, women 62)
- 1971 life expectancy at birth 72 years (men 69, women 75)
- 1990 life expectancy at birth 74 years (men 72, women 77)
- 1997 life expectancy at birth 77 years (men 74, women 79)

Life expectancy has increased, but **life span** has remained broadly the same. The UK population over 65 in:

- 1921 fewer than 3 million (less than 7 per cent)
- 1961 6.3 million (12 per cent of population)
- 1981 8.5 million (15 per cent of population)
- 1991 over 9.2 million (16 per cent of population)
- 2021 estimated 12.4 million (20 per cent of population)

Glossary

self-sufficiency: independence; being able to provide for self without requiring help from outside agencies

nuclear family: the structure often seen as the universal family unit, consisting of parents and dependent children

demographic: dealing with the statistical study of human populations (including birth, marriage and death rates)

hedonistic: the belief that a lifestyle based on pleasure is the chief good

life expectancy: the length of life an individual might expect at birth, granted personal circumstances

life span: the length of time between birth and death that the longest surviving member of a cohort might experience

Issues to be discussed

- What are the arguments for and against equalising retirement age for men and women at 65?
- Should retirement be optional rather than compulsory?
- Why have attitudes to old age changed?
- What are the advantages and disadvantages of a 'youth culture'?
- Why is old age so often regarded as a problem?
- Why has life expectancy increased?

Where now?

P. Laslett, *A Fresh Map of Life: the Emergence of the Third Age*, Weidenfield and Nicholson, 1989

www.helptheaged.org.uk   sosig.esrc.bris.ac.uk   www.acc.org.uk

What do you think?

Critically examine the way in which an increasingly ageing population affects society's values.

Will a society which has assumed the right to kill infants in the womb have difficulty in assuming the right to kill other human beings, especially older adults who are judged unwanted, deemed imperfect physically or mentally, or considered a possible social nuisance?

The next candidates for arbitrary reclassification as non-persons are the elderly. This will become increasingly so as the proportion of the old and weak in relation to the young and strong becomes abnormally large. The imbalance will cause many of the young to perceive the old as a cramping nuisance in the **hedonistic** life-style they claim as their right. As the demand for affluence continues and the economic crunch gets greater, the amount of compassion that the legislature and the courts will have for the old does not seem likely to be significant.

If we oppose euthanasia, we must also share the weight of caring for lonely or incapacitated older people who are not terminally ill. Our concern is more than not killing the elderly and the ill. It is giving them real life. Of course, there must be some facilities that care for the terminally ill. But, as long as possible the old, infirm and dying should be given the chance to be really alive in the midst of the whole spectrum of life. It becomes our responsibility when we quite properly say, 'Euthanasia is wrong'.

We must be realistic. The alternatives we have discussed will demand a high price. They will cost each of us some of our personal peace and affluence. But we must do them – first of all, because they are right. And, second, it will be a sharing of the burdens of life, and one day it will be our turn to be helped – and we will be glad when we are.

If we sit back and do nothing, our mere passivity and apathy will lead to actively evil results. As people we are only as good as our deep inner principles.

From Schaeffer and Koop, *Whatever Happened to the Human Race?*, Marshall Morgan and Scott, 1975, pp. 68–69; 95

Too old to live or too young to die?

Activities

1. Using the statistics on page 124 construct appropriate graphs to show:
   a changing life expectancy for men and women
   b the proportion of the population over 65 in 1921; 1961; 1981; 1991 and 2021
   c comment on any changes you identify.
2. Debate the opinion that 'old age is a state of mind rather than of chronological age'.
3. Construct a questionnaire to identify the attitudes of different groups of people to becoming old. Ask a sample of at least 30 people, representing 4 different age groups to complete the questionnaire. Analyse the responses and present your findings in tabular and written form.
4. What is meant by the 'arbitrary reclassification as non–persons' of the elderly?

Thinking and analytical skills

1. What types of knowledge do the authors of the passage use to justify their argument?
2. Identify and comment on any fallacies in the argument they present.
3. To what extent do the social values shown in the photograph support the conclusion of the passage?

(iv) Can we afford old age?

Links: 3.1 (i); 3.1 (iii); 3.1 (v); 4.7 **Key skills:** N3.2; N3.3; IT3.1; C3.1b;IT3.3

Introduction

It is often mistakenly assumed that all old people belong to a single **homogenous**, disadvantaged group. Conveniently the elderly can be divided into three **chronological** sections. These are: early old age, (65 – 75); late old age (75+); and extreme old age (100+). Although the elderly are expected to remain at about 16 per cent of the population, the proportion aged over 75 will increase from about 4 per cent to 9 per cent. The number of **centenarians** is increasing by 7 per cent per year.

Background

Retirement age in Britain is 60 for women and 65 for men, although from 2010 it will be equalised at 65 to stop discrimination. Retired people are usually economically inactive and unproductive. In the past, retirement generally came through ill health, but today it is usually determined by age, rather than physical condition.

Economic changes, including reduced income and changed lifestyle, are inevitable for many. Some retain a large income through investments, occupational pensions and savings, but most pensioners have less than half the average UK income and 15 per cent live in poverty, dependent on state support. This economic situation reduces social status and changes spending patterns. Average expenditure on essentials is about 40 per cent of income, but they cost married pensioners 53 per cent and single female pensioners 60 per cent of income.

Social issues may be more important than economic. Age Concern claims that the head of one-third of all households is over 60, while one-sixth consists of a single person over pensionable age and only 13 per cent of pensioners live with people other than their partner.

Commonly used terminology for the elderly reflects disrespect and lack of social status. Even the term 'senior citizen' implies lower status. Retirement brings changed routines. Lives that, throughout employment, were tightly structured must be adjusted to new patterns. Knowledge, skills and experience are often no longer required or valued. Old age can bring loneliness through loss of relationships with former colleagues and the death of partners, relatives and friends. Many experience more ill-health than during their working lives and restrict their activities through fear.

The cost of old age is high. Increased numbers of old people have been matched by reduced numbers in the workforce, meaning that a declining number of workers must pay for an increasing proportion of longer living elderly. In the short term this has been balanced by a reduced birth rate, which requires less expenditure on the young. However in the longer term fewer people must pay increasing costs.

Elderly people are a significant client group for health and social workers. This increases employment opportunities and costs. Care of the elderly absorbs an increasingly large share of National Income. In 1985 the government, recognising potential economic problems, changed the state pension scheme to encourage increased use of private schemes.

Ageism is often unintentional, but sees old age as a problem because of:

- changing value systems linked to fear of death,
- declining belief in afterlife,
- the emergence of a dominant youth culture,
- resentment at perceived costs of providing for the elderly, while also saving for their own future,
- doubt as to whether age is a biological or social problem,
- concern that state provision will be inadequate.

Earlier retirement may alter attitudes and increasing numbers may raise the political and economic power of the elderly.

Glossary

homogeneous: made up of parts that are all the same
chronological: an order fixed by date, time or age
centenarians: people who are aged 100 years, or more
ageism: behaving negatively simply on the grounds of age
mortality: the human state in being subject to death and dying
superfluity: an extra, unnecessary amount

Issues to be discussed

- Should the state be responsible for supporting the elderly or should individuals provide for themselves?
- How far are 'the problems of old age' matters of perception rather than of reality?
- Could national income spent on supporting the elderly be used more effectively to help the young or reduce taxes?
- Should there be a legal limit to the length of life?

Where now?

P. Laslett, *A Fresh Map of Life: the Emergence of the Third Age*, Weidenfield and Nicholson, 1989
G. E. Fennell, C. Phillipson and I. Evers, *The Sociology of Old Age*, 1994
www.helptheaged.org.uk www.statistics.gov.uk www.acc.org.uk

What do you think?

'Some have questioned the morality of devoting large resources to seeking to extend the lives of the elderly for what must be relatively short periods of time.' (DHSS 1976) To what extent do you agree?

People in advanced societies today are the first population to exist in which almost every individual has a chance of full experience of the world, full in the sense of being in it for as long as they are capable of living. How are we going to use this sudden, unprecedented, unanticipated release from **mortality**? How are we to conduct ourselves now that all of us can expect to live out something like the full natural span, whatever that may be?

In so far as this challenge has been recognised at all, the response has been one of fear and alarm, or so it seems to me. Instead of so rearranging our affairs, and so dividing up our lives, that we can begin to realise the full potential human experience for the first time in human history, we have taken fright. At the moment all that we seem able to see is the ever growing number of failing elderly people who weigh upon the individuals who support them. Ageing is seen as a burden on society at large because resources have to be found to give older people incomes, provide for their ever failing health, to maintain institutions for those who cannot be supported otherwise.

This sad story, which we perpetually repeat to ourselves, has a plot, which reaches a climax in the 1990s. The number of elderly, and especially of the very elderly, is growing very fast. Since they are living longer, maintaining them is becoming ever more expensive. Even providing them with company gets more difficult since the numbers of young are decreasing while the numbers of old are increasing. Our work force is ageing rapidly, losing its younger members and being unable or unwilling to retain its **superfluity** of older ones. Europe and the West are growing old and will never be young again.

From P. Laslett, *A Fresh Map of Life: the Emergence of the Third Age*, Weidenfield and Nicolson, 1989, p. 1

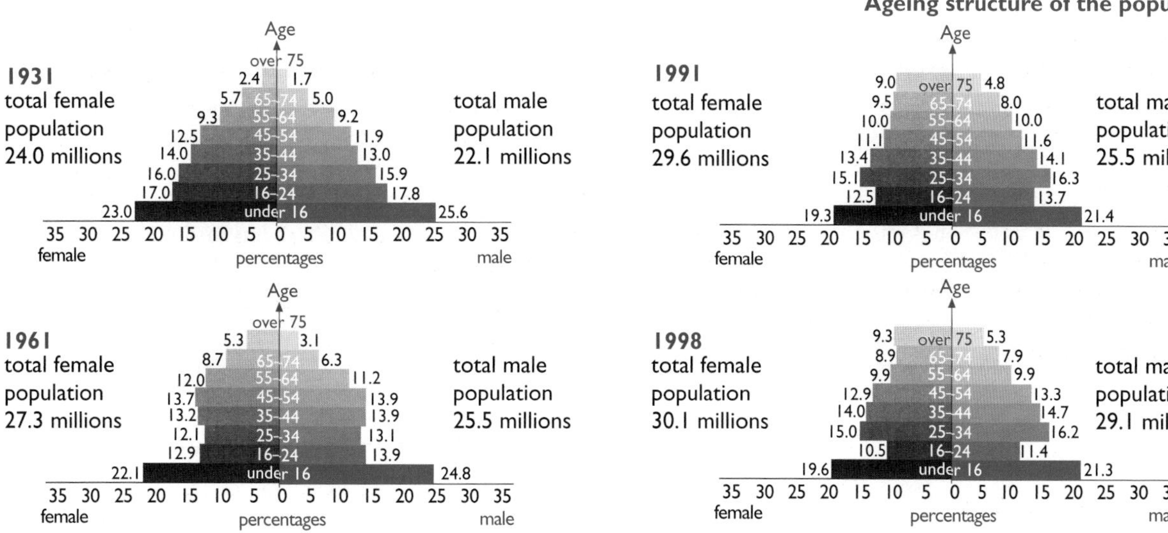

Source: *Social Trends 1995*, Office for National Statistics; www.statistics.gov.uk

Activities

1 Using the information in the graphs:
   a Draw line graphs to show population changes for males and females in each of the age group categories.
   b Calculate the percentage of the total population aged over 65 in 1961, 1981 and estimate that for 2021.
   c Show two other ways of giving the information contained in the graphs to show and compare the proportion of each age group.
   d Estimate the total expected population for 2011 and 2021.
2 Make a presentation on provisions for the elderly.
3 Assuming working life is from 18 to 65 years for both males and females, calculate the number and proportion of the total remaining population in Britain for 1951, 1981 and 2011.
4 Research the cost of one month's care for an elderly couple.
5 Investigate the proposals of each of the major political parties to deal with issues relating to age.
6 Debate the proposal that 'as a country we cannot afford to provide for the social and economic needs of the elderly'.

Thinking and analytical skills

1 Identify the stages in the argument presented by Laslett. How effectively is his conclusion justified?
2 What additional evidence might **a** strengthen his argument and **b** undermine it?

(v) Is disability a social or a personal issue?

Links: 3.1 (ii); 3.1 (i); 3.1 (vii) 4.6; 4.8 **Key skills:** C3.3; N3.1; N3.2; N3.3; IT3.1

Introduction

'Disability' describes a wide range of physical and mental conditions experienced by human beings. It is applied to restrictions resulting from **impairment** which prevent or restrict a person from behaving in a manner accepted as normal. The term also describes restrictions placed on individuals by the socially constructed environment, which is unsuited to the needs of impaired people. In both senses it can be a source of discrimination and inequality.

Background

In 1991 the United Nations estimated that 10 per cent of the world's population (about 500 million people) experienced some form of impairment, while almost 25 per cent of the total population were adversely affected. 60 per cent of the disabled live in the developed world but 20 per cent experience disability as a result of **malnutrition**.

Fourteen per cent of the UK's over 16 population suffer impairment. Twelve per cent of people aged 65 to 69 are disabled, but the figure rises to 80 per cent of those over 75. Often people with disabilities are treated as a homogeneous group. In fact there are just as many variations and differences as are to be found in the total population.

Traditionally the disabled were looked after by their own **extended families**. In extreme cases help came from the church or charity. The Industrial Revolution resulted in many social and economic changes. Large numbers left the country to find work in newly developing industrial towns. The old family structure broke down and was unable to care adequately for disabled members. Increasingly it was left to the state to cater for their needs through **workhouses**.

People who previously were included in society became increasingly excluded. Many disabilities were seen as medical rather than social issues and large numbers were institutionalised, being allowed only limited access to mainstream areas.

This paternalistic attitude was designed to provide support and shelter for people who, regarded as inadequate, were believed to be incapable of living a 'normal' life. Almost inevitably this changed into one of protecting society from the disabled.

In the 1980s attitudes began to change. The 1981 Education Act provided for the inclusion in mainstream schools of children with various physical and learning disabilities. In 1995 the Conservative Government passed a Disability Discrimination Act. In 2000 the Labour government, acting on recommendations of the Disability Rights Task Force introduced legislation to ensure that 'no disabled child, student or adult should ever again be excluded from the best that education can offer or from the choices and opportunities that have long been taken for granted by others'.

The cost of disability is considerable. Society generally lacks understanding of impairment, mainly because of the long-term **segregation** of the disabled. This has fostered fear, embarrassment and often a feeling that the impaired are 'inferior'. These attitudes can perpetuate ongoing discrimination, seen in employment figures. In 1997 the official rate of unemployment for the disabled was 21.2 per cent compared to 7.6 per cent for the able bodied. This is often justified on the grounds that disability imposes restrictions on the capacity to work. However, employers often express satisfaction with the quality of work produced by the disabled. Prejudice, rather than inability, creates disability.

Glossary

impairment: being damaged or weakened

malnutrition: insufficient nutrition as a result of a poor or unbalanced or inadequate diet

extended family: a family or household consisting of three or more generations, or including aunts and uncles and their dependent offspring

workhouses: institutions set up to provide relief to the poor, unemployed and ill in the nineteenth century

segregation: isolation or separation from other groups

Issues to be discussed

- How far is there discrimination against disabled people?
- Should the law impose sanctions to enforce equal treatment for all people, irrespective of disabilities?
- How can the employment opportunities of the disabled be improved?
- Examine the view that people with impairments should be provided for as of right and not from charity.
- Why and to what extent are people frightened of those with disabilities? How can these perceptions be changed?

Where now?

disabilitynow.org.uk
www.disabledperson.com

What do you think?

'It is the attitude of 'normal' people and not physical or mental impairment which is disabling'. Do you think that this opinion is accurate today? Explain and justify your view.

A woman who tried to book a trip for eight wheelchair users on the London Eye was told that only four wheelchairs are allowed per ride and that each wheelchair user must ride in a separate 'pod'.

Kim Swift, who has multiple sclerosis, tried to book the trip in May for the Social Activities for People with Multiple Sclerosis group.

She was told that a maximum of two wheelchair users from any one group were allowed on one trip.

'As there were eight of us who use chairs, our ride, including the changeover time, would take over two hours,' said Ms Swift, 41. 'It's ridiculous. My partner and I are both wheelchair users, and because of this rule we can't share the experience of seeing London from the Eye together.'

A spokesperson for the London Eye said: 'We have had hundreds of wheelchair users on the Eye since it opened in March, including Stephen Hawking.'

Gwilym Morris, campaigns officer for disability charity Scope, said: 'This is massively discriminatory. The Eye is a top London attraction and it's ludicrous that groups of wheelchair users shouldn't be allowed to enjoy the ride in the same manner as anyone else.'

'Disability Now' news story; www.disabilitynow.org.uk/news_6.htm

Prejudice, not inability, creates disability.

Activities

1 Research the provision made in your school or college to give free access to all facilities to people with disabilities. Present your findings in a report, making recommendations for improvement.

2 Investigate the cost of providing and fitting a chair lift in the home of an elderly person who has difficulty in coping with stairs. You should obtain at least three different estimates. Make a report of your recommendations, including full costs for fitting and either purchase or hire.

3 Design a questionnaire to find out what facilities are required by people with either visual or physical impairment. Ask 50 people of mixed ages to complete the questionnaire. Analyse the responses and present them in appropriate graphic form with a written commentary.

4 Research the help available from the Social Services and voluntary organisations for carers of people with moderately severe disabilities.

Thinking and analytical skills

1 Identify the different types of knowledge illustrated in the passage.

2 To what extent does the photograph support or undermine the justification offered by the spokesperson for the London Eye?

(vi) Are men still more equal than women?

Links: 3.1 (i); 3.1 (v); 3.1 (vii) **Key skills:** IT3.3; N3.2; C3.2; C3.1a; N3.3; C3.3; IT3.1; IT3.2

Introduction

For most of its history British society has been male-dominated. Feminism developed as a reaction to this prevailing **ideology**. Attitudes have changed and in theory women are the equals of, and should be given the same opportunities as, men. This is not always true in practice.

Background

Although the feminist movement takes various forms and has a range of aims, it is broadly committed to social equality.

The Suffragette movement believed that inequality could be overcome if women were **enfranchised**. This aim was achieved in 1918, but did not result in any significant change in the social or economic position of most women.

The Women's Liberation Movement of the late 1960s was part of a much wider pressure for radical reform. It focused attention on social and economic disadvantages and **discrimination**. Parliament responded with laws designed to remove inequalities. These have helped to narrow the economic gap between men and women, to open up opportunities for women and change social attitudes and values. However many inequalities still remain.

Legislation has been passed to improve women's social position. Some seek deliberately to increase equality of opportunity; others have a broader purpose. Early reforms have been added to and developed in recent years.

- 1967 Abortion was legalised under certain conditions and, when linked with the introduction of the contraceptive pill, is seen as a major stage in establishing female ownership and control of their own bodies.
- 1969 Divorce Law made divorce simpler. The number of divorce petitions, especially those sought by women, has increased dramatically.
- 1970 Equal Pay Act made it illegal to pay men and women different rates for the same jobs. Employers often found it relatively easy to evade its restrictions.
- 1975 The Sex Discrimination Act made illegal the unfavourable treatment of women in education, work and other areas. The Equal Opportunities Commission was established to ensure that the law was enforced. In spite of several high profile cases the Commission has not succeeded in transforming society.
- 1975 EU Equal Pay Act applied the 1970 Law to work to which equal value was attached.
- 1976 Domestic Violence and Matrimonial Procedures Act gave greater protection to victims of domestic violence.

Today women and girls:

- achieve better results than boys at school,
- enter Higher Education, in increasing numbers,
- are three times as likely as men to care for elderly or disabled relatives,
- are less likely than men to vote,
- despite **positive discrimination** by the Labour Party, make up less than a fifth of 659 MPs,
- provide half the workforce, but remain disadvantaged in pay, promotion and access to senior posts,
- make up an increasingly large proportion of the poor, especially single mothers.

Legal changes may make patterns of behaviour more acceptable, but cannot change deep-seated attitudes or ensure that discrimination does not occur.

Glossary

ideology: any system of ideas underlying and informing social and political action; or a system of ideas that justifies the subordination of one group by another

enfranchised: admitting a person to the right to vote

positive discrimination: social policies encouraging favourable treatment of disadvantaged 'minority' groups

discrimination: treating a socially defined group differently to others because of membership of that group

Issues to be discussed

- In what ways are females still subject to discrimination? What steps need to be taken to overcome this?
- 'It is men not women who are now disadvantaged'. Do you agree?
- What is 'equality of opportunity'?
- Should all people be regarded as the 'same and equal' or 'equal but different'?
- Can positive discrimination ever be justified?

Where now?

www.emplaw.co.uk
www.eoc.org.uk
www.org/conferences/women.org.uk

What do you think?

To what extent is it fair to say that governments have failed to provide equality of opportunity for women?

The journey to Equality of Opportunity for women has not yet been completed. Progress is still needed to reduce the sex segregation of jobs, the low pay ghettos that it permits, and the waste of potential female skills that it entails. Such progress will run into the familiar obstacles if measures are not also taken to recognise, support and share the unpaid tasks needed to maintain and reproduce the population.

Measures to improve women's access to education, training and remunerative jobs need to be complemented by measures to give families more choice about the management of their unpaid responsibilities. Examples of measures to support parents would be increases and improvements in childcare, for pre-school children and those of school age; to make parental leave available to parents of both sexes; to recognise childcare as a legitimate work expense for tax and benefit purposes; and to encourage the participation of fathers in child-rearing. This last suggestion might be taken more seriously as the working week gets shorter and if the pay penalties for devoting time to caring were reduced. Women on the whole have not achieved an equal economic footing with men in British society and they will not achieve it universally overnight. Meanwhile, it would be a mistake for legislation on divorce, tax or pensions to assume that they had. Equitable treatments must be devised that recognise economic sacrifices (whether they have been made by men or women) as well as economic achievements.

It is not at all clear that further progress towards improving the economic status of women would precipitate the demise of the British family or the dreaded (by some) 'twilight of parenthood'. Effective progress for women involves changes which recognise the family responsibilities of paid workers of both sexes. This should, if anything, strengthen the family and encourage childbearing.

From H. Joshi, *'The Changing Form of Women's Economic Dependency'* in H. Joshi. (ed.), *Changing Population of Britain*, Blackwell, 1989, p.173

Statistical information on women's pay and hours of work compared to men

Average gross weekly earnings (full time)(£)	April 1997	
	Men	**Women**
United Kingdom	**407.3**	**296.2**
North-east	360.1	269.0
North-west (GOR) & Merseyside	386.4	277.4
North-west (GOR)	387.4	275.8
Merseyside	381.7	284.4
Yorkshire and the Humber	363.9	268.9
East Midlands	369.2	260.3
West Midlands	375.4	268.5
Eastern	399.5	295.9
London	541.3	386.3
South-east (GOR)	428.3	306.5
South-west	382.4	274.8
England	**414.0**	**301.3**
Wales	**363.5**	**269.0**
Scotland	**378.0**	**272.4**
Northern Ireland	**355.9**	**265.3**

Source: *Office for National Statistics*; www.statistics.gov.uk

Employees by gender and occupation 1991 and 1999 in the UK expressed as percentages of total

	Males		Females	
	1991	1999	1991	1999
Managers and administrators	16	19	8	11
Professional	10	11	8	10
Associate professional and technical	8	9	10	11
Clerical and secretarial	8	8	29	26
Craft and related	21	17	4	2
Personal and protective services	7	8	14	17
Selling	6	6	12	12
Plant and machine operatives	15	15	5	4
Other occupations	8	8	10	8
All employees (=100%) (millions)	11.8	12.4	10.1	10.8

Source: *Social Trends 2000 Pocket Book Edition – Labour Force Survey*, Office for National Statistics; www.statistics.gov.uk

Activities

1 Using the categories in the table above, collect examples of employment opportunities in each category from your local newspaper. Analyse your collection to identify any features that are common to employment in which:
a the majority of workers are men,
b the majority of workers are women,
c numbers of employees of both sexes are similar.

2 Debate the opinion that 'it is unfair that women, who have a greater life expectancy, can retire earlier than men'.

3 Investigate the examination results in your centre for the last 10 years. Draw appropriate graphs to show the trend in:
a all grade A–C results at GCSE,
b female grade A–C results at GCSE,
c male grade A–C results at GCSE,
Do the same for A level results and comment on any trends that you can identify.

4 Investigate how gender roles are shown on television or in magazines. Write a report about your findings.

Thinking and analytical skills

1 Identify the stages in Joshi's argument.
2 To what extent can her conclusions be justified or challenged?

(vii) Is Britain a multicultural or multiracial society?

Links: 1.1 (iv); 3.1 (i); 3.1 (v); 3.1 (vi); 4.1 **Key skills:** C3.3; C3.1a; N3.1; N3.3; IT3.1; IT3.2

Introduction

Prejudice against minority groups is a common feature in human society. It is often ingrained and based on deep-seated, if unjustified, fears. It can exist under any circumstances and does not depend on obvious physical differences, although where these are present it may flourish. Prejudice often leads to open persecution of minorities and can be associated with ideological claims that the dominant group is superior to others.

Background

Immigration is a consistent feature of Britain's history. It peaked between about 1950 and 1975 with an influx of people from the Caribbean and southern Asia (the New Commonwealth).

Ethnic groups are often distinguished by shared history, language, culture, customs, beliefs, traditions and religion. Minorities may think of themselves as culturally different and seek to establish and maintain group boundaries to preserve their distinctive character. Ethnic differences are learned, but people perceive them as deep rooted.

A **pluralist society** exists if several culturally distinctive groups share the same social and economic structure. Such differences may be associated with inequalities of wealth, power and social status. Minorities can experience disadvantage through discrimination if the dominant group has rights and opportunities denied to others.

Physical and social separation from the larger community may cause minority groups to concentrate in certain neighbourhoods. Prejudice can link minorities tightly together, encouraging endogamy to maintain cultural identity. Racial antagonism can develop, especially if physical differences exist.

Race and ethnicity are often confused. Claims that racial differences and characteristics can be identified and classified are inaccurate. Genetic variations exist as often within an ethnic group as between groups. False 'scientific' evidence has often been used to justify racial conflict.

Since 1965 successive governments have tried to integrate all sections of society and combat racism and inequality by legislation. In 1968 the Home Secretary said integration was not 'a flattening process of assimilation, but equal opportunity accompanied by cultural diversity, in an atmosphere of mutual trust'.

Race Relations Acts were passed in:

- 1965 to set up the Race Relations Board, which was able to intervene in cases of proven discrimination on grounds of race,
- 1968 to prevent discrimination in housing, employment and commercial services,
- 1976 to replace the Board with the Commission for Racial Equality, which could conduct investigations, require changes, and check they were implemented.

Other Acts have affected race relations:

- 1962 and 1976 Immigration Acts restricted immigration,
- 1981 British Nationality Act distinguished between British Citizenship and British Overseas citizenship.
- 1991 Asylum Act restricted entry of political refugees.

These laws have failed to combat racism. The attitude of the government has often appeared to be 'too little, too late'.

Glossary

prejudice: preconceived opinions or bias

immigration: coming into a country to settle

pluralist society: a society where several ethnic groups coexist, living in communities largely separate from others

endogamy: marriage only within the kin or group

race: a discredited scientific term to describe biologically distinct groups

Issues to be discussed

- Is there a difference between ethnicity and race?
- Why does racial prejudice exist?
- Should the government try to assimilate all ethnic groups into a single culture or seek to preserve a pluralistic society?
- What are the benefits of life in a multicultural society?
- Why are minority groups often disadvantaged?

Where now?

H. Goulbourne, *Race Relations in Britain since 1945*, Macmillan, 1998

www.chronicleworld.org

www.cps.or.uk

What do you think?

To what extent is it possible to justify the claim that Britain is multicultural and a multiracial society?

The concept of a multicultural society in post-imperial Britain entails more than toleration of cultural pluralism. The ideology embraces notions of fairness and equality, and the proponents of multiculturalism presumably do not intend that celebration of difference should be used to justify inequality as the promotion of difference in apartheid South Africa was used to establish a grossly unjust social order. There are, however, considerable problems to be confronted in the endeavour to build a fair and equal multicultural society in Britain.

Some problems have been long-standing or historical, while others are of relatively recent origins. Both old and new problems reflect the increasingly complex incorporation or integration of new minority ethnic groups into British society. The historical problems have been characterised by struggles to achieve equality of opportunity in employment, fairness in the criminal justice system, equal access to good housing and obtaining a satisfactory education. Increasingly, however, the problems of health, social and community services, and representations of new minorities in the media have become important areas of concern for policy-makers, providers of services, community organisations and politicians, as new minorities become more easily identified as parts of the British social and political fabrics.

The issues mentioned here do not exhaust the new nor the old practical problems of the multicultural society in post–imperial Britain. Multiculturalism as policy and ideology has not succeeded in abolishing differential incorporation, because new ethnic groups suffer disproportionately from the ills of society and we will begin the next century and millennium with an accumulation of race relations problems. But when compared to the colonial degradation and imperial pomp with which the century, opened the poverty of multiculturalism in post-imperial Britain might appear to be less of a failure than we now think.

From H. Goulbourne, *Race Relations in Britain since 1945*, Macmillan, 1998, pp. 75; 98–99

Population by age as a percentage of each ethnic group, 1998–99

Great Britain

	Under 16	16–34	35–64	65+	All ages =100% millions
White	20	26	38	16	53.1
Black	29	33	33	6	0.9
Indian	24	32	38	7	0.9
Pakistani/Bangladeshi	37	35	24	3	1.0
Other groups					
Chinese	15	40	39	6	0.2
None of above	43	30	24	2	0.8
All other groups (including mixed origin)	38	32	27	3	1.0
All ethnic groups	**21**	**26**	**38**	**15**	**56.8**

Source: *Social Trends 2000*, Office for National Statistics; www.statistics.gov.uk

Activities

1. Examine the population table. Identify and comment on the trends shown by these figures.
2. What is the meaning of 'institutionalised racism'? In a group discuss how it can be identified and dealt with. Present your conclusions in a written report.
3. Discuss why racism has survived in spite of legislation and the passage of time.
4. Investigate the employment and unemployment figures in your area for members of the different groups listed in the table. Present your findings in appropriate tables or graphs.
5. Debate the view that 'a multicultural society is a richer and more interesting society'.

Thinking and analytical skills

1. What different types of knowledge does Goulbourne use?
2. How effectively does he justify his conclusion?

(i) What is the difference between the major UK political parties?

Links: 3.2 (ii); 3.2 (v) **Key skills:** WO3.1; WO3.2; C3.1b; C3.2; C3.3; C3.1a; N3.2; N3.3; IT3.1; IT3.2; IT3.3

Introduction

Britain's system of government is 'party political'. The government is chosen after an election from the political party that won most seats. The prime minister is usually leader of the largest political party in parliament.

Political parties are multi-interest groups which aim to win government office in order to carry out their policies. Many British political thinkers believe a multi-party system is essential for effective democratic government.

Background

In the UK, any group can set up a political party. Countries using **proportional representation** have many different parties, but the British '**simple plurality**' voting system makes it difficult today for new parties to win seats in parliament. Three parties have dominated UK politics in the twentieth century. Until 1918 the Conservatives' main rivals were the Liberals. As Liberal support declined, the Labour Party gradually emerged. Growing popular support for Nationalist parties in Scotland, Ireland and Wales has not led to a share in power because of the electoral system. It is sometimes said that Britain is governed by a two-party system.

Attempts to set up new parties have usually failed. The last real success was the foundation of the Labour Party in 1900. In the 1980s the Social Democrat party was established. After some early success, it merged with the Liberal Party in 1988 to form the Liberal Democrats. Although it has the support of about a fifth of electors, it failed to win many seats until the 1997 general election, when it won 46. Popular support for minority parties has recently increased faster than is reflected in national elections results.

Voting changes in 1867 and 1884 enlarged the electorate and encouraged the formation of a new type of political party to organise elections effectively. Each party has its own key beliefs, but most will change emphasis to win elections.

Why do we need political parties?

- Election campaigns and government action are based on party policy.
- Parties establish links between parliament, government and constituencies.
- Parties select and train people to enter public life.
- Parties bring together people with a range of different views to form consensus.
- Parties not in government provide constructive opposition.
- Parties organise the activities and efforts of their members during election campaigns.

Political ideals about policy may be very different. However, since the 1950s, the main parties have broadly agreed about social policy. This is called political consensus. Ideas may be presented differently but the three main parties agree on the need for the National Health Service and the Welfare State. They all claim to support the family and traditional moral values. Some critics say this general agreement makes it difficult for voters to choose between the parties. They say unless there is political competition, there will be no significant reform.

Glossary

proportional representation: MPs represent a party in parliament in proportion to votes they receive

simple plurality: a candidate with the largest number of votes is elected

paternalistic: acting in an authoritarian manner as is thought best for the country

laissez-faire: non-interference by government on limiting individual freedom

consensus: general agreement

Issues to be discussed

- To what extent should parties be prepared to change their policies in order to win elections?
- Are MPs delegates or representatives of the electors?
- What are the advantages and disadvantages of single-party government in comparison to a coalition?
- Why do third parties rarely succeed in UK elections?
- What do you understand by the term 'one nation' politics?
- To what extent does political **consensus** threaten social reform?
- Is there such a thing as 'a natural party of government'?

Where now?

J. Kingdom, *Government and Politics in Britain*, Polity Press, 1999

D. Kavanagh, *British Politics: Continuities and Change*, Oxford University Press, 1996

M. Kirby, *Investigating Political Sociology*, Collins, 1995

www.labour.org.uk

www.libdems.org.uk

www.conservative-party.org.uk

What do you think?

Would you agree that the only real differences between the major political parties is in presentation rather than policy? Explain and justify your answer.

Liberal Democrat leader Charles Kennedy has insisted no backroom deals will be done between himself and the prime minister over further cooperation with Labour.

The Liberal Democrats and Labour already cooperate on constitutional affairs, foreign policy and defence. Although Mr Kennedy stressed that he wanted the government to spend more money on health and education, a fully elected House of Lords and tougher freedom of information legislation, he said he was prepared to cooperate with the government where their policies tally.

BBC News, 8 November 1999

Speaking to the Keep the Pound Rally on 22 February, William Hague, leader of the Conservative Party said, 'Today I'm issuing a warning to all those who want to keep the pound but think it's safe to vote Labour because they'll get a referendum. We now know that Tony Blair fixes elections, has no respect for democracy and will stop at nothing to get his way. You can't trust Tony Blair with the referendum on the pound. He'll fix that too.

'Recent days have shown that he has got nothing but contempt for the democratic process and the pound. A referendum will be no different. But there's one vote even Tony Blair can't fix – and that's the vote at the next general election.'

Transcript of speech from www.keepthepound.org.uk

After 18 years in the wilderness, power is sweet. But the (Labour) party faithful are wondering whether it was worth it. The government is not even delivering on its limited election pledges.

In *Tribune* last week, Blair wrote, 'I am not interested in artificial divides between heartland areas and new Labour seats.' What he means is that he makes policy to appeal to the largest market. This middle-down alliance voted for Thatcher in the 1980s. Now it supports Blair. Blair's priority is, and always has been, votes and victories. It works.

The parties are becoming more alike. We live in a political market economy. Blair knows that as the political brands converge, they become commodity products and the voters become flighty.

From an article by Philip Oppenheim in *The Sunday Times*, 27 February 2000

The traditional distribution of British political parties

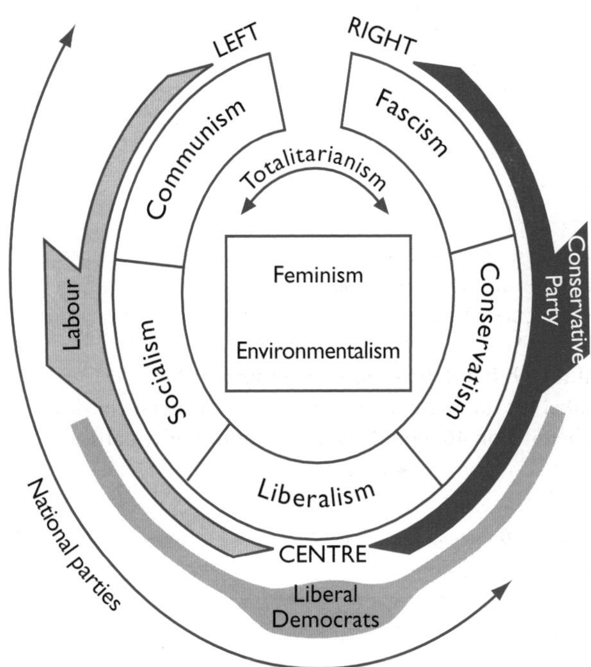

Activities

1 In a group, research the views of the major parties on one of the following issues: law and order, defence, environment, overseas aid or immigration. Present your findings in a report, identifying similarities and differences.

2 Debate the motion 'The rise of Nationalist parties will lead to the break up of the United Kingdom.'

3 Discuss arguments for and against the view that political parties have no future in view of the rise of single-issue protest movements.

4 Find the election results for your constituency (home or school) for the last five elections.
a Calculate the proportion of voters who did not vote.
b Calculate the number of electors in each election whose views **i** reflect, and **ii** do not reflect the result.
c Construct appropriate graphs or tables to illustrate these results.
d Explain and comment on the trends shown.

Thinking and analytical skills

1 What are the similarities and differences between the opinions of Hague and Oppenheim in the two extracts?

2 How does William Hague justify his claim that you can't trust Tony Blair?

3 How might you challenge the view in the third extract that the parties are becoming more alike?

(ii) Can we have both low taxes and high government spending?

Links: 1.1(v); 3.2 (i); 3.2 (iv); 4.15 **Key skills:** N3.2; C3.1b; C3.1a; N3.3; C3.2; N3.1

Introduction

Voters and political parties have different views about the role of government. Some believe that a government's involvement in economic and social matters should be confined to low taxes and limited public expenditure and regulation. Others believe that governments should direct the economy and support high taxation and spending policies and provide for the social and economic well-being of the population.

Background

Before 1945 the aim of most British governments was a **balanced budget**. In 1936, after the Great Depression, the economist J. M. Keynes advocated that governments should actively manage the economy and provide for the social needs of the population. He suggested high government spending in **recession** and low spending in times of high **inflation**. Between 1945 and 1979, most governments followed this approach.

At first this policy worked, but in the 1970s rapidly rising unemployment and inflation indicated that government management of the economy seemed to have failed. In 1975, after an economic crisis, the Labour government was forced to reduce public spending, cut borrowing and increase interest rates. Chancellor of the Exchequer, James Callaghan, said, 'We cannot now spend our way out of recession.'

Right-wing politicians like Mrs Thatcher believed there was 'too much government'. When she became prime minister in 1979 she adopted a **monetarist** policy, aimed at reducing government spending. In the USA, President Reagan followed a similar policy. The Labour government since 1997 has also followed a cautious policy, with tight controls on public spending.

Governments usually spend to provide public services, redistribute income through transfer payments and influence the economy. Money is raised from taxes, borrowing or profits from publicly owned businesses. Each government decides its own priorities.

The Treasury, headed by the chancellor, is responsible for government spending and allocating of resources. Traditionally it favours a cautious approach to spending and tries to control high-spending departments. Each year departments negotiate with the Treasury for their share of government money. Spending decisions effectively define government policy.

In theory, parliament controls government spending. Each autumn it is told about spending plans for the next financial year. In March, the chancellor announces the budget which outlines plans to raise government income. These plans result from extensive consultation and are supposed to be kept secret until budget day, but are often leaked to the press in advance. The government must have parliament's permission to collect taxes each year. This is done when the budget is accepted.

Over the years, the level of government spending has increased as a proportion of GDP. In 1890 it was only 9 per cent, but since 1945 it has usually been about 40 per cent. There are several reasons for this increase. Economic growth has made more resources available and population changes mean that more pensioners and schoolchildren need help. Electors demand generous spending programmes even though the costs of essential services provided by the Welfare State increase constantly.

Glossary

balanced budget: income and expenditure are the same

recession: a period of lower than average economic growth

inflation: increase over time in the general level of prices

monetarist: belief that control of money supply and credit is the way to manage the economy

transfer payments: redistribution of income by payments and grants from tax to those in need, in the form of benefits

GDP (Gross Domestic Product): the value of all goods and services produced in a country in a year

Issues to be discussed

- What services should the state provide for **a** all citizens, and **b** different needy groups (such as the elderly, the unemployed, the ill, single parents, children, etc.)?
- Does government spending on welfare encourage people to become too dependent on the state?
- Should governments take money from the rich in order to give to the poor?
- Do you agree that too much importance is given to the secrecy of the budget?

Where now?

J. Kingdom, *Government and Politics in Britain*, Polity Press, 1999

D. Kavanagh, *British Politics: Continuities and Change*, Oxford University Press, 1996 www.bankofengland.co.uk

www.conservative-party.org.uk www.libdem.org.uk www.hm-treasury.gov.uk

What do you think?

'Government policy towards taxation and spending is influenced more by the desire to win elections than by the needs of the economy.' Assess the extent to which this opinion is justified.

The Treasury believe that the public finances were not only healthy but, unless the chancellor took action to give some of the money back, the government would be looking at embarrassingly large budget surpluses for years to come.

Initially the idea was that a boost to spending in the priority areas of health and education would be combined with modest personal tax cuts. Brown boosted public spending by £4 billion, half of which went to health and £1 billion to education. He cut taxes by £1.3 billion.

Brown's planned spending rise over the next 12 months of 5.1 per cent in real terms represented the second largest annual increase in 25 years.

An economist said, 'Fiscal policy is being driven by the aim of boosting the government's popularity in the countdown to the general election rather than rebalancing the economy.'

Brown's boost to spending will last well beyond the election. 'I didn't expect to see the whiff of electioneering so early from the chancellor,' said the CBI's director general. 'He has missed an opportunity to help industry. I'm also disappointed that he wants to present himself as giving to people and not businesses. But people are businesses, and it is people who are going to suffer.'

Brown may have encouraged Labour's 'heartland' supporters, but he did nothing, for heartland business.

From The Sunday Times, 26 March 2000

The growth of GDP since 1981

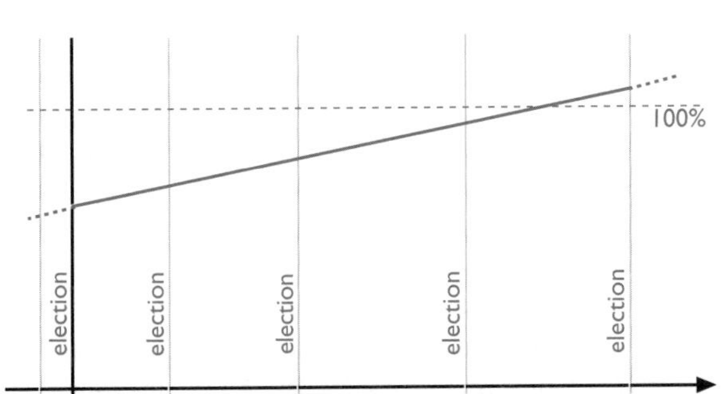

1981	1990	1995	1997
69.9%	92.4%	100.0%	106.1%
£498,314 m	£658,480 m	£712,548 m	£756,144 m

In 1975 GDP was approx. 75% (£493,860m) of the 1990 volume, while in 1951 it was approx. 39% (£256,807m).

The top line gives GDP (adjusted to 1995 figures) as a percentage; the lower figure, expressed in £millions, is at constant 1995 prices.

Source: Office for National Statistics, www.statistics.gov.uk

Selected government expenditure

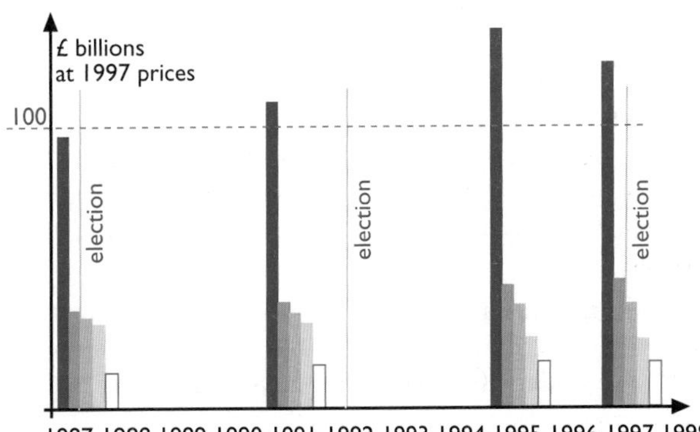

	1987	1991	1995	1997
Social protection	96	109	133	131
Health	33	37	43	44
Education	31	33	36	36
Defence	30	30	24	23
Law and order	12	15	17	16
All expenditure	280	301	338	331

Source: The Office for National Statistics, www.statistics.gov.uk

Activities

1 Compare proposals about taxation and spending made by the major parties in their most recent election manifestoes.

2 How far has Labour kept its election promises about **a** direct and indirect taxation, and **b** public spending on social provisions?

3 Calculate changes that might take place in government tax and spending plans over the next ten years, if trends since 1990 continue. Show the outcome in appropriate graphs.

4 Debate the view that 'Britain has too much government'.

5 Make a presentation to justify reducing government spending on state pensions.

6 Conduct a survey on whether people would support increased taxes to pay for more generous social security payments to:
a single parent families,
b unemployed youths,
c the chronically disabled.

Thinking and analytical skills

1 Identify the different types of knowledge used in the article above.

2 To what extent does the evidence of the graph support the argument?

(iii) Do we need regional government?

Links: 3.2 (ii); 3.2 (vi) **Key skills:** N3.2; N3.3; C3.2; C3.1b; C3.3; IT3.1; IT3.3

Introduction

The United Kingdom is dominated by England in terms of size, population and wealth. The United Kingdom is ruled by a central government and parliament in London. In the twentieth century, demands for independence or self-government resulted in the separation of Eire from the United Kingdom and some **devolution** for Scotland and Wales. Some people would like to see self-government for English regions.

Background

Since the early nineteenth century in Ireland there has been a strong movement for Home Rule or independence. In 1922, after civil war, Eire gained independence but Ulster stayed in the UK, with its own parliament in Stormont having devolved powers.

In 1972 **sectarian** violence resulted in the suspension of Stormont and the imposition of **direct rule**, which lasted until 1999. After the Good Friday Agreement and a referendum, the Northern Ireland Assembly was set up. Rival parties combined for a time in a new power-sharing government.

Scotland, Wales and northern England have long depended economically on declining industries, while the south-east attracts prosperous new industries and employment. In 1996 the EU reported that people in the south-east had a 20 per cent higher income per head, were better qualified, had larger houses and were likely to live longer than northerners.

Economic, political and social discontent led to demands that Scotland and Wales should be given their own governments. People believed they would be in closer touch with the needs of the region and would therefore take steps to improve conditions.

In the 1970s there was growing support for the Scottish and Welsh Nationalist parties. In 1979 the Labour government allowed **referendums** to be held, but there was insufficient support for self-rule. The new Conservative government was opposed to any form of devolution and adopted a highly centralised system of government. In the 1997 election, no Conservative MPs were elected in Wales or Scotland.

Labour's **manifesto** promised devolution to Scotland and Wales and regional assemblies in England. Referendums held in 1997 showed that Scotland wanted its own parliament, but that Welsh feeling was less clear. In May 1999 Wales and Scotland elected new governing bodies. The Scottish Parliament has much greater powers than the Welsh Assembly.

There is less demand for English regional assemblies, but Labour and the Liberal Democrats have promised to establish them if requested to do so by the local population and the Regional Development Agency.

The Liberal Democrats criticise Labour for delaying referendums on English regional governments. The Conservatives fear that regional assemblies will destroy the UK. Some people claim that England is disadvantaged because it lacks the same regional structure as the rest of the UK. Pressure for further devolution may force changes in England in the future.

The EU's support for regionalism may increase pressure for change. It prefers to work through regional bodies rather than national governments.

Glossary

devolution: state authority passed from one institution (parliament) to another (regional government)

sectarian: a body or group having distinctive beliefs which mark them as different to other parts of the community

direct rule: when the right of a region to govern its own affairs is replaced by control from central government

referendums: popular vote on a particular political issue

manifesto: set of policy promises made by a party before an election to win the support of electors

Issues to be discussed

- What are the advantages and disadvantages of power sharing in Northern Ireland?
- What are the benefits of regional assemblies?
- Will devolution break up the UK? If it does, will it matter?
- Why should the Scottish Parliament have more power than the Welsh Assembly?
- Should Welsh and Scots MPs take part in the Westminster parliament?
- Is there any point having a UK parliament at Westminster?

Where now?

J. Kingdom, *Government and Politics in Britain*, Polity Press, 1999

D. Kavanagh, *British Politics: Continuities and Change*, Oxford University Press, 1996

Budge, Newton et al, *The Politics of the New Europe*, Longman, 1997

www.gn.apc.org

www.europa.eu.int/index

www.charter88.org.uk

What do you think?

'Devolution in England would be a serious threat to the continued future of the United Kingdom.' Critically examine this view.

'If Old Labour attempt to buy off strong regional protest, it will be doomed to failure. Labour have had their fingers burned in Edinburgh, Cardiff and London. It now seems that they want a puppet committee in England with a Labour majority to stop the English peasants from revolting.

The Liberal Democrats are seeking to improve the proposal to give the committee some teeth and independence but we are under no illusion that it can be anything but a temporary stopgap. The people of the English regions deserve and need genuine decentralisation just as much as those in Scotland, Wales and London.'

Comment from Paul Tyler, Liberal Democrat, 11 April 2000, www.libdems.org.uk/index

The Labour Party's 1997 manifesto said that, 'We are committed to moving, with the consent of the local people, to directly elected regional government in England.'

Demand is growing for the swift introduction of directly elected assemblies, particularly in the north-east of England. The Campaign for a Northern Assembly (November 1997) published 'A Declaration of the North' in the *New Statesman*. It called for devolution of power to the northern regions of England. Supporters of the declaration urged the government to hold a referendum on establishing a directly elected regional assembly and claimed that the north of England was suffering from 'neglect and isolation from over-centralised government in London'.

From *Constitutional Reform and Devolution*, The British Council, 1999; www.britcoun.org/devolution/regions2

The UK in the mid 1990s population, share of GDP and regional aid received from the EU

	1	2	3
United Kingdom Total	**58.4 m**	**100**	**£1,005**
England	**48.7 m**	**102**	**£601**
North-east		85	£86
North-west		91	£216
Yorkshire and Humberside		89	£90
East Midlands		94	£31
West Midlands		93	£108
East		97	£8
London		140	£23
South-east		107	£4
South-west		95	£36
Wales	**2.9 m**	**83**	**£72**
Scotland	**5.1 m**	**98**	**£162**
Northern Ireland	**1.6 m**	**81**	**£170**

1 Population by region 1995 (millions) **2** Share of GDP by region per head of population 1996–97
3 Regional assistance received from EU structural fund (£ millions at 1994 prices). Figures all relate to UK in mid-1990s.

Source: The Office for National Statistics, www.statistics.gov.uk

Activities

1 Using the information in the table above, construct appropriate graphs to show:
a the proportion of GDP per head of population by regions,
b the allocation of EU resources to each region,
c the proportion of population in each region,
d account for any significant differences.

2 Construct a different type of graph to show the information in the table. What conclusions can you draw from this?

3 Research the possible benefits of regional government in your own locality. Produce a leaflet to argue either for or against local regional government.

4 Examine differences in power between the Scottish and Welsh assemblies.

Thinking and analytical skills

1 Compare the similarities and differences between the arguments presented in the two passages.
2 What different types of knowledge might Tyler use to justify his conclusion?

(iv) How important are pressure groups in the political process?

Links: 3.2 (i); 3.2 (v) **Key skills:** WO3.1; WO3.2; WO3.3; C3.1a; C3.1b; C3.2; N3.1; N3.2; N3.3

Introduction

Most political parties are multi-interest groups, with policies on various issues. Members may differ on some issues, but agree on major **policies**. Parties in Britain aim to gain enough popular support to win elections, to form a government (whether at local or national level) and to carry out their policies. Governments often claim a **mandate** as a result of electoral victory. However, elections do not show real strength of feeling on any single issue.

Background

Pressure groups are a vital part of the **constitution**. Since the range of policies supported by political parties is too varied to reflect any one individual's particular interests, many people join pressure groups. Unlike parties, these usually concentrate on a single issue. Members, drawn from different social groups, may not agree on other subjects. These groups rarely want power or political office, but seek to advance their aims by influencing groups with power. Pressure groups, like Militant Tendency or the Tory Reform Group, may exist inside a party, but generally they operate outside the party system. There are different types of pressure group.

Insider groups like the British Medical Association (BMA) or the National Farmers Union (NFU) often have direct access to relevant government departments. They are consulted on matters of policy and can influence legislation. Membership is restricted and is usually motivated by self-interest and self-promotion.

Promotional groups (like Child Poverty Action, Shelter and the National Viewers' and Listeners' Association) focus on a particular cause. Members are rarely motivated by self-interest but seek to influence both government and public opinion on behalf of disadvantaged groups. Membership is open to any concerned person, but may attract zealots.

Interest groups like the RAC, trade unions or professional associations exist to protect and promote the economic or social interests of their members. Membership is usually restricted to a particular interest group. Peak groups are similar but represent the views of a set of related interests. The Trade Union Congress (TUC), for example, represents affiliated trade unions and the Confederation of British Industry (CBI) represents different employers.

Episodic groups develop to pursue a particular project, over a limited time period. Membership is fluid and may come mainly from the area immediately affected by the project. Such groups may form to oppose a new motorway, the use of green belt for housing or the location of an industrial estate.

Most pressure groups use peaceful, legal means. They promote their aims through advertising, the media, direct contact with government and **lobbying**. Established groups expect to be consulted by government and opposition parties in the formulation of policy.

Other groups prefer to use **direct action** to draw public attention to their aims. Activities may include marches, demonstrations, civil disobedience, obstruction and direct breaches of the law. Recent examples include the anti-poll tax campaign and anti-road protests such as the Newbury by-pass. Direct action is high profile and confrontational.

Glossary

policies: proposals for action made by a political group

mandate: the approval given by an election victory to a set of policies presented by a political group

constitution: the rules, customs and conventions which define the powers of state institutions and the method of government. It may be written or unwritten

lobbying: attempting to directly persuade MPs to support a policy, usually by interview or face-to-face meeting

direct action: actions (other than the democratic process of voting) intended to bring pressure on the government or other authority to change policy

Issues for discussion

- In a democratic country, why do we need pressure groups?
- Are pressure groups the best way of encouraging change?
- To what extent are pressure groups anti-democratic?
- Should some pressure groups be allowed more easy access to government departments than others?
- Are police powers sufficient to deal with direct action?
- What type of pressure groups do the following belong to? Abortion Law Reform; Greenpeace; Campaign for State Education; the Police Federation; Age Concern; Salvation Army; Gay Rights; CND; Victim Support

Where now?

J. Kingdom, *Government and Politics in Britain*, Polity Press, 1999
D. Kavanagh, *British Politics: Continuities and Change*, Oxford University Press, 1996
M. Kirby, *Investigating Political Sociology*, Collins, 1995

www.foe.co.uk
www.freetibet.org
news.bbc.co.uk

What do you think?

Critically examine the claim that pressure groups exist in order to force the majority to accept the view of the minority. To what extent can this view be justified?

In the last twenty years there has been increasing concern about the environment. This has often led to direct action, greater media interest and a strong police response in opposition to planned developments. One such activity concerns a proposed toll motorway, the BNRR.

John Prescott has broken Labour's promise not to build the Birmingham Northern Relief Road – a 6-lane, 27-mile toll motorway through the West Midlands Green Belt.

We can still stop this!

There is a direct action camp which has been set up to oppose the building of the BNRR with tree-houses, tunnels and towers and cottages which have been squatted. But with 27 miles of route there's plenty of room for your ideas and energy. A possession order for eviction was granted on the 11th of September – this means eviction could come at any time.

The majority of local people oppose the BNRR and local support groups are being set up.

BUILD. Build defences. Build support. Build an unstoppable movement to defeat the transeuropean consortium responsible for more destruction, more pollution and more profit at our expense.

From a newsletter issued in early 1998; www.geocities.com/RainForest

In October 1999 President Jiang Zemin of China made a state visit to Britain. During his visit, protesters demonstrated against human rights abuses in China. There was a strong police response.

Activities

1 Working in a group, research arguments for and against the development of the BNRR (or a similar development that has aroused concern in your own locality). Debate the view that the police deserve full public support in the actions that they are driven to take against protesters.

2 Investigate the legal powers of the police when faced with direct action. Should they be increased or restricted? Justify your conclusions.

3 Discuss different types of direct action available to protesters. Do you agree that any form of action is justified in a good cause?

4 Conduct a survey to examine the attitude of a range of people to different types of action that a pressure group might take to oppose an environmental issue of your choice. Outline your conclusions, supporting your findings with appropriate tables, graphs and commentary.

Thinking and analytical skills

1 What type of argument is used in the passage about the BNRR? How effective is it?

2 What evidence might be used to **a** support it, and **b** challenge it?

3 Identify different values illustrated in the photograph taken during the state visit to Britain of the Chinese president.

(v) Should the voting system be reformed and, if so, how?

Links: 3.2 (ii); 3.2 (vi) **Key skills:** N3.3;N3.2; C3.1a; C3.2; C3.3

Introduction

In a **democracy**, those members of the public who are entitled to the franchise elect the **legislature**. In Britain most people over 18 are allowed to vote. Elections for parliament are held at least once every five years.

Critics of the British system claim it is unfair as it ignores many voters' views and claim that other methods give fairer results. Different voting methods are used in local, regional and European elections and in other democracies.

Background

The method of voting used in British elections is 'First Past The Post' (FPTP) or Single Member Simple Plurality (SMSP). The country is divided into 659 single-member **constituencies**. In each constituency the candidate who gains the most votes is elected, even if this is less than 50 per cent of the votes cast. In most elections, more people vote against the winning candidate than vote for him or her.

Single Transferable Vote (STV). Voters rank candidates in multi-member constituencies according to preference, irrespective of political party. If their preferred candidate does not need the vote, it is transferred to a second choice (and so on). This system is used in Eire, for the Australian Senate and in Northern Ireland for elections to the European parliament.

The Alternative Vote (AV). Electors, voting in single-member constituencies, rank candidates in their preferred order. Any candidate gaining 50 per cent of votes cast is elected. If no-one has a simple majority of votes, the candidate scoring least is eliminated. His or her votes are then re-distributed according to the second preference expressed by the voters. This process is repeated until one candidate gains a simple majority. The system is used for the Australian House of Representatives.

Party List Systems. In multi-member constituencies, voters have the same number of votes as there are seats. Instead of voting for a candidate, electors vote for a political party. In a 'closed list' system, the party ranks candidates in preferred order, giving voters little choice. In an 'open list' system, the voter can express a preference for individuals from the list. Each party is allocated seats in proportion to the votes received. Most European countries use this system. It was used in the 1999 European elections in the UK.

The Supplementary Vote (SV). Voters make two choices in single-member constituencies. If no candidate receives 50 per cent of first preference votes, the second preference votes of low-scoring candidates are redistributed to the two highest scoring candidates. The candidate with the highest vote wins. This system was used to elect the Mayor of London.

Additional Member System (AMS). There are several variations, combining the First Past The Post and Party List systems. Voters have two votes. The first vote elects a candidate in a single-member constituency, by a simple majority. The second is used in a multi-member constituency to choose from a party list, to 'top up' party candidates in proportion to the votes cast. It is used in Germany and New Zealand, and was used in the Scottish and Welsh Assembly elections in 1999.

The Alternative Vote Plus (AV+) is similar to AMS. Voters have two votes, one for a constituency MP and the other for a regional multi-member Open Party List. It is not in use at present, although it was recommended by Lord Jenkins' Independent Commission on the Voting System.

Glossary

democracy: rule by the people

legislature: the law-making institution within a state

franchise: the right to vote at public elections

constituency: body of voters who elect a representative; hence the areas into which a country is divided for the purpose of electing representatives

coalition: temporary combination, for a special purpose, of different groups which otherwise have distinctive principles

Issues to be discussed

- Why do we have elections?
- Is an MP a representative or a delegate?
- Should all electors be required to vote?
- Why do some political parties favour electoral reform?
- Discuss the different arguments for and against electoral reform.
- Does proportional representation cause weak government?

Where now?

J. Kingdom, *Government and Politics in Britain*, Polity Press, 1999

D. Kavanagh, *British Politics: Continuities and Change*, Oxford University Press, 1996

M. Kirby, *Investigating Political Sociology*, Collins, 1995

www.conservative-party.org.uk

www.libdem.org.uk

www.labour.org.uk

What do you think?

Critically examine the strengths and weaknesses of different types of voting systems.

Arguments for FPTP:

- Usually the majority party can form a strong government.
- It is simple to understand and is democratic.
- Voters express a view on their choice of government.
- It usually leads to a two-party system of government.
- It avoids weak coalition governments.
- It creates strong links between MPs and constituencies.
- Candidates with most support win in a fair process.

Arguments against FPTP:

- Some voters are not represented and votes are wasted.
- Some voters will never be represented.
- Parties not voters choose candidates.
- Voters are represented unequally.
- Results are distorted when votes are heavily concentrated.
- Negative voting against unpopular candidates is encouraged.
- Results can be affected by constituency boundaries.

Number of seats in parliament won by the main parties in UK general elections since 1945

Year	Labour	Lib Dem	Nat.	Con	Total
1997	419	46	28	165	659
1992	271	20	24	336	651
1987	229	22*	6	376	650
1983	209	23*	4	397	635
1979	269	11	4	339	635
1974 Oct	319	13	14	277	635
1974 Feb	301	14	9	297	630
1970	288	8	5	330	630
1968	364	12	1	253	630
1964	317	9	0	304	630
1959	258	6	0	365	630
1955	277	6	2	345	630
1951	295	8	3	321	625
1950	315	9	2	298	625
1945	383	12	6	210	640

* Figure includes MPs elected for both the Liberal Party and the Social Democratic Party. In 1988 these parties merged to form the Liberal Democrats

Source: Office for National Statistics; www.statistics.gov.uk

Proportion of votes in UK elections since 1945

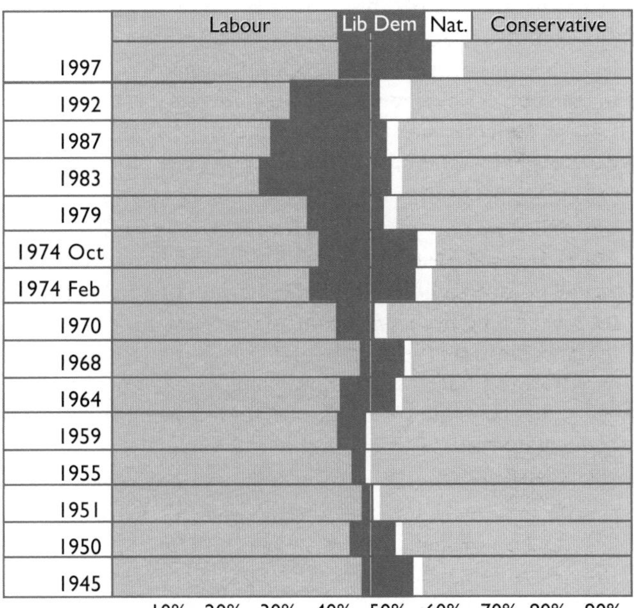

Source: Office for National Statistics; www.statistics.gov.uk

Activities

1. Draw appropriate graphs to show **a** the voting trend for the major parties (1945 to 1997), and **b** the proportion of seats gained by each of the parties in the 1945, 1974 (February) and 1992 elections.
2. Show how these results would have differed if a proportional system of voting had been used.
3. Find the 1997 election results for your own constituency. Estimate the outcome if a system of proportional voting had been used. Comment on your conclusions.
4. As a group, research the views of the major political parties on proportional representation. Critically examine the arguments they use to justify their position. Make an illustrated presentation of your findings.
5. Consider the benefits and disadvantages of the Party List system of voting. What arguments might you use in a debate to oppose or justify its introduction into UK elections?

Thinking and analytical skills

1. Identify and explain any fallacies in the argument that proportional voting is fairer than other systems.
2. Why might it be claimed that true democracy is impossible in a large modern society?

(vi) What is the European Union and how does it work?

Links: 3.2 (vii); 3.2 (iii) **Key skills:** N3.3; N3.2; C3.1a; C3.2; C3.3

Introduction

The European Union (EU) consists of 15 member states and grew out of the EEC. After the Second World War it was felt that economic co-operation would provide greater collective European security. In 1957, 6 countries signed the Treaty of Rome to set up the EEC. The EU has several governing institutions, staffed mainly by people directly appointed by member states; only MEPs are popularly elected.

Background

Britain's links with the USA and the **Commonwealth** delayed its entry into the EEC. Early applications for membership were rejected. Eventually in 1973 Britain was admitted. Since then both main parties have been split over the benefits of membership. Labour now seems to favour the EU, but Conservatives are divided. Liberal Democrats strongly support closer European links.

The Council of Ministers, the political head of the EU, is the legislative and decision-making body. The presidency is held for a period of six months by each member state in turn. Council members are national ministers or heads of the departments concerned with the issues under discussion.

The Council makes three types of decision. Regulations have the immediate force of law; directives are binding, but are open to interpretation; recommendations and resolutions are advisory. **Weighted voting** allocates votes according to the size of a country's population. Major decisions relating to the single market require that 10 countries and 62 votes are in favour. Otherwise voting is by simple majority. Individual states can **veto** decisions that threaten vital national interest.

The European Council meets two or three times a year. It consists of heads of state and foreign secretaries. It has no legislative power, but discusses major community issues.

The European Commission implements Council policy and is responsible for initiating Council policy discussions. It is effectively a European civil service, with twenty-three departments. It drafts the budget and negotiates with non-member states. Twenty commissioners, nominated by member states, serve five-year terms. The president of the Commission is appointed with the agreement of all member states and the approval of the EU parliament.

The EU parliament meets for one week each month in Strasbourg. Members (MEPs) are elected by proportional representation for five-year terms. There are no political parties, but MEPs sit in broad political groupings. The parliament's legislative powers, though limited, are increasing. As a consultative body it lacks executive powers, but may reject the budget and dismiss the Commission. Much of its work is done through committees that meet in Brussels.

The European Court of Justice meets at the Hague and is made up of a judge from each member state. It is an international court of appeal, review and referral. Its aim is to see that community law is uniformly enforced. Decisions do not have to be unanimous but are binding on members. The European Commission refers most of the cases considered by the Court.

Glossary

Commonwealth: a loose association of former British colonies, recognising the Queen as head of state

weighted voting: the number of votes is determined by the size of a country's population so that larger states have more votes

veto: the power to reject a proposal irrespective of its support from other involved states

federation: a system where states have voluntarily pooled their sovereignty to create a higher level of government

subsidiarity: different levels of government power should be as close to the people as is compatible with efficiency

Issues to be discussed

- Compare the EU institutions with those of Britain. What are the similarities and differences?
- Does it matter that there is little direct democracy in EU institutions?
- Does weighted voting give too much influence to smaller states?
- Is the EU too dominated by national interests?
- To what extent should the European Court be able to take decisions that are binding in Britain?
- Why does Britain seem to be a reluctant member of the EU?

Where now?

Budge, Newton et al., *The Politics of the New Europe*, Longman, 1997

J. Kingdom, *Government and Politics in Britain*, Polity Press, 1999

D. Kavanagh, *British Politics: Continuities and Change*, Oxford University Press, 1996

europa.eu.int/index

www.fco.gov.uk/europe/index

www.keepthepound.org.uk

What do you think?

Should the political powers of the EU be increased? How might change affect national sovereignty and democracy?

The impact of the EU in Europe is growing but it has yet to assume the structure, powers and functions of a **federation**. Consequently, the EU's power remains potential rather than actual. It has problems in translating aims and economic strength into collective action. With some notable exceptions, the EU still reaches decisions by adopting the lowest common denominator among the competing policies of member states.

The internal machinery must be reformed in such a way that decision-making effectiveness is enhanced alongside democratic control, while maintaining national control in areas marked out by the principle of **subsidiarity**.

Enlarged membership would enforce the streamlining of decision-making and demand significant institutional changes. This might involve: reducing the number of commissioners; altering the system of six-monthly presidencies; amending the weighted voting system; relying more on majority voting; and increased powers for the European parliament.

If it is to reap the full benefits from its new internal market, the EU will need to establish common policies in economics, finance, and social and environmental policy. Economic and Monetary Union (EMU) is intended to set up a single currency and establish a European Central Bank. Can EMU exist without political union or is political union a precondition for successful EMU? Germany is for a political framework, in particular a strengthened European parliament, to guarantee the complete independence of the new Central Bank.

Members will come under pressure to develop a common foreign and security capability in order to adopt a common approach in international affairs.

The Intergovernmental Conference (of 1996–97) may have the effect of enforcing more common policies. If so, certain members may be tempted to opt out of some aspects of EU activity. This may hasten moves to a multi-speed Europe. Britain seems more interested in using Europe as a framework for its own foreign and economic policies.

From Budge, Newton et al, *The Politics of the New Europe*, Longman, 1997

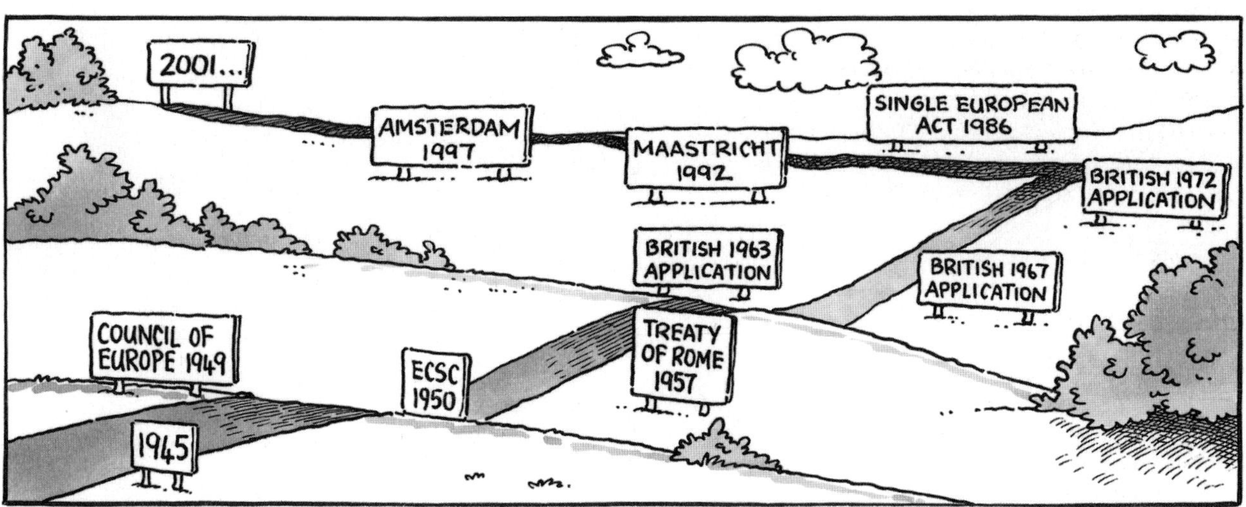

The road to European unity.

Activities

1 Find the results of MEP elections in your own constituency since 1979. Examine and explain **a** any voting trends, and **b** the impact of PR in the 1999 election.

2 Plot this information on appropriate graphs. Compare the results of European elections with general elections.

3 Debate the opinion that the British parliament has lost much of its power because of the development of the EU.

4 Investigate the reason for the dispersal of EU government agencies between Brussels, Strasbourg and Luxembourg.

5 Investigate whether European Heads of State summits achieve anything other than a 'media circus'.

Thinking and analytical skills

1 Identify the different types of argument used in the passage.

2 How effectively does the author of the passage justify the argument for closer political union?

(vii) What has Europe done for Britain?

Links: 3.2 (iii); 3.2 (vi); 4.17 **Key skills:** C3.1a; C3.1b; C3.3; C3.3; N3.2

Introduction

Since Britain joined the EU in 1973 there has been on-going debate over the benefits of membership. Major areas of concern are budget contributions, the impact of the Social Charter and sovereignty. The question of a single currency has been deferred. Business leaders and economists generally favour the EU, but many politicians and the public are more sceptical.

Background

As the size and function of the EU has expanded, its budget has grown steadily. Since 1988 the EU's revenue has been set as a proportion of Community **GNP**. The four sources of revenue are customs duties, agricultural levies, VAT and national contributions to cover any deficit.

Expenditure includes administration, agreed payments, the common agricultural policy, overseas aid and regional grants in support of European policy. Budget negotiations cause conflict between the EU Council and parliament, both of which want control. Richer countries try to limit contributions, while poorer countries want expenditure increased.

In 1996 the British contribution was £6,735.9 million and **return payments** were £4,834 million. The total projected EU budget for 1999 and subsequent years was £61 billion. In 1984 the Conservatives, wanting to reduce expenditure during a period of rising unemployment, claimed Britain's contribution was too high. After lengthy negotiations, the EEC conceded an annual rebate of £2.8 million on British payments. Other countries resent this, but attempts to reduce the rebate have been resisted by British governments.

The Social Charter to 'develop the social dimension of the single market' was introduced by the Maastricht Agreement. The Charter includes freedom of movement, better working conditions, social protection, collective bargaining, vocational training, equal treatment for men and women and worker participation in management.

All EU countries, except Britain, signed the Charter in 1989. The British government claimed it would reduce economic competitiveness and undermine the principle of subsidiarity. In 1998, however, the Labour government signed it claiming that a low wage economy with a poorly skilled workforce would not attract international investors and that continued rejection could cost jobs and reduce investment. As a result of the Charter the minimum wage was introduced.

Sovereignty is a major area of concern. By signing the Treaty of Accession, the government accepted – for the first time – a written constitution which meant European law took precedence over British law. Courts in the UK must accept European decisions and enforce them.

EU supporters claim there is no real loss of sovereignty as Britain can withdraw at any time. Parliament still controls foreign policy, exchange rate, monetary policy and defence.

Opponents fear the development of a superstate, claiming that **qualified majority voting** makes the national veto less effective in many areas of European legislation. The European Declaration of Human Rights limits parliament's power to make laws and the Court's right to enforce them. Sovereign power has also been lost through the devolution of powers to regional assemblies.

Glossary

GNP: the total money value of the final goods and services produced in an economy in any year

return payments: payments made, often as grants, by the EU to member states or regional bodies

sovereignty: the idea of where ultimate authority in a state is to be found

qualified majority voting: a vote in which more than a simple majority is required for success

Soviet bloc: those countries in eastern Europe which fell under the economic and military influence of the USSR

Issues to be discussed

- What is the effect of the Social Charter on employment in Britain?
- Is national sovereignty important? If so, why?
- To what extent do Britain and the other European member states mean the same thing by 'subsidiarity'?
- Why, in view of the aims of the EU, do 'richer countries try to limit their contributions while poorer countries want expenditure increased'?
- How does 'qualified majority voting make the national veto less effective'? Is this to the benefit of Britain?

Where now?

Budge, Newton et al., *The Politics of the New Europe*, Longman, 1997

J. Kingdom, *Government and the Politics in Britain*, Polity Press, 1999

B. Mill, *The European Union*, Heinemann, 1998

europa.eu.int/index

www.fco.gov.uk/europe/index

www.keepthepound.org.uk

What do you think?

'There is no such thing as a separate community interest; the community interest is compounded of the national interests of the member states.' Critically examine this opinion.

Europe has troubled the leaderships of the two main political parties more than it has the general public. The issue has proved more persistently troublesome in British politics than it has in the domestic politics of any other member state.

For most of the past three decades there has been something of a consensus among media, business, finance and Whitehall about the benefits of membership and of greater integration of the EU. The public has shown little enthusiasm for such goals as a single currency or a united Europe. Turnout in the European elections is about 35 per cent, by far the lowest in the EU and the British are usually among the least enthusiastic nations in support for Europe-wide initiatives.

Britain has usually resisted initiatives from the Commission or the Council of Ministers. This has been true of the creation of monetary and economic union, the Social Charter and efforts to forge a common defence and foreign policy.

The future seems to promise more difficulties for Britain's political leaders, particularly in the Conservative party who have been unhappy about the extension of qualified majority voting and moves to even more common policies. It is divided over whether Britain should sign up for a single European currency. The Commission wishes to extend integration even further and disapproves of Britain's existing exemptions or opt-outs from common policies. Britain has welcomed suggestions for the enlargement of the Union, including membership of former **Soviet bloc** states in eastern Europe. Their membership may lead to the EU's agenda being dominated by the concerns of small and medium sized states and extends the number of policy areas that will be subject to qualified majority voting.

From D. Kavanagh, *British Politics*, Oxford University Press, 1996, pp. 85–86

Members of the EU in 2000

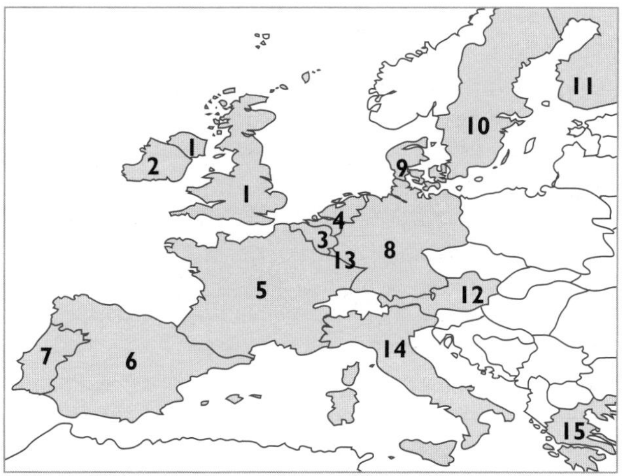

Source: D. Mall et al, *Business Studies*, Causeway Press, 2000

The annual contributions to and payments from the EU to member states (£ million)

Map ref.	Country	Paid in	Paid from
8	Germany	16,900.1	8,033.0
5	France	10,000.0	9,725.8
14	Italy	7,371.4	6,130.0
1	UK	6,735.9	4,834.0
6	Spain	3,694.0	8,554.0
4	Netherlands	3,609.0	1,618.0
3	Belgium	2,232.0	1,625.0
10	Sweden	1,593.0	980.0
12	Austria	1,524.0	1,302.0
9	Denmark	1,107.0	1,264.0
15	Greece	901.0	4,104.0
7	Portugal	737.0	2,995.0
11	Finland	782.0	708.0
2	Ireland	578.0	2,417.0
13	Luxembourg	133.0	68.0

Source: *Court of Auditors Report 1997*, www.news.bbc.co.uk/hi/english/world/europe/newsid

Activities

1 Investigate why Britain has been reluctant to enter the single currency. Write a report outlining the possible advantages and disadvantages of joining the system.

2 a Show the two sets of figures in the table in two different, appropriate forms of graph or diagram.
b Calculate the percentage of the EU budget contributed by the four largest and four smallest contributors.
c Calculate total payments made by the EU to the original six members. Show this as a percentage of the entire budget income from other member states.

3 Research and make a presentation on the impact of the European Court on British society on, for example, **a** the age at which people are entitled to state pensions, and **b** the nature of punishment in educational establishments.

4 Discuss the meaning of 'single market'. How does it affect British industry and commerce?

5 Investigate the meaning of the term 'democratic deficit'. Does it need to be reduced?

Thinking and analytical skills

1 Identify three different 'facts' and three 'beliefs' in the passage. How might the truth of the beliefs be established?

2 To what extent does the evidence contained in the map/table support the argument that 'the British rebate agreed in 1984 distorts the whole system of contributions'.

(i) What do social scientists do?

Links: 2.2 (i); 2.2 (ii); 3.3 (ii); 3.3(iv) **Key skills:** N3.3; N3.2; N3.3; C3.3; C3.1a; C3.1b

Introduction

The study of humanity differs from scientific research, since human beings are unlike natural objects. In social sciences the objects of study are people who interact with researchers. **Ethical** considerations impose restraint on the nature of research. Social science concerns the full range of human experience. Specialism and ideology determine research methods, perspective and focus of study.

Background

Positivist approaches look at the larger picture, identifying a world of impersonal laws where external social forces construct individual behaviour. They study social structure and use quantifiable data.

Interpretists adopt a smaller scale, more subjective view of society. They are concerned with the reactions of small groups and individuals. Accepting the objective nature of the world, they seek to identify with, share and interpret individual experiences. They emphasise richness of detail and **qualitative** data.

Other approaches combine qualitative and **quantitative** methods. Marxists, for example, believe that human behaviour is determined by economic factors and therefore look for a single causal viewpoint.

Laboratory experiment is unsuited to social research. People are not guinea pigs and it is impractical to establish genuine **control groups**. Comparison of similar social phenomena is as close as it is usually possible to come to laboratory methods since social scientists are bound by ethical rules. Since individuals behave individually, the social scientists cannot make precise predictions.

Sampling is necessary, since human populations are very large, and is applicable to any of the research methods. Choosing the size and nature of a sample is important – it can be random or representative. Different types of sampling vary in reliability and ease of administration.

Surveys are fact-collecting exercises and can be expensive and time consuming. Weaknesses include consistency of administration, reliability of responses, validity and difficulty of replication. Good results depend on appropriate questions, effective researchers, the quality of analysis and interpretation of responses.

Questionnaires can be administered personally or by post. Expensive and time consuming, they can be factually useful for supplying good quantitative data but less useful for opinions, unless questions are open ended. Analysis and quantification can give a false impression of precision, attitudes and behaviour.

Interviews are useful but should be carefully designed and administered. They suit small samples, but to be effective, should be used with other methods.

Observation, whether participant or non-participant, covert or overt, is time consuming but can provide rich information from small, unrepresentative groups. Covert observation may yield better results, but raises ethical and safety questions. Observation provides insights, but can produce false images and distorted behaviour patterns.

Secondary evidence, including statistics, is valuable, but needs to be interpreted. It can be unreliable, having been produced or collected for other purposes.

Social scientists may accumulate verifiable data that indicate trends, but they cannot produce absolute laws or precise forecasts. Individual behaviour cannot be predicted, although generalisations about group behaviour can be made.

Glossary

ethical: relating to the moral code of a person or society

qualitative data: data that cannot be expressed numerically e.g. the thoughts and feelings of a few people, in depth

quantitative data: data that can be expressed numerically

control groups: groups matched in every way with an experimental group except for the research variable

sampling: when a small group is used to represent a large group or population

Issues to be discussed

- What justification is there for covert observation? Why is it considered to be ethically wrong?
- If social scientists cannot make accurate predictions about future behaviour, is there any point in their work?
- Is laboratory experiment unsuited to all social research?
- Discuss the different types of sampling methods and identify their strengths and weaknesses.
- How can questionnaires be made more reliable?

Where now?

C. Court, *Introduction to Sociology*, Tudor, 1997
Marcus and Ducklin, *Success in Sociology*, John Murray, 1998
Sociology Review Vol 9, No 3 (2000)

www.stbrn.ac.uk
redrival.net/evaluation
sosig.ac.uk/

What do you think?

Social sciences can define problems but can't provide solutions. Do you agree? Justify your answer.

Once the forties were the prime of life; now the scrapheap beckons at 42. A study has shown that job applicants over that age face rejection, no matter how good they are. Ten years ago such discrimination seldom started until workers reached their fifties, but now the early forties – just when commitments are at their highest – are the age at which employment prospects become most fragile.

The research, commissioned by an employment consultancy, shows that, in many high-tech industries, ageism starts even before 42. Only in the north of England are older workers still acceptable, or in call centres, which take anyone with a good telephone manner.

The researchers interviewed 237 candidates over the age of 35 seeking professional jobs, plus 27 employers. About 51 per cent of the candidates of 44 and under described cases of age discrimination.

One victim of ageism lost his £50,000-a-year management post at British Steel when he was 41. He is still out of work. Another, with an IQ of 150, lost her executive job in 1982, when she was 42, and has not worked since. Last year AXA Sun Life insurance pensioned off almost all executives aged over 50. Barclays Bank ran into trouble with the Inland Revenue when it tried to retire executives in their forties – nobody can claim pensions until they are over 50.

Don Steel of the Association of the Retired and Persons Over 50, said it was wrong many jobs were open only to the young: 'In 1979, 93 per cent of the over-fifties were in work. Now it is 68 per cent. Prejudice is striking ever younger.'

From *The Sunday Times*, 19 March 2000

Why do most people retire at 65 – unless they belong to a privileged profession?

Activities

1 Design a questionnaire on the topic of ageism and unemployment.
  a Ask a mixture of people of different age groups, including people in employment and those who have retired early, to complete it.
  b Analyse your results and present them in appropriate graph form. Make a presentation of your findings.
  c Write a brief report to show whether your findings support or challenge the findings in the article.

2 Which research methods do you think were used for the study reported in the passage? Explain your answer.

3 Which of the research methods listed on page 148 is **a** most appropriate, and **b** least appropriate for a study of ageism in employment?

4 Debate the view that 'in employment it should not matter how old you are; all that is important is whether you can do the job'.

Thinking and analytical skills

1 Identify the different types of knowledge used in the passage.

2 What are the different stages of the argument?

3 How effectively is the conclusion in the passage justified by the evidence presented?

(ii) How scientific are the social sciences?

Links: 2..2 (iii); 2.3 (i); 3.3 (i) **Key skills:** WO3.1, WO3.2; C3.1b; C3.3; C3.1a; N3.1; N3.2; N3.3

Introduction

Social sciences concern the study of human behaviour. They investigate and seek answers to why human beings act as they do. They aim to be thorough and accurate in methodology in order to identify laws to explain and predict behaviour. Some claim human behaviour can be studied scientifically.

Background

The social sciences include the following:

- Political Science concerns processes which influence human government.
- Anthropology studies small-scale societies and 'man as an animal'.
- Economics is about the relationship between scarce resources and human competition for their use.
- Psychology studies human and animal behaviour, with particular reference to the mind.
- Sociology is the study of society as a whole in terms of organisation, institutions and structures.

Although there is considerable overlap between these areas, each has its own distinctive characteristics.

Natural sciences include astronomy, biology, chemistry and physics. They seek to explain the world of nature. Although dealing with different aspects of nature, they use similar methods, relying on theoretical thinking to develop a **hypothesis**, which is then assessed on the basis of available knowledge.

Verifiable knowledge is determined by a combination of experiment and observation. Experiment is seen as the most effective and reliable way to test a hypothesis. Observation requires precise, accurate measurement. It must be open to **replication** to establish the truth of initial findings: if circumstances are duplicated exactly identical results will be produced. When a hypothesis is confirmed, a 'law' will be postulated. Scientific laws are tentative but can be used to make predictions.

Early social scientists believed the methods of natural sciences could be used to study human behaviour. They hoped that scientific method would give legitimacy and respectability to their work.

They believed that if social facts or natural laws could be identified, they could be used to predict behaviour patterns. Their aim was to identify and verify such laws by observation and measurement. They hoped to use such knowledge to end social conflict and resolve social problems.

Objectivity is a key feature of scientific method. A '**value free**' approach should ensure that conclusions are valid and reliable. It is often claimed that human behaviour cannot be studied in a completely dispassionate way. Personal values may distort the interpretation of evidence and the validity of conclusions.

Since total objectivity cannot be achieved, researchers should acknowledge their personal perspective. Objectivity in methods of observation and argument are, perhaps, more important than in personal views. The main safeguard of objectivity is public and open scrutiny of findings. Critical assessment can maintain and preserve objectivity.

Glossary

hypothesis: a supposition made as a basis for reasoning or as a starting point for investigation

verifiable knowledge: knowledge the accuracy of which can be tested and confirmed

replication: the collection of data under the same conditions as a previous study to test and confirm the validity of findings

value free: research conducted without influence of the researcher's own values or beliefs

Issues to be discussed

- Is it possible for a researcher to be completely objective when studying human behaviour?
- Does the subject matter of the social sciences prevent a truly scientific approach?
- Are there fundamental social laws governing human behaviour that can be used to predict social developments?
- What similarities and differences exist between the methods of social and natural scientists?

Where now?

Sociology Review Vol 8, No 2 (1998)

T. May and M. Williams, *Knowing the Social World*, Open University, 1998

clearinghouse.net redrival.net/evaluation sosig.ac.uk/

What do you think?

'Since every individual is part of society, it is not possible for social scientists to be truly objective.' Critically examine this view, explaining and justifying your conclusions.

Sociology seeks to apply to the study of humanity and society the methods of science. It rests upon the assumption common to all the social sciences that the scientific method can make a significant contribution to our understanding of people's character, actions, and institutions, and to the solution of those practical problems that humanity faces in its collective experience.

What are the prerequisites for the scientific study of society and what are its essential characteristics? The term science has been given many meanings. Historically it once signified any branch of knowledge or study. In modern times science has come to be used chiefly in two distinct though related ways. It has been defined as any body of knowledge based upon reliable observation and organised into a system of general propositions or laws. It has also been taken to mean the methods by which systematic and accurate knowledge about the 'real' world is acquired, as opposed to the intuition, speculation, and more or less casual, though often penetrating, observations of literature, philosophy or theology.

The chief characteristic of both scientific analysis and observation is objectivity. The validity of any conclusion and the reliability of any observations are – or should be – independent of the values and beliefs of the scientist. Ideally, the scientist keeps his philosophical views, political allegiances, religious beliefs, social preferences and personal feelings from influencing his results in any way. Objectivity is likely to be far more difficult to achieve in all the social sciences than in the natural sciences, for people inevitably bring to their study of themselves and society a body of ideas that may affect their observations and bias their conclusions.

From E. Chinoy, *Society*, Random House, 1967, pp. 4–6

IF ONLY PEOPLE WERE ALL THE SAME. HOW DO THEY EXPECT US TO STUDY THEM PROPERLY ?

Activities

1 Working in a group, choose one of the following social issues and devise a method to investigate it:
a Do more boys than girls take part in team sports?
b What type of part-time jobs, if any, are available to: **i** people still at school, and **ii** people who have recently retired?
c What social facilities do unemployed people want?
Present your conclusion in a verbal report, using appropriate images.

2 Interview your science teachers about what they understand by 'scientific method'. Design a leaflet to explain it to the rest of your group.

3 Debate the opinion 'since all people are different, it is not possible to define normal human behaviour'.

4 Develop a hypothesis on a social issue of your choice. What is the best way to investigate and test your hypothesis?

Thinking and analytical skills

1 Identify examples of subjective and objective knowledge in the passage.

2 How far does the cartoon provide valid evidence in support of the conclusion in the passage?

(iii) What's the point of work?

Links: 3.3 (ii); 3.3 (iv); 3.3 (vii); 4.16 **Key skills:** N3.1; N3.2; C3.3; C3.1a

Introduction

Work is a feature of all human society. Since work is socially defined, any definition must be related to a particular society and a specific time to have meaning. In broad terms it is used to describe any activity which results in the production of goods or services. Most people are involved in some form of work activity.

Background

Work can be classified under four main headings:

- Formal work receives monetary or other reward. It is recognised by the state, officially recorded, subject to taxation and National Insurance and government inspection and regulation.
- Informal work, which is not officially recognised or recorded, is often described as the 'black economy'. Payment is often in cash or kind. People involved in the black economy may have other formal work or may be officially unemployed and claiming state benefits. Earnings are not declared for tax purposes.
- Household work does not receive formal reward and usually consists of domestic services to a family or household. It includes cleaning, shopping, cooking, childcare and do-it-yourself. Most domestic work is traditionally performed by women and has low social status. **Feminist** writers suggest that it exists to perpetuate the oppression of women and its real value should be measured by the cost of buying similar services in the employment market.
- Community or voluntary work is unpaid activity that takes place outside the household or family. It includes activities such as collecting for charity or social committee membership.

In some non-industrial societies, work is performed only out of necessity. For example, hunter-gatherers may only work until they have gathered sufficient food for their immediate needs. In Western society, many feel the need to work – a 1994 survey suggested many unemployed would prefer low-paid work to drawing benefit.

Individual reasons for work include:

- to earn wages to survive,
- for interest and enjoyment arising from the job,
- to have social contact with others,
- to help others,
- to escape from restrictive domestic circumstances,
- to gain an identity and an identifiable role,
- to obtain status as a worker and from a position in the occupational hierarchy,
- to achieve self-fulfilment,
- as an undesirable means to achieve a desired end.

Different perspectives explain societal reasons for work differently. In economic terms, work is necessary to produce the goods and wealth required by society. **Marxists** claim work **alienates** workers, exists to control the population and generate profits for the ruling class. A third view says the **work ethic** is deeply embedded in the social conscience.

Paid work fits into one of three categories. It can lead to self-fulfilment and satisfaction. It can reduce the worker to a mere appendage (exemplified in the term 'factory-hands'). It can be a neutral experience, merely something that must be done in order to make more enjoyable activities accessible.

Glossary

feminists: advocate the right of women to equality with men in all aspects of life

Marxists: believe that conflict between social groups is inevitable and has economic causes

alienates: brings about a sense of loss of control

work ethic: the belief that people have a responsibility to work, irrespective of satisfaction

Issues to be discussed

- Should people who choose not to work be regarded as inferior or second rate?
- Why do we think working is important?
- Does work have to be alienating and oppressive?
- How does work confer either status or self-fulfilment?
- Why does domestic work have low status?
- Does the 'black economy' give work a bad name?

Where now?

Sociology Review, Vol 8 No 2 (1998)

Madry and Kirby, *Investigating Work, Unemployment and Leisure*, Collins, 1996

dfee.gov.uk

stbrn.ac.uk

What do you think?

'New technology has brought wealth to a few but alienation and low pay to many.' To what extent can this view be justified?

Undoubtedly, developments in information technology offer opportunities for the transformation of work. Predictions based upon present trends suggest that in countries such as Britain manufacturing will cease to be a significant source of employment. If roughly 35 per cent of the workforce were engaged in manufacturing occupations in the late Seventies, by the year 2010 the comparable figure will be about 15 per cent. This will be because most of the world's manufacturing capacity will be concentrated in low labour cost regions.

This means that in the more advanced countries of Europe the major concentration of jobs will be services of one kind and another. Here it is important to differentiate between two types of occupation: on the one hand, there are the highly paid professional, technical and creative jobs; on the other, there are those that are low paid and low skilled. Performance within the educational system largely determines in which of these we will find ourselves in the labour market.

The information age will not eradicate poverty. All predictions suggest that there will be a continuing growth in the number of low-paid jobs. Because a service economy is labour intensive, the jobs created are poorly paid and often offered on a short-term and part-time basis. New occupations emerging are as arduous as any to be found in traditional manufacturing. There is no capacity for the exercise of personal discretion, judgement and control.

The future of work, then, will be shaped by developments in information technology. With the decline in manufacturing, one set of boring, low-paid jobs will be replaced by another set of such jobs. However, there are other currently privileged occupations that are likely to be transformed in more positive ways as a result of the impact of information technology.

From R. Scase, 'The Future of Work' in *Sociology Review*, Vol 8 No 2 (1998)

Check-out operators reply on high-tech equipment but are often regarded as low-skilled workers with low status.

Activities

1 Assume that a full-time worker earns £4.15 per hour and a part-time worker gets £3.85 per hour. Calculate the weekly and annual pay of **a** a part-time worker, employed for 18 hours a week, and **b** a full-time worker employed for 37 hours per week.

2 Assume that personal allowances exempt the first £4,335 from tax and the worker received no other allowances:
a What pay rise would the part-time worker need in order to start paying tax? (Express as a percentage and £p per hour.)
b How much tax would the full-time worker pay, if tax is at 10 per cent?
c How much extra tax would a full-time worker have to pay after a 5 per cent pay rise?

3 Examine newspaper adverts for jobs. How do employers try to make jobs seem interesting?

4 Present a report to explain why many women seem attracted to part-time employment.

Thinking and analytical skills

1 Compare the types of knowledge used in the passage with those shown in the photograph.

2 Identify the stages in Scase's argument.

3 Does the passage present a balanced argument? Explain and justify your answer.

(iv) How much unemployment do we need?

Links: 3.3 (iii); 3.3 (v); 3.3 (vi); 4.16; 4.17 **Key skills:** N3.2; N3.3; C3.3; C3.1a; C3.1b

Introduction

Unemployment means not being employed in paid work or self-employment, even though an individual is available for work. It is a state that should be considered from several different viewpoints. It affects individuals, their families and dependents, society as well as the local and national economies.

Background

Full employment (defined in the Beveridge Report of 1942 as 'when less than 3 per cent of the **workforce** is unemployed') was the aim of governments between 1945 and 1979. This was the result of the social and economic difficulties of the Great Depression. In the UK between 1921 and 1939, unemployment averaged 14 per cent and was never less than 10 per cent of the workforce. Between 1948 and 1966, unemployment averaged 2 per cent of the workforce.

A changing pattern of employment emerged in the late 1970s. By 1979 employment it had reached 6 per cent, by 1982 9.5 per cent and in 1986 peaked at 11.8 per cent (or over 3 million people). In 1993, after a drop, it rose again to 12.4 per cent of all males and 7.6 per cent of all females over 16. Since then the general trend has been downwards.

Reasons for these changes included new government economic policies. Before 1979 Keynesian theories of active government involvement were accepted. The 1979 Conservative government adopted a monetarist policy, aiming to reduce government spending and direct involvement in economic activity. It was believed that inflation, not unemployment, was the main threat to prosperity. The British economy was less competitive because of oil price rises and the emergence of low-wage economies in the Far East. The workforce grew as increasing numbers of married women looked for work.

Other important economic influences on employment included declining manufacturing industries, greater part-time employment, new technology, expansion of service industries and high youth unemployment, especially among males and **ethnic minorities**.

Regional unemployment has been high in certain areas. In 1997 the north-east, Yorkshire and Humberside, Scotland, Wales and Northern Ireland all had unemployment rates greater than 8 per cent when the national average was 7.1 per cent. In contrast, the rate was only 5.2 per cent in the south-east and south-west. Areas with higher unemployment were those with economies based mainly on traditional manufacturing and production industries. New light industries, which replaced them, could not make use of the skills of many of the unemployed males.

Social groups most at risk of long-term unemployment include unskilled and semi-skilled workers, while managers, professionals and the highly skilled are least vulnerable. Personal services and light manufacturing, which employ considerable numbers of women part-time, may also suffer variations in employment. Inner cities tend to have higher unemployment rates than rural or suburban areas. Unemployment among those over 45 is increasing.

It is claimed that the unemployment picture is not reflected accurately in statistics. Methods of calculation were repeatedly changed after 1980 so that unemployed people over 55, young people under 18 and many married women are no longer included.

Glossary

workforce: the population aged between the end of compulsory schooling and retirement age, who are economically active and available for employment

ethnic minorities: a group of people in a minority in a given society who, because of distinctive physical or cultural differences, are disadvantaged in society

hierarchy: any system of graded organisation

Issues to be discussed

- Are people unemployed in the long term because they choose not to take available jobs?
- To what extent has the increase in the employment of women created male unemployment?
- Why are there greater numbers of ethnic minorities in the unemployment figures?
- To what extent should part-time work be encouraged?
- Should the government seek to reduce unemployment?
- Is inflation more of a problem than unemployment?

Where now?

W. Hutton, *The State We're in*, Jonathan Cape, 1995
Madry and Kirby, *Investigating Work, Unemployment and Leisure*, Collins, 1996
A. Dunnett, *Understanding the Economy*, Longman, 1998

www.statistics.gov.uk
europa.eu.int
www.employmentservice.gov.uk

What do you think?

To what extent do you agree that we need unemployment if the economy is to be efficient and prosperous?

Employers are tough about the conditions on which they are prepared to employ unskilled workers at the bottom of the **hierarchy**. The impact of sustained high unemployment, the abolition of wages councils, the weakness of employment regulation and the growth of contracting-out have combined to expose growing numbers of unskilled workers to naked employer power.

Society is dividing before our eyes, opening up new social fissures in the working population. The first 30 per cent are the disadvantaged. These include more than 4 million men who are out of work, including those who do not receive unemployment benefit so do not count as officially unemployed. It also includes unemployed women and women married to economically inactive men who are unable to take work because the loss of their husband's income support would more than offset any wage they might earn. Altogether some 28 per cent of the adult working population are either unemployed or economically inactive. Add another 1 per cent who are occupied on government schemes to alleviate unemployment, and the proportion of the population living at the edge is close to 30 per cent. (This 30 per cent, with their children poorly fed, their families under stress and without access to amenities like gardens, are the absolutely disadvantaged.)

The second 30 per cent are made up of the marginalised and the insecure. This category is not so much defined by income as by its relation to the labour market. People in this category work at jobs that are insecure, poorly protected and carry few benefits. This category more than any other is at the receiving end of the changes blowing through Britain's offices and factories.

From W. Hutton, The State We're In, Jonathan Cape, 1995, pp. 105–06

Unemployment by age and gender

percentage of economically active people

	1991	1993	1995	1997	1999
Males					
16–17	15.4	18.5	18.9	19.3	21.6
18–24	15.7	21.1	17.7	14.8	12.5
25–44	8.0	10.9	9.0	7.0	5.6
45–54	6.3	9.4	7.4	6.1	4.9
55–59	8.4	12.3	10.2	8.0	6.4
60–64	9.9	14.2	9.9	7.6	6.4
65 and over	5.9	4.6	NA	4.0	NA
All 16 and over	9.2	12.4	10.1	8.1	6.8
Females					
16–17	14.3	15.1	15.6	16.0	14.0
18–24	10.5	12.9	11.5	9.7	9.3
25–44	7.1	7.3	6.7	5.4	4.8
45–54	4.6	5.0	4.5	3.8	3.2
55–59	5.5	6.0	4.7	4.8	3.6
60 and over	4.4	3.9	NA	2.0	1.9
All 16 and over	7.2	7.6	6.8	5.8	5.1

Size of the economically active labour force (male and female)

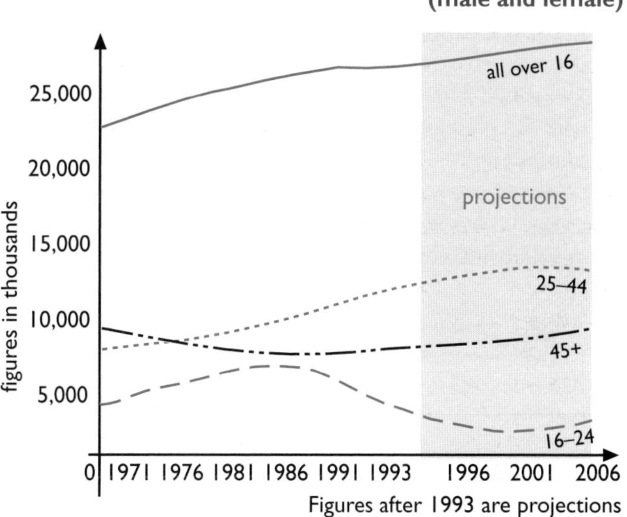

Figures after 1993 are projections

Source: Social Trends 1995, The Office for National Statistics; www.statistics.gov.uk

Activities

1 Discuss the view that unemployment is no longer a social problem because of welfare benefits.

2 Using the figures in the table construct:
a Appropriate graphs to show the trend of unemployment from 1991–99 for people in the age range 16–24.
b Appropriate graphs to show comparison of the proportions of males and females in each age group who were unemployed **i** in 1993, and **ii** in 1997.
c Comment on the trends shown in these figures.

3 **a** Using the table and the graph, calculate the number of the active labour force who were unemployed in 1991, 1993 and 1997 in each of the age groups.
b Show each of the proportions of employed to unemployed in two different graphic forms.
c Make a presentation based on your findings.

4 Investigate the number of unemployed in your locality and the range of jobs available to them. Present your findings in a report.

Thinking and analytical skills

1 In what ways does the author of the passage **a** appeal to the emotions, and **b** make use of knowledge to support his argument?

2 To what extent is the argument presented in the passage justified internally and supported by the tables?

(v) Who pays the price of unemployment?

Links: 3.3 (iv); 3.3 (ii); 3.3 (vi); 4.16 **Key skills:** IT3.1; IT3.2; IT3.3; N3.1; N3.3; WO3.1; WO3.2; WO3.3; C3.1a; C3.3

Introduction

Unemployment has become an accepted part of social and economic life, and we have become accustomed to thinking in large numbers. Factories close and job losses are counted in hundreds or thousands. The number of unemployed runs into millions and the rate of unemployment has often been well over 10 per cent. Under these circumstances, it is easy to forget that unemployment affects individuals and families.

Background

The unemployed fall into several different categories:

- Frictional unemployment is when people, in the normal course of events, are unemployed for brief periods.
- Seasonal unemployment occurs because of the time of year, like holiday camp workers or builders and farm labourers who are affected by inclement weather.
- Residual unemployment includes workers left over from the above categories, who cannot, for a time, be absorbed.
- Structural unemployment results from changes in the structure of the economy. It includes people whose skills do not match jobs available. Usually it results from an imbalance caused by the decline of one industry and the development of a totally different replacement. This type of unemployment was significant in the 1980s recession.
- Regional unemployment is when industries decline in one area and are replaced in another or when industry is unable to compete with cheap **imports** from abroad.
- Cyclical unemployment occurs if labour supply exceeds demand and is associated with changes in the **trade cycle**.
- Technological unemployment is when new technology reduces demand for labour. Old jobs are replaced with new ones that need fewer workers for the same or greater output.

Among the unemployed are also people who, though capable of work, do not seriously seek it and are content to rely on state benefit and perhaps the black economy.

Individuals react differently to unemployment. Some are **fatalistic** while others experience deep-seated psychological upset. Reactions often depend on whether unemployment is new or long-term. Work deprivation can result in apathy, depression, alienation and isolation from society.

Financial problems through loss of income can lead to poverty. The income gap between employment and benefit has increased since the Eighties through changes that link benefit to average prices rather than incomes.

Socially, unemployment has results that are difficult to **quantify**. It can bring social disorganisation, extra strain on marriage leading to a high divorce rate, loss of identity, reduced social contacts and restricted leisure activities. Workers who lack financial resources may lose job mobility.

High unemployment has twin economic effects on the state. Increased benefit payments result in upward pressure on taxes, and loss of revenue in taxation from the unemployed reduces state income.

The state is under pressure to intervene financially in areas of high unemployment to encourage job creation schemes. Some claim that although regional policies may create jobs, they are inefficient and adversely affect the **balance of trade.** Some claim that a reserve army of labour is essential if the economy is to expand.

Glossary

imports: goods that are brought in from other countries, rather than being produced in Britain

trade cycle: regular fluctuating phases in the economy

fatalistic: accepting that the individual has no control over events

quantify: to express in number or quantities

balance of trade: the financial difference between imports and exports

Issues to be discussed

- Are people entitled to jobs?
- To what extent are the social consequences of unemployment more significant than the financial or economic costs?
- What steps should the government take to ensure that all who receive unemployment benefit are genuinely seeking work?
- Is full employment at any price more important than business efficiency?
- What level of unemployment is acceptable in order to achieve general economic prosperity?

Where now?

C. Court. *Introduction to Sociology*, Tudor, 1997
J. Beardshaw, *Economics*, Pitman, 1992
Madry and Kirby, *Investigating Sociology*, Collins, 1996

www.dfee.gov.uk
www.cybercomm.no/work
www.the-arc.org/ep

What do you think?

'Unemployment is a nuisance, not a human problem as far as politicians are concerned.' Do you agree?

The unemployed will be delivered a blunt message by chancellor, Gordon Brown: jobs are available, so get to work. He will tell people in Britain's unemployment black spots that the only way out of their plight is through enterprise and hard work. There will be no new government hand-outs.

In what will be seen as an echo of Norman Tebbit's exhortation to the unemployed in the Eighties to 'get on your bikes', Brown's message is 'get off your backsides'.

A Treasury study on regional unemployment and job vacancies shows that even in areas of highest unemployment, there are plenty of job vacancies. The chancellor will insist that the problem in the regions is not lack of money, but a lack of enterprise and a failure to match up vacancies to people who could fill them.

'It is time to start dealing with the causes of unemployment and not just the consequences' he said. 'While more may have gone into these areas in social security benefits, less has gone in for training, enterprise and development.'

The chancellor believes that one of the main reasons why high unemployment co-exists with plentiful job vacancies is that many claimants work on the sly.

The Treasury's study of regional unemployment and job vacancies will show that there are more than 1m job vacancies in the economy, just slightly fewer than the 1.15m receiving unemployment benefit. In north-east England, Britain's highest unemployment area, officials estimate that there are more than 60,000 vacancies against a jobless total of just under 74,000. In the South-east, excluding London, there are more than 120,000 vacancies and just over 85,000 unemployed.

The chancellor's tough line on the unemployed is intended to show that there is no shift in policy. 'If people think that the solution lies in a return to the old ways, I will prove them wrong,' he said.

From *The Sunday Times*, 27 February 2000

The decline of Britain's traditional industries has led to high levels of unemployment in some parts of the country.

Activities

1. Research the amount spent by the government in unemployment benefit during each of the last five years. Present your findings in an appropriate written and graphic form. (Use http://www.statistics.gov.uk/statbase.)
2. Construct and administer to a mixed sample, a questionnaire on the social effects of unemployment. Analyse and comment on your findings.
3. In a group, prepare a list of arguments for and against the view that 'the unemployed ought to be worse off than people in work'. Make a presentation of your findings.
4. Collect examples of newspaper reports on unemployment. Analyse and write a report about the way different newspapers describe people who are out of work.

Thinking and analytical skills

1. Identify the different stages in the argument presented by *The Sunday Times* article.
2. How well does Gordon Brown, according to the report, justify his conclusions about the unemployed?

(vi) What should the government do about unemployment?

Links: 3.3 (iii); 3.3 (iv); 3.3 (v) **Key skills:** N3.3; WO3.1; WO3.2; WO3.3; C3.1a

Introduction

For much of the last twenty years, government policy has been to reduce direct economic involvement as much as possible. In the previous half century most governments were interventionist, but the Conservatives under Margaret Thatcher and John Major favoured a market policy. In 1997 Labour agreed to follow Tory policies in spending.

Background

Regulation of work and working conditions is generally accepted as a normal part of a government's responsibility. In Britain, for much of the nineteenth century, most governments were laissez-faire, believing that employers should decide matters of pay, hours and working conditions, and that regulation should be kept to a minimum.

In the twentieth century, membership of the European Union and acceptance of the Social Charter has resulted in considerable state regulation. Although there are different political perspectives about the specific nature of control, most politicians agree that some form of active government is needed to protect workers' interests.

To achieve this, laws have been made by Westminster and Brussels to define minimum acceptable working conditions: hours of employment are limited, health and safety regulations exist and a minimum wage has been introduced. To ensure that the laws are observed, the DfEE operates a system of inspectors.

The state is one of Britain's largest employers, although in recent years the number of state employees has been deliberately reduced. Few would argue that the civil servants and **bureaucrats** who are responsible for detailed work of government should not be directly employed by the state. However, some work traditionally done by state employees has been contracted out to the private sector.

The 1979 Conservative government believed the state was too involved in the economy. It believed that government should create conditions for prosperity and leave employment and training to **private enterprise**, claiming state ownership of industry was inefficient and expensive.

Consequently, the last twenty years have seen large-scale **privatisation** in the UK. This reduction of state control has ranged from the sale of the railways and coalmines to the privatisation of school dinner services. Some claim this has reduced state expenditure and increased efficiency by introducing the concept of profit and compensation in industries that used to survive on state subsidy.

State intervention in private industry has also been reduced. In the Seventies, as industries began to suffer from recession, various governments adopted an aggressive job creation policy. Investment in **depressed areas** was encouraged and incentives were provided to encourage the establishment of new industries. In the Eighties, this policy was reversed. It was claimed that although government incentives might ease the problem of unemployment, it had an adverse effect on the balance of trade. At the same time, the government attempted to reduce its costs by changing the benefit system. Some claim this policy has forced reluctant workers to seek employment. Others claim that it has caused unnecessary suffering to people who were unemployed through no fault of their own.

Glossary

regulation: rules laid down to control and restrict actions to ensure the requirements of authority are met

bureaucrat: officials who implement the rules made by government

private enterprise: businesses that are not owned or controlled by the state; operated for profit

privatisation: the sale or transfer of nationally owned industries to private ownership and control

depressed areas: areas with high levels of unemployment as a result of the closure of the main industry

Issues to be discussed

- Should the government provide work or should that be left to private enterprise?
- Should the government actively help the unemployed to find work? Justify your response.
- Are private businesses capable of protecting their workers' interests without state intervention?
- What changes have taken place in government policy to employment and unemployment since 1997?
- Does it matter if some areas of the country remain depressed or should the government intervene directly to help them?

Where now?

W. Hutton, *The State We're in*, Jonathan Cape, 1995

Madry and Kirby, *Investigating Work, Unemployment and Leisure*, Collins, 1996

http://scout.cs.wisc.edu/index.html

www.ilo.org.public

www.statistics.gov.uk

What do you think?

'The role of the government should be to create economic prosperity and not create jobs.' To what extent do you agree?

The phenomenal rise in social security spending has come about because the economy has been run in such a way that the numbers living in poverty and eligible for benefit have increased dramatically. There used to be 7 million claimants of income support in 1979; in 1993 there were 11 million.

It is mainly men who are the cause of the problem. Not only are there 1.7 million officially unemployed and dependent on income support – there are another 2 million who are no longer seeking employment because they know there is none. Over 70 per cent of them are completely unskilled – exactly the category in which the demand for labour has fallen.

The number of unskilled, jobless, male social security claimants has so increased under the impact of government policies, that expenditure increases more than offset any of the savings. Nor has there been any significant impact of the unemployed on wage setting in the wider economy.

The government's instinct has been to reduce state involvement. Neither Nigel Lawson, nor any of his successors, saw public money spent on training as a form of investment that might ultimately reduce the burden of social security.

From W. Hutton, *The State We're In*, Jonathan Cape, 1995, pp. 185–87

Comparable figures for regional unemployment (expressed as percentage of economically active population)

Percentages

	1990	1991	1992	1993	1994	1997
Great Britain						7.1
England and Wales	6.6	9.2	8.9	9.5	0.4	8.4
Scotland	8.0	9.2	9.5	10.1	9.9	8.5
Northern Ireland	13.7	14.1	12.1	12.5	11.5	7.5
North	8.6	10.6	11.2	11.2	11.7	6.9
West Midlands	5.9	9.0	10.7	11.6	9.9	6.8
South-east	3.9	7.4	9.4	10.3	9.6	5.2
South-west	4.5	7.7	9.1	9.2	7.5	5.2

Source: *Social Trends 1995*; www.statistics.gov.uk

Government expenditure on regional preferential assistance to industry (£ millions)

	88–89	90–91	92–93	94–95	96–97
Great Britain*	615.7	497.3	364.0	368.9	371.1
England	316.3	204.4	119.0	125.3	110.7
Wales	148.2	133.7	140.6	109.2	132.4
Scotland	151.2	159.2	104.4	134.4	128.2
Northern Ireland	138.3	132.1	105.6	132.9	137.1
North East	134.1	85.0	48.3	38.4	24.3
West Midlands	26.2	18.0	10.8	14.7	25.5
South-east	–	–	–	0.7	1.5

* *Not including figures for Northern Ireland*

Source: *Social Trends 1995*; www.statistics.gov.uk

Activities

1 Consider, compare and comment on the trends shown in the two sets of figures in the tables.

2 Investigate the availability of the New Deal programme in your area. Contact the Local Employment centre to discover:
a take up figures among unemployed groups,
b drop out rates,
c success rates in leading to full time employment.
Show your figures in appropriate graphs or tables.

3 Working in a group, compile a list of arguments for and against government involvement in job creation schemes.

4 Debate the opinion that government has a responsibility to support failing industry in order to avoid social problems in potentially depressed areas.

5 Display the trends shown in the tables above in appropriate graphs or tables for either the four countries or the four regions.

Thinking and analytical skills

1 Identify Hutton's conclusion and the stages of his argument.

2 To what extent is his conclusion justified by his argument?

3 In what ways and to what extent do the tables contribute to the validity of Hutton's argument?

(vii) How and why has the use of leisure time changed?

Links: 1.1 (ii); 3.3 (i); 3.3 (v); 3.3 (viii); 4.3; 4.4; 4.18 **Key skills:** C3.3; N1; N2; N3; C3.2; IT3.1; IT3.2

Introduction

Leisure activities are those things that people choose to do in their own time. As leisure time has increased, so has the range and nature of available activities. 'Leisure' has become a large and important sector of the economy. For some people leisure has become a central life interest, but for others it may remain largely inaccessible.

Background

Leisure time can be divided into three categories. Its most normal meaning refers to spare time when people are not engaged in paid employment, voluntary activities or domestic chores. Leisure time can result from non-work or unemployment. It can relate to those who are retired from employment.

Attitudes to leisure are often passed down the generations. Choice of leisure allows individuals to create a lifestyle around their own identity. Surveys show that men in full time employment generally have more leisure time than women and that married women working part time have least leisure time.

Several factors have combined to increase amounts of free time. During the early 1980s unemployment was at very high levels. This resulted in a large amount of free time for millions of people of working age. Changes in the nature of employment have meant that for many people the length of the working day has been reduced, although for others working hours have increased. Developments in technology, the decline of traditional heavy industries and the growth of the service sector have meant that more people are able to make good use of leisure time. At the same time full time employment has declined whilst part time work has increased. The **shake-out** in industry has resulted in a substantial number of healthy workers taking early retirement, whilst some employers often seem reluctant to take on older workers.

Factors influencing the use of leisure can include:

- age, **marital status** and responsibilities,
- health and physical fitness,
- the cost of activities and equipment,
- financial position and amount of **disposable income**,
- ease of access and availability of resources,
- available time occurring at the right time,
- gender, ethnicity and social class,
- fashion and the influence of the media,
- the influence of work colleagues,
- family and education.

Some people, for whom work is central in their lives, see leisure as an extension of employment, providing necessary refreshment to enable more efficient performance of tasks. Leisure time may be devoted to study for qualifications, or entertaining customers.

For others, leisure complements work. Their lives are clearly **segmented**, and work is often routine and boring. Leisure offers stimulation and excitement.

A third group find work alienating and treat leisure as an opportunity to forget their working lives. For example many people in dangerous occupations, like coal mining, may spend much of their leisure time drinking.

Glossary

shake-out: literally to empty a vessel of its contents; therefore in economic terms it refers to reducing the work force, by getting rid of surplus labour

marital status: whether a person is married, single, divorced or widowed; today it may not be restricted simply to formal 'marriage'

disposable income: income left after the payment of necessary expenditure

segmented: divided into distinct, separate sections

Issues to be discussed

- How might social or work status influence leisure interests and activities?
- Consider the different ways in which gender, ethnicity, age and disability might contribute to or restrict a person's use of leisure time.
- What factors might cause a person to choose active leisure pastimes rather than passive ones, or solitary activities rather than group ones?
- Is it possible to have too much leisure time?
- Why might some people find leisure activities 'inaccessible'?

Where now?

R. Hoggart, *The Way We Live Now*, Chatto and Windus, 1995

Madry and Kirby, *Investigating Work, Unemployment and Leisure*, Collins, 1996

www.english.sports.gov.uk www.ecna.org www.ramblers.org.uk

What do you think?

Do you agree that Hoggart presents an accurate picture of working-class leisure activities? Explain and justify your answer.

To appreciate the arts involves, first of all, the interplay of natural taste, talent and educational opportunity. The next major factor is social class, the differing physical and financial conditions within each class and, more important, their differing cultural conditions and assumptions. It cannot be convincingly argued today that most working-class people should not be expected to take an interest in the arts, on the grounds that their hours of work are long and arduous; for many this is no longer true. Generally, executives and managers work longer hours, and are under more strain.

To appreciate the arts can be expensive. Classical concerts are not cheap. Prohibitive cost is a favourite argument to explain why many people do not attend. It ignores the fact that a ticket for a pop concert can cost at least as much as one for a symphony concert.

More people than ever before have money to spend as they will, and exercise that right; those choices are educationally, socially and culturally conditioned.

The climate provided by class and occupation is much the most powerful element. Recreational habits of the working-class districts are heavily conditioned by age and sex. At the first level is the beer-and-bint culture of many young men in pubs and clubs (they have their female counterparts and both have their middle-class counterparts). Conversation after that age focuses on sport, cars, family problems, gossip about neighbours, what's been on the telly, royalty, crime, the cost of living, problems at work, and sex again. They divide also according to participant recreations, with gardening, DIY, and fishing predominant. What you would not expect is any talk about the arts, about plays or books or music or dance. They are simply not part of the culture.

From R. Hoggart, *The Way We Live Now*, Chatto and Windus, 1995, pp. 219–21

Activities

1 Investigate and compare three different types of leisure provision in your locality. Use your findings to make a presentation.

2 It is said that fishing is the most popular participant sport. Construct a questionnaire to ascertain why it has such popularity. Present your findings in a written report with appropriate graphs or tables.

3 Examine your local paper and make a list of the different leisure activities available. Present your results in a table, using appropriate headings and categories.

4 Use the Internet to identify the availability and cost of nationally significant leisure facilities within a fifty mile radius of your home. Design a leaflet to outline what is available.

Thinking and analytical skills

1 Identify and outline the stages of Hoggart's argument in the passage.

2 In what ways does Hoggart attempt to justify his assertions?

3 Is his conclusion valid?

(viii) Should government provide leisure facilities?

Links: 1.1 (v); 3.3 (iii); 3.3 (vi); 3.3 (vii); 4.4 **Key skills:** N3.1; N3.2; N3.3; C3.3; C3.1a; C3.1b

Introduction

Leisure facilities must be provided and maintained, even when they use natural resources (like rivers for angling, lakes for sailing or mountains for climbing). A major social and economic issue concerns the extent to which government should be involved. It has a clear role in regulation, enforcement of legal safety standards and general responsibility for the preservation of the natural **heritage**. But should it be involved commercially?

Background

The leisure industry has grown rapidly since the 1960s to match the steady increase in leisure time. Leisure provision falls into three distinct groups.

Private sector provision meets most demand at local and national level. **Entrepreneurs**, having identified demand, establish leisure-based businesses to make profit, exploit a **market niche** and deliver a service. They are entirely profit oriented.

Private provision may be large or small scale and local, regional, national or international in scope. Ownership may be in the hands of individuals, families, companies or international **conglomerates**. Income comes initially from investment or loans. Once established, customers generate income, although sometimes sponsorship may be available. The unique feature of private sector provision is the great variety offered. Only the profit motive is common to all.

Public sector provision takes various forms. It originates from either local or central government and is more often concerned with service than profit. It is usually intended, within broad **parameters**, to balance costs against income.

Start-up income usually comes from taxes, in the form of local or central government grants. A grant may be indirect, coming through government-sponsored agencies like the Sports Council. Ongoing revenue comes from charges, taxation, grants and income from **ancillary** services like restaurants at local authority swimming baths.

Since the public sector aims to provide a service, concessionary rates at off-peak times are often offered to the elderly, the poor or the unemployed. These groups have considerable leisure time but often lack sufficient financial resources or disposable income to benefit fully.

This sector often reflects prevailing political ideology and has been heavily **subsidised**. Some political groups believe the state and local authorities should provide equally for all citizens. Others feel the state should be a regulator and leave provision to private business.

Voluntary provision is usually non-profit making and seeks to provide services that might not otherwise exist. Examples include youth groups, the National Trust and interest groups like local orchestras, sports teams and rambling associations. Such groups have few paid employees, relying on the active good will of members. Local or central government may provide subsidies, but income generally comes from members' subscriptions.

Mixed provision can make up a fourth category. This occurs when central or local government combines with the private sector to fund facilities. This has happened with many expensive prestige projects, like the Dome, the National Exhibition Centre or the proposed rebuilding of Wembley.

Glossary

heritage: literally, anything that may be inherited

entrepreneur: a businessman who invests capital in a commercial activity to make profit

market niche: a section of commercial life, which has not been fully exploited previously

conglomerate: businesses made up of companies involved with a variety of different economic products or services

parameters: the boundaries, limits or constraints of a particular situation

ancillary: one service which is subservient to another

subsidy: a financial grant from a state organisation

Issues to be discussed

- Do we need state regulation of leisure facilities and providers?
- Should state agencies subsidise the private sector leisure industry in order to finance prestige projects?
- Are too many leisure time activities too passive?
- Would society be better off if leisure had not been reduced to a consumable commodity?
- Do entrepreneurs benefit more from leisure facilities than their customers?
- How true is it to say that the private sector is only interested in profit?

Where now?

Madry and Kirby, *Investigating Work, Unemployment and Leisure*, Collins, 1996

www.sosig.esrc.bris.ac.uk

www.english-heritage.org.uk

What do you think?

Are the leisure and entertainment industries simply about making profit or about social control?

Spending time and money on appearance, on entertainments and pastimes as if they were consumer items is taken as a sign of good fortune and social prestige. Fashions are mechanisms of social regulation, not because they direct us to follow certain styles of conduct but because they influence how we think about human conduct and social relations.

The entertainment industries have been successful in producing a continuous and growing interest in conspicuous consumption. For the most part, they are a diversionary institution in modern society, which manufacture partial interpretations of social reality by widely promoting a variety of illusions and desires. Most of the general public are well aware that the entertainment industries are in the business of marketing large-scale illusions and fantasies to millions of people. However, these industries are not generally regarded as sinister in any way. They are commonly valued for their creation of employment and their contribution to the economy.

Even if it is considered that the entertainment industries may exert an inordinate amount of influence over public knowledge, this is still not thought of as necessarily dangerous. If these industries do conceal the inequalities within a community by engrossing the majority of us in the pursuit of fantasies, or if they trivialise social reality by presenting simplistic analyses of human behaviour, or if they promote an ideology such as a belief in a meritocracy in a society that has clear class divisions and little social mobility, then it is still difficult to convince us that entertainment industries are promoting misleading views in order to inhibit the individual's ability to see how society works Even with some acceptance of the idea that the entertainment industries may definitely influence public culture, they are persistently seen as largely benign.

From J. Finkelstein, *'Fashion, Taste and Eating Out'*. Quoted in A. Giddens, *The Polity Reader in Cultural Theory*; Polity Press, 1994, pp. 280–82

Commercial leisure facilities.

Publicly provided leisure facilities.

Activities

1 Identify and then show in a table the ten most popular leisure facilities in your locality. How many are:
  a provided from the private sector,
  b provided by the public sector,
  c provided by volunteers?

2 Find out how much your local authority spent on leisure in each of the last five years. Show these figures:
  a in appropriate line graphs over time,
  b as a proportion of local authority spending.

3 Research how leisure activities in your area are publicised. Design either a publicity poster or leaflet for a regular activity that takes place in your school or college.

4 Debate the opinion that leisure facilities should not be subsidised, but should be commercially viable.

5 Conduct a survey to identify what facilities people of your age feel should be available.

Thinking and analytical skills

1 Identify the different stages of the argument presented in the passage.

2 What types of knowledge does the author use to justify her conclusion?

3 To what extent does the passage present a balanced argument?

(i) Why do we need law?

Links: 1.2 (i); 3.4 (ii); 3.4 (vii) **Key skills:** C3.1a; C3.1b; C3.2; IT3.1; It3.2

Introduction

Any society or group of people has its own set of rules to control the behaviour of its members. Such rules will define what acceptable or unacceptable behaviour is. Rules of conduct may change through time in response to changing circumstances. Different societies are likely to have different ideas of the type of behaviour they wish to encourage. Rules may be formal (written down) or informal (understood).

Background

Formal rules or laws exist to promote social order, establish **justice** and define relations between individuals and groups within a society. They also help to protect property rights, establish moral standards and give legal status to authorities. Laws underpin the freedom of citizens, guarantee certain civil liberties and provide a method of resolving disputes. In effect laws reflect and formalise the shared values of a society.

Positive law is defined by a human agency, such as a **monarch** or government. It is often based on custom or meets particular circumstances. It can be altered if attitudes or circumstances change. Different countries and times may have different laws. A belief in positive law implies acceptance that over time laws may change. Acceptance of this view may incline society to a liberal or radical approach.

Natural law is fundamental to all societies, according to those who believe it exists. It is unchangeable, not subject to the whim of individuals. Such law is believed to apply equally everywhere and at all times, and is more binding than local law or customs. In more religious ages, natural law was believed to come from God and to be linked to natural rights. Some societies, such as France and the USA have attempted to define these principles in a **Bill of Rights**. This idea underlies the European Declaration on Human Rights. Belief in natural law may incline society to a more conservative approach, resisting change.

In England and Wales, there are three different types of law. (The Scottish system is different.) Common law has developed over time. It consists of rules or practices which have the force of law in a court. **Statutes** are laws passed by parliament and written in the statute book. Case law consists of court rulings and interpretations of points of law. The UK's membership of the EU has introduced European law, which can take precedence over all other forms of law in the UK.

The existence of law creates a belief that it is morally right and should be obeyed. It also creates crime since criminal behaviour is defined in terms of breaking laws, and is open to a range of sanctions.

Respect for the law will exist if it is regarded as reasonable. If a law is thought unreasonable, pressure for change will develop, either by parliamentary means or by direct action. This happened in the successful anti-poll tax campaign. Law is usually a compromise between different views and is often open to interpretation.

Courts are independent of government and exist to defend the values of society against law-breakers. Their function is to provide fair trials and sound verdicts for people accused of offences, to demonstrate equality of treatment for all regardless of social position and to allow accused people the right of defence.

Glossary

justice: fairness; the exercise of authority to maintain what is right

monarch: a supreme ruler, such as king, queen or emperor; the position is usually hereditary

Bill of Rights: a constitutional document guaranteeing the rights of individuals

statute: a written law of a legislative body or parliament

Act: law passed by parliament

Issues to be discussed

- Can law be unbiased? Does it reflect the views of the population or of a dominant group?
- How does law reflect the values of society?
- Why do most people who obey most laws choose to break some laws?
- If there is such a thing as natural law, how should it be defined and identified?
- Does it matter that European law takes precedence over UK law?

Where now?

M. J. Allen, *Textbook on Criminal Law*, Blackstone Press, 1996

J. Kingdom, *Government and Politics in Britain*, Polity Press, 1999

www.homeoffice.gov.uk www.stbrn.ac.uk

What do you think?

'The Law is impartial and exists to protect the rights of individuals and society, without favour or prejudice.' To what extent do you agree with this opinion?

One view claims law is the reflection of the will of the people, but another suggests it is a reflection of the will of the powerful, although this may not always be immediately apparent.

Critics argue that, as economic power guarantees political and social power, the rich are able to manipulate the rest of us and pass laws which benefit them. There are basically two ways in which the ruling class ensures that laws favourable to them are passed.

First, the manipulation of values ensures that the debate on law and order is conducted within a framework of values sympathetic to the ruling class – this is known as setting the agenda. An example is the 1994 Public Order and Criminal Justice Act. This gave the state new powers to prevent gatherings of quite small numbers of people, in effect taking away civil liberties from the majority of the population.

A second method is through the use of pressure group activity. Changes in the law generally result from pressure groups lobbying the government. Organised pressure groups, which carry out their activities in public, are the most visible. But critics point to the power of the City of London to lobby the government in informal ways behind the scenes.

Not all laws, however, are seen to be entirely for the benefit of the ruling class. Clearly, many laws do protect ordinary people. Genuine concessions can be gained when the interests of the powerful and of the ordinary people overlap or when representative pressure groups are able to push through reforms in the interests of the wider population. On other occasions the law may not obviously reflect the will of the powerful, most notably when there are divisions between members of the ruling class.

From S. Moore, *Investigating Crime and Deviance*, Collins, 1997, p. 71

Anti-road building protesters demonstrate against the construction of a new motorway. The right to civil protest against a perceived wrong is guaranteed by law.

Activities

1 Why was the anti-poll tax campaign able to enforce a change to the law?

2 Identify one new law proposed by the government for the present session of parliament.
a Conduct a survey in your area to discover popular feeling about the proposal.
b Compare how the proposal is treated in different parts of the media.
c Make a presentation of your findings.

3 Do you agree that only criminals should fear the law?

4 If you were able to make any new law, what would it be? Outline the purpose of your proposal and the main points you would include.

5 Debate the opinion 'good laws should be obeyed but bad laws should be ignored.'

Thinking and analytical skills

1 Identify the strengths and the weaknesses in the argument used in the passage.

2 What values are represented in the photograph?

3 How do the values shown in the photograph contribute to the arguments in the passage?

(ii) Does the law make things right?

Links: 1.2 (ii); 1.2 (iii); 1.3 (vi); 3.4 (iii); 3.4 (vi); 4.12 **Key skills:** C3.2; C3.3; C3.1b; C3.1a; WO3.1; WO3.2; WO3.3; N3.1; N3,2

Introduction

The difference between right and wrong and good and bad is a moral judgement. The meaning of these terms may differ between cultures, societies and over time. Some societies hold generally accepted absolute values without argument, often influenced by religious belief. For many people today, religion has little significance which means they may lack moral certainty. Right and wrong then becomes a personal judgement.

Background

The law defines what society sees as acceptable and unacceptable conduct. Actions in accordance with the law are right, but breaches of the law are wrong. The law says it is wrong to drive over 70mph on a motorway. Speeding drivers may agree it is wrong to break the law, but might not consider their actions to be evil.

For a legal system to be effective, any law must have the majority support of the population. Where that support is missing, laws are often ignored, broken or are the subject of pressure for change.

Changes to the law occur throughout history. The Suffragette movement was a famous and dramatic campaign in the early twentieth century for votes for women. Some historians feel that the confrontational nature of the campaign delayed **emancipation**. Other dramatic changes in the law and in the values the law upholds have included: divorce reform, abortion reform, the abolition of the death penalty, equal opportunities and opposition to racial and sexual discrimination.

Some changes in the law, such as the Dangerous Dogs Act, the imposition of speed limits and the breathalyser, have reduced individual freedom. At present, there is pressure to change the law on fox hunting, the age of consent for homosexuals, soft drugs, **euthanasia** and organ donation.

Pressure for change can come in various ways:

- New knowledge may make changes possible or necessary.
- It may come from changing attitudes and values.
- Moral crusaders campaign for changes to 'wrong' laws.
- Moral campaigns may be supported and encouraged or even led by the mass media.
- Moral panics may create a sense of fear and concern in society leading to demands for new laws.
- Pressure groups may seek to influence the government and public opinion.
- The structure of society may change over time and make new laws necessary or old laws inadequate.
- As society becomes increasingly multicultural and multiracial, there may be demands to change the law.
- Membership of the EU means that European law takes precedence over UK law, making some changes necessary.
- The media and **globalisation** may raise awareness of attitudes and beliefs in other countries.
- Dominant groups, especially political parties, have an agenda for change which they implement when in power.

As far as the law is concerned, right and wrong is not absolute. It is simply a reflection of socially accepted attitudes at a particular time in history.

Glossary

emancipation: literally freeing a slave population; hence freeing women of society's restrictions

euthanasia: mercy killing, bringing about an easy death for someone who is suffering.

globalisation: the development and diffusion of worldwide social and economic ties

humanistic: a central focus on human needs without recourse to religious beliefs or practices

Issues to be discussed

- Should people refuse to obey laws with which they disagree?
- How far should people who disagree with a law be allowed to go in persuading the government to change it?
- Does society make law or does law make society?
- How can new knowledge make change possible or necessary? Identify examples of this type of change.
- Identify examples of changes to the law demanded or achieved by each of the types of pressure listed above.

Where now?

Schaeffer and Koop, *Whatever Happened to the Human Race?*, Marshall Morgan and Scott, 1980

A. Giddens, *Sociology*, Polity Press, 1993

www.iaetf.org www.ves.org.uk

What do you think?

'If the law is bad any method of forcing it to be changed is acceptable.' Critically examine this view.

Cultures can be judged in many ways, but eventually every nation in every age must be judged by this test: how did it treat people? The final measure of mankind's humanity is how humanely people treat one another.

There is a 'thinkable' and an 'unthinkable' in every era. One era is quite certain intellectually and emotionally about what is acceptable. Yet another era decides that those 'certainties' are unacceptable and puts another set of values into practice. On a **humanistic** basis, people drift along from generation to generation and the morally unthinkable becomes the thinkable as the years move on. By 'humanistic base' we mean the fundamental idea that men and women can derive the standards by which to judge all matters. For such people, there are no fixed standards of behaviour, no standards that cannot be eroded or replaced by what seems necessary or even fashionable.

The most striking and unusual feature of history is the speed with which eras change. Looking back in history, we note that cultures such as the Indus River civilisation lasted about a thousand years. Today the passing of eras is so greatly speeded up that the 1960s stand in sharp contrast to the 1970s. What was unthinkable in the 1960s is unthinkable no longer.

The thinkables of the 1980s and 1990s will certainly include things which most people today find unthinkable and immoral, even unimaginable and too extreme to suggest. Yet when these become thinkable and acceptable, most people will not even remember that they were unthinkable in the Seventies. They will slide into each new unthinkable without a jolt.

What we regard as thinkable and unthinkable about how we treat human life has changed drastically in the West.

From Schaeffer and Koop, *Whatever Happened to the Human Race?*, Marshall Morgan and Scott, 1980, pp. 2–3

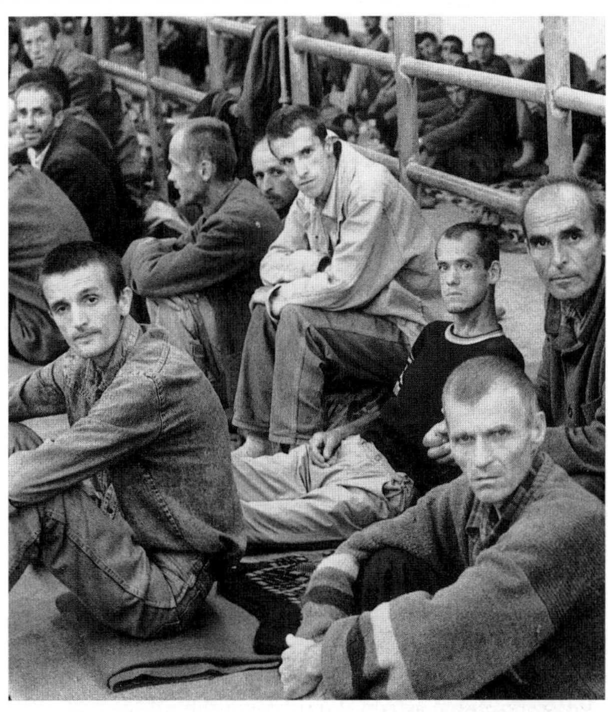

Inside the Bosnian camps: allegations about mistreatment were borne out when the Press were allowed into the Manjaca camp. This was legal but is it right?

Activities

1 Explain what Schaeffer and Koop mean by 'thinkable' and 'unthinkable'.

2 Write a response from a humanist perspective, to the argument presented in the passage.

3 In a group, discuss what present-day 'unthinkable' might become acceptable in the next 20 years. Write a short pamphlet to explain why you feel it should be accepted.

4 Choose any of the changes to the law listed on page 166. Working in a group, research the arguments and methods that were used to bring about a change in the law. Make a presentation of your findings, including statistical or graphical evidence to show the effect of the reform.

5 Review newspaper and/or television reports of any current campaign to change the law. Conduct a survey to discover local feelings. Write a report of your findings.

Thinking and analytical skills

1 Schaeffer and Koop make use of both subjective and objective knowledge. Identify examples of each.

2 How might the argument in the passage be justified?

(iii) What is the point of punishment?

Links: 1.2 (ii); 3.4 (i); 3.4 (iv) **Key skills:** IT3.1; IT3.3; N3.3; N3.2; C3.3

Introduction

Law is an instrument of social control and sets out sanctions for offenders. These are intended to protect the interests of society rather than individuals. Parliament makes the law, the police investigate offences, and the judiciary judge and sentence offenders. The purpose of punishment is a question that can generate considerable debate. In the UK, punishment varies according to the crime committed.

Background

Since the abolition of capital punishment, imprisonment is the most severe penalty in the UK. Other punishments include fines, probation, **parole**, community service and **electronic tagging**.

Is punishment too harsh or too lenient? Reasons to justify punishment fall into two broad categories: to punish offenders and to reassert society's moral values.

Retribution, based on the idea of 'just deserts,' expresses society's moral objection to crime and hatred of criminal activity. It reflects a communal desire for revenge and reaffirms the values upheld by the law. When passing sentence, a judge should not be motivated simply by the desire for revenge. Punishment should be reasoned, reasonable and designed to remove any advantage gained through criminal activity. Punishment should be proportional to the harm caused.

Deterrence is both particular and general. It is 'particular' in attempting to discourage re-offending and 'general' because it aims to persuade potential criminals not to offend through fear. Some judges impose **exemplary sentences** for serious, frequently recurring crimes. Severe penalties seem not to discourage re-offending. The possibility of capture by the police is a greater deterrent. Fear of punishment may affect people sharing mainstream values more than those who are **marginalised**.

Incapacitation means removing offenders from society. Punishment exists to protect society from those who, if at liberty, might continue to offend. Reform and rehabilitation of criminals were once believed to be the main purpose of punishment. The aim was to help offenders to accept mainstream values and conform to society. In 1964, Prison Rules were introduced to encourage training and counselling. Probation was introduced as an alternative to prison so that criminals could live a normal life. Closely supervised help and guidance would replace loss of liberty. The 1967 Criminal Justice Act introduced parole and remission for good behaviour.

Recently thinking has changed. Increasing prison population and overcrowding has made rehabilitation impracticable. The Conservative government introduced a harsher regime with the 1991 Criminal Justice Act. Penalties were to reflect the seriousness of offences. The 1997 Crime (Sentence) Act imposed mandatory prison terms for certain offences and a life sentence for offenders convicted for the second time of a serious violent or sexual crime. Other methods of punishment were applied to lesser offences, emphasising retribution not rehabilitation. Judges were discouraged from imposing lighter sentences. Labour adopted a similar policy in their 1998 Crime and Disorder Act, which imposed more severe penalties and required reparations for certain victims. Reformers claim that criminals' families are the real sufferers from imprisonment and that loss of liberty, constant supervision and isolation from normal social life makes prison itself punishment.

Glossary

parole: early release of prisoners on promise of continued good behaviour

electronic tagging: method of tagging prisoners so they can serve their sentence in the community, under restrictions and electronic supervision

exemplary sentences: more severe punishment that is normally expected to act as a warning or example to others

marginalised: the process of being and feeling excluded from mainstream society; not receiving sufficient prestige

Issues to be discussed

- Should criminals in prison be punished or is loss of liberty sufficient penalty?
- Are prisons too comfortable to deter repeat offenders?
- Is there a case for part-time prison sentences?
- Should we try to change society before we try to change criminals?
- Why do 'people sharing mainstream values' fear punishment 'more than those who are marginalised'?

Where now?

M. J. Allen, *Textbook on Criminal Law*, Blackstone Press, 1996

A. Giddens, *Sociology*, Polity Press, 1993

www.homeoffice.gov.uk

web.ukonline.co.uk/howard.league

www.tphbook.dircon.co.uk

What do you think?

'Prison does not work.' To what extent do you agree with this statement? What real alternatives are there for the punishment of serious, persistent or violent offenders? Justify your conclusions.

- Who are we locking up? During 1995, 20,742 people were sent to prison for non-payment of fines; 749 for non-payment of TV licences.
- The average remand population in 1994 was 12,400. Over 63 per cent did not receive a prison sentence.
- Over the last 10 years, 453 people have killed themselves in prison. In 1995 alone, 9 were under 21 years old.
- During 1993/94, it cost an average of £548 per week to keep someone in prison. A community based sentence costs £25.
- In 1995 the chief inspector of prisons withdrew his inspection team from a women's prison because of overzealous security, prisoners being locked in cells 23 hours a day and in very dirty conditions.
- Fifty-one per cent of all prisoners discharged from custody in 1992 were reconvicted after 2 years. This rises to 89 per cent of all 14–16-year-olds.

Adapted from a fact sheet from the Howard League for Penal Reform; www.ukonline.co.uk

As part of a two-pronged approach to crime, the Government is to introduce three-year minimum sentences for those convicted of a third offence of domestic burglary. Home Secretary, Jack Straw said: 'The fight against crime is at the centre of our commitment to make Britain a better place to live. Crime diminishes the lives of innocent people, restricts their freedoms and causes fear, anger and loss. Our strategy is to tackle crime and its causes. At the same time we are determined to ensure proper punishment for those who break the law. I have therefore decided to bring into force a three-year minimum sentence for those convicted of a third offence of burglary. These criminals will receive the tough penalties they deserve. We need to combine preventing crime with punishing criminals.'

From a speech made by Jack Straw, 13th January 1999; www.ukonline.co.uk

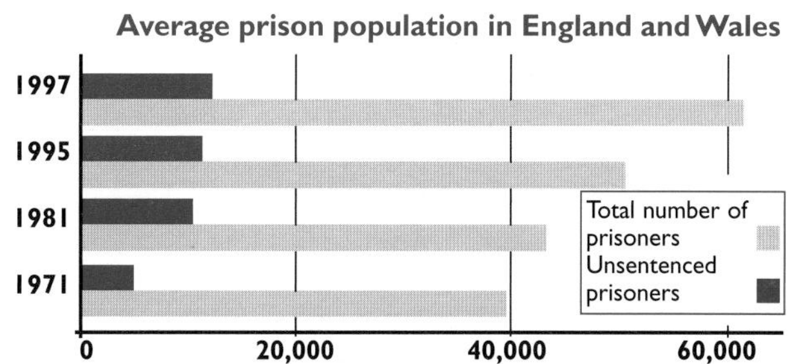

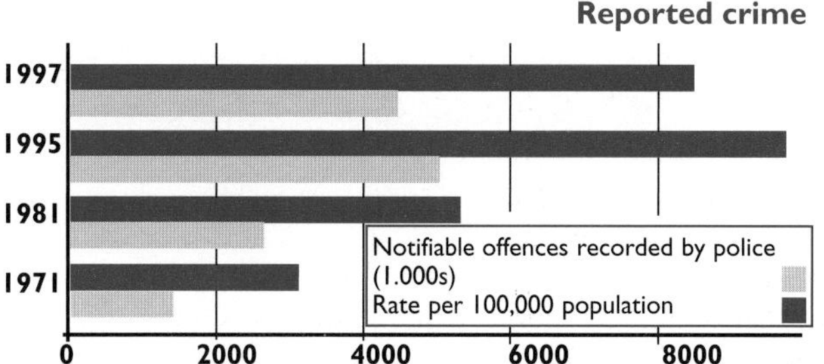

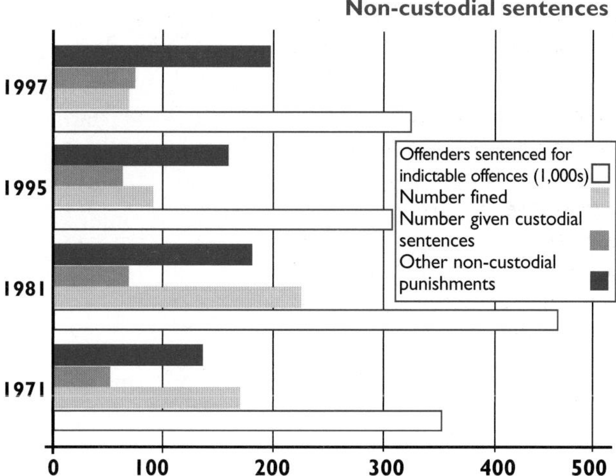

Source: Office for National Statistics; www.statistics.gov.uk

Activities

1 Investigate the figures for crime and punishment in the area where you live, over the last five years.
a What trends can you identify? **b** Which crimes receive the most severe sentences? **c** Is there any relationship between rising crime figures and levels of punishment?

2 Show the information in the graphs in a different graphic or tabular form.

3 Investigate the steps taken by the present government 'to tackle crime and its causes'.

4 Conduct a survey to investigate attitudes to the purpose of punishment. Present your findings in a report, including graphs and statistics. Include any recommendations you would make to the Home Secretary to make punishment more effective.

Thinking and analytical skills

1 Jack Straw uses both objective and subjective knowledge in his argument. Identify and comment on examples of both in the passage.

2 What arguments are implicit in the Howard League fact sheet? How effectively are they justified?

(iv) Should capital punishment be restored?

Links: 3.4 (i); 3.4 (iii); 4.8 **Key skills:** IT3.1; IT3.2; IT3.3; N3.1; N3.2; N3.3; C3.1a; C3.1b; C3.3

Introduction

Capital punishment is the lawful infliction of death on an individual as a sanction for breaking certain laws. Formerly it was practised by most states but today has been abolished, or effectively discontinued, in over one hundred. This reflects a major change in attitudes towards **social control**. In the past, emphasis was placed on publicly inflicted pain but now the emphasis is on changing the attitudes of criminals.

Background

In Britain execution was by hanging and, until 1868, in public. A minimum age limit of 16, fixed in 1908, was raised to 18 in 1933. Changing attitudes developed after the Second World War because of:

- concerns raised by several high-profile cases,
- the cruelty of **Nazi death camps**, which sickened people who feared misuse of power by governments,
- media publicity raising awareness of criminals' humanity,
- changing attitudes and values in society,
- the Home Office operating systems unfairly,
- the seeming unfairness of one person – the Home Secretary – having the power of life or death.

The average number of executions a year between 1900 and 1965 was 11. This punishment, inflicted upon a few, was applied too inconsistently to deter others. 'Life imprisonment' (for 10 to 15 years) for reprieved criminals did not compare with the severity of hanging.

The 1957 Homicide Act was an attempt to reduce confusion. Only five categories of murder were punishable by hanging. The Act, which introduced the concept of '**diminished responsibility**', increased confusion.

Capital punishment for murder was suspended for five years in 1965 and totally abolished in 1969. In 1998, execution for military crimes was ended. Attempts to restore hanging have failed to gain parliamentary backing, even though there is strong popular support for it.

Why should capital punishment be restored?

- It has a long tradition and is taught by many religions.
- It removes evil people who threaten society.
- Other methods of punishment are expensive.
- It is a real punishment, making criminals suffer.
- It will deter others from committing a similar crime.
- It is less cruel than life imprisonment.
- Most people want capital punishment restored.
- Lack of execution may encourage worse crimes.

Why should capital punishment remain abolished?

- It is cruel and unnatural and brutalises society.
- It is not an effective deterrent.
- It can easily be extended to other crimes.
- It is irreversible and beyond compensation.
- Life imprisonment is more rational and humane.
- It may make juries reluctant to convict.
- It causes immoral suffering to the offender's family.
- Race, class or gender may influence its use.

Glossary

social control: practices developed by groups to enforce conformity and deal with behaviour that violates norms

Nazi: German totalitarian political party and government 1933 to 1945

death camps: concentration camps used in Germany to contain and then destroy enemies of the state, like the Jews

reprieve: remission or commutation of a capital sentence

diminished responsibility: a legal defence, used in murder trials, that the accused was not responsible for his actions

Issues to be discussed

- Should capital punishment be restored in the UK for:
  a the most serious cases of murder?
  b all cases of murder?
  c serious crimes of violence as well as murder?
- How might the influence of race, class or gender on the imposition of execution be investigated?
- Should the government hold a binding referendum on the restoration of capital punishment? Why?
- Would a more humane form of execution be acceptable?

Where now?

R. Hood, *The Death Penalty: a World-wide Perspective*, Clarendon Press, 1996
www.amnesty.org
www.geocities.com/CapitolHill/6142

What do you think?

'Capital punishment is the only fair and reasonable sanction for those who unlawfully take life. It should be reintroduced and applied rigorously without reprieve.' To what extent can this opinion be justified?

Britons on Florida's death row may be asked to agree to their hearts, livers and other organs being given to transplant patients.

Proposed changes to the state's law would allow execution by drugs, which induce brain death while the heart remains beating. Organs would be passed to hospitals.

More than 160 British passport holders are in prison in Florida. At least 15 have been convicted of murder and one faces execution. This weekend his lawyer reacted with anger to the suggestion of using execution victims as organ donors. 'He is not about to participate in a Frankenstein experiment by the twisted state legislature. We are confident that he is not going to be in prison much longer.'

Until this year Florida, which has 368 prisoners on death row, used an unreliable electric chair, which caused one victim to catch fire. The state has now introduced a cocktail of three drugs and the advent of lethal injection executions gave Bill Andrews, a Republican politician, the idea for his bill. He argues that body parts such as heart valves, skin and bone marrow can be recovered without any alteration to the existing drug combination. Retrieving a beating heart would, however, require a modified execution method.

Transplant organisations have expressed concern about the risk of Aids or hepatitis infection, but have raised no moral objections.

A British lawyer, based in New Orleans, who has waged a long campaign against the death penalty, condemned the plan. 'It is like hanging, drawing and quartering someone – it is revolting.' he said.

From *The Sunday Times*, 9 April 2000

In spite of protests, executions still take place in America.

Activities

1 Using www.statistics.gov.uk, examine statistics on murders in the UK between 1950 and 2000.
  a Plot these figures on an appropriate graph, marking in the 1957 Homicide Act, and the suspension and abolition of capital punishment.
  b Examine and explain any trends.
  c Is there evidence that execution was or was not a deterrent?
  d What other evidence might you require?

2 Debate the opinion that 'restoration of the death penalty would encourage our desire for revenge but would not reduce criminal behaviour'.

3 Research attitudes of different religions to capital punishment and write a report comparing your findings with present-day practice.

4 Research and make a presentation on the Universal Declaration of Human Rights and capital punishment. (Use www.statistics.gov.uk and www.un.org/rights.)

Thinking and analytical skills

1 Consider the arguments for and against restoration of capital punishment. Identify those which are **a** beliefs, **b** factual, and **c** fallacy.

2 Does the argument in the newspaper article appeal to emotion or reason? How might its claims be justified?

(v) Can we afford legal aid?

Links: 3.4 (i); 3.4 (vii) **Key skills:** N3.1; N3.2; C3.1b; C3.2; C3.1a

Introduction

If a legal system is to be fair it must be equally available to all citizens and must provide the same level of justice for all. In theory, the law is impartial – any person having recourse to the law should feel confident that they will receive the same justice as everybody else. This ideal is rarely, if ever, achieved in any society.

Background

Legal expenses are often a major barrier to fairness. **Litigants** generally require the services of a **solicitor** or **barrister**. The side that can afford the best lawyers often wins. Good lawyers can be expensive and trials, lengthy.

Each side must pay its own legal costs, although the court sometimes makes the loser contribute to the winner's costs. As a result, lawyers' clients are usually wealthy middle-class people who can afford justice. Poorer people may be forced to suffer injustice rather than face ruinous legal bills.

Legal aid was introduced in 1949 to help poorer people who might otherwise be unable to afford to seek legal help. This was a major step forward for law and democracy. It would be a significant denial of human rights if the state failed to help poor people meet legal costs.

The operation of legal aid has been severely criticised and frequent attempts have been made to reform it. Originally, the Law Society managed the system, but in 1989 responsibility was transferred to the Legal Aid Board. Extensive reviews of the legal aid system in the mid-1990s led in 1997 to proposals for fundamental reform. These came into force in April 2000 for civil legal aid and will be in place for criminal legal aid by April 2001.

There are three types of legal aid: civil proceedings, criminal cases and legal advice (known as the Green Form Scheme). Civil grants fall into three groups: free aid; partial assistance, subject to contribution; no aid. In criminal cases fees are either paid in full or not at all. In lengthy and expensive cases 'applicants with reasonable means may be granted legal aid'. Under the Green Form Scheme, limited assistance and advice can be given to anyone, regardless of needs.

Claimants must satisfy two tests. Financial resources are **means-tested** in terms of disposable income and disposable capital. **Civil claimants** must establish the merits of the case, showing it is 'a reasonable case with a reasonable chance of success'. In criminal cases, claimants must establish the case is 'in the interests of justice'. In civil cases, the Legal Services Commission, which replaced the Legal Aid Board in April 2000, conducts assessments, but applicants for criminal aid are considered by the court.

Criticisms:

- Wealthy people often find technical reasons to claim.
- The system is expensive and costs are rising rapidly.
- Middle-income earners are effectively excluded from going to law. They can't afford the cost or get legal aid.
- The legally aided have advantages over the non-aided when deciding whether to continue with litigation.
- Eighty per cent of claimants do not make contributions.
- The proportion of households able to claim legal aid fell from 77 per cent to 61 per cent from 1979 to 1990.
- Ninety-nine per cent of those tried in criminal cases have legal aid, irrespective of how they plead.

Glossary

litigant: someone who goes to law

solicitors: lawyers who traditionally deal with out-of-court matters; there are about 35,000

barrister: traditionally a specialist advocate who appears in court on behalf of a litigant; there are about 5,000

means-test: a measure of financial resources against clearly defined criteria

civil proceedings: legal action involving the relationship between one citizen and another, rather than with the state

Issues to be discussed

- Would democracy and human rights be diminished if legal aid were abolished?
- Why do 99 per cent of people tried in criminal cases receive legal aid?
- What are the main weaknesses of the legal aid system and how might it be improved?
- Does it matter if wealthy people receive legal aid?
- How and why are middle-income people penalised by the legal aid system? What steps are needed to protect them?

Where now?

M. Zander, *Cases and Materials on the English Legal System*, Butterworths, 1996

P. Cane Atiyah, *Accidents, Compensation and the Law*, Butterworths, 1993

www.poptel.org.uk/cab/

www.coe.fr/eng/legaltxt

www.open.gov.uk/lcd/leg-aid

www.legalservices.gov.uk

What do you think?

'Legal Aid is intended to help the poor, but it has simply made the rich richer.' To what extent do you agree ?

An attempt by Kevin Maxwell's lawyers to claim more money for their work on his 1996 fraud trial is being challenged by Lord Irvine, the Lord Chancellor.

The case, which ended with Maxwell's acquittal, has already cost taxpayers £30 million, a British fraud trial record. In March a senior costs judge ruled in favour of the lawyers' additional claim.

Irvine's intervention is the latest move in a long crusade against high-charging lawyers. Just before Christmas Irvine warned lawyers he was ready 'to bear down very, very hard' on high legal aid earnings. The annual civil and criminal aid bill is about £1.6 billion.

Legal teams worked on Maxwell's case for more than four years, the trial lasted eight months and the entire costs were borne by the public purse. Irvine's attacks on some lawyers' inflated earnings started two months after he became Lord Chancellor. He criticised '£1m-a-year lawyers' and said it was 'staggering' that the top 1 per cent of criminal cases consumed 24 per cent of the £566m legal aid bill.

In 1998 he provoked fury among lawyers by publishing a top 40 league table of the barristers and solicitors who earned the most from legal aid. The table showed that one solicitor's firm was paid £8.5m in the 1996–97 financial year. Seven of the top earning criminal barristers were involved in the Maxwell fraud trial.

Irvine is driving through legal aid reforms, so that by 2002 solicitors and barristers will be paid fixed sums for high-cost cases, not hourly fees, which can reach £315 for top QCs.

From *The Sunday Times*, 30 April 2000

Legal Aid gross expenditure, 1990/91–1996/97

£millions	1990–91	1991–92	1992–93	1993–94	1994–95	1995–96	1996–97
Civil legal aid	380.0	513.2	686.9	828.0	929.7	1030.1	1110.9
Criminal magistrates courts	174.0	212.0	200.7	193.9	204.7	214.7	228.9
Criminal higher courts	157.8	187.5	221.9	237.8	263.9	287.6	314.8
Green Form Scheme	76.1	99.7	123.6	145.7	141.5	145.0	153.3
Assistance by way of representation	19.2	22.8	21.8	18.8	13.5	12.1	11.9
Duty solicitor schemes	44.1	61.6	71.6	78.0	80.5	94.9	103.8
TOTAL	**852.0**	**1,096.8**	**1,326.5**	**1,502.2**	**1,633.7**	**1,784.4**	**1,923.5**

Source: *The Legal Aid System – an overview*; www.open.gov.uk/lcd/laid/leg-aid.htm

Activities

1. Draw appropriate graphs to show the growth in legal aid expenditure between 1990 and 1997. Comment on the trends your graphs show.
2. Research and make a presentation on the Green Form Scheme. In what ways should it be reformed?
3. Investigate the proposed reform of the legal aid system to be completed by 2002. How far will these reforms resolve criticisms of the system?
4. Debate 'society can no longer afford legal aid'.
5. Conduct a survey in your locality to discover the general level of awareness about legal aid. Present your findings and conclusions in written and graphic form.
6. Using the Lord Chancellor's statistics (Legal Aid acts of assistance at www.open.gov.uk/lcd/laid/leg-aid.htm) and the table above, calculate the average contribution made by the legal aid system to each claimant, for each of the categories in 1990–91 and 1996–97. Compare and comment on your findings.

Thinking and analytical skills

1. In what ways is Irvine's criticism of high earning lawyers one-sided?
2. Identify the different types of knowledge used by the article in *The Sunday Times*.

(vi) Does society benefit from deviant behaviour?

Links: 1.2 (i); 1.2 (iii); 1.2 (vi); 3.4 (ii); 3. 4 (i) **Key skills:** C3.1a; C3.3; WO3.1; WO3.2; WO3.3; N3.2; N3.3

Introduction

Society is held together by a set of commonly held beliefs about the types of behaviour that are good and bad. Societal norms and associated value systems will vary between cultures and at different times. It is likely that there will be different but broadly overlapping value systems within different sub groups in a society.

Background

People who accept and conform to social values are regarded as 'normal'. Although individuals are occasionally **deviant,** most people usually conform to society's expectations. Among the reasons for this are:

- genuine commitment to society's values,
- socialisation has embedded values in their personality,
- fear of the social or legal consequences of not conforming.

Anyone choosing not to behave according to society's values is 'abnormal'. Behaviour that simply offends society's morals or values is deviant, but conduct going beyond this, breaking the law and perhaps causing harm to others, is criminal.

Deviance in society is **universal** and normal. It is claimed that when social controls become so extreme that there is no deviance, society will stagnate and collapse. **Totalitarian** and **theocratic** states are, in theory, non-deviant societies.

Societies where deviance is totally out of control may collapse, since the values that should unite them will be destroyed. It is suggested that this is why the Roman Empire collapsed.

The healthiest societies seem to be ones with limited amounts of deviance, where social norms remain strong, without being unduly repressive. Modern democratic countries fall into this category.

Society can respond to deviance in several ways. The most frequent response is disapproval and negative sanctions because deviance is seen as a challenge to accepted social norms. Society will attempt to enforce conformity. Offenders may be marginalised or excluded. Unacceptable behaviour may be criminalised if society's hostility towards it is particularly strong or conduct is very different to the norm.

Eccentricity, by definition deviant, may be ignored or treated with amused tolerance, since it is unlikely to threaten social stability. Common, less threatening deviant activities (like exceeding speed limits) are accepted as neither unusual nor socially disturbing.

Some deviant behaviour may be approved, although many may choose not to copy it. Such behaviour may create demands to change the law or modify attitudes. In this way a previously condemned action may become acceptable.

Positive deviant behaviour:

- Resisting bullies, irrespective of consequences.
- Trying to save life, even at personal risk of death.
- Refusing to conform in a deviant subculture.
- Campaigning to right perceived wrongs (like anti-**vivisectionists**).
- Raising public awareness of the need to change laws.
- Refusing to accept orthodoxy and developing new areas of knowledge (like Darwin).

Deviant behaviour can benefit society by raising public awareness, questioning rules and testing boundaries of acceptable behaviour. It can help change and develop society and help draw society closer together.

Glossary

deviant: an individual some of whose behaviour departs from that regarded as 'normal' or socially acceptable

universal: actions, standards or values which are found and accepted in all societies

totalitarian: a system of government that allows no rival loyalties or political parties

theocratic: a system of government ruled directly by God, or by the rule of a single religion

vivisectionists: people who experiment on live animals

Issues to be discussed

- What justification is there for the claim that society needs some deviant behaviour?
- What types of deviant behaviour might be approved, even though many may choose not to copy it? Explain why it generates this type of response.
- Identify and discuss examples of how different cultures view particular actions differently.
- Who or what within society determines whether behaviour is deviant?

Where now?

S. Moore, *Investigating Crime and Deviance*, Collins, 1997
Marcus and Ducklin, *Success in Sociology*, John Murray, 1998

sosig.ac.uk
www.yahoo.society.ac

What do you think?

Critically evaluate the view that 'There is nothing about an action that makes it deviant. Deviancy is created by the ideas and values that prevail in society.'

It is the relations of men to one another, the roles they play, their institutions and values, and the connections among these variables that affect the definition, rate and distribution of deviant behaviour. There are always tendencies towards deviance inherent in society itself. The strength of these tendencies varies with the extent of social disorganisation.

Social disorganisation sometimes takes the form of inconsistent or contradictory norms and values that seem to require different kinds of conduct in the same situation. Shall the businessman be scrupulously honest or shall he use a stratagem of doubtful legality to increase his profits? Should the politician speak his views forthrightly or tailor his public pronouncements in the interest of political expediency? Should the child of immigrant parents obey the values of his parents or the standards of the new society in which he finds himself? Such cultural contradictions often impose difficult choices. If opposing values are widely accepted as valid, people find it difficult to accept one and reject the other. Instead, without openly rejecting either value, the individual frequently offers some socially acceptable reason for apparently ignoring one of them. The businessman guilty of a lapse of ethics argues that, as no law was violated, no moral failure has occurred. The politician who jettisons his principles for the sake of his office emphasises the contribution he can make while denying his violation of any moral rule.

A continuing clash of values, however, may progressively weaken attachment to both alternatives, thus increasing the possibility that neither can serve as an effective guide to action.

From E. Chinoy, *Society*, Random House, 1967, p.471

If everybody was deviant, how long could society continue in its present form?

Activities

1. Debate the opinion that 'Society would be happier if there were fewer rules to break.'
2. Investigate the sanctions used in your school or college to discourage deviant behaviour among the students. Write a leaflet to explain how they are justified.
3. Investigate the extent to which refusal to obey a particular law has caused the government to change it.
4. Why do people claim that they support rules and laws and yet often justify their own conduct in breaking them?
5. In a group, choose three of the basic rules of conduct in your school or college. Conduct a survey during the course of a single day to establish the proportion of students who break or ignore them. Present your findings in appropriate tables or graphs.

Thinking and analytical skills

1. What values are implied in the cartoon? To what extent can they be justified or challenged?
2. Chinoy supports his argument with analogy. How effective is this in justifying his views?

(vii) Does Britain need a Declaration of Human Rights?

Links: 1.2 (iii); 1.2 (iv); 1.2 (v); 3.4 (iv); 3.4 (vi); 4.10 **Key skills:** C3.1b; C3.2; IT3.1; IT3.2; C3.1a

Introduction

Most European countries have a Declaration of Rights **entrenched** in their constitutions. Until recently the United Kingdom was unusual in not having a formal statement of rights. Traditionally it was believed that rights in Britain were protected by the law. Critics of this view have demanded that rights in Britain should be defined and guaranteed by law. Some adopt a more extreme view and argue also for the recognition of animal rights.

Background

Human rights are based on the belief that **fundamental rights** exist at all times in all societies. Human rights are sometimes associated with **civil liberties**, but a significant problem is how they can be identified, defined and agreed. Culture influences thoughts about what they are and how they originated. It is generally accepted that fundamental rights cannot be revoked by a legislature without the consent of the people.

In the late seventeenth century John Locke claimed that people originally consented to be governed in return for a guarantee that the basic liberty or security of 'life, limb and property' would be defended. This influenced the United States' Declaration of Rights. **Ratified** in 1791, it recognised and guaranteed that all men were 'endowed by their creator with certain unalienable rights'.

In France in 1789 the corruption of government was blamed on general ignorance of the rights of man. Rights were described as 'natural, unalienable and sacred' in the Declaration of the Rights of Man and the Citizen.

In 1948 the United Nations issued its own Universal Declaration of Human Rights. The introduction stated that 'recognition of the equal and inalienable rights of all members of the human family is the foundation of freedom, justice and peace in the world'.

The European Convention for the Protection of Human Rights and Fundamental Freedoms was ratified by Britain in 1951. However, it was not incorporated into UK law until 1998 and did not come into full effect until 2000. The Convention forbids a range of **discriminatory practices** and guarantees a variety of freedoms and rights. Since 1966 British citizens who have felt their rights are being infringed can appeal to the European Court of Human Rights, but could not appeal to British Courts on the same grounds.

Until the new Act became law in Britain, there was nothing to prevent a future government removing or limiting rights that had previously been taken for granted.

The law assumed that a citizen could do anything not explicitly forbidden, and which did not interfere with others' freedom. Some people believe that a number of recent laws (such as laws dealing with equal pay, sex discrimination and race relations) have restricted individual rights.

In 1995 the UN Human Rights Committee claimed that the UK had failed to secure basic Human Rights for citizens. The European Court has found the British government in breach of Human Rights legislation more frequently then any other signatory. The government has set up a Human Rights Committee to review all future legislation to ensure that it meets the demands of the Convention. Critics claim that the government must raise public awareness and understanding of human rights.

Glossary

entrenched: a constitutional provision that cannot be changed by the normal law-making procedure

fundamental rights: basic rights to which all citizens are entitled

civil liberties: the rights which an individual has as a citizen and which cannot be infringed by other citizens or the state

ratified (-ication): the process by which a document is formally confirmed and validated

discriminatory practices: actions or behaviour which sets up or observes a difference between individuals

Issues to be discussed

- To what extent are there 'fundamental rights'? How can they be identified?
- Are the 'fundamental rights' contained in the various declarations relevant to all cultures?
- Should the interests of the state be more important than the rights of individuals?
- Does it matter that the early declarations of rights were male centred?
- Do you agree that animal rights are just as important as human rights and should have the same protection?

Where now?

J. Kingdom, *Government and Politics in Britain*, Polity Press, 1999

www.nara.gov

www.un.org/rights

www.liberty-human-rights.org.uk

www.coe.fr/eng

www.constitution.org

www.amnesty.org.uk

www.charter88.org.uk

What do you think?

Critically examine the claim that there is no such thing as 'a fundamental human right'. Those rights included in declarations simply reflect the cultural influences experienced by the authors.

Why the UK needs a declaration of human rights

- To bring the UK into line with the rest of Europe.
- The executive is becoming too powerful.
- Ordinary people are ignorant of their rights.
- Courts are failing to defend the rights of individuals against the state.
- The government has continually been criticised by the European Court of Human Rights for violations of the Convention.
- Rights would be guaranteed and no longer subject to government whim.
- Only agreement by 'the people' can change rights.
- 'Rights' are seen as a privilege but are an entitlement.

Why the UK does not need a declaration of human rights

- Rights already exist and are protected by law.
- A Bill of Rights would reduce not increase freedom.
- Emphasis should be placed on the responsibilities of citizenship rather than the rights of the individual.
- A Bill of Rights would reduce parliamentary sovereignty.
- At present the legislative activities of parliament are not restricted by the decisions of earlier parliaments.
- Britain has a tradition of strong government and does not need written controls.
- The UK constitution is based on the balance of powers and would be upset by a Bill of Rights.
- A Bill of Rights could lead to challenges to existing laws.

We work on a very wide range of issues, including the right to a fair trial; freedom from cruel, inhuman and degrading treatment; freedom from unlawful detention; privacy and family life; freedom of expression and assembly; and freedom from discrimination.

The Human Rights Act 1998 is the most significant reform in Liberty's 60-year history, and we campaigned for its introduction for many years. The Act will provide legally enforceable civil and political rights in our domestic courts for the first time, and all public authorities will have to act in compliance with it. Although its impact will be profound, the Act will not solve all human rights problems or remove the need for further legal reforms.

Conservative Party press release, 6 March 2000; from a statement published by Liberty; www.liberty-human-rights.org.uk

Newspaper reports claimed that Government officials pressured police to clamp down on human rights protesters during the Chinese state visit in 1999. If these reports are accurate, then this is one of the most blatant cases yet of the Government's hypocrisy. On human rights, Labour says one thing and does another. Robin Cook has postured to the world as a defender of human rights yet in Britain Mr Cook's officials actively pressured police to limit the fundamental right of self-expression. If any ministers ordered or pressured the police to try to deny basic rights then those ministers should resign. Many people throughout Britain, from all political backgrounds, will feel a sense of shame that the government would be willing to tarnish our reputation in order to ingratiate itself with any foreign government. We have a duty to respect the right of people living in Britain to express their views.

From Francis Maude MP, www.tory.org.uk/news/releases

Activities

1 List and justify your choice of the five most important 'fundamental rights'.

2 Research a recent decision against the British government by the European Court of Human Rights. Make a presentation of the case put to the court and the verdict reached. Your presentation should show the effect of this decision on the sovereignty of the British parliament.

3 Debate the view that 'declarations of Human Rights are designed to protect the interests of those in power rather than those of ordinary people'.

4 What further legal reforms may be needed to help solve all human rights problems?

Thinking and analytical skills

1 Which of the arguments for and against a British Declaration of Human Rights are based on belief? Which would you regard as being fallacies?

2 In what ways and with what success does Maude justify his argument?

(i) What are families and why do we need them?

Links: 1.2 (vi); 3.5 (ii); 3.5 (v); 4.5 **Key skills:** N3.1; N3.2; N3.3; IT3.1; IT3.2; IT3.3; C3.2; C3.1a; WO3.1; WO3.2

Introduction

It is claimed that a form of family exists in every society. The term can mean different things to different individuals and societies. Most people accept their own family experience as normal. Since it is claimed that family fulfils a key role in society, both personally and individually, the ideology of family is given a high public profile. Key issues are: what is family and are the **functions** which only family can perform?

Background

The media picture of a 'normal' family implies that other structures are inferior, inadequate or incomplete. It is to this idealised norm that politicians refer, when urging a return to 'family values'. However, claims are made that the traditional 'normal' family is no longer necessary or desirable, and perhaps never really existed.

Nuclear families are often thought of as 'normal' in Western society. **Stereotypically**, these consist of a male and female adult in a socially approved sexual relationship plus dependent children. It is claimed that this structure is the basic, **irreducible** building block of society and that all other family structures develop from it. A nuclear family may be free-standing or part of a larger, extended **kinship** group. Members are related by ties of blood, birth or marriage, or other legal provision.

A contrasting view is that 'family' can describe any group of people offering mutual support to each other. Relationship by blood or legal ties is less significant than a sense of identifying with each other as a supportive unit.

Those who believe that families are a positive good, see them as providing:

- individual sexual needs and gratification,
- the effective reproduction of humanity,
- child-care and child rearing during dependent years,
- **socialisation** of the young, to prepare them for society,
- the transmission of society's beliefs, values and norms,
- stability and structure for individual personalities,
- the various needs of the economic system,
- protection for society from undesirable changes.

Negative views of modern families claim they:

- may damage individual personality, by creating a limiting environment,
- may make individuals too inward-looking and over-dependent on one other,
- create friction, as members temporarily ally with each other in order to get what they want,
- create unrealistic and unattainable expectations,
- support capitalism and the exploitation of the poor,
- subsidise labour costs through the unpaid domestic labour of women,
- make women dependent on men's wages,
- reinforce the need to work by creating and perpetuating financial commitments and encouraging consumerism,
- perpetuate stereotypical gender roles.

Do we need family? There are contrasting views on the need for families. Radicals claim that families do not benefit society and are no longer needed since other institutions can fulfil its various roles more effectively. Others feel that family is still essential, contributing significantly to the well-being of society.

Glossary

function: any action which is properly performed in order to fulfil a purpose

stereotype: a predetermined fixed mental impression, which is used instead of individual judgements

irreducible: something that cannot be simplified further

kinship: blood or birth relationship

socialisation: the social process of instilling norms and values in an individual, usually a child

Issues to be discussed

- Discuss and explain which of the two views of family is the most useful.
- Are there any roles required by society which can:
  a best be provided by family,
  b only provided by family,
  c be provided better by other institutions?
- Why are there radically different views on family?
- Is family effective in socialising children?

Where now?

N. Jorgenson, *Investigating Families and Households*, Collins, 1995

Marcus and Ducklin, *Success in Sociology*, Murray, 1998

sosig.ac.uk   europa.int/index

What do you think?

"The traditional view of family has little of value to offer to the twenty-first century.' Critically examine this view.

What has been happening to the American family constitutes part of a process of differentiation. This process has involved a further step in the reduction in the importance in our society of kinship units other than the nuclear family. It has also resulted in the transfer of a variety of functions from the nuclear family to other structures of the society. This means that the family has become a more specialised agency than before, probably more specialised than it has been in any previously known society. This represents a decline of certain features, which traditionally have been associated with families; but whether it represents a 'decline of the family' in a more general sense is another matter. We think the trend of the evidence points to the beginning of the relative stabilisation of a new type of family structure, one in which the family is more specialised than before, but not in any general sense less important, because the society is dependent more exclusively on it for the performance of certain of its vital functions.

The first consideration is that 'loss of function' means that the family has become, on a large-scale view, almost completely functionless. It does not itself engage in much economic production; it is not a significant unit in the political power system; it is not a major direct agency of integration of the larger society. Its individual members participate in all these functions, but they do so as 'individuals' not in their roles as family members.

The most important implication of this view is that the functions of the family in a highly differentiated society are not to be interpreted as functions directly on behalf of the society, but on behalf of personality.

From Parsons and Bales, 'Family, Socialisation and Interaction Process' in M Anderson (ed.), *Sociology of the Family*, Penguin, 1980, pp. 185–97

The family still has certain vital functions to perform.

Activities

1 Compile a questionnaire to investigate whether people of different age groups have different views on the purpose of marriage. Administer the questionnaire to at least 20 different people, including men and women, representing different age groups and different marital status.

2 Collate and analyse your findings. Present them in appropriate written and graphic form.

3 Research the trends in family size since 1900. Show your findings in written and graphic form.

4 Read the passage above and in a group, make a list of functions that the family performs on behalf of individuals, rather than society. Put them in the order of their importance to society and justify your choice.

5 Debate the opinion that families are of more benefit to men than to women.

6 Examine the photograph. In what ways is the picture of family that it presents unreliable?

Thinking and analytical skills

1 Identify the different stages in the argument presented in the extract.

2 On what different types of knowledge is the argument based?

3 To what extent do you feel the conclusion can be supported?

(ii) How many types of family does society need?

Links: 1.2 (vi); 3.5 (i) 3.5 (iv) **Key skills:** N3.1; N3.2; N3.3; IT3.1; IT3.2; IT3.3; C3.1a; C3.1b

Introduction

Politicians and the media often imply that one type of family is dominant in Western society. In 1998–99 almost three-quarters of the UK population lived in couple-based families, but fewer than 40 per cent belonged to traditional nuclear families. Family life is marked by **diversity** rather than uniformity.

Background

Family diversity can result from changed social attitudes towards family. People increasingly choose to live on their own, rather than in large households. This trend, especially for people under pensionable age, is expected to continue. Single-parent families with dependent children have also increased because of the increasing divorce rate and changing attitudes towards **illegitimacy**.

Economic circumstances contribute to diversity. Increased employment opportunities and welfare benefits have given women greater economic independence. Women used to rely on a male partner's income but today can support themselves and their children.

The cultural impact of **migration**, the influence of ethnic minorities, the decline of religious belief and the globalising effect of the media have all contributed to the development of different family types.

Extended kinship groups, seen as dominant family types in pre-industrial societies, may take various forms:

- Vertical groups consist of three or more related generations living together.
- Horizontally extended groups consist of several related adults and dependent children.
- In some societies the degree of kinship is close, but in others, it can be wider, based on shared descent.

Polygamy, or plural marriage, not legal in Britain, is found in some societies. Polygyny is practised in some primitive rural societies where women undertake productive work and men hunt. **Polyandry** exists where there is a shortage of women or where men are frequently absent.

Mother-centred families, increasingly common, occur for various reasons. They may result from death or divorce, but in the UK some women choose female-headed families. It is claimed that **matrifocal** families among the USA's black population are a cultural legacy of slavery or the product of economic hardship. Faced with extreme poverty, men may desert or be driven out of their families. Matrifocal families may be vertically and horizontally extended, consisting of related adult women, dependent children and short-term resident males.

Collective or communal families were a deliberate attempt to escape the traditional family structure. Most were relatively short-lived. In some, children were raised separately from their biological parents. In others, they were treated as belonging to the community. Modern examples of communal families are found in Israeli Kibbutzes or among New Age Travellers.

Until recently, families with parents of the same sex experienced considerable social stigma and opposition, but social and legal attitudes have now become more tolerant. Reconstituted, or re-ordered, families are increasingly common, consisting of family units which, having been broken through death or divorce, are reformed by remarriage. Such families generally include step-children and step-parents.

Family diversity suggests that family is adaptive, changing to meet specific needs of society at any given time.

Glossary

diversity: variety; unlikeness

illegitimacy: literally 'not lawful'; children born to parents who are not legally married to each other

migration: movement from one place to another

polyandry: a system of marriage where a female has more than one husband at the same time

matrifocal: a female-headed family

Issues to be discussed

- Why does the media present the nuclear family as the 'ideal family type'?
- Why are extended families more common among the working and upper classes than among the middle classes?
- What more do communal or collective families have to offer than traditional families?
- Should the state try to encourage one type of family?

Where now?

N. Jorgenson, *Investigating Families and Households*, Collins, 1995
www.statistics.gov.uk
sosig.ac.uk

What do you think?

Critically examine the view that family diversity creates a stronger society.

A report published in May 1998 by the International Planned Parenthood Federation found that 87 per cent of all births to teenagers in the UK occurred outside marriage – the highest proportion in the world. Women in Britain are also starting to have pre-marital sex earlier than elsewhere. Of all children in Britain, 20 per cent now live in one-parent families; fewer than half of all people live in the traditional family unit of a married couple with their own children. Some of this is due to a rise in lesbian and gay partnerships, but the number of first marriages is also falling and the number of divorces and remarriages is rising. Does this mean that the family and family relationships are declining in importance?

Francis Fukuyama argues in *The End of Order* (1997) that rising female employment is at the heart of a 'great disruption' in the family in the Nineties. The real problem is that men now see women as being more independent and more able to look after the children that they father. The old obligation young men once felt for parenting is now replaced by a new freedom and irresponsibility. There is no deficit of mothers and motherhood; there is, however, a serious deficit of fathers and fatherhood.

Exactly how to respond to this crisis in male parenting is also causing ructions. Feminists want to resist any return to what they see as the repressive 1950s family model or to economic disincentives for women to work. Those with a more functionalist leaning warn of what has been called a 'female supremacism', which makes men irrelevant to the family and threatens to change masculine identity and socialisation, with potentially alarming social outcomes. Which way forward then, for the family and gender identities?

From J. Williams, 'The Family and Gender Identities' in *Sociology Review,* Vol 8 No. 3 (1999)

People in private households: by type of household and family in which they live

Great Britain — Percentages

	1961	1971	1981	1991	1998–99
One family households					
Living alone	4	6	8	11	12
Couple					
No children	18	19	20	23	26
Dependent children	52	52	47	41	39
Non-dependent children only	12	10	10	11	8
Lone parent	3	4	6	10	11
Other households	12	9	9	4	4
All people in private households (=100%) (millions)	–	53.4	53.9	55.4	
People not in private households (millions)	–	0.9	0.8	0.8	
Total population (millions)	**51.4**	**54.4**	**54.8**	**56.2**	**57.5**

Source: *Social Trends 2000,* Office for National Statistics; www.statistics.gov.uk

Activities

1 Using the figures in the table, construct appropriate graphs to show:
a changes in the proportion of different types of family in the UK since 1961,
b the proportion of the population living in different types of family in 1961 and 1991.

2 Use www.statistics.gov.uk to research information to compare the frequency of different types of family or households in the member states of the EU. Present your findings in appropriate form.

3 Examine whether particular family types are more common:
a in different regions of the UK,
b among different ethnic groups,
c among different social or economic groups.

4 Why does Western society not approve or practise different types of polygamy?

5 In a group, discuss what type of family organisation will be most appropriate for the twenty-first century.

Thinking and analytical skills

1 What different types of knowledge are used in the passage to support the author's argument?

2 To what extent does the table support the argument of the passage?

3 What weaknesses can be identified in the conclusion of the passage? What evidence might help to overcome these weaknesses?

(iii) Have attitudes to marriage changed?

Links: 1.2 (vi); 1.3 (i); 1.3 (vi); 3.5 (i); 3.5 (iv); 3.5 (v) **Key skills:** N3.3; C3.3; C3.1b; IT3.1; IT3.2; IT3.3; N3.1; N3.2; C3.2

Introduction

Marriage is a formal, public and legally recognised contract between two adults. In Western society, it is marked by a civil or religious ceremony in which two people commit themselves for life to a faithful social, economic and sexual partnership built on romantic love. Traditionally it is associated with child bearing and rearing.

Background

Traditionally marriage was based on economics not romance and was actively encouraged by church and state. Marriage was regarded as **indissoluble**, needing to be worked at, or at least, endured. Only the wealthy could afford divorce.

In rural economies, marriage provided mutual support and protection, cheap labour for the family 'business' and care during illness, infirmity or old age.

Industrialisation led to many economic and social changes, some of which affected family life. Medical improvements reduced infant and female mortality rates. Consequently marriages lasted longer and the number of children was limited. Marriage became **affectionate**, rather than **companionate**, and families became more child-centred. Expectations of marriage increased.

Attitudes have been changing since the 1950s. The 1969 Divorce Reform Act caused an explosion in the divorce rate. Divorce once carried a **stigma** but is accepted today. The media report celebrities who agree divorce terms before marriage. From 1951 to 1969 **divorce petitions** increased from 28,767 to 51,310 and by 1992 reached 189,864. Most divorces are sought by women.

Marriage is no longer seen as a lifelong commitment and proposals for short-term, renewable, legally binding marriage contracts have been put forward.

Cohabiting, or consensual union, has become increasingly common. It has always been practised and is now seen as an alternative to marriage. It used to be treated as a short-term measure, either because one partner was legally unable to marry or as a 'trial' marriage. This change may reflect a decline in how society values marriage or it may be a reaction to the high cost of weddings or a response to the uncertain future of marriage. The number of cohabiting couples cannot be exactly calculated.

Some communities have arranged marriages. Criticisms of this practice may reflect ignorance of religious and cultural practices. In the UK, arranged marriages are changing. Many young people are now allowed some choice under the influence of Western attitudes and practices. Divorce in arranged marriages is about a third of the national figure.

Declining marriage rates suggest a loss of confidence in marriage, especially among women. Once many young females made marriage and family a high priority, but today a career is often seen as more important.

In 1997 there were 310,000 marriages in Britain, of which only 181,000 were first marriages for both partners, compared to almost 350,000 in 1970. Over 40 per cent of marriages in 1997 involved remarriage. Remarriage has increased rapidly since 1960 and today usually at least one partner is divorced.

Glossary

indissoluble: lasting or stable; something that cannot be dissolved or ended except by death

affectionate marriage: a marriage entered into on the basis of mutual attraction or love

companionate marriage: a marriage entered for mutual benefit rather than for emotional reasons

stigma: a stain or mark on an individual's good name or character

divorce petition: the legal application for a divorce as opposed to the decree which makes divorce a fact

Issues to be discussed

- Is marriage threatened because divorce is too easy?
- Has the decline in religious belief been significant in encouraging the decline in marriage?
- What are the advantages and benefits of an 'arranged' marriage compared to a 'romantic' marriage?
- How far has the increased financial independence of women encouraged them to seek divorce rather than to work at an unsatisfactory marriage?
- What do increased remarriage rates say about the way people value marriage today?

Where now?

N. Jorgenson, *Investigating Families and Households*, Collins, 1995

D. Clark, *Marriage, Domestic Life and Social Change*, Routledge, 1991

www-news.uchicago.edu www.statistics.gov.uk

What do you think?

'Is it really worth getting married?' Analyse and evaluate arguments for and against this question.

The government offers few financial incentives to get married. The married couple's allowance has been cut back by successive governments and it will disappear in April for couples under 65.

William Hague, leader of the Conservative party, has criticised the government for abolishing the allowance – although Tory chancellors have contributed to its decline over the years. Hague has also pledged to reinstate the tax benefit should he ever come to power. He believes that people should be rewarded for 'doing the right thing'.

The rules that govern capital gains tax are kinder to married couples. You are liable for the tax not only on gains, but also on gifts – unless the gift is to your husband or wife. You can minimise any Capital Gains Tax (CGT) bill by giving assets to your spouse. But cohabitants gain the advantage over married couples if they own two homes. Normally you must pay CGT on the sale of any property other than your principal residence. Unmarried couples can legitimately avoid the tax by putting each home in a different name. The loophole is not open to married couples.

Rules on inheritance tax favour married couples. You can bequeath your estate to your husband or wife when you die and they will not have to pay tax. If you are not married, you could be in a precarious position when your loved one dies. If there is no will, intestacy laws do not necessarily recognise a cohabitant, even if you have lived together as man and wife for many years. It is also rare for personal pensions or company schemes to grant automatic rights to a girlfriend or boyfriend. If you die after retirement, there is no guarantee that the person living with you will receive a widow or widower's pension.

John Whiting, an accountant, says: 'The tax system is neutral. The government could certainly demonstrate its commitment to marriage by skewing the system in its favour.'

From *The Sunday Times*, 19 March 2000

Marriages and divorces in the UK, 1961–97

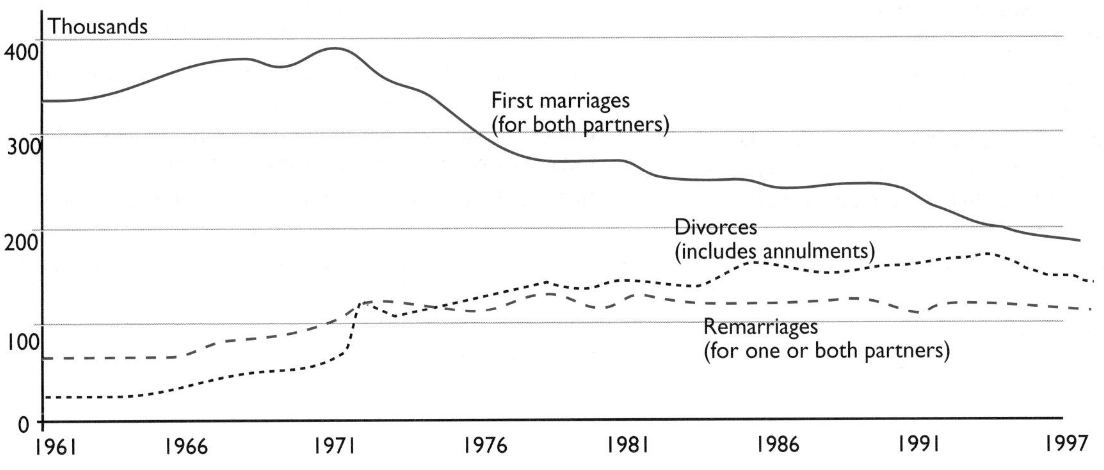

Source: *Social Trends 2000*, Office for National Statistics; www.statistics.gov.uk

Activities

1 Research any legal or economic changes made by the last two governments which have adversely affected marriage.

2 Describe and explain the trend shown in the graph.

3 Investigate and make a short presentation, using overhead transparencies, on changes in divorce laws between 1950 and the present day. In your presentation you should make use of appropriate graphs and tables.

4 Conduct a survey to investigate attitudes to marriage, cohabiting and divorce. You should investigate the views of people of different ages and marital status.

5 Compare the words of the civil marriage service with those used by different groups.
a Are there any significant differences?
b What similarities are there?
c Are the words appropriate to the twenty-first century?

Thinking and analytical skills

1 Identify the stages in the argument in the passage.

2 What different types of knowledge are used in the passage to support the argument?

3 To what extent do the graphs and tables support the conclusion in the passage?

(iv) Are single-parent families a social problem?

Links 1.2 (vi); 3.5 (ii); 3.5 (iii) **Key Skills:** C3.3; C3.1b; N3.2; N3.3; C3.1a

Introduction

During the last 30 years there has been a dramatic rise in the number of families headed by single parents. In 1991, lone parents headed 20 per cent of families with dependent children. This represents 1.3 million parents and 2.1 million children. Mothers head most single-parent families. There is a tendency to group lone-parent families together, forgetting that they come about for different reasons and experience widely different circumstances.

Background

Origins and types of lone-parent families:

- Some result from the death of one parent. No choice is involved.
- Some women deliberately choose to have children without a permanent partner. This is becoming more frequent.
- It has been claimed that young women deliberately get pregnant in order to be rehoused by Social Services.
- Males who do not contribute financially may be expelled from the household in times of economic hardship, either as a means of gaining benefit or to reduce costs.
- Changes in sexual morality result in some unintentional pregnancies. Partners may be casual associates or disappear when faced with responsibilities.
- Families can be split for economic reasons. This can occur if one parent works away from home for long periods of time or during financial hardship. In either case, lone-parenthood is expected to be temporary.
- Desertion, when one parent simply leaves the home and 'disappears', causes lone parenthood. This may result from boredom, disappointed expectations of marriage, economic failure or alternative interests.
- Over 60 per cent of single parent families come about today as a result of the rapid increase in divorce.

The main causes of single parenthood today involve economic pressures, changed social attitudes and increased expectations. Greater prosperity, increased employment opportunities for women and the potential for independence make it easier to leave unsatisfactory relationships.

Financial hardship is experienced by many single parents, especially mothers. Former partners often do not contribute to child-care costs and full-time, well-paid employment is rarely available, especially for mothers of young children. This can lead to reliance on state benefit.

Government efforts to reduce dependence, through the Child Support Agency and child-care schemes have had limited success, with the result that state expenditure on lone-parent families is among the lowest in Europe.

Some claim single parenthood adversely affects children, that it limits educational attainment, encourages **juvenile crime**, leads to poor health and creates many other social problems. This can help to develop stereotypical images and expectations of single-parent children. Evidence is limited, but generally it seems that children brought up in two-parent households do better. The reasons for this are unclear.

Many, especially **custodial** fathers, see lone parenthood as short-term. Remarriage offers an attractive route to a **reconstituted** family. Politicians voice concern about single parenthood because of its cost and its apparent threat to the traditional family pattern. Although the state pays lip service to the idea of family values, it does little practically to support them.

Glossary

juvenile crime: crime committed by young people; from this the term describes certain types of crime particularly associated with young people (e.g. 'joy-riding')

custodial (parent): the parent with whom a child lives and who has legal responsibility for its care and welfare

reconstituted marriage: the marriage of people previously married who bring to the new partnership offspring of a previous relationship (hence 'step-families')

Issues to be discussed

- What are traditional 'family values' and how may they be threatened by single-parent family life?
- Do children of single-parent households always suffer when compared to children living with both parents?
- Who should pay the increasing costs of lone parenthood?
- How can the government give practical help to lone-parent families? Should it do so?
- Are lone-parent families always deprived?

Where now?

A. J. Cherlin, *Marriage, Divorce and Remarriage*, Harvard University Press, 1992

N. Jorgenson, *Investigating Families and Households*, Collins, 1995

www.gingerbread.org.uk www.clasp.org/pubs/childrenforce/ssi.htm

What do you think?

'Children who live with both parents have better life-chances than those in single-parent households.' To what extent can this view be justified?

Studies of children show negative effects of divorce are real and persistent, but only a minority experience severe negative consequences. The 1981 National Survey of Children found that adolescents who had experienced the divorce or separation of their parents differed only modestly on average, from those whose parents remained married, on a wide variety of outcomes such as school achievement, delinquency and psychological well-being.

Not all children respond similarly to divorce. Some children are simply more resilient to stress than others. Some manage to find safe niches that insulate them from the trauma of divorce. Not all divorces have the same consequences for children.

Nevertheless, two conclusions can be drawn. First, children do better when the custodial parent can re-establish an orderly and supportive household routine. When the custodial parent can keep the house in order, get the children to school and to bed on time, maintain disciplinary standards consistently and provide love and warmth, children can draw support from the parent.

Second, children do better when there is less conflict between their parents. This principle applies to intact two-parent homes as well as to families of divorce. In fact, studies show that children living with a single parent show fewer behavioural problems than do children living in homes in which two angry parents argue persistently.

In the 1981 survey, children who had regular visits with their non-custodial parent were just as likely as those with infrequent visits to have problems in school or to engage in delinquent behaviour or early sexual activity.

From A. J. Cherlin, *Marriage, Divorce and Remarriage*, Harvard University Press, 1992, pp. 77–79

Lone parent families in Britain, 1991

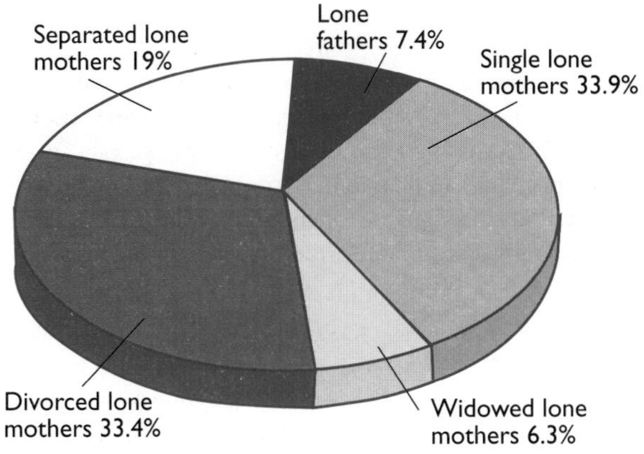

Source: N. Jorgenson, *Investigating Families and Households*, Collins, 1995, p.142

Families with dependent children, by family type, 1971–95

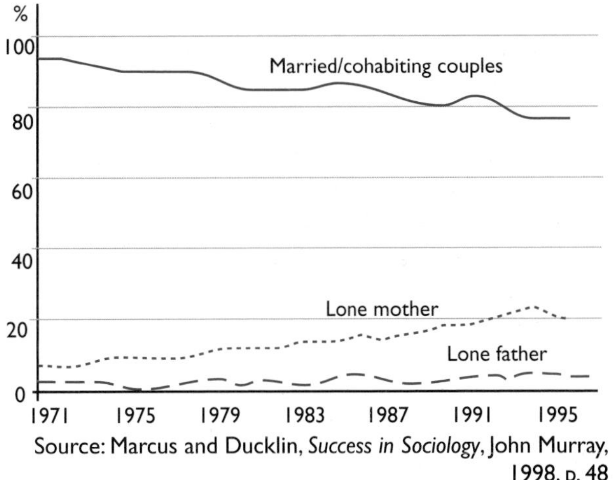

Source: Marcus and Ducklin, *Success in Sociology*, John Murray, 1998, p. 48

Activities

1 Investigate evidence which suggests that children who grow up in single-parent families may:
a achieve less in education,
b become more involved in delinquent behaviour,
c become single or lone parents themselves.
Suggest reasons for your findings.

2 Design a leaflet and present a report to explain why the proportion of single-parent families has increased in the last 30 years. Support your work with a graph or table.

3 Research the provision made by the government to support single-parent families. In what ways would you change this provision? Explain your reasons.

4 Choose a family issue and collect newspaper reports about it, using a variety of different newspapers.
a Compare the language and images used for families living with single, both natural and step-parents.
b Outline any similarities and differences you are able to identify.

Thinking and analytical skills

1 What is the main conclusion about children in single-parent families in the passage?
2 What different types of knowledge or argument are used in the passage?
3 Comment on the graphs, explaining whether they support or justify the conclusion in the passage.

(v) How have demographic changes affected family life?

Links 3.1 (iii); 3.5 (i); 3.5 (ii); 4.7 **Key skills:** N3.1; N3.2; N3.3; IT3.1; IT3.2; IT3.3

Introduction

Demographic changes have a major impact on families. In 1911 average **life expectancy** at birth for males was 50.4 and for females 53.9 years; for 1951 it was 66.1 and 70.9, and for 1997, 74.6 and 79.6 respectively. It is estimated that by 2021 the figures will be 78.6 and 82.7. As the population has increased, so it has become older.

Background

Increased **longevity** has implications for both society and the family, especially in terms of the social and economic costs of caring for the elderly and the young. Pension funds, for example, may no longer provide adequate support. Political parties urge that families, not the state, should care for elderly relatives. Where possible, savings must pay for residential care.

Old age affects families in three ways. Income must be diverted to support the elderly for their extended lives, inheritance will be **deferred** and may even be reduced to pay for care. Expectations that elderly people will live with relatives rather than in residential care can put intolerable strains on family relationships.

Greater longevity leads to longer marriages. Couples sharing more time together between children leaving home and retirement may benefit. For others, longer marriages create tension and conflict. Divorces for couples married between 15 and 25 years have increased from 14 per cent of all divorces in 1961 to 23 per cent in 1996, but for couples married for more than 25 years it has fallen from 21 per cent to 11 per cent.

Family size has changed. Live births have fallen from almost 1,100,000 in 1911 in a population of 38,237,000 to about 785,000 in a population of 50,287,000 in 1951. By 1997 there was an average of 750,000 live births in a population of 59,009,000. By 2021, live births may be about 694,000 in a population of 61,000,000.

Women born in 1930 averaged 1.9 children by age of 30, those born in 1957 averaged 1.5 children at 30, while 30-year-olds in 1997 averaged 1.3 children. Average family size has become smaller, often leading to improved **lifestyle**. Reasons for this include ease of abortion and contraception, declining infant mortality and increased prosperity.

Having smaller families reduces the length of parental child-care and encourages mothers to resume careers, leading to greater independence after children have grown up. This can also put increased pressure on marriages.

Children are financially dependent for longer than ever before. In 1900, children could work from 12, but now cannot leave school until 16. Greater numbers stay in education for longer. In 1986, 55 per cent of 16–18 year olds were in full-time education or training. By 1998, the figure was 75 per cent. The proportion in higher education rose from 23 per cent in 1991 to 31 per cent in 1998.

Increased family costs are imposed in two ways. Earning power is deferred during education and parental costs to support children through education have risen considerably with the introduction of tuition fees and removal of maintenance grants. Many young people leave education to enter employment with heavy debts.

The **life cycle** has changed. Marriage and the birth of a first child occur later than previously. Increased freedom after children leave home may be curtailed by caring for elderly parents. Longer retirement has also altered lifestyle.

Glossary

life expectancy: the number of years a child born in a particular year might normally expect to live

longevity: long life

deferred: put off or postponed

lifestyle: the manner in which an individual or group lives

life cycle (or life course): the various stages of life from infancy to old age, each stage having different social and economic characteristics

Issues to be discussed

- Examine reasons why parents might choose to defer marriage and families and limit the number of children.
- What might be the consequences of such deferment?
- How has increased geographical mobility affected family life for: **a** parents, and **b** children?
- What social and economic pressures have contributed to changes in family and family life?
- Why does longevity adversely affect pension funds?
- Why has life expectancy increased and what consequences may it have for society?

Where now?

N. Jorgenson, *Investigating Families and Households*, Collins, 1995

Population Trends, The Stationery Office (published regularly)

www.statistics.gov.uk

What do you think?

'Changes in population and economic pressures will lead to the re-emergence of extended families.' Critically examine the arguments for and against this view and justify your conclusions.

Average family size in many modern societies has stabilised at around 1–2 children per family. Thus in some it has actually fallen below the replacement level of 2.1 children per family. However, the position is very different in many Third World societies, where a larger average family size reflects higher infant mortality rates, a younger population and labour-intensive subsistence economies where the work of children is a vital source of family support.

In most European countries, including Britain, average life expectancy has increased. By the year 2000 it is expected to be 80 years for women and 75 years for men. Birth rates have fallen throughout the century, so the balance of the age structure of the British population has shifted and there are now larger proportions of old people compared to young people and children.

On average, people now have living grandparents for a greater proportion of their lives than they used to. A complicating factor is a trend towards later marriage and childrearing, which is partly a reflection of the expansion and extension of educational opportunities to a later age and of the increased numbers of working women who give their career and occupations high priority. The average age of bearing a first child is creeping upwards to the late twenties and is around 30 in the middle classes. Similar trends are emerging with male parenthood.

The implication of this trend is that the younger grandparent, aged in the late thirties or early forties, who married at seventeen and had a daughter or son who also married at a similar age, will become more of a rarity. In the near future, grandparenthood could commonly begin in the early sixties. Since members of the present older generation are on average fitter and healthier and will consequently live longer than their parents, 'later' grandparenting may be less of a problem.

From N. Jorgenson, *Investigating Families and Households*, Collins, 1995, pp. 162–64

Changes in life expectancy can lead to multi-generational family units.

Activities

1. Research changes in average life expectancy for males and females of different ethnic origin. Construct appropriate graphs to compare this information.
2. Investigate the size of families represented by members of your group and for their previous two generations. Use the figures you discover to calculate the average size of family represented by the group today and for previous generations. Show your findings in tables or graphs.
3. Research and construct your own family tree for the last three or four generations.
   a As far as you can, show ages, places of origin, numbers of children born to each parent.
   b Comment on any trends you can identify.
   c Calculate the average length of life for males and females in each generation.
   d Compare your findings with the figures given on page 186.

Thinking and analytical skills

1. Identify the main conclusions in the passage.
2. What different types of knowledge and argument are used to support these conclusions?
3. How far are the conclusions supported by **a** evidence used in the passage, and **b** the photograph?
4. Does the photograph offer valid evidence on which to base conclusions?

(vi) Is society too youth centred?

Links: 3.1 (iii); 3.5 (i); 3.5 (v); 4.17 **Key skills:** WO1; WO2; N3.1; N2; N3.3; C3.1a; C3.3

Introduction

Families used to be economic units of production as well as **consumption**. Members worked together, under the direction of a **patriarchal** father, in the family 'business', often a farm or domestically based manufacture. Childhood lasted only until infants could take their place in the workforce. Today this has changed. Family has become a unit of consumption. Workers are employed as individuals, not family members.

Background

Consumption is essential to any economic system. Goods are produced and labour employed to meet consumer needs. Increased demand encourages manufacturers to increase supply, which usually leads to greater prosperity. It is in the interests of the economy to encourage demand.

People have certain essential needs like food, shelter and clothing. Wants, like designer clothes or bigger cars, are desirable, if unnecessary. Needs are constant, but wants vary between individuals according to circumstance. Advertising focuses on wants not needs, to encourage consumption and increase production and profit.

Patterns of consumption change during an individual's life cycle, according to disposable income. Young families spend significantly on child welfare; retired people often spend less on non-essentials. Most people have their greatest personal disposable income between leaving school and starting a family, and between children leaving home and retirement.

Youth culture implies that young people form a separate market. Since the Fifties, this has been economically significant. Advertising has focused on this market to create a 'must-have' lifestyle. Fashion, style and the 'right label' are **yardsticks** for success. Much economic production is specifically geared to supplying this market. Many consumer products are specifically aimed at the young. The media reinforces this image of young people as major consumers. Important factors in the 'youth market' are:

- a marked decline in infant mortality,
- the extension of education for many to 18 or even 22,
- delay in entering the labour market,
- the growth of part-time 'student work',
- the development of teenage fashion,
- deferment of marriage,
- the influence of the media,
- increased overall prosperity.

However, even though high consumption expectations exist among the young, not all benefit. Many, especially students, have found that ease of consumer purchase and changes in the financing of higher education have led to intolerable debt.

Not all young people have the resources for participation in the youth market. Many have difficulty finding employment or may receive low pay. Changes in benefit rules mean the unemployed under 18 cannot claim and remain dependent on parental support.

It is perhaps coincidence that the peak age for male law breakers has risen. Before 1972 (when the school-leaving age was raised) it was 14, but increased to 18 between 1988 and 1998. Female offenders have retained a constant peak at 14 to 15 years. In 1997, 9 per cent of 18-year-old males and 2 per cent of 15-year-old females were either cautioned or found guilty of **indictable offences**.

Glossary

consumption: literally 'using up', hence in economic terms the purchase or use of goods

patriarchal: rule by the male head or leader of a family, group or tribe; often the oldest living relative

yardstick: an ideal to which an individual's achievements may be compared

indictable offences: an offence of sufficient seriousness to cause a person to be accused in court

Issues to be discussed

- How does the media encourage a separate youth market?
- To what extent do demands by consumers create supply rather than advertising create demand?
- How important to the economy is the youth market?
- Is there a link between youth crime and growing consumerism?
- Are teenagers an invention of the twentieth century?

Where now?

N. Jorgenson, *Investigating Families and Households*, Collins, 1995

Social Science Review (various volumes)

www.statistics.gov.uk www.yahoo.com/social_science

What do you think?

'Since all people are consumers, it is unreasonable to talk about a separate "youth market".' To what extent do you agree?

The material conditions for the recognition of youth as a distinctive social group lay in the displacement of young people from the environment of rural communities to newly developed urban spaces. In traditional village society young people were subject to the social control of peers and elders in their transition from the irresponsibility of childhood to the responsibility of adulthood.

In modern industrial societies, with their complex social systems, the roles performed within the family ceased to be harmonious with the wider social system and thus identification with members of the family did not ensure full social maturity and status in the social system.

Youth subcultures usually had important positive functions in easing the transition from the security of childhood to that of full adult in marriage and occupational status. In providing a bridge to adulthood, these subcultures also transformed the traditional value system where it had become outdated. Parsons' picture of youth culture reflected the social climate of the postwar period in western Europe and North America, characterised by notions of the affluent society, the right to leisure and the expression of self through consumption. A key player in this affluent society was the teenager, who rapidly became identified as a new economic actor with distinctive patterns of consumption. Consumption included not only particular products but also media forms and the style creation that went with the arrival of rock'n'roll.

Girls are no longer seen as wholly defined by their consumption. The consumption of youth styles via clothes, music and cosmetics is more properly seen as one element of girls' cultural activity. The practice of consumption indicates neither passivity nor gullibility on the part of girls.

From H. Pilkington, 'Youth Cultural Studies' in *Sociology Review*, Vol 7, No 1 (1997)

'Have now, pay later' consumerism is probably targeted at young people.

Activities

1 Examine and evaluate a range of adverts aimed at young people.
a In what ways are they similar to each other?
b How do they differ from adverts aimed at other markets?
c How are they similar to adverts aimed at other markets?

2 Imagine you are a member of an advertising team. Plan an advertising campaign for a new product (of your choice) aimed at the youth market. Your plans should include posters, leaflets, graphics and a written plan.

3 Design a questionnaire to investigate the reasons why young people made recent purchases.
a Draw up a table showing the different purchases made, the frequency of such purchases and expenditure.
b Construct graphs to illustrate different spending patterns between males and females and for different age groups.

4 In a group, draw up a list of guidelines for advertisers in the youth market. Justify the choices you have made.

Thinking and analytical skills

1 What is the main argument in the passage?
2 What types of argument or knowledge does the author use?
3 To what extent is the author's conclusion justified?

4.1 Should ethnic minorities be fully integrated into society?

Links: 1. (iv); 1.3 (ii); 1.3 (iv); 3.1 (vii); 3.5 (ii); 3.5 (v)

'By maintaining a unique culture – music, art, film, literature – and religion, ethnic minorities preserve a separate identity at the expense of complete social integration.' Examine this view from cultural, social and scientific perspectives.

Introduction

The United Kingdom has always been made up of different ethnic groups; these different groups have contributed to a rich and diverse culture. Until the middle of the twentieth century, assimilating different cultural groups may have appeared easier because most immigrants were of western European origin. From the early 1950s immigrants coming predominantly from south-east Asia and the Caribbean had different cultural, economic and social backgrounds from the majority population. They spoke a variety of languages and dialects. This linguistic diversity has continued: a 1991 survey showed that over 160 different languages and dialects were spoken by children in London's schools.

Some people claim it is possible to distinguish distinctive cultures in different parts of the world. For example, they claim to be able to identify a broadly based south-east Asian culture which is distinctly different from that of western Europe or West Africa. Although there are regional differences within each of these cultures, they also share common central values.

In Britain there are inevitably many different subcultures. Welsh and Scottish nationalism is based as much on perceived cultural differences as on different political backgrounds and aspiration. Despite this, Britain seems generally to be a culturally integrated country. Does the existence of contrasting cultures and subcultures make closer social integration impossible or does it promise the development of a richer and more varied society?

In the1970s, many Pakistani organisations presented poetry readings in Urdu. The formal teaching of Indian languages was steadily taken over by religious institutions. Mosques and Islamic cultural centres often taught Arabic and Urdu, languages that share a common script.

Even if children did not learn to read and write in their language of origin, they grew up speaking it at home and with other Indian and Pakistani children. Though parents wished their children to have a British education, they did not necessarily want them to forget their mother tongue or disown their cultural heritage. The vast majority of people of Indian, Pakistani and Bangladeshi origin in Britain did not wish or intend to give up completely their socio-cultural identity.

Indian and Pakistani societies can best be described as pluralistic, where many linguistic, religious and racial groups coexist peacefully. Indians and Pakistanis, therefore, grew up accepting and respecting the religious, linguistic, dietary and sartorial differences of their fellow nationals. Adherence to the 'different and equal' concept, whether applied within their own communities or with respect to the British, was maintained when they migrated to Great Britain. None of these cultural differences disturbed or agitated the Indian or Pakistani settlers. They did not aspire to a stifling uniformity in culture or language. Yet there was a unity in diversity among them. People of Indian, Pakistani and Bangladeshi origin shared common attitudes towards birth and death, marriage and family, parents and teachers, money and education.

From D. Hiro, *Black British, White British, a History of Race Relations in Britain*, Grafton Books, 1991

Issues to be discussed

- Why is Asian music described as 'ethnic' while Welsh and Scottish language songs are considered mainstream?
- Should schools popularise minority ethnic culture more actively? If so, how best can it be done?
- Should Lottery money subsidise ethnic culture?
- List aspects of ethnic culture that have become part of mainstream culture. Why has this happened?
- Is ethnic culture likely to become a preserve of the elderly as time passes and the majority of the ethnic groups are assimilated?
- Why are immigrants from the old Commonwealth not described as 'ethnic'?
- Do you agree that fear and ignorance are the main reasons why many people are hostile to various aspects of ethnic culture?

Where now?

D Hiro, *Black British, White British, a History of Race Relations in Britain*, Grafton Books, 1991

T. Eagleton, *The Idea of Culture*, Blackwell, 2000

Cultural perspective

- It is not possible to map culture effectively. There is always overlap and intermixing between subcultures; an illustration of this is the conflict in the former Yugoslavia.
- Attempts have been made to map the different cultural groups in the British population on the grounds of origin (by place of birth or descent). However, these attempts have not taken into account regional subdivisions or marriage and other social contact between groups from different backgrounds.
- All cultures are dynamic and change over time as they encounter other cultures and incorporate different strands into their own culture.
- A group's culture is influenced by its relationship with other groups. For example, hostility may cause its identity to be reasserted.
- The media set the 'tone' of culture. Dominant culture often has a better press and greater exposure than minority cultures, which can be presented as inferior.
- Ethnic groups are usually identified by their distinctive cultural features which appear significantly different from the dominant culture. The term is often applied to small, powerless groups.
- No culture is internally uniform. There are always some members of a group who are less committed to the shared values of others.
- Minorities are often shown as conservative, seeking to cling to 'traditional' values. In reality, all cultures evolve. Young people, who are attracted to new cultural movements, may reinterpret old traditions.

Scientific perspective

- The dominant religion in a culture sometimes has an overwhelming effect on the development of science and other intellectual activities, for example, the experience of Galileo with the Catholic Church. Galileo also had to take into account the views of his conservative sponsors.
- Some people have identified culturally distinct forms of science, for example, Chinese medicine and Islamic science. The danger here is that artificial boundaries may be placed on what may be studied or investigated.
- Similar religious arguments arose in the mid-nineteenth century, when Darwin put forward the theory of evolution which was supported by a great deal of observed evidence.
- Scientific study of ethnic groupings shows differences that are sometimes easy and sometimes difficult to explain. Some research, for example, into supposed differences in the intelligence of various groups, has had a hidden, racist agenda. The most serious problem with all such studies is to eliminate the effect of environment in their experimental design.

Social perspective

- A shared culture can give a group a strong sense of belonging and can provide regular social interaction.
- Groups that set their own goals and maintain their own independent values can often come into conflict with other groups which do not share the same values.
- New Right theorists contrast a 'traditional' homogeneous British culture with what they see as the 'inferior' culture of ethnic minorities. These assumptions are usually highly stereotypical.
- Britain has a stable society but it is not really homogenous since there is little real consensus over values and norms.
- 'Cultural racism' is when attitudes, ideas and ideologies are based on mistaken beliefs about racial groups. This leads to cultural prejudice.
- Early legislation aimed for cultural assimilation in order to achieve a monocultural society. More recently, it has been accepted that there should be cultural pluralism, based on mutual respect and tolerance.
- Race conflicts are often disputes over cultural differences, disguised as racial in origin.
- Ethnic minorities are presented as a threat to 'the traditional British way of life' which, if not contained, will destroy the homogeneity and unity of society.
- In 1983 a legal judgement of the House of Lords said a group with a shared history and distinctive cultural traditions was an 'ethnic cultural minority'.
- Early migrant groups gravitated to inner city areas not only for economic reasons but also as a way of maintaining a shared identity and a separate culture.

Thinking and analytical skills

1. What different types of knowledge would be useful when arguing that ethnic culture is not inferior to mainstream culture?
2. Consider the views of the New Right. What are the strengths and weaknesses of their claims about ethnic culture?

4.2 Can a modern society afford not to have an integrated transport policy?

Links: 1.6 (v); 2.1 (ii); 3.1 (i); 3.2 (iv); 3.3 (vii)

Everyone agrees that cars are a problem, but no-one is sure what the solution is. Give a justified explanation of what you think the problem is and how it might be satisfactorily resolved. In your answer you should consider the issue from different viewpoints.

Introduction

Since the 1950s the total distance travelled in the UK, excluding freight, has trebled. Although governments and pressure groups have tried to encourage the use of public transport, people prefer cars. In the 1990s, over 86 per cent of the distance travelled by passengers was in cars, vans or taxis and less than 15 per cent was by bus or train.

Car ownership has increased steadily over the years. In 1998, 70 per cent of households had at least one car and 28 per cent had two or more. There are now 10 times more cars in Britain than in 1950 and, as a result, road traffic has increased considerably. In 1951, about 60 billion kilometres were travelled by road vehicles, compared to 455 billion in 1998. This is expected to reach 524 billion by 2006.

Between 1996 and 1998, one-quarter of all journeys were for social purposes, the majority by car. Half of all journeys made by children were by car, compared to only a third on foot.

Although traffic has increased, overall speed has decreased. Motor vehicles averaged 56 miles per hour on motorways in 1998 compared to 63 miles per hour in 1995, while average speeds on built-up roads fell from 34 to 30 miles per hour. However, in 1998 more than half the cars using motorways exceeded the speed limit.

In 2000, public transport suffered. Concorde was grounded after a fatal explosion. Railtrack imposed speed limits and carried out extensive safety checks and repairs following a fatal rail crash. In the autumn, concerted protests against high petrol prices forced the government to modify its policy. Proposed budget changes in November in effect recognised the primacy of the car.

Road traffic will regularly grind to a halt and train services will increasingly be disrupted as a result of global warming. The average temperature of the world is now 0.8 °C higher than it was in 1900 and is expected to rise by a further 3 °C by 2100. As the world warms up, extreme weather will become more common

Trains will be held up by the wrong kind of ice. There will be fewer dry, frosty winter mornings, but more nights when rain and melted snow freeze on the conductor rails. Heavy rain will cause flooding and landslides which could badly affect railways. Trees are more likely to be brought down by high winds, damaging overhead power supplies.

Lightning will become common throughout the year in Britain. A spokesman for Railtrack said, 'Last year was the worst ever for lightning strikes.' In 1999, lightning caused four times more delays to passengers than delays in the previous years. Railtrack has set up a lightning task force to find ways of preventing power surges caused by strikes to overhead wires and conductor rails, which bring the trains to a halt.

The warmer weather will disrupt transport systems throughout the world although, ironically, transport is one of the key sources of the carbon dioxide emissions that are warming the world.

Adapted from *New Scientist*, 1 July 2000

Issues to be discussed

- Is the possession and use of private transport a right or a privilege?
- How real are concerns that cars are doing irreparable damage to the environment?
- What are the forms of private transport most likely to replace the car?
- Would governments be more effective in reducing reliance on cars if they set a better example?
- What realistic alternatives are there to fossil fuels and why have they not been developed for public use?
- Is punitive taxation an effective way to reduce reliance on cars? What is the best way to achieve this?
- What steps can be taken to develop a more effective and reliable system of public transport?

Where now?

www.foe.co.uk
www.eta.co.uk
www.parliament.the-stationery-office.co.uk
www.detr.gov.uk

Cultural perspective

- The media (advertising) can be irresponsible in the way it encourages car ownership and use.
- Modern culture, as reflected in television and film, is based on car ownership which is seen as an essential status symbol and social necessity. Not having a car is seen as evidence of poverty.
- Car design is a major area of innovation and has contributed to many aesthetic developments.
- Car ownership and use may increase individual happiness but can harm the interests of the social group, especially in the long term.
- Is it morally right to use cars for journeys that could be made by public transport?
- We should be more concerned about future generations and less concerned about our own comfort.
- Some cars are glamorised as sex or power symbols.
- Unless a significant number of people change their behaviour, it is pointless anybody changing.
- Public transport is less environmentally harmful and makes greater economic sense.
- Government has a responsibility to fund research into alternative, effective forms of transport.

Scientific perspective

- The increased use of off-road recreational vehicles is damaging environments that were previously inaccessible or were accessible only to walkers.
- The continued use of non-renewable resources, such as gas and oil, is short-sighted. For as long as they are still relatively inexpensive (and in some countries subject to very low taxation), research into alternatives is inhibited.
- Other forms of pollution, for instance noise, are produced by the car and road transport generally. There is scarcely a place in England where traffic cannot be heard.
- Fuel and carbon dioxide taxes could accelerate the search for cleaner, renewable resources for personal transport. Such research is continuing and the hydrogen fuel cell is being developed as an alternative to oil, gas or petrol.
- The use of fossil fuels wastes irreplaceable resources and environmental pressure groups claim it damages the environment. They want restrictions on road transport to protect the environment.
- Use of the car for every journey, however short, is damaging the nation's health. Children and adults are more overweight and are less fit than ever before. Walking more and further would help them.
- The development of other forms of technology may reduce the need for personal transport – for example, electronic communications and home-working, video conferencing and virtual reality experiences.
- Stress induced by driving on more crowded roads is showing itself in increased irritability and 'road-rage' incidents.

Social perspective

- Industry wants better roads to cut freight costs.
- Householders are concerned about threats to safety and property caused by new and existing roads.
- Political parties are under pressure to reduce environmental damage, improve public transport and build better road communications.
- Transport difficulties can influence how people vote.
- Only government can develop and implement effective integrated transport policies.
- The government is faced with European directives to reduce environmental pollution.
- Governments could price cars off the road with road tolls and taxes on town centre parking.
- Car manufacture is an important part of the economy.
- More effective legislation is required to protect society from careless drivers who flout existing laws.
- Unlimited importing of cars is harmful to the economy.
- Many workers are employed in the car industry.
- Car ownership produces considerable revenue for the government through taxes.
- Public transport is slow, expensive and inconvenient.
- Road building is an investment for the future as it can reduce the costs of industry and preserve the built environment.
- The police should spend less time persecuting car drivers and more time catching real criminals.

Thinking and analytical skills

1 What different types of knowledge and argument does the author of the passage use?
2 How justifiable is the claim that cars are, in part, responsible for global warming?

4.3 How real are soap operas?

Links: 1.1 (iii); 1.6 (i); 1.6 (v); 4.1 (i); 4.1 (viii)

'Soaps show life as we would like it to be, rather than as it really is.' Assess this opinion from social, moral and cultural perspectives.

Introduction

Soap operas gained their name from the earliest form of the genre on American radio. The term has since been used to describe similar types of programme. Targeted at a primarily female audience, soap operas are serials that are screened several times a week and contain various interlocking story lines and characters.

The most popular soaps are broadcast in the early evening. Broadcasters hope that viewer inertia will cause audiences to continue watching later programmes. British television shows a considerable number of such programmes that, generally, do attract large audiences.

In a fairly typical week soaps dominate the top ten list of programmes watched. *EastEnders* usually fills the top three slots for BBC1, with about fourteen million viewers, while *Coronation Street* dominates ITV, with slightly larger viewing figures.

Most British soaps deal with the 'normal' everyday life of ordinary people. Some imported soaps, especially those from America and Australia, are more upmarket.

Soaps aim to build up and retain audiences by cleverly extended dramatic story lines. Each broadcast tends to end with a cliffhanger, designed to retain viewers' interest. Emphasis is usually placed on 'realism' so that viewers will identify with the different characters.

The pursuit of realism has been an impetus for change in British soaps, but the bedrock of the appeal to realism has remained the same – a value placed on a particular setting, an 'authentic' regional experience and a particular class representation.

In their different ways, all four of the British soaps on which I am focusing (*Coronation Street, Crossroads, EastEnders, Brookside*) work with these concepts. The settings are specific – a street, a motel, a square, a small housing development – and are defined geographically so that the audience builds up a precise sense of place. In all cases, this regional authority gives the soaps a sense of specificity crucial to realism and the ability to work with regional characteristics. In themselves, such characteristics may be clichéd and sweeping, but they form part of the way in which British culture absorbs, uses and contributes to regional differences. And finally, the setting and region give each soap the opportunity to present working-class characters. The commitment to bring to the screen working-class accents, mores, problems and pleasures – still largely absent from much of British television – is an important element in the soaps' claim to realism.

Soaps do not offer a coherent aesthetic experience and, in particular, they do not work entirely in the realist tradition which is so valued in Britain. Instead, soaps deploy a range of aesthetic elements and offer a mix of generic conventions, which confuse or make them an object of scorn to those who seek to confine them to a particular format. This shifting between the different traditions contributes to the experience of engagement and distance which is so characteristic of soap viewing. But the values of light entertainment, melodrama and realism do not always fit smoothly together.

From Christine Gerraghty, 'Women and Soap Opera' in *The Polity Reader in Cultural Theory*, Polity Press, 1994

Issues to be discussed

- Why are soaps often regarded as a useful way of conveying important ideas and information to the public?
- Should the writers of soaps have a moral responsibility to their viewers or is their job simply to provide entertainment?
- Why do many characters in British soaps have a working-class or lower middle-class background while American soaps, like *Dallas*, focus on wealthy people?
- Why do viewers identify with some of the characters in soap operas?
- Why are British soap operas consistently among the most popular programmes on television?
- How important are spin-offs of soaps (like fan clubs and magazines, holiday tours, characters opening supermarkets and shows) in **a** establishing realism, and **b** ensuring continuing popularity?

Where now?

C. Gerraghty, 'Women and Soap Opera' in *The Polity Reader in Cultural Theory*, Polity Press, 1994
N. Abercrombie, *Television and Society*, Polity Press, 1996
www.findarticles.com

Cultural perspective

- *The Archers*, Britain's longest running radio serial, was developed to convey up-to-date agricultural information to farmers. Characters and settings were deliberately chosen so that the audience would identify easily with the characters and story lines. *The Archers* is still used to convey useful information.
- Many soaps are designed to be pure entertainment, providing escapism for viewers.
- Story lines are based on the everyday life of 'ordinary' people and stereotypical characters to make it easier for viewers to identify with the programmes.
- Most people can accept that soaps are fiction, but some believe they are true and that the characters are real. For example, some actors have been attacked in real life because of the unacceptable actions of the characters they portray and viewers regularly contacted ITV to ask if they could hire the Crossroads Motel for weddings, conferences and other private functions.
- Soaps are in competition with each other and often have similar story lines.
- Realism is achieved through story lines that often do not have happy endings.
- The media often mock soaps as poor examples of popular culture. Nevertheless, successful soaps achieve tremendous popularity and easily attract the largest regular TV audiences.
- When, in the 1970s, the viewing time of *Crossroads* was changed from 6 pm to 4.30 pm, female factory workers in Devon went on strike because they couldn't watch their favourite programme.
- Successful story lines can engage popular opinion; for example, there was a campaign to 'Free the Wetherfield One' when Deirdre Rashid, a character from *Coronation Street*, was wrongly imprisoned. A question was asked in parliament about it.
- *The Archers* is still billed as 'an everyday story of country folk'.
- Since soaps thrive on drama, producers rely on births, murders, weddings and accidents to keep their audiences.
- The subject matter of story lines is usually true to life. (Although realism is lost by the frequency with which different disasters strike the same individuals.)
- Stories and characters' behaviour are often predictable.

Social perspective

- Successful soaps often have marketing spin-offs which can be extremely profitable. They can provide employment and income for a locality as well as leisure pursuits, like tours of Coronation Street, Emmerdale village and Holmfirth where *Last of the Summer Wine* is set.
- Royals, celebrities and politicians have appeared as themselves in soaps which gives credibility to 'realism'.
- Soaps can deal with real, significant issues and raise public awareness more effectively than a factual or documentary programme.
- Story lines have included living with AIDS, teenage pregnancy, drug addiction, transsexuality, adoption and the influence of religious cults.
- Many soaps feature dysfunctional families and the pressures and problems they face. Some critics claim this is simply a reflection of society, while other say it creates patterns of behaviour that society will follow.
- Soaps are relatively cheap to produce but attract large advertising revenue because of their large audiences. This makes them attractive and profitable for the TV companies.
- Characters in soaps can become so real that their names and characteristics become part of everyday speech. For example, Benny, the simple-minded handyman in *Crossroads*, gave his name to a type of woollen hat or a simple gullible person.
- Most soaps revolve around the idea of community, showing both its tensions and strengths. This can present a significant ideal in a largely anonymous urban environment.
- Most soaps deal with leisure-time activities and rarely focus on issues of employment.
- Time is distorted and events are structured so that every programme ends in a cliffhanger.
- Soaps challenge accepted value systems. Good people are often depicted as losers and bad people are shown to succeed.
- Speed of production and the fragmented nature of story lines mean that programmes can be easily adapted to reflect and include contemporary issues, thus contributing to the sense of realism.

Thinking and analytical skills

1 Identify the different types of knowledge used in the passage.
2 What are the strengths and weaknesses of the arguments used? How effectively are they justified?

4.4 Is the abuse of drugs killing sport?

Links: 1.2 (iii); 1.3 (vi); 2.1 (iii); 2.4 (ii); 3.1 (ii); 3.4 (i); 3.4 (vi)

Many people are disturbed by the thought of sportsmen and women using performance-enhancing drugs, but they are perfectly happy to use the latest technological aids to achieve success in their work. Discuss arguments for and against the view that the use of performance-enhancing drugs should be legalised in sport.

Introduction

There has been considerable media interest recently in the use of performance-enhancing drugs in sport. Several prominent athletes have been identified as drug takers by official testing programmes.

However, drug use in sport is not new. In Ancient Greece mass spectator sport and rich prizes led to the development of professionalism in sport. Bribing and cheating were the norm and some competitors used performance-enhancing substances, like mushrooms and plant extracts. Whenever sport is about reward, rather than personal enjoyment, some competitors will seek unfair advantage.

Many sports list banned substances and operate systematic or random testing programmes to discourage drug use. However, since different drugs produce different effects, substances banned in one sport may be acceptable in another. For example, anabolic steroids, which help build muscle to make competitors stronger and faster, might help a sprinter or shot-putter, but could disadvantage an archer or shooter who requires steady hands, not strength and speed. 'Masking agents' are banned, not because they improve performance but because they can hide banned substances.

Some claim that athletes must have talent to succeed and that drugs merely enhance these natural gifts. Others claim the use of any artificial aids to improve performance should be banned and records achieved through drug use devalue sporting competition.

We expect our athletes to celebrate nature and the body beautiful, but we also demand that they win competitions.

Florence Griffith Joyner (Flo-Jo) died, aged 38, from heart seizure this week. Even before her untimely death, there were whispers that Flo-Jo used performance-enhancing drugs.

Her death will throw the spotlight back on to the debate over drugs in sports. Earlier this month another athlete, the US baseball player, Mark McGwire, hit the most home runs ever in a single season. He is the first athlete in history to break a record while publicly admitting his use of performance-enhancing drugs. So far, the use of drugs has not doomed baseball. As in many walks of life, unbridled success is able to sweep any latent misgivings neatly under the carpet.

The moral crusade against the use of drugs in sport, like most moral crusades, is surrounded by myth. One of the myths is that fans won't pay to see drug-aided athletes perform. A second myth is that using drugs means that athletes don't have to work for their achievements.

It is undoubtedly true, nonetheless, that the idea of using performance-enhancing drugs is deeply disturbing to a great many people. John Whetton, former Olympic 1,500 metre finalist said, 'Using chemicals to do what your body isn't capable of doing is cheating, but it is a form of cheating that is hidden and therefore it is a nasty form of cheating.'

Opposition to using drugs in sport is based on more than the fact that it is simply not allowed by the rules.

From *New Statesman*, 25 September 1998

Issues to be discussed

- To what extent is it true to say that in sport it is more important to take part than to win?
- How far are young people influenced by whether sports stars take drugs or not?
- Does it matter whether competitors in the Olympic games use drugs in their training?
- Does modern technology give some athletes an unfair advantage? If so, should it also be banned?
- Is the use of performance-enhancing drugs in sport a concern of government or should it be left to the sports controlling bodies?
- What steps might a scientist or other researcher take to determine whether sports records have been unfairly distorted by the use of drugs?
- What steps can be taken to prevent the use of banned substances in sport?

Where now?

www.sportrec.qld.gov.au/infopaper/drugsinf.html
news2.thls.bbc.co.uk/hi/english/uk/scotland
www.findarticles.com

Cultural perspective

- Drug taking in sport is a professional, not a legal, issue.
- Sport is a major social institution and athletes are under increasing pressure to succeed.
- If a sportsman's rivals are using drugs, it is only sensible for him or her to use them as well.
- The expectations of family, friends and trainers can put athletes under pressure to succeed.
- The known use of drugs in sports like cycling and baseball has not driven spectators away.
- If a safe performance-enhancing drug improved every athlete's performance to the same level, there would be no point taking it.
- Ordinary people who play sport to improve the quality of their lives may be exposed to drugs.
- The use of performance-enhancing substances is cheating, which is contrary to sporting ideals.
- Sport ought to be a fair competition between highly skilled performers who have developed expertise through natural ability and hard work.
- Drug taking is unfair because some athletes, especially those in poorer parts of the world, are disadvantaged anyway because of a lack of resources.
- The media want better results all the time and may encourage the use of drugs to improve performance.

Scientific perspective

- Much drug testing is ineffective because careful planning can ensure that traces of drugs disappear from an athlete's body before a competition while still enhancing his or her performance.
- The human body naturally produces some banned substances. This means that testing can never be really relied upon.
- If sufficient money were invested, it would be possible to develop effective performance-enhancing drugs that do not have harmful side effects.
- The use of drugs in professional sport may contribute to the development of increasingly sophisticated performance-enhancing drugs.
- Banned substance may cause short- and long-term damage to athletes' health.
- Injured athletes may use drugs to enable them to compete, even though they are not fully fit. This may cause them lasting damage.
- Sport is an expression of the Darwinian concept of the survival of the fittest.

Social perspective

- World-class athletes are geographically mobile, so it is very difficult to enforce any realistic control unless there are worldwide laws against drug taking in sport.
- Sporting success is regarded as a national as well as a personal triumph. Sporting success should be encouraged, whatever methods are used.
- Unless drug taking is legalised, most of the records set in the last 50 years may be challenged as being unreliable.
- Athletes only have a short time at the top and therefore need to take advantage of every opportunity to win the rich prizes and endorsements that are available.
- Drugs are here to stay, so the sporting authorities ought to work with them, rather than try to prevent their use.
- Drug taking in sport may involve not only the use of illegal substances (whether banned by the sports organisation or the law of the land), but also the abusive consumption of legal drugs.
- The standards accepted in sport are a reflection of the standards adopted by society.
- Taking drugs in any form or circumstance is interfering with nature – and breaking divine law.
- Many governments oppose the use of drugs in sport.
- Sports stars are heroes for many young people. Their example of drug abuse (or of rejecting drugs) may encourage similar behaviour in fans.
- Sport is big business. Sponsors are entitled to get value for their money. If competitors need to take drugs in order to win, this should be accepted.
- Sports organisations fighting against drugs in sport can be a focus for a broader campaign against drugs.
- Organisations which ought to stamp out drug taking have a financial interest in not wrecking the reputation of their sports, so they cover up drug abuse.

Thinking and analytical skills

1 What different types of knowledge are used in the passage?
2 Identify and explain any flaws or weaknesses in the argument.
3 To what extent does the author of the passage justify the conclusion?

4.5 Should adoption be made easier in this country?

Links: 1.1 (iv); 1.3 (ii); 3.4 (i); 3.4 (ii); 3.5 (i); 3.5 (v)

Critically examine the view 'Since every woman is entitled to a child, whatever the cost, governments should remove restrictions on adoption and other methods of providing children for women who want them.' In your answer you should consider adoption, surrogacy, artificial insemination and other ways to have a baby.

Introduction

In January 2001 the purchase of two babies for adoption over the Internet raised a number of concerns:

- the use of the Internet for this purpose,
- that this type of adoption, legal in America, allows British citizens to evade tighter UK adoption laws,
- the suitability of the couple to be parents,
- the apparent lack of checks as to suitability,
- the morality of purchasing or selling babies,
- the need to change British legislation in order to speed up the process of adoption,
- the large number of children who are in care but, for legal reasons, cannot be adopted, even though large numbers of potential parents want to adopt.

During this media-inspired controversy, the British government said it would speed up changes in the law to improve the adoption process and ensure that wealthy people could not easily evade its provisions.

Fostering, whether short or long term, is an alternative to adoption. Although it helps unfortunate or disadvantaged children, it does not give their carers full parental rights.

Medical science has developed techniques to enable some infertile women to become pregnant. However, fertility treatment can be an uncertain and expensive process.

In recent years there has been controversy about surrogate parenting. In Britain, surrogacy for profit is illegal, but is big business in the USA and in other parts of the world. Payment for surrogacy raises many practical, legal and ethical issues.

Try as I might, I cannot convince myself that buying babies is anything other than corrupt. The defence argues that there is nothing intrinsically wrong with acquiring babies in this way. Why should an adoption agency not be run on a profit-making basis?

Given the lamentable state of the adoption services in this country, it has a point. It is also difficult not to feel some sympathy for the other argument put forward by the buy-a-baby crew that providing an unwanted child with a loving environment remains a Good Thing.

But I can't surmount my distaste. People aren't pets and babies aren't a commodity. To suggest that they are, is morally bankrupt. Where do you stop? Since when did 'caring' come with a price attached?

Arranging adoptions is laudable, but why should anyone pay for rescuing a child and wanting to love it? How can this be anything other than sick? Human life is sacred; it should not, must not carry a price tag.

In the past 25 years the number of adoptions in Britain has fallen from 22,000 to 6,000 a year, while unplanned teenage pregnancies have soared and there are many more career women warming to the joys of motherhood too late to achieve a successful pregnancy of their own.

It now takes an average of six years for a child to be adopted. Trying to get a faster result by buying babies is not the answer. We need a wholesale review of the adoption system. Quickly, please.

From a column by India Knight, *The Sunday Times*, 21 January 2001

Issues to be discussed

- What criteria should be used to decide whether adoption can take place?
- Does it matter whether children go to adoptive parents of the same ethnic group as themselves?
- Is surrogacy right or wrong? What restrictions should there be on payment?
- Is it true that every woman is entitled to have a child of her own? Justify your answer.
- Why are adoption and surrogacy political issues?
- Many people who want to adopt children are disqualified because they are over 35 years old. Should age on its own be a sufficient reason to prevent adoption?
- Why should adoptive children be entitled to know who their natural parents are?
- How would you speed up the adoption process?

Where now?

www.guardianunlimited.co.uk/Archive
www.doh.gov.uk
www.findarticles.com
www.adoption-net.co.uk
www.surrogacy.org.uk

Cultural perspective

- Is there moral justification for claims that all women are entitled to a child? And if women are, why not men?
- Morality demands that society should be concerned about the needs of children as well as adults.
- Is it morally right to buy or sell children, even for the best of motives?
- How can the wellbeing of children who are sold for adoption be safeguarded?
- Can we be sure that children advertised, bought and sold are not wanted for immoral or other purposes?
- Should single-sex couples or single people be allowed to adopt? Do they provide the right role model or does their situation create social problems for the children?
- Is surrogacy right morally or religiously?
- Is the media really concerned about children's needs or just about sensationalism and increased circulation?
- Can the needs of emotionally disturbed or handicapped children who are adopted be safeguarded?
- Are there any circumstances in which it is acceptable for the media to advertise children for sale, whether by adoption or surrogacy?
- Should the media be criticised for highlighting abuses?
- Have the media and media personalities created an artificial want by suggesting that women and families can only find fulfilment through children?
- Children from ethnic minorities form a fifth of those available for adoption, but there are few prospective ethnic parents seeking to adopt.

Scientific perspective

- Just because science has made it possible for us to perform a medical procedure (like surrogacy) doesn't mean that it is right to do so.
- The need for adoption might be averted if improved medical procedures (for example, IVF and male fertility improvements) enabled more women to conceive and have children.
- Surrogacy involves surgical procedures. These are expensive and mean that only those who can afford treatment can benefit from it.
- Scientific study of the behaviour of related and adoptive parents may affect the procedures of adoption and the training of adoptive parents.
- DNA analysis and matching now enable very confident identification of natural parents. Adopted children have the right, in the UK, to be informed who their natural parents are.
- Extensive artificial changes in the ways in which families come to have children have implications for 'natural' families, with unknown consequences on the behaviour of children and, later, adults.
- Changes in communications – notably the Internet – and the ease of international travel make it possible for adoptions to be made in other countries and for UK laws to be broken or side-stepped.

Social perspective

- Adoption is a slow process and can take several years.
- The government wants to increase the adoption rate.
- Since keeping children in care is expensive emotionally and financially, it makes sound social and economic sense to encourage adoption.
- The care system has been discredited through recent bad publicity about cases of child abuse and neglect.
- There are more children available for adoption than there are potential adoptive parents.
- The national system lacks consistency, which leads to wide variations in local adoption procedures.
- There may be a social stigma attached to adoptive parents whose sexuality varies from the norm.
- Regulating adoption procedures can guarantee protection of children's rights.
- Procedures need to be tightly controlled in order to 'weed out' undesirable applicants.
- Children's needs are more important than adult wants.
- Every child is entitled to be loved, cared for and wanted.
- Just because the law allows something, does it automatically make it right?
- Should the age or physical condition of a prospective adopter affect whether adoption is allowed?
- In July 2000 the government promised to set up an adoption register, setting out the national standards.

Thinking and analytical skills

1. Does the writer of the passage present a sound argument? Identify its strengths and weaknesses.
2. What different types of argument and knowledge are used in the passage?
3. How might an opponent of the writer's views respond to her arguments?

4.6 Should one person ever be allowed to help another 'die with dignity'?

Links: 1.2 (iii); 1.3 (vi); 3.1 (ii); 3.1 (iii); 3.1 (iv); 3.1 (v); 3.4 (ii)

Many supporters of euthanasia argue that every individual has the inalienable right to choose how and when their life will end. Critically examine arguments for and against this view.

Introduction

The term 'euthanasia' can mean different things. Literally, it means 'a good death'. The Pro-Life Alliance define it as 'any action or omission intended to end the life of a patient on the grounds that his or her life is not worth living'. In contrast, the Voluntary Euthanasia Society say it is 'a good death brought about by a doctor providing drugs or an injection to bring a peaceful end to the dying process'. Popular usage means any termination of life by a doctor, but Dutch law adds 'at the express wish of a patient'. In 2000, the Netherlands became the first developed country to legalise euthanasia.

Three classes of euthanasia are generally identified:

- Passive euthanasia is when life-sustaining treatment is withheld because doctors agree that continued treatment would serve no good purpose. In 1993, a legal decision classed basic nutrition and hydration as treatment and gave doctors authority to cease treatment of a patient 'in a persistent vegetative state'.
- Physician-assisted suicide is when a patient, in full command of their mental capacities, repeatedly and consistently asks a doctor to ease their suffering by helping to deliberately end their life.
- Active euthanasia is when a doctor consciously and deliberately administers medication knowing that it will inevitably shorten a patient's life without the patient's knowledge or agreement.

Research showing that terminally ill cancer patients can long for death one day, but cling to life the next has illustrated the potential risks of legalising euthanasia.

The recommendation is that, should voluntary euthanasia be legalised, patients should have a 'cooling off period' during which they can change their minds. The study found that a patient who strongly expressed the desire to die could say the opposite even 12 hours later. 'The likely transience of a request to die is important. Demonstrations of a sustained wish to die must be part of evaluating any death-hastening request' the report states.

Physician-assisted suicide is currently illegal in this country. The British Medical Association (BMA) states: 'The normal duty of a doctor is to attempt to rescue the would-be suicide. Considerable moral and practical confusion for doctors could be generated by the imposition of a duty to assist it.'

The Voluntary Euthanasia Society said a 15-day cooling off period 'is an integral part of any proposal that we are making'. Studies have shown links between a patient's interest in physician-assisted suicide and depression, pain and other distressing symptoms.

The researchers are hopeful that understanding this link could help provide better pain control and palliative care to cancer patients. But they conceded that their work could not be used to predict the will-to-live of patients with other illnesses, such as Aids or progressive disorders.

From news.bbc.co.uk, 3 September 1999

Issues to be discussed

- What are the political arguments for and against the legalisation of euthanasia?
- Could relatives of terminally ill patients encourage euthanasia in order to gain access to their property?
- Is the main duty of doctors to preserve life at all costs or to ease suffering?
- Should doctors who assist a person to die be accused of murder or manslaughter?
- Should euthanasia be legalised? Justify your answer.
- Is there any difference between a doctor and a non-medical person assisting with euthanasia?
- Is there any moral difference between a doctor who allows a patient to die and one who speeds up the process of dying?
- If euthanasia was legalised what safeguards should be in place to ensure that doctors were really carrying out the wishes of their patients?
- Under what medical circumstances is it justifiable to break the law?

Where now?

news.bbc.co.uk
www.didina.demon.co.uk
www.guardianunlimited.co.uk
www.prolife.org.uk/
www.euthanasia.org/dutch.html
www.ves.org.uk/
www.legaltheory.demon.co.uk

Cultural perspective

- If life becomes unbearable, it is a kindness to the individual and their family to help them to reach a dignified end.
- People are entitled to choose how and when their life ends.
- If it is morally acceptable to allow pain relief that shortens life, it must be right to allow termination of life when a patient wants it.
- It is an essential part of civilisation to be allowed to die with dignity.
- Refusing help is morally wrong and may cause a person to attempt unassisted suicide. If this is unsuccessful, it can lead to even greater distress.
- Some religions teach that life is sacred and should be preserved at all costs.
- Many people believe 'while there is life there is hope' and that if there is enough research, a cure for any illness may be found.
- Euthanasia would devalue human life. If we accept the voluntary killing of the terminally ill, what is to stop the killing of those with severe mental or physical disabilities?
- Advocates of euthanasia have a utilitarian view of humanity, but every life is unique and deserves absolute respect.
- Doctors are committed to preserving life.

Scientific perspective

- Computer-controlled injection devices allow a terminally ill patient to administer a lethal injection for themselves. The intention is to allow the patient a choice in the face of unbearable pain. The supply of such a device and instructions on how to use it could be interpreted as assisting suicide.
- Euthanasia is a step towards eugenics, which was one of the great evils of the Nazi regime in Germany.
- It is better to deep-freeze terminally ill patients rather than to aid their deaths. In the future scientific discoveries may make a cure possible.
- The science of pain relief within the hospice movement provides opportunities for dignified death, but the starving and dehydration of passive euthanasia can cause massive suffering.

Social perspective

- Suicide has not been a crime since 1961, so why should physician-assisted suicide be a criminal offence?
- Laws banning euthanasia are bad laws because they are unenforceable and are regularly broken.
- An ageing population will not only increase disability, illness and suffering but will increase health costs.
- It makes better economic sense to help people who want to die to do so, than waste the limited resources of the National Health Service on their care.
- Holland has one of the highest levels of health care in the world yet has legalised euthanasia.
- It is legal to give a patient massive doses of morphine (that lead to death) to ease pain and not to resuscitate a patient who has had a massive heart attack.
- Opinion polls show that many people support the idea of a change in the law.
- Living wills are legal, but euthanasia isn't.
- The law defines death as 'brain-stem death', but there is no agreed definition of when this occurs.
- Why should brain death count as the death of the person if other organs continue to function?
- People broke the law in order to legalise abortion; people will break the law to legalise euthanasia. If this happens, how can we expect other laws to be respected?
- Appeals to legalise euthanasia are based on emotion rather than reason.
- Euthanasia is simply the intentional killing of the sick, the elderly and the infirm.
- Legalisation of euthanasia will lead to the wholesale killing of the elderly. In Holland, old people are afraid to go into hospital for fear of involuntary euthanasia.
- Euthanasia turns people into commodities that can be disposed of when they're no longer wanted. Society objects to this attitude to pets, so why should we accept it for human beings? If we accept it for the old and sick today, how long will it be before we apply it to the mentally or physically disabled or to unwanted children?

Thinking and analytical skills

1. What different types of knowledge might be used to justify or challenge the rightness of euthanasia?
2. What different types of argument are used in the passage?

4.7 Will we soon be able to live for ever?

Links: 1.2 (iv); 1.3 ( ); 1.3 (v); 3.1 (iii); 3.1 (iv); 3.3 (viii); 3.5 (v) 4.6

Scientists claim that they will soon be able to extend the span of human life to hundreds of years. Is this likely to be the greatest prize for mankind or a terrible curse? Justify your answer by referring to scientific, cultural and social perspectives.

Introduction

The one thing we can be sure of in life is death. In contrast to earlier times and other cultures, death is a taboo subject in modern Western society. Although we acknowledge its inevitability, we often try to ignore it and pretend it won't happen to us. Nevertheless, throughout history people of all cultures have asked, 'What happens after death?'

Most people would like to avoid death or at least delay it for as long as possible. Some seek immortality by:

- having sons, to ensure their family name carries on,
- creating lasting monuments bearing their name,
- leaving a lasting legacy, like a research or artistic foundation.

Some try to extend life by:

- having their bodies frozen when they die, until such time as medical science is able to cure them of the disease that killed them,
- spending fortunes on cosmetic surgery,
- encouraging cloning to produce replacement organs to allow life to be extended.

Scientists and doctors are more concerned with saving and extending life than with whether there is an afterlife. Recent discoveries suggest that scientists are on the verge of discovering the secret of life itself. Life expectancy has increased steadily over the last century and many believe that it will continue to increase, soon reaching 120. Some scientists claim that there is no medical reason why life expectancy cannot increase to 300 or more.

At present there is little suggestion that science can enable people to live for ever, but there are doubtless some people who would be prepared to pay for the secret if it existed.

All share a common destiny – the righteous and the wicked, the good and the bad.

This is the evil in everything that happens under the sun: the same destiny overtakes us all … There is madness in their hearts while they live, and afterwards they join the dead. Anyone who is among the living has hope – even a live dog is better off than a dead lion!
For the living know that they will die,
but the dead know nothing;
they have no further reward,
and even the memory of them is forgotten.
Their love and their hate
and their jealousy have long since vanished;
never again will they have a part
in anything that happens under the sun.

Ecclesiastes 9 verses 2, 3–6

Lord … you turn men back to dust, saying, 'Return to dust, O son of men' … You sweep men away in the sleep of death; they are like the new grass of the morning – through the morning it springs up new, by evening it is dried and withered … All our days pass away under your wrath; we finish our years with a moan. The length of our days is seventy years – or eighty, if we have the strength; yet their span is but trouble and sorrow, for they quickly pass, and we fly away.

Psalm 90 verses 3, 5, 9–10 (New International version)

Issues to be discussed

- Why does modern Western society find it more difficult to think about death than previous generations?
- Should scientists be concerned only with how to extend life or should they accept some responsibility for the quality of life that their discoveries make possible?
- Should births be limited to avoid overpopulation resulting from increased longevity?
- What would be the advantages and disadvantages of living for longer periods?
- Do people really want to live for ever?
- Who should pay for the costs of increased life expectancy and consequent health care?
- What are the political and legal implications of an increasingly ageing population?
- What are the moral implications of offering extended life to some people but not to others?
- Is it morally right to spend money extending life for some, when others in poorer parts of the world have a very short life expectancy?

Where now?

www.findarticles.com

W. F. Nolan and G. C Johnson, *Logan's Run*, Buccaneer Books, 1999

Cultural perspective

- Most religions incorporate beliefs about death and afterlife.
- Buddhism teaches that we undergo serial reincarnation, but our aim should be to achieve nirvana, the state of eternal nothingness.
- The Hindu Gita teaches that the human soul is immortal and cannot be killed.
- The Koran teaches that on Judgement Day the evil will be punished and the good will live for ever in paradise.
- Many Christians believe that after death the soul goes to heaven. Others believe Judgement Day will bring resurrection and either reward or punishment.
- Some believe that scientists are wrong to 'play at God' by trying to extend life.
- Will longer life increase the sum total of human happiness or will it lead to greater misery?
- Philosophers try, on grounds of reason, to determine whether or not there is an afterlife.
- Humanists believe mankind only has one life and should make the best possible use of it.
- The media often print stories about people who claim to have died, visited heaven and returned to give eyewitness accounts of the glories of the afterlife.
- Media stories about scientific discoveries raise hopes that medical knowledge may enable us to live for ever.
- Would it be aesthetically pleasing to experience long life?

Scientific perspective

- Very few vertebrate animals live extremely long lives – there may be a good evolutionary reason for this.
- Another attempt to achieve a kind of immortality is by freezing the body or just the brain. The idea is that they will be resuscitated when a cure is found for the disease from which they died.
- When a person dies, many of the body's cells continue their function for some time afterwards. In Britain, death is legally defined quite arbitrarily as 'brain-stem death'.
- Stem cells may be used to produce replacement organs to transplant into their owner when their organs start to deteriorate or are damaged through illness.
- Cloning from a person's stem cells would not mean that person would live longer, since the cloned individual (like identical twins) would not be identical because their experience and environment would be different, even though their genes were the same.
- If the life expectancy of many people increased radically, it would have a serious effect on the age structure of the population; the long-term effects of this are unknown.
- A significant unknown is the psychological effects that greater life expectation will have on an individual.
- If science can increase life expectancy indefinitely, individuals must be allowed to choose when to die.

Social perspective

- Increased longevity means longer retirement, but society cannot afford increased longevity since pension and welfare benefits will be insufficient to meet increased demands.
- Do we need good health as well as long life? If so, how can we ensure that most people experience both?
- Should the state or families or private enterprise be responsible for the care of the very old?
- Welfare and medical needs increase with age.
- Does longer life guarantee better life?
- How will laws need to be changed to meet the demands of a much older population?
- Will increased longevity raise the status of old people or increase the generation gap?
- How should families plan for the needs of members who may live longer than previously expected?
- Will greater longevity lead to a reduction in productivity and national wealth or to a longer working life?
- Should governments place limits on medical research in order to restrict developments in longevity?
- Will increased longevity lead to greater loneliness and isolation for the elderly or revive the extended family?
- What are the implications of an increasingly elderly population in the developed world and of a significantly younger population in the developing world?

Thinking and analytical skills

1 What types of knowledge would be used by **a** a scientist, **b** a doctor, **c** a theologian, and **d** a philosopher if they were discussing the merits of extending life expectancy?

2 How would **a** a humanist, and **b** a Christian respond to the passages quoted from the Bible?

4.8 Should organ donation be made compulsory?

Links: 1.2 (i); 1.3 (v); 3.1 (ii); 3.4 (i); 3.4 (ii); 3.4 (vi); 3.4 (vii)

Critically examine the opinion that doctors should be legally able to remove organs from dead bodies without the consent of relatives.You should consider scientific, moral, religious and political perspectives.

Introduction

There are three main demands for human organs:

- for transplant surgery to replace deteriorating or worn-out organs to help save, extend or improve life,
- for research, to increase anatomical and physiological knowledge. Animals, however close they may seem to humans, cannot give doctors the detailed knowledge that is needed to treat the human condition,
- to develop medical treatments and drugs.

The first recorded organ transplant took place in 1936 in the then-USSR. The first successful living donor kidney transplant took place in the USA in 1954 and in 1967 the first successful heart transplant was undertaken in South Africa.

Since the Sixties transplant surgery has increased rapidly, both in the number and variety of operations. By 1983 doctors had successfully developed immunosuppressive drugs to control rejection of transplanted organs.

However, potential recipients far outnumber potential donors. Possible solutions include:

- conscriptive donation, whereby everyone is assumed to agree to organ removal unless they refuse consent,
- using animal organs to replace human organs,
- a central register of donors whose wishes would be binding after death, overriding the wishes of relatives,
- legalisation of sale and purchase of organs,
- developing scientific procedures for growing or regenerating organs (in animals or by cloning),
- media campaigns to change awareness and attitudes.

Organ donation and transplant create conflict. Our ethical and emotional objections conflict with our desire to use all possible methods to save or enhance life. A further limiting factor is the law which at present allows relatives to override the known wishes of the person who has died.

A damning report into the scandal of 3,500 organs removed from dead babies will attack a widespread culture among doctors that the practice is acceptable.

Alan Milburn, the health secretary, will tell doctors they must consult relatives on what they intend to remove and why. Milburn is expected to tell doctors: 'For trust to thrive between patients and the NHS, there has to be informed consent, not tick-in-the-box consent. The NHS must actively seek the consent of relatives.'

The report recommends that hospitals must be compelled to be clearer about what they are asking permission for – at the moment, organ removal is legal only if a relative agrees that 'tissue' can be removed. The report will show that the practice of organ removal is widespread and that there are an estimated 40,000 body parts stored around the country.

Ian Cohen, a Liverpool solicitor representing more than 150 families whose dead children had body parts removed without their parents' consent, said a number of large organs, such as livers and spleens, had never been traced and returned to the families for burial.

From *The Sunday Times*, 28 January 2001

Issues to be discussed

- Are organ transplants from donors simply a matter for science?
- What ethical arguments might be used to **a** justify, and **b** condemn payment for organs?
- Is animal organ transplantation (xenotransplants) an acceptable procedure?
- What criteria would you use to determine priorities for receiving organ transplants?
- Should Britain have a law of 'presumed consent', by which everyone is assumed to agree to organ donation after death unless they specifically opt not to?
- Does it matter if rich people have better access to transplant surgery than poor people, since they are already able to afford better medical treatment?
- Who should say when death has occurred – politicians, scientists, ministers of religion or doctors?

Where now?

www.findarticles.com
www.christianliferesources.com
www.law.indiana.edu
www.mssc.edu/pages/chart425/organ.htm
www.observer.co.uk/uk_news/story

Cultural perspective

- The gap between organ supply and demand is greater in countries with strong religious or cultural beliefs about the nature of death.
- Some people believe donating a dead relative's organs is an act of love and will preserve their memory.
- Organ transplants are about prestige for doctors not about giving patients a better quality of life.
- In 2000 the Pope said that organ donation was an act of love, but using discarded or cloned embryos was wrong. He accepted experiments with animal organs.
- There is no universally accepted definition of when death occurs. Doctors talk of brain death, but some religions say that death is when the spirit departs the body.
- Most people believe organ transplants are morally right, but only a third of deaths actually result in a donation.
- Some religious groups distinguish between accepting replaceable tissue (like blood) and refusing irreplaceable tissue (like hearts).
- Organ donation can improve the quality of life of sufferers and of the relatives who care for them.
- An organ bank would make it easier to provide immediately for those waiting for transplants.
- Many fear unscrupulous doctors may speed the death of patients in order to obtain organs.
- Some religious people believe they need to preserve a whole body for the Day of Resurrection.

Scientific perspective

- Transplanting animal organs could transmit deadly new diseases. Pig hearts and kidneys, for example, carry potentially deadly retroviruses.
- It can take many years before diseases passed on through animal organ transplants become apparent.
- Patients receiving animal organs are likely to be on complex and expensive drug regimes for the rest of their lives, in order to prevent rejection of the foreign tissue.
- Demands for animal transplants are encouraged by business interests, which stand to make billions of pounds of profit from them.
- In 1999 the UK government imposed standards for patients receiving animal organs. They included no unprotected sex and informing the authorities and doctors about each new sexual partner.
- Stem cell surgery (using a patient's own cells to grow new organs) may reduce the need for organ transplants.
- If the supply of organs were increased, doctors would improve their skill and thus increase success rates.
- Human organs are cheaper and more efficient than technological devices. It makes good economic sense to increase the supply of donors.

Social perspective

- Brazil, India and China, which rely heavily on organs from living donors, experience higher rates of infection than the USA, Canada and western Europe.
- The rich would benefit more from paid-for organ donation than would the poor, but they benefit from better health care anyway.
- Globalisation has led to worldwide trade in bodies and body parts.
- The main direction of sales of organs is from poorer countries to richer ones. In some countries a 'body-mafia' exists to locate paid donors.
- In 1994 the World Medical Association banned buying the organs of executed criminals, although this is still legally practised in China.
- Organ transplants and follow-up medicine are very expensive; the money could be better spent on less glamorous treatments.
- There are close links between criminal organisations and the sale of organs in some areas of the world.
- The Pope condemned transplants that did not 'respect human dignity'.
- Does it infringe on human rights to compel a person to donate organs if they do not want to do so?
- Since everyone, except the donors, benefits from donation shouldn't payment be allowed to compensate their families?
- Wealthy patients in countries where transplants are discouraged may buy organs and operations in countries where it is allowed.
- Relatives can often deny or override the wishes of donors, through either ignorance or emotion.
- What criteria should be used to determine priorities in places where supply of organs does not meet demand?

Thinking and analytical skills

1 What types of knowledge and argument are used in the passage?
2 How might you argue against the conclusion in the passage?

4.9 Should embryos with inherited diseases be aborted?

Links: 1.2 (i); 1.3 (v); 2.4 (ii); 3.1 (vi); 3.4 (ii)

'Modern medicine enables problems before birth to be detected. This means there is no medical reason for allowing disabled children to be born.' Evaluate the moral, social and scientific arguments for and against this point of view.

Introduction

A wide range of techniques is now available to detect that a developing foetus has problems such as an inherited disease or an acquired infection. Tests include:

- Ultrasound scans, which are very much safer than X-rays, are used to examine the baby in the womb. They can be used to detect physical abnormalities of the skeleton, limbs, intestines, heart, lungs and brain but only, of course, when these organs have started developing.
- Amniocentesis is a process whereby a small amount of the amniotic fluid surrounding the baby is removed. The foetal cells in this fluid can be tested for inherited diseases such as Down's syndrome. It is not completely without risk to the baby and is only carried out when other tests indicate that there might be a problem.
- If both parents' genes are known, then the chances of the baby having certain diseases can be predicted with varying degrees of certainty. Known as genetic counselling, this is likely to develop very quickly now that the Human Genome Project has established all the genes present in humans.

Cystic fibrosis (CF) is the most common inherited disease in Britain; five babies are born with it every week. But unless they are screened at birth, the disease can go undetected for months: more than one-third of cases are not diagnosed until after the child's first birthday. The disease causes the body to produce a thick, sticky mucus which builds up and eventually clogs the stomach and, more dangerously, the lungs.

The National Screening Committee, set up last year to investigate CF testing for all newborn babies, is due to report this summer. Dr Martin Scott, of the Cystic Fibrosis Trust, cannot understand the delay.

'Cystic fibrosis can be controlled very effectively with drug treatments. In neonatal babies who are tested, there are clear signs of presymptomatic damage, such as early lung inflammation and infection. On moral grounds, any prevarication seems unethical.' The cost of screening is about £1.50 per child – a small price to pay, says the CF Trust, for diagnosing our most prevalent genetic disease.

'Meanwhile, thanks to developments in conventional drug treatments, the life expectancy of a CF patient has tripled over the past 30 years. The median survival age is now 30 and many go well beyond that.'

Equally cutting-edge is some of the antenatal treatment being offered. It has been pioneered by Professor David Brock of the Human Genetics Unit at the University of Edinburgh. In the past five years around 30,000 women at the city's antenatal clinics have been offered a simple mouthwash test to find whether they carry the CF gene. If they test positive, their baby's father is offered the test; if he is also positive, they are given the option of an in vitro examination (amniocentesis or CVS) to determine whether their baby has CF. Nine women have had terminations after the tests on their foetus proved positive.

'We have reduced the incidence of CF in this area by two-thirds,' says Prof Brock. 'It is not ideal and many people will find it repugnant but, nonetheless, it is an option that 70 per cent of our patients want.'

From *The Daily Telegraph*, 19 April 1997

Issues to be discussed

- If termination of disabled foetuses is accepted, how long will it be before we terminate those who lack features their parents desire?
- Does disabled mean defective or socially unable? Why should either of these definitions justify the termination of a human life?
- Some cultures favour boys over girls. If society decides that being female is a disability, would termination be justified?
- If we have the science to detect abnormalities, surely we also have the science to make the lives of the disabled and their carers more tolerable? Do you agree that today it is easier to abort than to care?
- What types of disability should society try to remove?
- If every child should be a wanted child, should parents be entitled to demand the termination of an embryo if they felt they would be unable to give it the necessary love and care?

Where now? F. Schaeffer and C. Koop, *Whatever Happened to the Human Race?*, Marshall Morgan and Scott, 1980

Cultural perspective

- The main moral issue is to decide when a foetus becomes an individual and at which point the removal and death of the foetus becomes unacceptable.
- Most regard the ability to live independently as the criterion. However, life support systems for babies are increasingly effective. What will happen when an egg can be raised into an independent being outside the womb?
- All doctors take the Hippocratic oath, by which they promise to do all they can to preserve life. If they help abort disabled embryos, surely they are breaking their oath?
- Many religions teach that life is God-given and, as such, is sacred. Any action taken to destroy life is therefore contrary to their beliefs. Some religions believe that life starts at the point of conception.
- Is it more acceptable to use scientific knowledge to detect and avoid a possible problem before conception than to terminate a life, however blighted that life may be?
- Doctors who recommend termination because of perceived disabilities are playing at being God.
- What is the difference between killing a disabled foetus and killing a person who becomes disabled?
- Some philosophers believe that decisions should be taken in the best interests of society simply for individuals. Others believe that society has an obligation to care for everyone, irrespective of disability or disadvantage.
- Is it permissible to end the life of an embryo only because of physical disability or should the same opportunities exist where there is mental disability?

Scientific perspective

- The technology for detecting problems is good and getting better. In countries with well-supported health services, care systems for pregnant women make use of all available tests.
- Genetic counselling allows couples to decide, based on known risks, whether to have their baby.
- The risks of termination to the mother are not negligible and they increase with the age of the foetus. This practical problem has to be considered alongside the moral issues of terminating a pregnancy.
- It is unlikely that predicting disability with absolute certainty will ever be possible. It is also difficult to predict the level of disability.
- The extent of disability varies. Anencephaly (having very little or no brain tissue) is incurable; what might be done about polydactyly (extra fingers or toes) or the various degrees of cleft palate?
- As can be seen with cystic fibrosis, the treatment of some inherited diseases is improving all the time. Is it right to deprive a disabled foetus of the chance of subsequent acceptable health? (Gene therapy may mean that we never have to consider this question again.)
- Making sure that particular genes are not passed on to offspring is a form of artificial selection and we do not know where such selection might lead.

Social perspective

- Antenatal detection and elimination of abnormalities creates divisions of opinion in society, which are not easily resolved.
- If a pregnancy is either terminated or continued, expensive litigation, threatening or illegal behaviour and a lot of unhappiness may result.
- Does a foetus have human rights? If so, who decides whether such rights are being infringed?
- Is termination done for the sake of the embryo, the parents or society as a whole?
- How do we balance the problems of being disabled against the right to life, even if its quality is uncertain?
- If we accept the termination of disabled foetuses, what does it say about the value that society places on human life and our attitude to disability?
- Caring for the severely disabled is too expensive and should not be necessary.
- The social costs of disability are very high, especially in terms of strain and distress for families.
- Should termination on the grounds of serious disability be legally controlled like any other form of abortion?
- Just because we can detect abnormalities, doesn't mean we have to do it.
- Some very great people have suffered disability from birth. If they had never lived, society would have been much poorer.

Thinking and analytical skills

1 Identify the stages in the argument presented in the extract.
2 To what extent does the argument and evidence justify the conclusion?
3 What arguments might be presented by someone who took an opposing view?

4.10 Do animals have rights?

Links: 1.2 (i); 1.2 (ii); 3.1 (i); 3.4 (vii)

'Animals, as sentient beings, have equivalent rights to human beings. There is, therefore, no possible justification for experimenting on any animal, even if it benefits humankind.' Critically evaluate this statement from scientific, moral, religious and social perspectives.

Introduction

Animals and man have had a very long association:

- they have been beasts of burden and were used as transport,
- they are hunting assistants,
- they provide protection and companionship,
- they provide food and clothing,
- more recently, we've used them for medical research.

Human beings have used selective breeding and culling for hundreds (and probably thousands) of years to produce varieties of animals that are most suitable to these functions and to satisfy the whims of owners. Domestic animals are no longer likely to do well in the wild.

The use of animals has been subject to UK legislation for a long time, with the object of preventing cruel treatment of domestic and farm animals and to regulate the use of animals for research. The argument for this is that treating animals badly is a reflection of poor general moral standards, is not necessary and indicates little respect for all living things, including human beings. These are supported by scientific and self-interest arguments as well: unhappy or badly treated animals are unlikely to have the qualities for which they have been bred or kept in the first place.

The words we have used here – unhappy, respect, cruelty – show how we attribute feelings and emotions to animals that are akin to ours. This is known as anthropomorphism. While it is quite possible, indeed likely, that vertebrate animals feel pain in just the same way as we do, it is not at all clear that other emotions (particularly those that we infer from facial expressions and body posture) are like ours at all. For example, the wild chimpanzee's grin is an indication of fear and annoyance and in some varieties of dog, selective breeding is responsible for facial characteristics that resemble human babies: short muzzle, flat open face and large forward-looking eyes.

All this means that we cannot directly judge an animal's state of mind simply because it adopts an apparently human posture. And it also means that consciousness in a vertebrate animal, used with reference to humans, cannot be assumed from its expression or behaviour.

Rights and equal treatment for all humanity have a long history, but it is not always generally accepted that we are all equal. Many classical and some modern civilisations have regarded some human groups as expendable beasts of burden. The idea that we all have rights is comparatively new. It is still a contentious subject – and there is a general view that if society grants rights to its members, then we as individuals have responsibilities and duties towards each other.

The concept of animal rights is newer still, although some religions have always afforded special consideration to some or all animals. Strands of the argument used to support the idea of animal rights are:

- Man, as a sentient being, has rights.
- Sentient beings feel pain and unhappiness.
- Animals are sentient beings.
- Animals have rights.

These rights are presumed to be those of a peaceful and happy existence.

Any justification of animal rights must accept the world as it is and also that living organisms have evolved in complex environments where some live by harming others.

Issues to be discussed

- Who grants rights to humans or animals?
- Do wild animals have rights?
- Do animals have rights that are morally equivalent to human rights?
- What does sentience have to do with arguments about animal rights?
- Who should decide whether animal testing should be allowed? Should it be the British government, the European parliament or the United Nations?
- What realistic alternatives are there to animal testing?
- Should plants have rights?

Where now?

www.ampef.org/violent.htm
www.animalaid.org.uk/
caat.jhsph.edu/

Cultural perspective

- Cultural values differ between societies. Some may accept and others reject animal testing.
- Animals cannot express their own views, so any rights they have must be defined and conceded by human beings. Who determines what these rights should be?
- Many constitutions and declarations of rights outlaw the infliction of 'unnatural' cruelty. Surely animal research is unnatural?
- Although animals feel pain, they may not experience it in the same way a human being does.
- Animal research benefits humanity. Such good must outweigh the wrong of causing animals to suffer.
- Should animal rights supersede human needs?
- Utilitarians believe that right is determined by the greatest happiness of the greatest number. Should animals be included in this?
- Many religions teach that animals are part of a divine creation. Some claim that they are created equal with humanity and, therefore, should have similar rights. Others say they exist for the good of mankind.
- Eugenics and associated research carried out in Nazi Germany was condemned. How can similar research on defenceless animals be justified?
- Research conducted for genuine medical reasons should be distinguished from that carried out for its own sake or for social and cosmetic purposes.

Scientific perspective

- Animals are used, under controlling legislation, to test vaccines, produce vaccines, test drugs and to provide scientific evidence for the biochemistry and physiology of living organisms. Criteria for such research are laid out so those scientists who use animals in this way have clear guidelines on what they may and may not do.
- Animals are also used for teaching purposes (in dissection, for example) so that trainee scientists and doctors are able to develop skills that would be impossible to gain in any other way.
- The great majority of licensed experiments on animals are minor and usually do not cause pain, suffering or death for the animals concerned.
- Is the use of films of dissection different morally from actually performing the dissection?
- Although most scientists would prefer not to kill animals in order to carry out their work, the majority regard work that will save human life (and for veterinary scientists, animal life) as being more important than the lives of individual animals.
- Some scientists are actively developing alternatives (such as cultured human or animal tissues) to using whole animals.
- The use of animals in research is just the same as rearing and killing animals for food, and most people are omnivorous.

Social perspective

- Human rights legislation, only recently accepted in British law, says nothing about animal rights.
- If animals have rights, should plants and other inanimate objects have rights as well?
- Animal rights groups hold their views sincerely, but have been associated with terrorism and violence against humans. How can this be reconciled?
- Testing will take place whatever the law says. It is better to be legal and controlled, rather than illegal and not properly supervised.
- Attitudes to animal research are changing rapidly.
- If animals and animal rights protesters have rights, so do the scientists who carry out research on animals. They should be safe to carry out legally permissible actions.
- Many lives have been saved and the birth of children with genetic defects avoided as a result of animal testing.
- Animal experimentation is essential because alternatives are slow, unreliable and expensive.
- It is unthinkable for society to allow experimentation or testing of drugs on children, the elderly or disabled people, so how can we justify this treatment of animals?
- Is it the responsibility of the law to enforce the law, irrespective of whether it is good or bad?
- We can tell a lot about the values of a society by its attitude to other, less powerful groups.
- Any action that is within the law and can reduce human suffering must be acceptable.

Thinking and analytical skills

1. Evaluate the opposing arguments for animal rights.
2. What similarities and differences might exist between the arguments of a scientist, a theologian and a philosopher on the issue of animal rights?
3. List examples of the forms of knowledge used in these arguments.

4.11 Does the pursuit of science lessen the need for religion?

Links: 1.1 (i); 1.2 (i); 1.3 (i); 1.3 (v); 3.1 (i); 3.1 (ii); 4.12

'Science and religion can coexist comfortably as long as one does not pronounce on the basic principles of the other.' Evaluate this assertion with reference to the development of cosmology, evolution and the social sciences.

Introduction

In earlier times science and religion were closely interlinked. Very often the leaders of organised religion defined the boundaries of acceptable scientific knowledge and procedures. Scientists whose ideas did not conform to accepted beliefs could be punished, forced to change their views or prevented from working.

Three major developments in western Europe changed this. The Protestant Reformation in the sixteenth century destroyed the absolute authority of a single universal church and encouraged a spirit of enquiry. In the eighteenth century, the Enlightenment encouraged rational thought, established generally accepted scientific procedures, and challenged traditional beliefs. The third development was the popularisation of the theory of evolution in the mid-nineteenth century. These changes meant that many people were now faced with the intellectual challenge of reconciling apparently contradictory views on the nature and origin of life.

By the late 1990s, it was often claimed that religion no longer had a part to play in society. This 'secularisation theory' resulted from the declining numbers of people who claimed religious conviction and took part in religious activities. There was an overwhelming belief that science had found more acceptable answers than religion to the traditional life-questions.

A prediction that science would increasingly turn people away from God is proven wrong today by a survey showing that scientists are as faithful now as they were eight decades ago.

The proportion of scientists who believe in a god has remained almost unchanged for the past 80 years, despite the enormous leaps of discovery made during this century. However, during the same period, there has been a fall in the percentage of scientists who believe in immortality or desire it.

Prof James Leuba, the American academic who made the original prediction, caused a scandal 80 years ago when he announced that 60 per cent of scientists did not believe in God. However, a rerun of his survey, published today in *Nature*, shows that the 40 per cent figure for believers is still true today.

The results of the survey have prompted a mixed reaction from the research community. 'I am quite surprised,' said Lord Winston, the test-tube baby pioneer. 'It suggests that scientists are not out of touch with ordinary people. I think that is very important for society.'

Prof Peter Atkins of Oxford University felt that the results of the survey probably applied more to American than British scientists, arguing that it was not possible to believe in gods and be a true scientist. Last year, he told the British Association for the Advancement of Science that belief in gods was a 'worn-out, but once useful, crutch in mankind's journey towards truth'.

But Prof Lewis Wolpert of University College London said the finding was understandable. 'It is perfectly reasonable to be both deeply religious, as Newton was, and a brilliant scientist, so long as you don't let the one influence the other.'

From *The Daily Telegraph*, 3 April 1997

Issues to be discussed

- Is it a waste of time arguing about the differences between religion and science?
- Darwin said to someone he thought was unconvinced by evolution: 'My hope is that at least it may stagger you in your certainties.' What did he mean?
- Do you agree that science needs religion in order to exercise moral control and restraint over its discoveries?
- In times of distress, do we need religious belief to provide us with the comfort that cannot be provided by science?
- How true is it to say that science can only tell us that we will die, but religion can give us reasons why?
- Discuss the view: 'For most people science has simply replaced the supernatural power of religion (God) with the equally supernatural power of knowledge.'

Where now?

D. D. Riegle, *Creation or Evolution?*, Zondervan, 1975

G. Vanderman, D. T. Gish, M. de Groot, J. Gallagher and J. Walton, *God's Wonderful World*, The Stanborough Press, 1992

mercur.usao.edu/www/faculty/shaferi/relsci.html

Cultural perspective

- There is no generally accepted definition of religion. A narrow definition emphasises the supernatural, but a broad definition simply stresses the existence of a belief system.
- Science is the systematic pursuit and formulation of knowledge.
- Religious texts like the Bible or the Koran do not claim to be scientific texts but revelations of sacred things that supernatural beings want mankind to know and do.
- Some believe sacred texts are written in language and terms that are accessible to all people, irrespective of that state of scientific knowledge.
- Fundamentalists claim that their scriptures are right and that scientific discoveries must either be reconciled with sacred teachings or be dismissed as wrong.
- Religion defines its territory as that which is unknowable and must simply be believed. A group's agreed beliefs will constitute a large part of its 'culture'.
- Religion gives a strong base for a group's culture because its members must agree with its beliefs.
- Religion has been the source of many great works of art that could only be realised as a result of scientific and technological discoveries.
- A scientific culture is less stable than a religious one because its basic ideas will change continually.
- 'The effort to understand the universe is one of the very few things that lifts human life a little above the level of farce and gives it some of the grace of tragedy' (Steven Weinberg).

Scientific perspective

- Science is based on existing explanations of the world or universe and tries to increase and improve these explanations.
- The starting point for any scientist is to believe that there is a rational, causal explanation of phenomena; to believe otherwise makes investigation impossible.
- It is a perfectly reasonable scientific exercise to try to discover why humans appear to need or believe in religion. It is also reasonable for religion to have a supernatural explanation for scientific behaviour. The two cannot be separated.
- The Big Bang theory shows that the world was not created in the way described in the Bible. The story in the Bible is therefore not meant to be taken literally.
- The theory of evolution shows clearly how new species can arise and the fossil record gives ample evidence of organisms that have become extinct. There is, therefore, no need to believe in a creator.
- Scientists do not accept that anything is 'unknowable'.
- Religion makes predictions that cannot be tested; scientific predictions will either fail to overturn an existing explanation or will result in the need for a new one.
- 'Science must begin with myths and with the criticism of myths.' (Karl Popper)
- 'Science without religion is lame, religion without science is blind.' (Albert Einstein)

Social perspective

- Religion is the only possible basis for a stable society. Science develops and changes too quickly to allow for stability but religion is essentially conservative.
- Religion creates social stability by promulgating, transmitting and maintaining shared beliefs and values.
- In the past, religious observance brought members of society together in shared acts of worship and the rituals of worship. In the modern age, sporting activities and pop concerts fulfil this function more effectively.
- Religious cultures are usually conservative, but science and technology tend to provoke change.
- Science binds people together through shared discovery and experience, but religion causes conflict, and division.
- Religious beliefs created the concept of racial differences, but science has proved that these differences do not exist.
- Science has created a meritocratic society but religion creates a sense of equality and the brotherhood of man.
- Religion gives authority for morality and law.
- 'So far as I can remember, there is not one word in the gospels in praise of intelligence.' (Bertrand Russell)
- The scientific concept of survival of the fittest has led to the development of modern economic theories of supply and demand and success or failure. Religion teaches that the love of money is the root of all evil and its pursuit causes destructive and divisive patterns of behaviour.

Thinking and analytical skills

1 Identify the different stages in the argument presented in the Introduction.
2 What types of knowledge are used and how reliable are they?

4.12 Does society still need religion?

Links: 1.1 (i); 1.2 (i); 1.2 (iv); 1.3 (i); 1.3 (ii); 1.3 (v); 3.1 (i); 3.1 (ii); 4.11

'In spite of the progress made by science most people still need a religious dimension to their lives.' With reference to science, culture and society, critically examine the extent to which this statement is justified.

Introduction

Is religion in terminal decline or is it emerging as a potent, if different, force in modern society?

It is often claimed that scientific discoveries have reduced the need for organised religion; many say it will disappear as its role is replaced by other institutions. Most British people claim not to have strong religious beliefs, yet many happily believe in a supernatural power or being.

Religion can generate intense feelings among believers and non-believers alike. Tension often exists between different religious groups. Throughout history religious minorities have been persecuted; such action was often organised by religious leaders and enforced by their followers. In spite of this, religion has survived, often becoming stronger under pressure.

Karl Marx said that religion would disappear when capitalism was destroyed. After the Bolshevik Revolution in 1917, acts of religious faith were forbidden in Soviet Russia and churches were closed. However, religious beliefs survived, emerging after the collapse of the USSR in 1991. Christianity is now growing more rapidly in Russia than in any other part of the developed world.

Since the Sixties, the number of people joining new religious movements has increased rapidly throughout the world. Since the Eighties, religious fundamentalism has been a major political influence in the Islamic world. In addition, alternative belief systems, like paganism, witchcraft and astrology, have gained increasing support.

The publication of the human genome puts in front of us in graphic detail just how complex – and yet how elegant – is the structure of our very being. We cannot help but feel both wonder and awe when we view the intricate biochemical matrix that makes human life possible. This is clearly an event in which science and religion should be at one in rejoicing, for now we know just how much wisdom God demonstrated in making us as we are. We also should rejoice over the many positive implications of this new knowledge. Scientists have already identified the genetic mutations that are at the root of a number of diseases, raising hope that we will soon find cures for them. In Judaism, physicians and those who do medical research are God's partners and agents in the ongoing act of healing. Moreover, in so doing, we will be relieving human suffering and that too, as Judaism sees it, is an unmitigated good, indeed, a divine demand.

The more we can do, the more we have to ask whether we should do what we can. As we learn not only to identify the human genome but to manipulate it, we will increasingly and inevitably face the question of whether we should make changes of a certain sort. Put theologically, when do we cease being God's partner and instead play God? The answer is not to avoid modern developments at all costs. We must learn, rather, to sharpen our skills of moral discernment so that we can identify good and bad uses of our new knowledge. We must then make sure that only the good uses are pursued.

As much as we stand in pride, awe, and wonder at this new knowledge, then, we must also recognise that it brings us a new, heightened level of moral responsibility to use that new knowledge well.

Statement by Rabbi Elliot N. Dorff, Ph.D., University of Judaism, Los Angeles, USA, 12 February 2001

Issues to be discussed

- Since religion and science deal with different aspects of life, should one be in conflict with the other?
- How can the survival of religion be explained when there is so much scientific evidence that contradicts its claims?
- Do you have to believe in a supernatural power in order to be religious?
- If religion still has an important contribution to make to society, how should religious leaders make the practice of religion more attractive to more people?
- Why do you think many scientists express religious beliefs?
- Discuss the view that scientists need to know, but in religion it is only necessary to believe.

Where now?

Stephen J. Gould, *Rocks of Ages*, Jonathan Cape, 2001
Richard Dawkins, *The Blind Watchmaker*, Buccaneer Books, 1999

Cultural perspective

- Between 1975 and 1995, membership of the Muslim, Sikh, Hindu and Jewish religions in the UK increased from 0.76 million to 2 million people.
- Religious values are still the basis of morality, even if they have been transformed to meet the needs of a secular society.
- The influence of religion can be seen in many cultural activities (especially art and music).
- Most people need something to believe in and religion offers a belief system that many find acceptable.
- Places of religious worship often fulfil a wider role in society as community centres.
- Religion is a major unifying factor for ethnic minorities and helps to define and preserve their separate identities.
- Religion is a dynamic force that adapts and changes to meet new circumstances.
- In 1998, 72 per cent of people questioned in the UK said they believed in some sort of god or supernatural being; 21 per cent of the sample 'knew', without doubt, that God existed, while 37 per cent expressed belief occasionally or only when in difficulty.
- Religion can be one of the major causes of war and violence (think of the Middle East, Northern Ireland, Afghanistan).
- Intolerance (of others' faults, practices and lifestyles) has frequently been associated with some religious groups.
- Religion can still offer answers to some questions that are beyond science – like what happens after death.
- New Age movements reject the authoritarianism of science.
- Science and religion are about different types of knowledge and belief.

Scientific perspective

- Science has offered alternative explanations to religion of many phenomena (such as creation).
- Science is about possibilities but religion is about absolutes.
- Scientists cannot admit that anything in the universe is unknowable or beyond comprehension. But there is a neat solution to this – anything that is unknowable is, therefore, religion and not science.
- Science may be seen to have replaced religion because it provides better explanations to phenomena that seemed inexplicable.
- Religious belief can help people to come to terms with the effects of disaster or with tragedy.
- Scientific discoveries in cosmology, for example, may bring scientific and religious explanations closer together.
- Medical science recognises that religious faith can help those with medical and psychological problems.
- Scientific discoveries that can be used for both good or harm make it more important (rather than less important) that society has a firmly based moral code. Generally a moral code stems from a set of religious beliefs.

Social perspective

- The industrialisation of society (one of the results of scientific and technological developments) has taken over some of the traditional functions of religion, for example, education, health care, care for the elderly, social welfare, etc.
- In an increasingly anonymous society, religion offers stability to people who might otherwise be aimless.
- For some groups in society, especially the elderly, religion can offer hope, comfort and reassurance, whereas science can create fear, confusion and uncertainty because of the rate of change and the development of new technologies it is responsible for.
- Religious organisations can provide care for the lonely and elderly that is no longer provided by families as a result of industrialisation.
- People need ceremony, ritual and a sense of belonging. Religion can provide this better than any other institution, especially at times like birth, marriage and death.
- Legal changes have removed some of the functions of religion. At one time religion, by confirming marriage, preserved and justified inheritance laws. Modern DNA techniques mean that it is scientists and not religious leaders who decide on questions of descent.
- Religion is more geared towards old people because it gives them comfort when they are approaching death or losing friends, but it is largely irrelevant to young people who find the answers they are looking for in science.
- Religious beliefs may seem to oppose progress in some contexts (for example, in relation to birth control).

Thinking and analytical skills

1 How effectively does Rabbi Dorff justify his conclusion?
2 Find examples of subjective and objective reasoning in the passage.
3 What different types of knowledge might be used to answer the arguments in the passage?

4.13 Is there anybody out there?

Links: 1.1 (i); 1.3 (i); 1.3 (v); 2.1 (i)

How do we justify using valuable resources trying to discover if there is sentient life in other parts of the universe? If such life were to be found, what would the implications be for science, religion and society?

Are we alone in the universe? When I was a student in the Sixties I was convinced that the answer was 'no'. This put me at odds with the prevailing scientific view. The orthodox position at that time was summed up by the French biologist Jacques Monod when he wrote of the 'unfeeling immensity of the universe' and declared that we had emerged from it alone and by pure chance. It was an opinion echoed by many other leading scientists. American palaeontologist George Gaylord Simpson, one of the giants of modern biology, described attempts to search for life elsewhere in the universe – especially intelligent life – as 'a gamble of the most adverse odds in history'.

Thirty years on, there has been a remarkable U-turn. Take Christian de Duve who, like Monod, is a Nobel prize-winning biologist. In his book *Vital Dust*, published in 1995, de Duve suggests that life is 'a cosmic imperative' bound to arise wherever conditions allow. His stance is shared by many at NASA, where their astrobiology programme is dedicated to seeking out alien life forms. Meanwhile, a team of enthusiastic astronomers sponsored by the SETI Institute in California is sweeping the sky with radio telescopes in the hope of stumbling across a message from ET. Journalists, Hollywood producers and schoolchildren likewise assume that the universe is teeming with life.

This shift in opinion has little to do with advances in understanding. True, we now have concrete evidence of planets in other star systems, but most astronomers believed all along that they were there. Biochemists have inched forward in their attempts to synthesise the building blocks of life, but creating life in a test tube remains a distant dream. We may soon discover evidence for past life on Mars but, if so, it will almost certainly have arrived there from earth, in rocks blasted off our planet by large asteroid impacts.

Yet the question of whether life is widespread in the universe is important. Researchers are making plans to search for earth-like planets around other stars, chiefly because they hope to find alien life there. The assumption that life should arise inevitably, given earth-like conditions, is known as biological determinism. But it is hard to find any support for it in the known laws of physics, chemistry or biology. If we relied solely on these laws to explain the workings of the universe, it would be reasonable to conclude, like Monod, that life can only have arisen by sheer good luck – and that it is therefore exceedingly unlikely to be found elsewhere.

From *New Scientist*, 18 September 1999

Issues to be discussed

- Do you agree that the only justification for research is to find new knowledge or should it always have a practical purpose and application?
- It is sometimes claimed that if alien life is discovered, the only way to communicate will be through mathematics. Why is this?
- If there is life on other planets, is it possible to continue believing in religion?
- What rules should be made to govern relations with new life forms discovered on other planets? Who should make the rules and how can they be enforced?
- Alien life forms could be a serious threat to the survival of humanity on earth. Would it not be better to stop all such research rather than face the possible dangers?

Where now?

www.themestream.com/articles
www.popsci.com/news
www.discovery.com/guides/space/aliens.html
www.enn.com/news

Cultural perspective

- It is often assumed that alien life forms would be inferior to human beings. It might be destructive to our culture if a superior form of alien life were discovered.
- If alien life has developed on other planets, will it be possible to retain belief in one god or even in the idea of supernatural powers?
- If alien life were discovered, is there any guarantee that communication between them and us would be possible?
- Morality in western Europe and America is based largely on the Judaeo-Christian ethic. How would humanity adjust to a system of morality that might have a totally different base?
- Do we want to discover alien life simply for the sake of meeting them or as a means of extending human power?
- How would alien life influence our culture? Would it contribute new art forms and aesthetic values or would it make no impact at all?
- If there is alien life on other planets, is it likely that they are looking for us in the same way that we are looking for them? How are we likely to respond if contact is ever made?
- Are we likely to be prejudiced against alien life forms because of the images created in our minds by media representations of 'little green men from Mars'?

Scientific perspective

- If we find evidence of life on the near planets, our technology is good enough to find out if this life has anything in common with terrestrial life. If it does, then it may be difficult to decide whether life arose on earth and spread to other planets nearby or whether earth was seeded with living organisms from space.
- The statistical chances of sentient life elsewhere are very good, simply because it has been estimated that there are billions of star systems containing planets similar to ours.
- Would it be sensible to send out signals to other star systems? (Remember, the signals could only travel at the speed of light and the nearest star systems are some four light years away.)
- If searches for life in other star systems detect signals from them, they will be difficult to interpret.
- Attempting to discover anything about other life forms in the universe is important because of what it might teach us about ourselves.
- The recent discovery of several planetary systems around nearby stars is exciting, but the planets that have been discovered are not similar in size and density to earth.
- One of the most important qualities that humanity possesses is a spirit of enquiry. Any research activity that extends the boundaries of our knowledge must be a good thing.

Social perspective

- The process of searching may lead to the development of knowledge and skills which will be of direct benefit to people on earth.
- Searching for extraterrestrial life could be a reason for international co-operation. This could only benefit society in general.
- Humanity's history of contact between different cultures (the discovery of America and Australia, for example) is not good. It resulted in destruction, exploitation and conflict.
- There is so much poverty and suffering on earth – the money could be better spent here.
- Spending on research, in whatever area, leads to investment, employment opportunities and profit.
- Any government that supported a successful search for alien life could gain great international prestige.
- If alien life does exist, it may attack earth or introduce diseases against which we have no defences.
- To be effectively controlled, research should be a co-operative effort undertaken by the United Nations or the European Community and not left to a single wealthy country, like the United States, which might do it for the wrong reasons.
- If alien life is discovered, it would have major implications for international law.
- If alien life is discovered, it is likely to be so distant from earth that it will be impossible to develop any meaningful links.

Thinking and analytical skills

1 Outline the different stages in the argument presented in the extract to support the conclusion.
2 What types of knowledge does the author make use of?
3 What response might a theologian or a politician make to the ideas in the extract?

4.14 Are art and science totally different activities?

Links: 1.1 (i); 1.4 (all); 1.5 (i); 1.5 (iii); 3.5 (ii)

'Art is meant to disturb; science reassures,' said Georges Braque, a highly innovative early twentieth century Cubist painter. How true is this statement? Illustrate your answer with reference to the concept of culture from artistic, scientific and social perspectives.

Introduction

In this context, art may refer either exclusively to the visual arts (often called painting) or, in broader terms, can embrace the entire range of plastic, creative and performing arts (including literature, theatre, dance, music, film, photography, architecture). Sometimes art can describe a particular type of skill. Braque, himself a noted painter, used the term in the first sense.

Similarly, the term science can be applied to a specific approach to the acquisition and testing of knowledge (empirical research). It can also relate to those separate and distinct disciplines variously described as 'the sciences': biology, chemistry, physics, astronomy and perhaps geology. It might even be applied to any defined body of knowledge which is assumed to be accepted and unassailable.

Whichever definitions are used, it is necessary to distinguish between types and objectives. For example, there is Art and there is art. The former implies quality and uniqueness, setting it apart from other work, whereas the second is a general all-embracing term.

Braque was a painter who used a form derided by contemporary critics because it deliberately flouted conventional standards and techniques. Critics were often those who claimed to be able to identify 'good art' because it conformed to well-established rules. In the comment above, Braque was defending Cubism and other forms of innovative art against those who said 'it isn't art because it doesn't obey the rules'. It is in this context that he used the term science. He was not claiming that it is the role of science to reassure. Rather, he was criticising the reduction of art appreciation to a set of approved rules – almost a form of painting by numbers – which can be learnt, known and applied. The science he attacked was the science of the cognoscenti not of the innovator.

Art, we have long known, originates in our irrational half – but then, for many of us, art is a dangerously anarchic activity and artists borderline mental patients whose art, as well as their traditionally irregular behaviour, threatens our respectability. But the human unconscious is also the driving-force behind our rational science. Science has long been depicted as a process of wholly conscious thought, which fuses our practical wishes, our reasonable cogitation and the innate curiosity which is one of our more respectable irrational drives, invited into the parlour because it is useful. True enough – in its final stages it is and does. But people become scientists and study particular topics with engagement for reasons as deeply rooted in their childhoods and their unconscious as any work of art, and the imaginative process which leads to original thinking about scientific matters is as Dionysian as any other 'creative' inspiration. The scientist has to be reality-centred thereafter, in order to work out his inspirational hunch and see if it really squares with the external world, but his ability or compulsion to settle particular questions, as well as his ability or inability to see particular facts, depend wholly at root on the same irrational mechanisms as other human creativity, insights and blind spots.

From Alex Comfort, *Nature and Human Nature*, Penguin, 1966

Issues to be discussed

- How far can science be called an 'unconscious activity'?
- Does the fact that the quotation is by a successful artist make it more, or less, verifiable?
- How can art improve the quality of life of ordinary people?
- Do you agree that art is for the rich and privileged but paintings are for ordinary people?
- If everything made by humanity is a work of art, does it follow that we should consider scientific discoveries to be works of art as well?
- Is it true that we admire science because we can't understand it, but we despise art because we think we understand it too well?

Where now?

www.wellcome.ac.uk/en/1/sci.html
www.eng.cam.ac.uk/
www.creative-science.org.uk/main.html

Cultural perspective

- Art is usually the work of single individuals who must produce new art forms to be successful. To do this, the artist is forced to use more unconventional materials and ideas which may shock people.
- Some artists are so unconventional that they are regarded as insane, hence disturbing.
- Some artists set out to shock deliberately, but this does not guarantee art that is successful.
- Art is about exploring feelings and ideas to achieve understanding, but science is about the pursuit of knowledge and answers.
- The attitude of many people to works of art is 'I know what I like and I like what I know'.
- Some artists (Damien Hirst, for example) may shock people by the use of particular materials.
- Art is imaginative and many consider it to have no boundaries or no-go areas; therefore all ideas and expressions in art are valid.
- Innovative art is designed to challenge convention and can be deliberately provocative, but when it becomes established and respectable, it develops its own comfortable language and vocabulary.
- Art seeks to express universally acknowledged truths, but science seeks to discover new truths.
- Art reflects what the artist sees but science describes facts that all can discover.

Scientific perspective

- Science is the outcome of enquiring minds; it is not its function to reassure.
- Science and technology use concepts and theories to provide solutions to problems and to reassure people that all problems can be solved.
- Science can be very disturbing. It may force people to re-examine their fundamental beliefs about the world and the way in which it works.
- Scientists find satisfaction when they have provided explanations for complex problems.
- Scientific theories are more satisfying when they are simple and explain many things.
- People are happier when they know that there are scientific explanations for phenomena.
- Both science and art can be experimental, but art is expressive while science is deductive or inductive.
- Science is an appeal to reason, but art is an appeal to emotion.
- Scientists experiment to test and confirm hypotheses and artists experiment to discover new boundaries and meanings in life.
- Science has undermined the stability of society by damaging religious truths and moral certainties, but throughout history art has reinforced social stability.
- Some of the world's greatest artists have also been scientists: Leonardo and Michelangelo studied anatomy and technology; the great Russian composer Borodin was a professor of chemistry.

Social perspective

- Art is something that everyone can understand, so when unconventional artistic ideas are expressed, they may affect many people.
- Works of art must be and can be interpreted in various ways according to time and circumstance, but science sets unchallengeable rules on the basis of experiments that can be replicated.
- Much science requires training to understand; it is for this reason that people have great respect for, and are reassured by, scientific experts.
- Art is an aspect of culture that binds society together. Schools and types of art exemplify different societies.
- Art explores and expresses society's values; science is about improving society's facilities.
- Many great artists experience poverty and rejection in life, yet after death their works increase in value and they become famous. A scientist can achieve fame and fortune in life thanks to the commercial exploitation of chance discoveries.
- Businessmen and governments sponsor art for prestige, but fund science for financial reward.
- Some art forms are more comfortable than others. Most people can like a work of art even if they can't appreciate it as an expert might, but science deliberately creates mystery and becomes inaccessible to ordinary people.
- People see the eccentric scientist as a figure of fun, but the bohemian artist as a drain on society.
- Art and science can both improve our quality of life.

Thinking and analytical skills

1 Identify examples of subjective and objective knowledge in the passage.
2 To what extent does the author successfully justify his conclusion?

4.15 Why should society fund scientific research?

Links: 1.1 (v); 1.2 (i); 2.4 (iii); 3.2 (ii); 3.3 (viii)

Vast sums of money from business and the taxpayer are devoted to research in science and technology. Much of it is obviously beneficial, but some of it could be questioned. Justify this use of public resources and critically evaluate the different ways in which these funds are allocated to particular areas, referring to the different perspectives in your answer.

Introduction

We might justify public funding of research by utilitarian arguments ('because science can provide us with better things, a better way of life and better ways of defending ourselves'). However, 'research' includes a multitude of activities, not all of which are beneficial to everyone. We may also consider that only a proportion of our resources should be used in this way.

Funds for research come from two main sources:

- Government allocates money to research institutions such as universities and institutes and to approved business contractors. Allocations are made by the Treasury and managed by national research councils.
- Private funds which can come from businesses (and are probably spent on research that enhances the business) or from charities whose funds are donated.

Bids for all research these days usually have to be able to show direct, immediate and publicly beneficial outcomes.

How is any particular area of research justified? Consider these points:

- There could be a financial return to society greater than the investment made.
- Problems identified by society may be solved.
- Nations, companies or individuals may perceive that successful research proves or maintains their political, economic or moral superiority over others.
- It may simply be that it is interesting to explore a particular area and therefore satisfy a few individuals' interests.

Identify examples where these justifications apply.

The long-standing 'academic' view of research is that value judgements should not be applied to it. The fact that a piece of research appears to be devoted only to expanding the frontiers of human knowledge and to developing better explanations of the world we live in, is sufficient justification to allow it to continue and perhaps even to fund it. One of the arguments supporting this point of view is that it is impossible to predict the usefulness of any additions to knowledge or the outcomes of any explanations – and there are many examples of apparently esoteric research, particularly in mathematics, which have been crucial to new and important technological improvements.

Issues to be discussed

- Should scientists be concerned with knowledge for its own sake?
- How far should decisions on the use of scientific discoveries be decided by political processes?
- To what extent should business and industry decide on the funding of scientific and technological research?
- Are discoveries only good if society benefits from them?
- Where should the funding for research come from, if not from private business and the taxpayer?
- Should the state take a percentage of the profits accruing to discoveries funded by taxpayers' money?
- What legal and moral restrictions should be placed on scientific research?

Where now?

www.research-councils.ac.uk/
www.research.microsoft.com
www.wellcome.ac.uk/
public.web.cern.ch/Public/Welcome.html
public.web.cern.ch/Public/bs_l.html
www.britcoun.org/science
www.icnet.uk/index.html

Cultural perspective

- Business interest in funding research may be more motivated by profit than by concerns for morality.
- There has been genuine concern that British business is more concerned in investing in consumer certainties than in innovative design, especially in technology. It is often left to foreign entrepreneurs to exploit British discoveries.
- It is not possible to say whether research will be of obvious benefit to society until discoveries are made. Many discoveries find a use that was not envisaged at the time of the original research.
- What criteria are to be used to decide and who is to determine whether a discovery is good, justified or in the public interest?
- If government is involved in research sponsorship, it can ensure that society's moral values are upheld.
- If investment in scientific and technical research is left to private industry, public funds thus released could be used to support and subsidise the arts.
- Is the philosophy of 'only do it if there is obvious social benefit' not in itself immoral?
- Research is expensive. The level to which a nation is prepared to support and justify such long-term contributions is a measure of a society's values.
- A company can gain a better reputation by supporting research.
- Government is likely to adopt a more conservative approach than private enterprise and so is likely to inhibit innovation.
- Governments are answerable to taxpayers for the way in which state resources are used.

Scientific perspective

- Much research has outstripped the ability of individuals or small groups to afford it, for example, nuclear physics, astronomical and cosmological research and cancer research.
- Other types of research require minimal resources, such as ecological or taxonomic research. Comparatively low spending is incurred on research such as the naming, classification, evolution and ecology of living organisms.
- Most research on these topics is carried out in universities, assisted by grants acquired from academic, charitable or government sources. It doesn't sound very exciting, but the correct identification of living organisms is absolutely basic to all biological studies, including medicine. If incorrectly identified, other research on an organism may be worthless.
- Ecological studies are essential in studying changes to the global environment. However, this research is difficult to fund and it is becoming harder, because gene sequencing and biomedical research is grabbing so much attention. Much taxonomic research is either a part-time professional, or even an amateur, occupation. Britain has a particularly strong tradition in this work and has a long history of amateur natural historians who have made very significant, but unsung, contributions to science.

Social perspective

- Much of the incentive for business subsidies for research is to increase profits and increase market-share and stay ahead of competitors.
- Money devoted to research is not simply subsidy but is an important investment for the future.
- It often pays companies to employ leading scientists to undertake what may prove to be unprofitable research in order to prevent their rivals from employing them.
- Government funding of research can attract commercial sponsorship, which might otherwise not be forthcoming.
- Government support for research may encourage leading inventors and scientists to remain in this country rather than become part of the brain drain.
- Support for research will ensure that future generations of students will benefit from high-quality teaching.
- Companies are accountable for expenditure and cannot afford to waste investment, but governments are not accountable and will be less influenced by commercial motives in their scientific and technological decisions.
- Support for non-commercial sponsorship of research can be used to reduce tax liabilities.
- Private companies may exploit discoveries made from research that resulted from taxpayers' money and benefit from large profits. Government, in turn, will benefit through tax revenue.
- Government investment, especially in expensive new areas, ensures that beneficial research occurs.
- Is it better to use government funds to support research that may lead to investment and employment opportunities in depressed areas, rather than simply to finance the benefit system?

Thinking and analytical skills

1 What types of knowledge would be needed to answer the question posed at the beginning of this section?
2 What similarities and differences might exist between the arguments of a scientist, a charitable fund-raiser and a politician?

4.16 Does more technology lead to happier working lives?

Links: 1.1 (i); 1.6 (i); 1.6 (iv); 2.6 (ii); 2.6 (iii); 3.3 (iii); 3.3 (vii); 3.3 (viii)

'Advances in science and technology lead to more effective working, increased leisure and greater happiness for workers in a developed society.' To what extent is this true of the UK?

Technology has always had a mixed press. Today, computers are reviled for putting people out of work and then tomorrow – without apparent pause – for keeping us all at work for all hours. The doomsayers say that our dependence on computers has stripped us of our humanity. Kurt Vonnegut, an American novelist, says 'computers are cheating people out of their sociability and also out of relations with other people – out of something as exciting as food or sex'. Nowhere is our schizophrenic approach to technology – and information and communication technologies in particular – more pronounced than in relation to work. On the one hand, ICT offers us the opportunity to ditch mundane work, to work more flexibly both in terms of time and space, to make work better. On the other hand, laptops and mobile phones can be seen as electronic tags, keeping us enslaved to the capitalist machine.

The truth is, of course, somewhere in between. The impact of technology on the way we work depends on us, on our individual attitudes and on corporate structures. Technology has the potential to be liberating in the workplace as it opens up companies to more diverse workers and more diverse ideas. There is a theoretical danger that overreliance on screens and keypads means we will lose the human touch – Vonnegut says only Luddite children will make interesting adults – but it seems a remote one.

Technology has loosened the ties between work and place. Mobiles, laptops, email, voicemail, personal organisers – the well-equipped manager is available for work night and day, wherever in the world he or she may be. This model of work obviously has benefits for all concerned but it also has its drawbacks. While reports of the death of the traditional office are exaggerated, it is certainly true that many workers have cut the apron strings to the corporate HQ. At least two million British employees already work from their home, car or wherever they happen to be. British Telecom predicts that within 25 years, 1 in 4 of us will be working out of the office.

The benefits of mobile working seem clear: staff spend less time commuting to work, which is also good for the environment, there is less need for expensive office space and productivity is boosted. Some firms have reported cuts in office space of between 25 and 65 per cent. Scottish Widows and Xerox claim productivity improvements of up to 60 per cent since allowing staff to work 'remotely'. But the costs – loneliness, lack of communication, an erosion of the corporate culture and higher job turnover – are harder to measure. It is also impossible to know what is lost from staff not being able to chat informally over the water cooler. People want flexibility, but they also want contact time.

From *Inside Learning Technologies*, January 2001

Issues to be discussed

- Do you agree that new technology has led to more effective working or has it simply increased the amount of work that has to be done?
- It is said that working from home can lead to isolation. How important is it for people to be able to meet and talk to colleagues?
- Has new technology destroyed creativity?
- Should there be legislation to control the working conditions of people who work from home rather than in an office?
- Is it practical to talk about domestic robots that will remove the drudgery from domestic work? If they become reality, will human happiness be increased?
- Does technology really contribute to improved leisure time or does it simply encourage a 'killing time' mentality?
- Has our happiness been increased by easy worldwide communication that makes us aware of major disasters as they occur?
- Has technology increased the happiness of the unemployed?

Where now? Lazlo Solymar, *Getting the Message*, Oxford University Press, 1999

Cultural perspective

- Computer games and other technological developments take people away from other more creative activities.
- Television is a major leisure activity. Although often instructive, it is passive entertainment.
- 180 million CDs (first introduced in 1983) are sold each year in the United Kingdom.
- Although British inventors have demonstrated considerable creativity in scientific and technological discovery, British entrepreneurs have commercially exploited relatively few of their inventions.
- Technology has led to cultural globalisation. Many cultures are threatened with westernisation.
- New art forms use new technology.
- Utilitarian philosophers would welcome the contributions of science and technology if they genuinely increased the sum total of human happiness. However, they would condemn them if they increased the happiness of some at the expense of others.
- Social Contract theorists would argue that it is the duty of the state and employers to do all they can to encourage the use of new technology in order to improve the quality of life of the population.
- The changes in technology resulted in unemployment for many whose skills do not match new demands.
- New technology has helped spread new religious movements but may have helped to cut church attendance.

Scientific perspective

- Robotics is a subject that is advancing rapidly and, in the future, will play an even greater part in the manufacture of goods and in making workers' lives easier.
- Intelligent home appliances that reduce the time we spend cleaning, cooking and maintaining a household will increase our leisure time.
- Increasing use of mobile phones and computers may damage health, especially that of young people.
- Many older people, however, regard mobile phones as intrusive, noisy and time-wasting.
- Repeated use of keyboards has led to a new illness, known as repetitive stress syndrome, which costs many working days through absence due to ill-health.
- There are many scientific discoveries that have improved working and living conditions. Teflon, first developed for the space race, has made a major contribution to easing domestic work.
- 'White goods' are now affordable, reliable and accessible and have improved most families' quality of life.
- The use of mobile phones has transformed communication, especially among young people.
- There are no signs that science or technology will ever stop rapid progress. This might be due to the link between technology and economic success.
- New technology is creating new applications for phones, televisions and computers at an ever-increasing rate.

Social perspective

- Scientific discoveries mean large numbers of the working population have had to learn new skills.
- The employment market has been transformed. Very few companies offer a 'job for life'.
- New inventions have reinforced the must-have mentality.
- Working from home has transformed relations between many workers and their families.
- Working from home could ease many of the problems caused by traffic jams and pollution.
- New technology has concentrated considerable wealth and power in few hands.
- Although electronic 24-hour banking is more convenient for customers, it has led to widespread unemployment among bank employees.
- The impact of new technology has emphasised social divisions between the rich and the poor.
- New technology has led to new types of crime such as computer hacking and the creation of computer viruses.
- New laws, like the Data Protection Act, are needed to safeguard individual rights.
- Scientific and technological discoveries have increased national and individual wealth, especially of investors.
- Technological developments have resulted in the decline of traditional low-skill manual employment and increased part-time female employment.
- Scientific discoveries have benefited wealthy industrialised countries, enabling them to exploit poorer, less developed countries.

Thinking and analytical skills

1 What types of knowledge are used in the passage?
2 To what extent are these views justified? How could they be refuted?

4.17 Are large multinational companies bad for us all?

Links: 1.1 (i) 1.2 (i); 1.2 (ii); 1.6 (ii); 1.6 (iii); 3.1 (ii); 3.3 (v)

'Multinational companies are able to utilise huge resources to solve big problems, but because they have to make profits, they do not always work in the best interests of humanity at large.' Critically evaluate this assertion from cultural, social and scientific perspectives.

The arguments over affordable life-saving medicines for the developing world intensified yesterday when it was revealed that the multinational pharmaceutical company Glaxo Wellcome has blocked imports of cheap copies of one of its Aids drugs into Ghana.

The revelation came as South Africa announced it had done a deal with a second company, Pfizer, over supplies of the drug Fluconazole to treat infections that often kill people whose immune systems are wrecked by the Aids virus HIV (such as meningitis).

Under pressure from campaigners, who began bringing a cheaper version of the patent-protected branded drug into South Africa which massively undercut the usual Pfizer price, the company has agreed to supply Fluconazole free.

But although aid organisations such as the charity Médecins Sans Frontières (MSF) hailed the deal as an example of what can be achieved if countries show a willingness to turn their back on the pharmaceutical giants and buy copies, Britain made it clear yesterday that it was not in favour of such tactics.

Trade minister Richard Caborn told activists from the London-based organisation Action for Southern Africa (Actsa) that such measures 'are not the answer here'.

Campaigners insist that developing countries must use every possible means to get hold of affordable drugs that can stop people dying. But Western governments say the companies have a right to protection for the drugs they sell at high prices in order, the companies argue, to recoup research and development costs.

The West says the right approach is for countries to negotiate discounts with the companies. But African nations say they cannot afford the drugs even at the discount prices offered in May this year by five multinationals. Only Senegal has so far taken up the invitation to negotiate a deal.

The giants take very seriously the threat of competition. Glaxo Wellcome has blocked the import into Ghana of a version of its Aids therapy Combivir made in India by Cipla.

It is argued by campaigners that impoverished countries faced with a health emergency have a right under international trade legislation to buy generic drugs. The African Regional Industrial Property Organisation was quoted yesterday as saying that if Glaxo went to court, it believed it would lose. But poor countries fear confrontation will upset relations with the West.

From *The Guardian*, 2 December 2000

Issues to be discussed

- Is there any difference between large multinational car manufacturers who improve their products through intense global competition with others and multinational drug companies who are accused here of making excessive profits and restricting the availability of their drugs?
- How can the political influence of large organisations be controlled?
- How can poor nations acquire affordable drugs?
- Are multinationals entitled to recover research costs by charging poor countries high prices for their products?

Where now?

www.foundation.novartis.com/multinational_companies.htm
hivinsite.ucsf.edu/social/spotlight/2098.4374full.html
www.expressindia.com/fe/daily/19971120/32455173.html

Cultural perspective

- Scientific research is not the sole domain of one country or culture.
- Different countries have different attitudes to aspects of medical research such as the ethical use of animals or the testing of drugs in controlled trials on patients.
- Wealthy, developed countries should control the actions of multinational companies more strictly.
- Multinational companies should be subject to ethical controls.
- Multinationals can practise cultural colonialism. By selling Western technology to developing countries, they reinforce dependence on the supplier and retailer, and restrict the development of home-grown talent.
- Multinationals are governed by profit and don't need to have any form of cultural loyalty.
- Multinational companies can respond very effectively to the needs of small countries since they have such large resources.
- By creating global uniformity of products, multinationals destroy creativity and innovation in poorer countries.
- Multinationals bring prosperity to developing countries through investment and so help remove the economic instability that so often leads to conflict and civil war.
- Some multinationals sponsor ethnic art and, by displaying it to worldwide audiences, have created interest and demand for it. This has helped increase prosperity.

Scientific perspective

- Medical research is very expensive and therefore it is sensible for resources to be organised and planned by one company.
- Medical research requires skills and knowledge from many disciplines and is therefore best carried out by teams of scientists. Such teams can only be supported by very large organisations.
- It is not sensible to have important medical research in the control of a business whose interests might not be served by the outcome of the research.
- Scientists employed by a powerful company with many interests in different countries and products may not be free to follow some lines of research.
- Scientific discoveries are usually too expensive to be of benefit to the people of developing countries, who are often the ones in greatest need.
- Multinationals should be compelled to subsidise the costs of their products to make them more readily available in the developing world.

Social perspective

- A company has to be allowed to make profits, otherwise it will go out of business.
- Large multinational organisations are in the best position to utilise global resources effectively and efficiently.
- Large multinational organisations are only concerned to maximise the returns to their shareholders and employees and will therefore not consider the effects of moving their activities from one country to another to find the cheapest place for their work.
- A multinational company is in a very good position to support developing countries because it provides employment and a boost to their economies.
- It is possible for a multinational company to make unscrupulous use of the different laws and legal systems in different countries.
- Because of their effect on the economy, large multinationals can exert some political influence in any country, but more so in poor countries.
- In a free market society, allowing large businesses to become bigger is the best way to get things done.
- The formation of a few, very large multinational companies restricts competition, which is a bad thing in a free market economy.

Thinking and analytical skills

1 Compare the contrasting arguments presented for and against Glaxo Wellcome.
2 Evaluate the moral position taken by Médicins Sans Frontières and Richard Caborn.

4.18 Should Sunday be a special day?

Links: 1.3 (i); 1.3 (ii); 1.3 (vi); 3.1 (i); 3.3 (viii); 3.4 (i); 3.5 (i)

'In any civilised society, at least one day in the week should be very different from the rest.' Evaluate the arguments for and against this point of view, considering both cultural and social perspectives.

A large majority of people on the strongly Presbyterian islands of Lewis and Harris now want ferries on Sundays, according to a poll. Yet islanders, who also showed they wanted air services on Sundays, still seem to regard it as a special day of rest. Most of those who took part in the survey were against local shops in Stornoway opening on the Sabbath. Ferry company Caledonian MacBrayne now says it would put on Sunday services if asked by the islands' transportation committee. Although there are likely to be calls for a further referendum before any change is made, all previous polls carried out in the last decade have shown a strong majority against Sunday travel to and from the two islands.

A Mori Scotland poll asked 750 people on Lewis and Harris about their attitude to Sunday transport and shopping. The research was carried out between 29 February and 4 March.

A clear majority of 72 per cent said they would like a referendum on Sunday travel to and from the islands. It also found that 61 per cent either strongly supported or tended to support ferry services starting on Sundays. Only 24 per cent stated they strongly opposed Sunday sailings, while another 9 per cent said they tended to oppose them. On the question of Sunday flights, 62 per cent of islanders said there should be such a service. Only 20 per cent of those asked were strongly opposed to Sunday flights, with another 12 per cent tending to oppose them.

Councillor Donald John Macsween, who has been a minority voice on Western Islands Council campaigning for Sunday ferries, said: 'I'm delighted with the result. It marks a sea change in opinion about transport links with the mainland. It was a very high poll and is bound to be an accurate reflection of opinion.'

He said he would now write to the chairman of ferry operator Caledonian MacBrayne to ask for a Sunday ferry service 'as soon as operationally possible'.

'It is also incumbent on Western Islands Council to ensure that they recognise that the vast majority in Lewis and Harris want Sunday ferries and they should work to facilitate that.'

Reverend John Macleod, of the Free Presbyterian Church in Stornoway, said he did not trust polls in general. 'We do not know how the interviewees were chosen. Did they put out the light and put pins in the phone book or did they deliberately choose who to phone? I don't know about Mori's techniques but it is surely possible that non-locals were targeted if, for example, they had non-local surnames.' Mr Macleod said it was not a case of majority or minority but what was in scripture. He said: 'If only one per cent say that what the divine law says – that only work of necessity and mercy should be done on the Sabbath – it is still that one per cent that is correct.'

CalMac said it had no plans for Sunday ferries but a spokesman added: 'However, we will do so if asked by the Western Islands Council's transportation committee or by the Scottish Executive.' Opinions were strongly against Sunday shopping, with two-thirds who took part in the poll not in favour.

From BBC News (Scotland), 16 March 2000

Issues to be discussed

- What are the beliefs of different religions on this topic?
- What do the results of the Mori poll in the article indicate?
- When the strongly held beliefs of minorities conflict with the wishes of the majority, how may confrontation be avoided?
- Is it possible to 'live and let live'?
- Is it important for society to have a regular rest day, whether or not it is linked to religious beliefs?
- Has the relaxation of rules about Sundays improved or harmed the quality of life of the majority of the population?

Where now?

www.rmplc.co.uk/eduweb/sites/sbs777/saccal/sunday.html
www.hmso.gov.uk/acts/summary/01994020.htm
www.write-on.co.uk/sabbath_and_lords_day.htm
www.agd.nsw.gov.au/lrc.nsf/pages/R37CHP2

Cultural perspective

- The designation of one day in the week to observe religious routines and rest has a long history. Most religions do so.
- Communities work better together if they share common cultural traditions, including that of a special day in the week.
- Since communities usually have a common religion, it makes it easier to set aside a certain time for common worship.
- The Jewish religion had a rest day on the 'Sabbath' or seventh day of the week. As many early Christians were also practising Jews, they observed Jewish worship on the Sabbath. However, they also celebrated the Resurrection of Jesus on the following day, the first day of the week, as they believed the Resurrection gave humanity a new beginning. This fitted in with the Bible story of creation, where the first day of the week represented a new beginning.
- Forcing people to have a day of rest is an infringement of individual freedom. People should be allowed to do whatever they want on any day of the week.
- A special day of rest is less significant in communities that have prayers and services every day.
- If we don't have a recognised day of rest, workers can be exploited by having to work whenever employers expect or want them to.
- Outmoded religious rules should not be allowed to affect everyone.
- During the French Revolution (1789–95) traditional religion was replaced with the worship of the Supreme Being. In 1792, an attempt was made to change the traditional seven-day week; the new week (or 'decade') had ten days. Sunday was abolished and a rest day allowed every tenth day.
- The beliefs of a few should not be forced on the majority.
- Families will be happier and more integrated if they can come together on a day when there are no other distractions.
- Making every day the same means that people will lose the simple pleasures of life.

Social perspective

- It is good for families to be able to gather and share a day together each week, for social reasons.
- Having one day in the week that is different provides a useful break in routine.
- The main reason for designating Sunday as a day of rest was to allow workers to recover and work better on the other six days.
- People should be allowed to work on Sundays if they wish to because they can earn more money and better support themselves and their families.
- It is impossible to have one non-working day a week set aside for everyone, since hospitals, power stations and transport systems have to be kept going.
- Making Sunday like every other day will have a profound effect on our way of life and should, therefore, be resisted.
- Making Sunday like every other day is what most people want and therefore change is inevitable.
- Changes in shop opening hours and times when sport and entertainment are available are having a negative effect on the structure of our society.
- Allowing unrestricted working days and hours will lead to exploitation of workers.
- Shops opening at all hours and on all days is good for business and also for workers.
- Shops opening at all hours and on all days prevents a concentration of shopping activity and transport on Saturdays.
- People suffer too much stress which will only be made worse if there is no special day when they can wind down.
- If people have too many recreational opportunities at weekends, they may work badly on Mondays or even not turn up for work at all.
- Sunday sport has been encouraged by television companies who want to use it to fill their schedules and attract audiences and advertising revenue.
- In the late twentieth century, public houses in certain areas of Wales were not allowed to open on Sundays. Referendums showed that most people wanted to keep this, but many of the voters drank in 'wet' counties or in working men's clubs where Sunday drinking was allowed.

Thinking and analytical skills

1. Compare and evaluate the arguments put forward in the article by Councillor Macsween and Rev Macleod.
2. Name and list examples of different types of knowledge used in the article.

Introduction

General Studies offers a number of opportunities for the practice, development and demonstration of competence in the various Key Skills at each level. In Units 1 to 3 you will find activities that can generate individual items of evidence for the Key Skills portfolio.

Ordinary class work can provide abundant opportunities to demonstrate mastery of Key Skills. For example, in Communication at Level 3, such opportunities might include:

- in Unit 3.2, taking part in a group discussion about the role of the monarchy (C3.1a),
- in Unit 2.1, making a presentation using graphs and diagrams about an aspect of a scientific discovery (C3.1b which could also contribute evidence for IT3.1),
- in Units 1.4 and 1.5, reading and synthesising information from a newspaper report and a textbook on an architectural style or building (C3.2),
- writing an essay in response to one of the questions in this book or writing a report on a piece of research you have completed as for C3.2 (C3.3).

Similarly, for Application of Number at Level 3, you might be asked to investigate evidence suggesting that the family has been irretrievably damaged. In Unit 3.5, you might:

- seek statistical evidence to show the increase in divorce and single-parent families (N3.1) (this could also contribute evidence for IT3.1),
- carry out various calculations (like the total number of divorced couples who remarry; the proportion of marriages ending in divorce) (N3.2),
- present findings in appropriate graphical and diagrammatic form (if combined with writing, this could also contribute to C3.3),
- carry out further research using the Internet and statistical information enter on a spreadsheet and used to make projections about future developments (IT3.2).

The examples in this section show how a single piece of work can satisfy the requirements of the General Studies course and, at the same time, can provide evidence of competence in a number of different Key Skills. For each assignment, the left-hand column outlines activities while the right-hand column details the particular skill achieved and the evidence required for the portfolio. These assignments are all pitched at Level 3, but can be modified to meet requirements at other levels. Candidates do not have to present evidence at the same level in all of the Key Skills. You could, for example, achieve Level 2 in Number, Level 3 in Communication and Level 4 in IT, depending on your individual ability.

Assignment 1

Assignment 1 is an example of a complete piece of work designed to address the demands of coursework and, at the same time, provide opportunities for producing most of the evidence required in the three assessed Key Skills. In particular, it is designed to produce a 'substantial activity' in Number and IT as is required in these two Key Skill areas. A substantial activity is defined by QCA as 'an activity that includes a number of related tasks, where the results of one task will affect the carrying out of the others'.

The example used is based on the Edexcel Specification for AS level, based on Unit 3 (Social Perspectives).

Assignment 2

Assignment 2 is an example of how a unit of work in the Cultural Domain (Unit 1), taking place over a number of lessons, could generate evidence for Use of Number. There are opportunities to obtain evidence in the other Key Skills, but these are not signposted.

Assignment 3

Assignment 3 is designed to provide the opportunity to produce evidence for Key Skills in Communication. It is based on the Scientific Domain (Unit 2). As with other assignments, it can be used to produce evidence for other Key Skills. In this assignment, attention is paid to C3.1a, C3. 2 and C3.3.

Assignment 4

Assignment 4 is based on the Social Domain (Unit 3) and relates to the strand 'Examination and appreciation of ideologies and values in society'. It is designed to produce evidence for Key Skills in IT and Communication C3.1b. It could be adapted to generate evidence for other Key Skills as well.

For further information on Key Skills requirements, consult the QCA publication *Introduction to Key Skills, Levels 1–3 in Communication, Application of Number and Information Technology* (1999).

Assignment I

'At one time there was a dominant family type in this country. During the last 30 years, as a result of various factors, family structures have changed so that it is no longer possible to identify one single dominant type.' Critically examine the arguments for and against this view. To what extent do you agree that it is true at both local and national level?

Aim and purpose

This assignment is an example of a piece of coursework designed to meet the requirements of the Edexcel Specification, Unit 3 at AS level. It addresses the issue of social and economic trends and constraints through the specified theme of 'Family Life'.

The task is to produce a folder of about 1,500 words in length which satisfies the subject content of Unit 3. It should demonstrate independent study and provide evidence of ability to meet all four of the Assessment Objectives. If all students in the centre are pursuing the same activity, there will be opportunities for collaborative as well as individual work, although the final piece of coursework will be individually produced.

Some additional activities that might not be required simply to satisfy coursework requirements have been provided in order to provide evidence of attainment in the Key Skills. Although this assignment will not produce all of the evidence required in the portfolio, it will generate a substantial amount. Examples of other evidence that might still be required are listed at the end of the assignment.

Activities within the assignment	Evidence required for Key Skills portfolio
1 Set up a group discussion/brainstorm to agree: **a** a definition of family, **b** a list of different family types **c** a broad outline of the requirements of the assignment **d** distribution of tasks to be undertaken on behalf of the group.	C3.1a **Contribute to a group discussion about a complex subject.** Evidence to include in the portfolio could include: **a** a record of the decisions taken, **b** a tape recording/video of the discussion to show the part played by each individual. This could consist of excerpts showing evidence of: **i** appropriate contributions, **ii** listening skills, **iii** creating opportunities for others to contribute. **c** a witness statement from a teacher who has observed the discussion.
2 Produce a brief summary statement of the definition and listings agreed. This could consist of: **a** the names of people involved in the discussion, **b** an agreed definition of family, **c** a list of different family types, perhaps with a brief explanation of each, **d** a summary of tasks and allocations.	C3.3 **Write two different types of documents about complex subjects.** This could be the first of the required two pieces of writing. *Style and language should be appropriate to a short memorandum rather than an extended piece of work. The audience is internal, in that it consists of the members of the group. The document's purpose is to serve as a reminder of discussion and agreement.*
3 **a** Research possible definitions of family and the topic of family types, using: **i** sociological textbooks, **ii** specialist books on the subject of family, **iii** newspaper and magazine articles. The aim of this section is to develop a theoretical background and awareness of the topic so that the student can identify issues that will be examined later in the assignment. As such, it is essentially an information-gathering exercise. **b** Select and briefly summarise (in note form) relevant information. Compare and collate different ideas from different sources. (Use this later to aid the writing of the coursework study.)	C.3.2 **Read and synthesise information from two extended documents about a complex subject. One of these documents should include at least one image.** *The need for images will be covered by the use of graphs and tables of figures contained in the textbooks or photographs illustrating different family types (e.g. P. Taylor, J. Richardson, A. Yeo, I Marsh, K. Trobe and A. Pilkington, Sociology in Focus, Causeway Press, 1999 or N. Jorgenson, Investigating Families and Households, Collins, 1995)* Evidence for both parts could consist of a list of the books and other reference material used, together with an annotated copy of the notes.

4 Research historical aspects of the topic for purposes of comparison. This can be done by reading historical studies, such as P. Laslett, *The World We Have Lost*, (Routledge 1999). Statistical information could contribute to the calculations and comparisons required later in the study (Stage 6).

C3. 2

Evidence could include notes of what has been read, copies of statistical information obtained, copies of any images available and summary notes of relevant content.

---

5 Use the Internet to find sites containing statistical information relating to the topic. The simplest approach would be to use British figures, perhaps using www.statistics.gov.uk. You could go on to explore sites that give comparative information for the European Community and/or the USA. (Alternatively, obtain and use information from printed sources, such as *Social Trends* or textbooks.)

N3.1 **Plan and interpret information from two different types of sources, including a large data set (over 50 items).**
IT3.1 **Plan and use different sources to search for, and select, information required for two different purposes.**

Evidence for both could be:

a a written plan indicating the purpose and method to be used to obtain information and how the plan relates to the activity,
b criteria to be used in searching for information,
c copies of the source material obtained, in the form of printouts if the Internet is used or photocopies if printed sources are used,
d a witness statement confirming that the research work has been properly completed,
e an outline of how the material is to be used and interpreted,
Sources used should be clearly annotated. Evidence could include an assessor's witness statement recording the nature of the search and copies of print-outs. There should be a written assessment of the relevance and quality of the material obtained in terms of the assignment. It helps if the evidence is cross-referenced back to the initial planning.

---

6 Using and interpreting statistical information: this could involve various calculations and extrapolations as well as the construction of graphs and tables, depending on the nature of the evidence obtained. Possibilities might include:
a Use of figures for the total number of families and percentages of types of family to calculate the number in each type. This could be done for a single year or for a number of different years. Using evidence from a number of different years allows figures to be interpreted, comparisons to be made and trends to be identified and interpreted.
b Construction of different types of graphs to illustrate the figures. Line graphs, for example, show trends over time, bar charts allow the comparison of years and types of family, pie charts allow comparison of proportion in each type and allow use of formulae, tables allow comparison of figures. If you use figures for several types of family and a number of different years, there should be sufficient evidence for using a large data set (over 50 items).
c Use of trends to project likely future developments, perhaps to calculate rates of growth.
d Use of figures from questionnaires to compare local, regional, national and international figures to look for similarities and differences.
e A written interpretation of the figures, drawing conclusions from them.

N3.2 **Carry out multi-stage calculations to do with:**
a amounts and sizes,
b scales and proportions,
c handling statistics,
d rearranging and using formulae, working with large data sets on at least one occasion.

IT3. 2 **Explore, develop and exchange information, and derive new information to meet two different purposes.**

Evidence could consist of:

a the different graphs and tables together with copies of calculations,
b written commentary on the figures and trends.

Some evidence could be transferred to spreadsheets and used to make calculations. In turn, these could be used to generate graphs and other images for other parts of this section.

N3.3 **Interpret results of calculations, present findings and justify methods. Use at least one graph, one chart and one diagram.**

C3.3

Evidence might include, as above, graphs and tables, calculations and a written commentary interpreting the results and explaining the choice of method as well as the relevance of the work to the study of family types.

IT 3. 3 **Present information from different sources for two different purposes and audiences, including at least one example of text, one example of images and one example of numbers.**

IT can be used to combine number work, charts and graphs from spreadsheets into a word processed report, in which the findings of the calculations and research are interpreted. *This would address one of the audiences required (the teacher) and would provide evidence of text, number and images.*

IT3. 2

The report could be emailed to members of the group and the teacher. *This would then provide evidence of two different audiences and the electronic exchange of information.*
IT evidence could consist of annotated print-outs or an observation record from an assessor, together with notes of automated routines used.

---

7 In a group, formulate a questionnaire/survey that will be administered to a representative sample to examine types of family and attitudes to family diversity. The survey should consist of perhaps 5 closed questions, either with yes/no or category based responses, to facilitate analysis. Draw up a plan to determine the nature of the sample and the number to be administered, taking into account age, gender and ethnicity.

- Each member of the group should administer (say) 10 questionnaires.
- At least 50 questionnaires should be completed. (If a larger number are used it will introduce a slightly more complex calculation to convert the figures to percentages.)
- Responses must be pooled to form a shared data base.
- Students working individually can use the collected data to: **i** analyse and interpret the data, **ii** construct graphs and tables and compare with national data. (A useful image might be a map showing the location of each of the respondents, perhaps broken down into totals for areas.)
- Compile a written report, based on the findings.

N3. 1; N3. 2 and N3. 3
C3. 1a; C3. 3
IT 3.2; IT 3. 3

A variety of forms of evidence can be produced for each of these:

a record of planning discussions and allocation of roles,
b discussion/compilation of questionnaire,
c use of email to distribute questionnaires; possible use of chat rooms to pursue questionnaires with strangers or contacts,
d collation of responses and associated calculations,
e graphs, tables and charts,
f written report.

---

8 Make a short presentation, based on the findings of the questionnaire, making comparisons with national and historical patterns.

C3.1b **Make a presentation about a complex subject, using at least one image to illustrate complex points.**
C3. 3 IT 3. 2. IT 3. 3

Evidence could include:

a assessor's witness statement (of how evidence from different sources was merged to produce the materials used in the presentation,
b working drafts to show how presentation was developed,
c handouts containing written summary of findings (C3.3),
d overhead transparencies used in presentation,
e copies of graphs and tables constructed/used.

---

9 Written outcome: produce a coursework folder, based on research and containing graphs and tables, addressing all four General Studies Assessment objectives.

C3. 3 etc.

Evidence would consist of the completed coursework folder. (All written work should show the 'ability to select an appropriate style and organise material coherently'.) In particular, this section of the work allows students to demonstrate their command of vocabulary, grammar, spelling and punctuation. It also provides the best opportunity to demonstrate ability to redraft, proofread and correct.

It should be remembered that the completed coursework will be assessed for the Quality of Written Communication through General Studies AO2.

This piece of work could be extended over the equivalent of one-third of the General Studies course, since the outcome is the equivalent of one examination unit. It can provide opportunity for the compilation of most of the evidence required for, at least, the three Key Skills of Communication, Number and IT. This structure can be adapted to fit a variety of themes and topics suitable for use as coursework in each of the Specifications. Centres would need to provide adequate supervision and guidance to ensure that students have the opportunity to develop relevant skills and to produce a final piece of work that meets all coursework requirements. Further evidence would probably be needed to support some aspects of N3. 2. Additional activities will be required for IT 3. 1, IT 3. 2 and IT 3.3 in order to meet the requirement to serve two purposes, two audiences and perhaps three forms of presenting work (IT3. 3). The assignment could be modified in such a way as to meet the requirements of Level 2, or even Level 1 in some or all of the Key Skills. There is also adequate opportunity to demonstrate competence in the other three Key Skills of Problem Solving, Working with Others and Improving Own Learning and Performance.

Assignment 2

> Investigate either the effects of advertising or newspaper ownership in the United Kingdom. Produce a brief written account of your findings using graphs, tables and other images. Your response should include a variety of different calculations and some interpretation of your figures.

Aim and purpose

This is a topic-based approach to the Media and Communication strand in the Cultural Domain. The topic, lasting for three or four lessons, is designed to examine ways in which the media influences public opinion, moral issues arising from its activities and current developments within the media. The topic is based on OCR Unit 1 (the Cultural Domain), but could meet some of the demands of either Edexcel or AQA specification A. The task, forming part of the topic, is designed to explore advertising and newspaper ownership and contribute evidence for a 'substantial activity' in Key Skills in the application of Number, Level 3. (It can also supply evidence for other Key Skills.) Students are required to research and produce an individual piece of work based on either of these two aspects of the media. The assignment may not provide all the evidence required for the Application of Number.

Activities within the assignment	Evidence required for Key Skills Portfolio
a Identify the terms of the assignment, whether it is newspaper ownership or advertising. (The example is based primarily on newspaper ownership.)	N 3.1 **Plan and interpret information from two different types of sources, including a large data set.** Evidence to be produced: **a** A written description of the task (an annotated task sheet) explaining how the task is to be taken forward.
b Determine the types of evidence required and the likely sources of information.	**b** A written note of the evidence required and how it is to be obtained, with copies of material used.
c Conduct necessary research: **i** Research statistical information using either the Internet or printed source material about newspaper ownership and newspaper circulation over a period of, perhaps, 20 years. **ii** Construct and administer a questionnaire, producing at least 50 responses. (In order to generate sufficient responses in the limited time available, this could be a collaborative effort.) The purpose of the questionnaire is to examine patterns and frequency of newspaper purchases.	**c** A print-out of statistical information or photocopy if printed material.
d Analyse responses to questionnaires. Express figures in rounded numbers and convert to percentages.	**d** A copy of the questionnaire and a summary of responses.
e Review statistical information obtained from the research and decide how this is best shown (e.g. tables, types of graphs, charts, etc.).	**e** A breakdown of respondents (age/status/background), etc. This could be done in the form of a table in which the responses are quantified.
f Compile a written record/print-out of the information obtained.	**f** A statement of how the material is to be used and the way in which it will contribute to the research.

2 Make calculations, using the evidence obtained.

a Using the responses to the questionnaire:

i Calculate the number of respondents who take each newspaper. Reduce responses to three headings: Regularly, Sometimes, Rarely.

ii Create a table to show these figures both as raw figures and as percentages of the whole.

iii Subdivide the newspapers into four categories: broadsheets; middle-of-the-road tabloids, 'popular' tabloids, free papers.

iv Calculate the number of respondents taking each type of newspaper and distribute them as before under the three headings.

v Show these figures in an appropriate table.

vi Construct appropriate graphs for each of the four types of table to show the proportion of the respondents who take each type of newspaper.

b Using the figures on newspaper ownership and circulation, construct a graph to show:

i How ownership has changed over the years.

ii How circulation figures have changed over the years.

iii Calculate the number of readers committed to each major newspaper owner (irrespective of newspaper read) on a national scale as close to the present day as possible. Convert the raw figures into percentages.

iv Construct an appropriate table to show these national percentages. Compare the national figures with the responses to the questionnaire (in **2 a (ii)** and **2 a (v)** above). Present your conclusions in a written form.

v Using the figures obtained for **2 b (i)** and **2 b (ii)**, calculate the average number of readers of each newspaper and newspaper owner over the last ten years.

vi Assuming the trends shown in your graphs for **2 b (i)** and **2 b (ii)** continue steadily, estimate the expected number of newspaper readers in 2021 in total, and for each newspaper and newspaper owner.

N 3. 2 **Carry out multi-stage calculations to do with:**

a amounts and sizes,

b scales and proportions,

c handling statistics,

d rearranging and using formulae.

You should work with a large data set on at least one occasion.

Evidence will include:

a Copies of tables and graphs.

b Records of the calculations made to show working out and checking. (There should be an indication that figures might be larger than 100 per cent because some people may have more than one newspaper.)

c Graphs ought to include pie charts or bar graphs to show proportions.

Probably a line graph. It will need to be labelled and annotated.

Make copies of calculations and collation of figures under given headings.

Calculations, working and answer with some evidence of how the answer was proved.

---

3 Compile a written report, using the graphs and tables produced.

a Graphs and charts should be clearly and appropriately constructed and labelled.

b The report should interpret the graphs and tables in order to outline the present and past ownership of newspaper ownership.

c Draw comparisons between national and local reader loyalty.

d Estimate the likely impact of national owners in the locality.

e Identify and comment on any trends shown in the graphs and tables.

f Justify the methods used to illustrate the figures. This should involve considering the different types of graph or chart and the reason why the chart or graph chosen was the most appropriate.

g Identify any difficulties encountered in finding, using and interpreting the figures.

h Explain how the work relates to and satisfies the requirements of the task.

N3. 3 **Interpret results of your calculations, present your findings and justify your methods. You must use at least one graph, one chart and one diagram.**

Evidence required:

a Much of the evidence required will be shown in the working and results for Section 2.

b A written report must include calculations, graphs and tables.

Assignment 3

Choose one recent scientific or technological discovery. Investigate the possible moral implications of the discovery. Do you agree that scientists' only concern is to make discoveries and that other people have the responsibility to decide how those discoveries are used?

Aim and purpose

The task is designed to give you the opportunity to engage in discussion on a significant issue, conduct your own research into specified aspects and then produce an essay or piece of extended writing on the given theme. It is designed to generate evidence for C3.1a; C3.2 and C3.3. If C3.3 is replaced with C3.1b, it could modify the assignment, allowing you the opportunity to make a presentation rather than to write an extended answer.

This assignment could form part of a topic-based approach to the strand of 'Moral responsibility: the social, ethical and environmental implications of scientific discoveries and technological development'. It is based on a two- or three-lesson unit in Science from AQA Specification A, dealing with the moral responsibilities of scientists. It could apply equally to the Edexcel AS Science units or the OCR A2 unit.

Activities within the assignment	Evidence required for Key Skills portfolio
1 An introductory teacher-led session could describe a number of recent scientific or technological developments or discoveries that have been applied in both a negative and a positive way. These might include issues like nuclear power, air transport (civilian transport and bombing raids), cloning and genetic modification and should raise the central issue of who holds the responsibility for the application and consequences of such discoveries.	
2 This should lead into a discussion that involves all students. The teacher should become a facilitator and observer rather than a central participant. Ideally students should be able to apply some of the skills and knowledge learnt in the Culture unit on 'Beliefs, values and moral reasoning' as well as to demonstrate an ability to contribute clearly and coherently to a discussion, putting forward and justifying their own views, while listening carefully to and taking account of the opinions of others.	C3.1a **Contribute to a group discussion about a complex subject.** Evidence for the portfolio could include: **a** A written record of the issues discussed and points made. **b** A tape recording/video of the discussion to show the part played by each individual. This could consist of excerpts showing evidence of: **i** appropriate contributions, **ii** listening skills, **iii** creating opportunities for others to contribute. **c** witness statement from a teacher who has observed the discussion. **d** record of any conclusion reached.
3 Conduct further research, prompted by the discussion. **a** This could involve using the Internet, reading appropriate sections of this text, consulting magazine articles or reading relevant sections of appropriate books *(the Key Skills element involves reading complex texts).* **b** Read extended documents to identify relevant information and different opinions on the issue under consideration. **c** Make a brief synopsis of the evidence obtained, making sure to give alternative views equal weighting. These notes should contribute to the completion of the written task.	C.3.2 **Read and synthesise information from two extended documents about a complex subject. One of these documents should include at least one image.** Evidence could include: **a** a written note of texts and other sources consulted, **b** notes constructed on the basis of reading and research, **c** written evidence, in the form of a summary, that the work has been synthesised.

4 Write an essay on the given topic. This should address the appropriate Assessment Objectives defined in the mark scheme of the particular board. It should:
a look at both sides of the issue,
b be clearly and coherently organised, using specialist vocabulary where appropriate and be written in a style appropriate to its purpose.
c present argument rather than assertion and be supported by evidence,
d reach a justified and supported conclusion,
e show mastery of the communication skills defined in AO2,
f be legible with accurate spelling, punctuation and grammar.

C3.3 **Write two different types of documents about complex subjects. One piece of writing should be an extended document and should include at least one image.**

The evidence required is the completed essay.

Further appropriate evidence would be copies of early corrected drafts to show the process that had been followed.

This assignment could be used to produce evidence for the other Key Skills. In particular, it would lend itself to aspects of IT. If adapted, it could produce evidence for the Application of Number, in the provision and interpretation of supporting statistical information.

Assignment 4

'It is a well-established fact that the population of the United Kingdom is ageing – the proportion of people over the age of 65 continues to increase, while the proportion of the population under the age of 16 is decreasing.' Investigate the evidence to support this statement and make a presentation on the effect of an increasingly ageing population on the economy.

Aim and purpose

This task is designed to explore the nature of and reasons for Britain's ageing population. The focus of the task is to prepare and deliver a presentation using IT skills. There is opportunity to show other skills, particularly N3.2 and N3.3 and perhaps C3.3. You should research and produce an individual piece of work. There is some opportunity for collective activity.

This assignment is based on the Edexcel Specification in which ideologies and values are examined through the themes of race, gender, age or disability. The emphasis at AS is placed on issues relating to age. This topic forms perhaps a third of the theme. The task can be modified for use with AQA Specification A at AS and the OCR Specification at A2.

Activities within the assignment

Evidence required for Key Skills portfolio

1 The assignment is likely to follow a general introductory lesson in which the nature and development of social values is discussed. Emphasis should be placed on formative influences and attention directed to issues of old age.

2 Outline the task and the nature of the Key Skills evidence to be produced. Working either individually or in a group, you should consider and determine the most appropriate approach to the activity. This should include:
a identifying the nature of the information required to meet the demands of the task,
b identifying sources of relevant information and determining techniques for carrying out appropriate searches (the most obvious routes to obtain statistics are either Internet searches using www.statistics.gov.uk or using the CD-ROM *Social Trends 1970–1995*),
c undertaking research for factual information to support and interpret the statistical information,
d sifting information obtained for relevance and suitability to the task.

IT 3. 1 **Plan and use different sources to search for and select information required for two different purposes.**

Evidence could consist of:
a a description of the activity,
b a written plan explaining how the information is to be searched for,
c a statement of how criteria are to be determined to judge the relevance of material,
d annotated print-outs of the information obtained,
e a list of sources and search methods used to ensure the search is effective.

3 Use the statistical information to produce appropriate text, graphs, tables and images for use in the presentation.

- **a** Evidence is likely to take the form of numerical information on the size of the population, broken down into age groups at different periods of time. Projections of future trends will also be required.
- **b** Calculations could be done using a spreadsheet.
- **c** Produce written text based on research.
- **d** Produce images for use on overhead transparencies (OHTs) and/or word-processed handouts.
- **e** Copies of handouts could be emailed to group participants prior to the presentation.
- **f** Future trends could be extended beyond, say, 2021, using a spreadsheet to change values in order to produce alternative levels of growth, dependent on different circumstances.

IT 3. 2 **Explore, develop and exchange information and collect new information to meet two different purposes.**

Evidence could include:

a annotated print-outs,
b an assessor's record of observation of the use of IT,
c documentation produced at different stages of the task to show how information was developed, changed and explored,
d documentation to show how new information was developed.

---

4 Draft an essay in response to the assignment question. The finished product should contain text, images and numbers. Discuss the content and layout of the presentation materials with other members of the group and make appropriate changes to improve them. Show, through copies of the drafts, how the work has been improved by making changes to the text; indicate how you developed OHTs or perhaps power point to enhance your presentation. Produce a hard copy handout, importing graphs, tables and illustrations. Check text for accuracy. Save the presentation on disk.

IT3. 3 **Present information from different sources for two different purposes and audiences. The work must include at least one example of text, one example of images and one example of numbers.**

Evidence could include:

a working drafts,
b assessor's record of observation of screen displays,
c print-outs and copies of computer-generated images,
d handouts showing final product, including examples of text, images and numbers and a disc copy.

---

5 Present work to a selected audience. Ensure that:
a speaking/delivery style is appropriate to the purpose of the presentation and the audience,
b the work is logically structured and organised so that a sound and valid argument is presented in order to reach a justified conclusion,
c images are used to illustrate the presentation.

C3.1b **Make a presentation about a complex subject, using at least one image to illustrate complex points.**

Evidence could include:

a an assessor's record of observation of the presentation,
b notes used to prepare and deliver the presentation,
c copies of images used, including handouts and OHTs.

These assignments are samples of the type and variety of work that can be used in General Studies to produce evidence for Key Skills, while at the same time addressing the requirements of the General Studies course. If assignments are designed, it is important that reference is made to the QCA document 'Introduction to Key Skills'. It should never be assumed that you automatically possess these skills. You need to be given opportunity to develop, practise and improve them.

We are grateful to the following for permission to reproduce copyright material:

Allen Lane, The Penguin Press for an extract from BAROQUE (1977) by J. R. Martin; Philip Allan Updates for adapted extracts from 'Youth cultural studies' by H. Pilkinton in SOCIOLOGY REVIEW Vol. 7 No. 1 1997, 'The future of work' by R. Scase in SOCIOLOGY REVIEW Vol. 8 No. 2 1998, and 'The family and gender identities' by J. Williams in SOCIOLOGY REVIEW Vol. 8 No. 3 1998; Humphrey Burton, writer and broadcaster, for an extract from an article in CLASSIC FM magazine, November 1997; Cambridge University Press for adapted extracts from CULTURE AND ANARCHY (1932) by Matthew Arnold, THE ROMANTIC AGE OF BRITAIN (1989) edited by B. Ford and THE FORCE OF KNOWLEDGE (1976) by John Ziman; Centaur Publishing Ltd for an adapted extract from article 'Marketing Week' Jan 20 2000 on www.findarticles.com © 2000 Centaur/Gale Group; Collins Publishers for adapted extracts from INVESTIGATING CRIME AND DEVIANCE (second edition 1997) by Stephen Moore 1997, and THE RELIGIOUS EXPERIENCE OF MANKIND (1984) by Ninian Smart; the author, Dr David Demick for an extract from his article 'Mutations – evolution or degeneration?' on www.christiananswers.net; Victor Gollancz Ltd for extract from A SHORT HISTORY OF RELIGION (1957) by E. E. Kellett; Grolier Electronic Publishing for an adapted extract from an article on CLAUDE DEBUSSY, jagor.srce.hr/~fsupek/debussy.html; Guardian News Services for extract from THE NEW INTERNATIONALIST issue 284 and extract from article 'Glaxo stops Africans buying cheap Aids drugs' by Sarah Boseley, THE GUARDIAN 2.12.00; the author, John Harris, for an adapted extract from his article 'On the education of revolutionary physicists: W C Roentgen and A H Becquerel' in SCHOOL SCIENCE REVIEW September 1995; HarperCollins Publishers for an adapted extract from ETHICS (1994), by McInerney and Rainbolt; Harvard University Press for an adapted extract in MARRIAGE, DIVORCE AND REMARRIAGE (1992) by A. J. Cherlin Copyright © 1981, 1992 by the President and Fellows of Harvard College; The Controller of Her Majesty's Stationery Office for an abridged extract from 'Progress, conclusions and recommendations' sections of SCIENTIFIC COMMITTEE ON SMOKING AND HEALTH REPORT 1998; Hodder & Stoughton Ltd for extract adapted from ADVANCED LEVEL MEDIA (1999) by Ball, Joyce and Rivers; ITPS Ltd for adapted extracts from LIVING PHILOSOPHY (1993) by R. Billington published by Routledge, EDUCATION, JUSTICE AND CULTURAL DIVERSITY (1998) by H. Halstead published by Routledge & Kegan Paul and A THEORY OF LITERARY PRODUCTION (1978) by P. Machery published by Routledge & Kegan Paul; Macmillan Inc for an adapted extract from MASS CULTURE: THE POPULAR ARTS IN AMERICA (1957) edited by Rosenberg & White; John Murray (Publishers) Ltd for an adapted extract from CIVILISATION (1979) by Kenneth Clark; National Gallery of Art for an extract from 'Just one big ego trip' by Waldemar Januszczak in THE SUNDAY TIMES 1.10.00; Marshall Morgan & Scott for adapted extracts from WHATEVER HAPPENED TO THE HUMAN RACE (1980) by Schaeffer and Koop; New Scientist Publications for adapted extracts from the articles 'Is there life out there?', by P. Davies, NEW SCIENTIST 18.9.99, 'Lost and found', by M. Chown, NEW SCIENTIST 13.5.00 'New Item' in NEW SCIENTIST 16.5.00, 'Expect serious delays', by M. Hamer, NEW SCIENTIST 1.7.00 and 'Take a chance' by N. Pidgeon in NEW SCIENTIST 12.8.2000; New Statesman Ltd for extract from article 'Drugs and Darwin fuel athletes' by Matt Barnard, NEW STATESMAN 25.9.98; News International for extracts/adapted extracts from 'Workers face the scrapheap at age of 42' by Leake & Bozras in THE SUNDAY TIMES 19.03.2000, article by Eleanor Mills in THE SUNDAY TIMES 26.03.00, 'Return to tax and spend' by David Smith in THE SUNDAY TIMES 26.3.2000, 'Donor plan for death row Britons' by Lois Rogers in THE SUNDAY TIMES 09.04.2000, 'Mass media' by Bryan Appleyard in THE SUNDAY TIMES 16.04.00, 'Working classes prefer arts to 'snobby' football' by R Brookes in THE SUNDAY TIMES 25.06.2000, 'Loo for two sets off chain reaction', by Tom Robbins in THE SUNDAY TIMES 3.9.00, 'Failing the family', editorial, THE SUNDAY TIMES 3.9.00, 'Just one big ego trip' by Waldemar Januszczak in THE SUNDAY TIMES 1.10.00, 'Mission impossible' by Hugh Pearman in THE SUNDAY TIMES 9.4.00, 'The oversold gene project' by Nigel Hawkes in THE TIMES 27.7.00, 'I don't buy the baby story', by India Knight, THE SUNDAY TIMES, 3.1.01, 'Hospital inquiry hits at baby organ doctors', by Lois Rogers, THE SUNDAY TIMES 28.1.01 All © Times Newspapers Ltd 2000, 2001; Oxford University Press for an adapted extract from BRITISH POLITICS (1990) by Dennis Kavanagh; Pearson Education Ltd for extract from THE POLITICS OF THE NEW EUROPE (1997) by Budge, Newton et al. published by Longman; Penguin Books Ltd for adapted extracts from THE SIMPLICITY OF SCIENCE (1959) by S. D. Beck published by Pelican, A HANDBOOK OF LIVING RELIGIONS (1991) by J. R. Hinnells and FAMILY SOCIALISATION AND INTERACTION PROCESS (1980) by Parsons and Bates; The Editor, The Prisons Handbook for an extract from a speech by Jack Straw quoted in THE PRISONS HANDBOOK, www.tphbook.discon.co.uk; HRH Prince of Wales/Respect for the Earth (2000) Profile Books Ltd in association with the BBC, for an extract by HRH The Prince of Wales from Reith Lectures 2000 (BBC Website); Random House Inc for an adapted extract from SOCIETY (second edition 1967) by E. Chinoy; The Random House Group Limited for adapted extracts from THE WAY WE LIVE NOW (1995) by R. Hoggart, published by Chatto & Windus, and THE STATE WE'RE IN (1996) by Will Hutton published by Jonathan Cape; The Social Affairs Unit for an adapted extract from 'Toleration and the currently offensive implication of judgement' by John Gray in THE LOSS OF VIRTUE (1992) edited by D. Anderson; Thames & Hudson Ltd for an extract from WHAT IS A MASTERPIECE? (1979) by Kenneth Clark; Telegraph Group Limited for 'God defies the laws of science', by Roger Highfield, THE DAILY TELEGRAPH 3.4.97, 'A test that changes lives', by Catharine O'Brien, THE DAILY TELEGRAPH 19.4.97, 'AstraZeneca to lift research spending abroad', by Suzy Jagger, THE DAILY TELEGRAPH 25.2.00; Weidenfeld & Nicolson Ltd for an adapted extract from THE STATE IN A CAPITALIST SOCIETY (1973) by R Millbrand, published by Unwin Hyman; Zondervan Publishing House for an extract CREATION OR EVOLUTION (fifth printing 1971) by D. Reigle.

We have been unable to trace the copyright holders of THE GREAT CHEMISTS (1929) by E. J. Holmyard and PRINCIPLES OF ETHICS - AN INTRODUCTION (1975) by P. Taylor and would appreciate any information that would enable us to do so.

We are grateful to the following for permission to reproduce copyright photographs:
theartarchive/Musée d'Orsay, Paris/Dagli Orti: p.63; photos from www.JohnBirdsall.co.uk: pp.35, 129, 161, 163l; The Banquet of the Gods, Ceiling Painting of the Courtship and Marriage of Cupid and Psyche (detail) by Sanzio of Urbino Raphael (1483-1520)(after), Villa Farnesina, Rome, Italy/Bridgeman Art Library: p.39, Exterior view of S. Maria del Fiore, 1294-1436 (photo), Duomo, Florence, Italy/BAL: p.49, The Calling of St. Matthew, c.1598-1601 (panel) by Michelangelo Merisi da Caravaggio (1571-1610), Contarelli Chapel, S. Luigi dei Francesi, Rome, Italy/BAL: p.51, Miss La La at the Cirque Fernando, 1879 (oil on canvas) by Edgar Degas (1834-1917), National Gallery, London, UK/BAL: p.57, Self Portrait, 1661-62 by Rembrandt Harmensz van Rijn (1606-69), Kenwood House, London, UK/BAL: p.61l, Self Portrait, 1887 (oil on canvas) by Vincent van Gogh (1853-90), Musée d'Orsay, Paris, France/BAL: p.61r, Apollo and Daphne by Matthias Rauchmiller (1645-86) (marble), Sculpture Gallery, Künsthistorisches Museum, Vienna, Austria/BAL: p.67l, Venus, lateral view, 1810 (marble) by Antonio Canova (1757-1822), Palazzo Pitti, Florence, Italy/BAL: p.67r, Landscape with viaduct: Montagne Sainte Victoire, c.1885-87 (oil on canvas) by Paul Cezanne (1839-1906), Metropolitan Museum of Art, New York, USA/BAL: p.71, The Honeymoon, illustration from 'The English Dance of Death', pub. by R. Ackermann (colour engraving) by Thomas Rowlandson (1756-1827), The Stapleton Collection/BAL: p.69; Camera Press/Lionel Cherrugult: p.149, Camera Press/Benoit Gysembergh: p.167; Collections/Yuri Lewinski: p.53bl; Donald Cooper, Photostage: p.23; English Heritage Photographic Library: p.53tl; Paula Solloway/Format: p.29, Maggie Murray/Format: p.187; Richard Greenhill: p.179; Hulton Archives: p.123; Peter Arkell/Impact: p.125, Alex Macnaughton/Impact: p.165; 'With kind permission from the Imperial Cancer Research Fund': p.112; Matchmaker/Miramax (courtesy Kobal) p. 17; National Trust Photo Library/Matthew Antrobus: p.53br; Mike Goldwater/Network: p.27, Michael Abrahams/Network: p.37, John Sturrock/Network: pp.153, 157; © Nick Newman/Sunday Times: p.15; 'NI Syndication/Simon Walker, The Times, London': p.77, 'NI Syndication, The Sun, London': p.83; Christa Stadtler/Photofusion: p.163r; Reuters/Popperfoto: p.141; PA Photos/EPA: pp.13, 171; Rex Features: p.121; Skyscan Balloon Photography Copyright: pp.41, 65; Press Association/Topham: pp.33, 59; Janine Wiedel Photo Library: p.189; Andy Williams Photo Library: pp.53tr, 55.

Crown copyright material is reproduced under Class Licence Number C01W0000039 with the permission of the Controller of HMSO and the Queen's Printer for Scotland.